12/10

NEDRA, I LOOK FORWARD TO BEING WITH YOU
AND THE CHILDREN ON TUESDAY. THANKS FOR YOUR
LOVE AND PATIENCE. WITH LOVE AND PRAYERS.

J

a special gift

_____

presented to:

_____

from:

_____

date:

"A new command I give you: Love one another.
As I have loved you, so you must love one another."

—John 13:34 NIV

The Women's Devotional Series

Among Friends

The Listening Heart

A Gift of Love

A Moment of Peace

Close to Home

From the Heart

This Quiet Place

In God's Garden

Fabric of Faith

Alone With God

Bouquets of Hope

Colors of Grace

Beautiful in God's Eyes

A Word From Home

Morning Praise

Heaven's Whisper

Grace Notes

Sanctuary

Love Out Loud

To order, call **1-800-765-6955.**
Visit us at **www.reviewandherald.com**
for more information on other Review and Herald® products.

love one another as I have loved you

Love
Out Loud

Ardis Dick Stenbakken, editor

REVIEW AND HERALD® PUBLISHING ASSOCIATION
Since 1861 | www.reviewandherald.com

Review and Herald® titles may be purchased in bulk for educational, business, fund-raising, or sales promotional use. For information, e-mail SpecialMarkets@reviewandherald.com.

The Review and Herald® Publishing Association publishes biblically based materials for spiritual, physical, and mental growth and Christian discipleship.

The author assumes full responsibility for the accuracy of all facts and quotations as cited in this book.

This book was
Edited by Penny Estes Wheeler
Copyedited by Kathy Pepper
Designed by Patricia Wegh
Cover photos © 2010 iStockphoto
Typeset: Minion 10.5/13.5

PRINTED IN U.S.A.

14 13 12 11 10   5 4 3 2 1

Library of Congress Cataloging-in-Publication Data
Love out loud / edited by Ardis Dick Stenbakken.
    p. cm.
1. Seventh-Day Adventist women—Prayers and devotions. 2. Devotional calendars—Seventh-Day Adventists. I. Stenbakken, Ardis Dick.
  BV4844.L68 2010
  242'.643—dc22
                 2010011257

ISBN 978-0-8280-2514-0

There is an aspect of this book that is unique.

None of these contributors has been paid—they have shared freely so that all profits go to scholarships for women. As this book goes to press, 1,671 scholarships have been given to women in 112 countries.

For more current information, or to contribute to these scholarships, please go to http://adventistwomensministries.org/index.php?id=60. In this way, you too can provide a sanctuary, a safe haven for others.

Waiting Patiently

I waited patiently for the Lord; and he inclined unto me, and heard my cry.
Ps. 40:1.

THIS VERSE MAKES ME THINK of the mother cat who comes each morning to our door and sits there looking intently through the screen. When she sees me, she meows but keeps waiting until I bring out a bowl of milk. Regardless of how slow I am, she still waits for me.

I am not by nature a patient person. I want things to happen now! But how often I still have to wait: at airports, traffic lights, check-out lines, and offices.

Sometimes I've even had to wait for my husband. The longest I ever had to wait for him was more than two hours. He left me at the supermarket, saying, "I'll be back shortly. I just have to run over and drop off this check."

Half an hour later I pushed a full cart out onto the parking lot looking for Ron. No car. No husband. I waited . . . and waited . . . and waited. I pushed my cart back and forth wondering and worrying, pacing and praying. What had happened to my usually prompt husband?

Closing time came. The parking lot emptied. The supermarket doors were locked. It began to get dark. This was in the days before cell phones and I had no way to contact him. I had no choice but to wait.

After two hours I saw his car drive into the now empty lot. He pulled up to my cart and jumped out to load the groceries in the trunk. "I'm so sorry," he said. "I forgot about coming for you and went home. When it got dark, I wondered why you weren't home fixing supper. Then I remembered. I am really sorry for making you wait so long!"

The poor man looked so repentant that there was nothing to do but laugh. At least he had come. My waiting was rewarded at last. — Bob's Story

~~However,~~ I often have to wait much longer than two hours for God to answer my prayers. I am trying to learn to wait patiently for Him to work things out in His own time. If I will wait and not give up, then I will be rewarded by His presence and an answer to my prayers. Waiting means to trust that He has heard my cry and will give me what I need. That is, of course, what David learned and tells us in today's text.

Lord, at the start of another year give me the patience I need to wait upon You, knowing that You hear my cry and will answer in due time.

Dorothy Eaton Watts

Resolutions

Be still, and know that I am God.
Ps. 46:10, NKJV.

A NEW YEAR BEGINS. Promises are made, resolutions are written. As we do this, we must remember that there is nothing as important as the Lord Himself. He knows the beginning from the end, so why not let Him just lead us in each day, in each thought, in each decision we make? Then we will know that our every act and every thought will be in tune with God and His will.

Some women are happy-go-lucky with no worries, letting God take care of everything. But that's not us, is it? We get in a big hurry. We're impatient. We're spoiled. We want what we want when we want it. It's hard to wait on the Creator of our souls when we're opening a business, buying a house or car, or even dating—finding that right mate. We should ask God what to do. We should invite Him into our lives. But when He says, "I don't think you should buy that car or marry that man," we argue, *It's OK, Lord, I can handle it.* We make excuse after excuse even though He's said, "No, my child. Wait on Me. What I have for you is so much better than what you want now." But we're impatient, aren't we?

Wouldn't it be nice if we learned from our mistakes? Wouldn't it be even better if our children and grandchildren learned from our mistakes? God made us with minds of our own—free to choose to listen, if we'd just do it.

I surely never thought this world would be around this long. But I do know that the Lord is coming soon. I want to see that! But what we fail to realize is that the Lord loves each and every one of us so He patiently waits for us to be ready to meet Him. His love for us is so great that He has extended time in hopes that when He does come, we will be ready. His heart will remember for all eternity if Micah or Peggy or Javene is not in heaven with Him. He thinks, *There's so much I wanted to share with her. I had such dreams for her.* So He waits and waits, saying, "Just a little longer. She'll be ready soon. She'll realize she can't live without Me." The Lord says this about each one of His children.

Our New Year's resolution should be, *I will not make the Lord wait on me anymore. Rather, I will serve Him and listen to what He wants me to do. I will truly wait on Him.*

Tammy Barnes-Taylor

Never Say Never

The human mind plans the way, but the Lord directs the steps.
Prov. 16:9, NRSV.

I LOVED TYPING CLASS because I loved the teacher. Also the class was made up of just girls, and we had great fun when the teacher would give us a break. But I was not that good at actually typing. "I'm never going to use typing anyway," I told the teacher. "I'm going to be a nurse, so I won't need typing." That was, of course, before nurses kept their records on computers. And it was also before I changed my mind about nursing and my college major to English. It was also before I married a ministerial student and typed his major papers through three years of seminary—long before the days of personal computers.

In fact, it seems that I have spent most of my life typing. I typed a seemingly endless number of papers while pursuing the English major and an advanced degree. I have typed innumerable articles for magazines and newspapers. I have typed multiple years' worth of church newsletters and church bulletins. And as I traveled the world working with women's ministries, I gave countless seminars, sermons, talks, and keynote addresses. They all had to be typed. And of course there has been constant typing involved in editing these devotional books. I've gotten better at it through the years, but I'm still not a great typist.

Despite my wrong-headedness back there in typing class, God has been good and has given me the ability to do what He has asked me to do. I think the Bible talks about this when it says, "I will lead the blind by ways they have not known, along unfamiliar paths I will guide them; I will turn the darkness into light before them and make the rough places smooth. These are the things I will do; I will not forsake them" (Isa. 42:16, NIV). Isn't that amazing?

I have met women who feel like they can't do so many things, so they never try. And I have met other women who have done incredible things, way beyond what one would think they could do. Several years ago when I was facing great challenges a friend shared a text with me: "Not that we are competent in ourselves to claim anything for ourselves, but our competence comes from God" (2 Cor. 3:5, NIV). That meant a lot to me. And in my Bible I have it cross-referenced with 1 Peter 4:11: "Whoever serves must do so with the strength that God supplies, so that God may be glorified in all things through Jesus Christ" (NRSV). I think that says it all.

Ardis Dick Stenbakken

Pretend You Are Here

Meanwhile his disciples urged him, "Rabbi, eat something."
John 4:31, NIV.

RAYS FROM THE SETTING SUN streamed in through the open window. Melissa's hair shone burnished gold. The child sat at the head of the table, her little face wreathed in anticipatory smiles, the unique "my birthday" plate in front of her.

"Would the birthday girl like to say grace?" Melissa's father asked. Immediately she stretched out two small arms and soon 12 pairs of hands were joined in a circle. Scrunching her eyelids closed, her sweet voice floated out over the table. "Dear God, I'm so glad it's my birthday," she began, "and that everyone is here." Pause. "Thank You for not sending Arlene any inwit . . . inwit . . . ," ["invitation" prompted her mother] "yeah, for today, so she could make my favorite desert." Pause. "I'd share some with You if You could come." Pause. "I'll just pretend You're here! And please eat something You really like. Amen."

Opening her eyes, Melissa broke the silence. "Can I start with 'tistachio' pie?" She looked directly at me. "You always say that if you're gonna eat dessert, eat it first!" I smiled and waved a hand to defer to Melissa's mother, who nodded permission.

"Whatever prompted you to tell God to eat?" demanded Melissa's much older cousin.

"My teacher said the disciples had to beg Him to eat 'cause He was so-o-o-o busy," Melissa explained. "They're all dead now, so I reminded Him." Again she paused. "I wonder if He likes birthday pie better than birthday cake, like me."

"Honestly, Melissa," her mother began, "I don't know where you get some of your harebrained . . ." Her voice trailed off, a deer-in-the-headlights expression on her face.

Lively conversation followed, punctuated by appreciative murmurs about the tasty food, but my mind was busy processing Melissa's personal view of the Deity. How precious to hear her wish aloud that she could share her birthday pistachio pie with God.

Oh Melissa, I thought, *keep pretending that God is here. Soon it will be a reality!* You too will be able to eat with Jesus, and it won't be pretend: "Listen! I am standing at the door, knocking; if you hear my voice and open the door, I will come in to you and eat with you, and you with me" (Rev. 3:20, NRSV).

Arlene Taylor

Give It to Jesus

*And it shall come to pass in that day, that his burden shall be taken away
from off thy shoulder, and his yoke from off thy neck, and the yoke
shall be destroyed because of the anointing.*
Isa.10:27.

DURING THE EARLY YEARS of my marriage my husband, Bill, and I were avid sports fans. We were glued to the television set during baseball season. We thoroughly enjoyed basketball and football. It was a joy to go to Madison Square Garden to the basketball games and to Yankee Stadium to the football games. How I loved the Morgan State and Grambling College Classics. I don't know which I enjoyed most, the game or watching the bands perform. Bill, who had two years of training with the Golden Gloves, had a special love for boxing. However, I lost interest in boxing in the 1960s after I saw an opponent carried out of the ring and I read about his death a few days later. Although I did not know him personally, it saddened my heart to know he lost his life under such circumstances. I think boxing is brutal.

And then there is wrestling—both men and women wrestlers. Although it seemed somewhat barbaric, I still found myself watching it every Saturday night.

Needless to say, wrestling is an activity in which we all participate as we wrestle with our sins, our spouses and children, educational status, finances, selfishness, unforgiveness, insomnia, insecurity, anger, emotions, confusion, depression, rejection, our church family, and even God through His Word. The list goes on and on. There is something to wrestle with 24/7.

But I am tired of being placed in a headlock, fingered in the eyes, and knocked to the ground. I don't like lying on my stomach with my arm twisted behind me, pressure on my back and neck, my leg bent inches from my hip, my foot in intense pain, and not being able to turn my head to the right or left. I don't want my shoulders pinned to the floor until the count of three. That hurts! Psalm 55:22 states, "Cast thy burden upon the Lord, and he shall sustain thee: he shall never suffer the righteous to be moved."

Sister, please pray this prayer with me: "Father, I place my burdens on You. Please deliver and sustain me from these wrestling matches. I cannot handle them. I give them to Jesus. I ask it and thank You in the name of Jesus. Amen."

Cora A. Walker

Bridging the Gap

And I sought for anyone among them who would repair the wall and stand in the breach before me on behalf of the land, so that I would not destroy it; but I found no one. Eze. 22:30, NRSV.

I ENJOY LISTENING to a nightly radio program titled *Lovers and Other Strangers*. Its host has one of the most soothing voices I have ever heard. The format includes poetry, stories, and musical pieces—each one fitting nicely with the night's theme.

One particular night my attention was especially drawn to the story being told. Two brothers had a slight rift which they allowed to fester into a full-blown argument until they were no longer speaking to each other. Then the younger brother widened the creek that separated their farms to prevent the older from crossing it. One day a stranger arrived at the older brother's door carrying a carpenter's toolbox. The brother asked the carpenter to build a fence at least eight feet high between his and his brother's property so that he would not have to look at his brother's farm. He gave the stranger the required measurements and materials and left on a trip.

Returning home, he found a well-done job—but totally different from what he'd instructed. Instead of a fence to hide his brother's farm he saw a beautiful bridge, complete with handrails, spanning the wide creek from his property to his brother's. And there was his brother running toward the bridge with outstretched arms! The brothers met in the middle of the bridge and threw their arms around one another in a long hug. Then they turned and saw the stranger packing up his tools. "Stay with us a little longer," they pleaded.

"I can't," he said kindly. "I have too many bridges yet to build."

The purpose of a bridge is to connect two points. Bridges vary in size and design from the simple and rustic to astonishing feats of engineering science. Some are for cars or wagons while others are designed for walkers. Like this stranger, each of us have many bridges to build in our relationships. They may be at home, work, school, church, or in our community. God has designed the best bridge of all—Jesus, our connecting link between heaven and earth. No one waits in line to cross this Bridge. We have simultaneous access to God through Christ Jesus.

I believe all are connected by the bridge of love. I pray God will help me today to be mindful of the bridges I must build.

Avis Mae Rodney

God Guides Us!

And we know that all things work together for good to them that love God.
Rom. 8:28.

WHEN I WAS A CHILD and our family lived in California, we moved around a lot. So I attended school in many different towns from central to southern California.

When I was in the last part of fifth grade I moved to Glendale Elementary School, located just a little more than a mile from my home. I became acquainted with Nancy who lived around the corner from me. We grew to be great friends and spent a lot of time together, including walking to and from school every day.

One afternoon Nancy and I were walking home as we always did, down one side of the street to the corner, across the street, and on home. We were strolling along when just a little way before the corner a voice said to me, *Cross the street right now*. I couldn't understand because we always crossed at the corner. Besides, it was against the law to jaywalk. Again the voice spoke, more urgently: *Cross the street right now! Hurry!* So I grabbed Nancy's arm and we ran across the street. Right then a car careened around the corner, lost control, and slammed into the corner house, up onto the porch and right on into the front bedroom.

We stood across the street, breathless and stunned, realizing how blessed we truly were. We knew that if we hadn't hurried across the street when we did, we would have been exactly where the car jumped the curb. I know our guardian angels were with us that day, preventing serious injury or even death.

In heaven it will be interesting to find out from our guardian angels how many times they have saved us. So often we aren't even aware of the dangers from which we've been rescued.

God has sent us a letter, the Bible, so that we will have His written blueprint of His plans for us. In other words, He guides us. Do we take time daily to study the blueprint, or do we let the business of life crowd out the time we should spend with our Lord? That's what Satan wants for us—to be too busy to live close to God. We need to stay so close to the Lord that we can hear Him when He talks to us. As my son says, "No time, no power; little time, little power; much time, much power—power for victory, power for transformation, power to become the witness God calls you to be."

Anne Elaine Nelson

Blisters on my Soul

Deliver me from mine enemies, O my God: defend me from them that rise up against me.
Ps. 59:1.

AS A YOUNGSTER, I thought new shoes caused blisters on everybody's feet the way they did on mine. I wore my old shoes for as long as I could for two reasons. First, they cost more money than we had during the 1940s, and my father, a garage mechanic, had no extra money. He was trying to rear my two brothers and me alone, since my mother and stepmother had both passed away. And second, every time I got new shoes they made blisters on my feet, especially on my heels. I later learned that I had narrow heels. With the shoe heels wider than my heels, my feet rubbed the heel of the shoe and made the blisters.

Whenever I get upset with someone, especially someone in church, I think about the blisters on my soul. Does everybody get them like I do? Someone makes a remark and I take it personally, even though the speaker meant nothing personal at all. And it makes a blister on my soul. It sort of festers and makes a bump and just sits there for a while. Finally I talk to God about it. And then I think of all the things our Savior lived through here on this earth. He was the God of the universe, Creator of our world. Yet He cared enough about you and me to leave heaven and come to earth as a newborn baby to learn and grow—finding favor with God and man—and to live and work with 12 difficult men. These 12 were dense, slow to learn, and wanted to see Him crowned king of their world. They made many blisters on Jesus' soul, yet He didn't leave His blisters to fester. He turned to His Father in prayer—often praying all night long. He prayed for His disciples, for His family, for His friends. He kept on doing His Father's will. He kept on healing, preaching, teaching. He never had it easy; I wonder why *we* expect life to be easy?

The Bible doesn't teach that life will be easy. However, "The Lord is good, a refuge in times of trouble" (Nahum 1:7, NIV). God cares for those who trust in Him, and Jesus has promised to give us His peace to cope with trials. He has also promised to give us a home in heaven and life eternal if we are faithful and follow His plan for us.

The next time you have a "blister" on your soul, turn to God. He is a good listener.

Loraine F. Sweetland

On Following the Golden Rule

Therefore all things whatsoever ye would that men should do to you,
do ye even so to them: for this is the law and the prophets.
Matt. 7:12.

DO WE NEED TO FOLLOW the golden rule with animals as well as humans? One day our young son ran into the house calling, "Mama, Mama! Tiger's swimming! Come see!" Following him outside, I saw our gray-and-white-striped kitten paddling away, but it didn't look happy.

"Get him out—now!" I ordered. "He doesn't like that! Did you put him in there?" Rick silently set Tiger gently on the grass. "Bengal tigers are the only cats I know of who like to cool off by swimming," I told Rick. I didn't question him further, figuring a word to the wise was sufficient.

I recalled Kitt, the clandestine pet in our dorm at the Christian boarding school I attended. Most of us girls had fed and pampered him. Kitt enjoyed taking bubble baths, and maybe Rick had gotten his idea from my sharing that story with him and Julie.

Years later I noticed that Catie (pronounced Katie), our marmalade-colored tabby, was intrigued with how water disappeared down sinks, tub drains, and toilet bowls in funnel-like fashion. She often sat on the tub's edge when I drew water, dipping a paw in or letting her tail get wet.

Maybe, I thought, *Like Kitt, she'd enjoy a bubble bath*, so I put her in the tub. Wailing like a banshee, she shot through the open doorway and stood in the hall, shaking water everywhere. My moment of middle-aged madness had created quite a mess!

Then I thought, *I can't swim. So I know I wouldn't like it if someone threw me in the water.* Feeling small and humble, I toweled Catie dry and promised, "I'm sorry. I won't do that to you again." She began to purr. She apparently forgave me, for we still have a loving relationship. Many animals respond well to kindness.

I had parented well with the advice I had given to Rick. And I should have followed up on it myself.

Do we need to apply the golden rule to how we treat animals? I'm firmly convinced that our world would be a better, nicer place if we all did!

Bonnie Moyers

The Tag That Made the Difference

Now therefore, our God, we thank thee, and praise thy glorious name.
1 Chron. 29:13.

TRAVELING FROM WASHINGTON, D.C., to the Philippines, I had my laptop computer, Bible, a book, and some personal items in my one carry-on bag. There was no problem at all until I reached the segment to Bacolod, a city in the province of Negros Occidental. I was stopped at the gate because they said my carry-on was over the 7 kilogram limit. They wanted me to check it. I explained to them that I came from an international flight and I could not check it as I had my computer and my reading books there, but they wouldn't give in.

Finally the supervisor sarcastically said, "Well, go ahead, talk to the manager." The way he said it gave the impression that the manager would say, "No," anyway. But I am not one who will give in without trying, so I responded to him politely, "Yes, please, may I speak with the manager?" He pointed out the manager who was busy with other passengers. I waited patiently, all the time praying for God's intervention. The man working on my boarding pass was now getting impatient, so I prayed more.

He checked my bag, verified the weight, and said, "It's a little heavy, but let me just put an orange tag on it." Then he said, "Thank you, Ma'am. You should be OK."

I expressed my appreciation and proceeded to my gate without any problem. The orange tag made the difference. It opened the way for me.

As I contemplated that experience, I said to myself, *That's why he is the manager.* He weighs the situation and gives a decision according to the need of the passengers. The first lesson that this situation taught me is that God knows that we carry a heavy load, but He understands. Second, in spite of our heavy load, if we come to Him, He will make the load lighter. Then He puts—not an orange tag on our load—but the "red tag" which represents His blood on the cross, His blood that opened the gateway of heaven for those who come to Him.

My prayer today is that we will be truly grateful for His love that is beyond human understanding—or the "red tag" that gave us the passage to our heavenly home. The tag that makes the difference.

Jemima Dollosa Orillosa

The Universe Is Fleeing Sin

And they heard the voice of the Lord God walking in the garden in the cool
of the day: and Adam and his wife hid themselves from the presence
of the Lord God amongst the trees of the garden.
Gen. 3:8.

RECENTLY I READ AN ARTICLE that stated that our moon is on a spiral that takes it a couple of millimeters further away from the earth every year. I was reminded of the time my college astronomy teacher lectured on the "fleeing phenomena." The teacher said one of the proofs of the big bang theory is the fact that astronomers had documented that all visible heavenly bodies were moving out and away from a center point. Someone asked where the center was. The teacher answered that, as our planet was on an edge of our own galaxy it was impossible to determine where the universal center was. At the time I had thought to myself, *Everything is actually fleeing this world because we are in rebellion against the "Center of the Universe,"*—God.

The entire universe is repelled by earth's rebellion against God. I believe that every visible heavenly body is putting as much distance between themselves and our sinful world as God's law of physics allows. But God didn't flee from us. Instead, He came to earth to look for us. He lived with us, He died for us, and now He woos us back to His love. "For God so loved the world, that he gave his only begotten Son, that whosoever believeth in him should not perish, but have everlasting life" (John 3:16).

Yes, the entire universe is fleeing sin because it separates from God, while we, the receptors of God's overriding love, grovel in sin's debasing influence. In 1 Tim. 6:11 Paul tells us to flee too, to "flee these things; and follow after righteousness, godliness, faith, love, patience, meekness." Praise God, our sin does not cause God to leave us, turn Him against us, or keep Him from loving us.

Beloved heavenly Father, thank You for loving us when the rest of the universe is appalled at our rebellion. Thank You for not leaving us in our debased natures. Thank You for wanting to associate with us so badly that You sent Your only begotten Son to die in our place. Thank You for promising heaven to those who reject sin and turn to You. Amen.

Darlenejoan McKibbin Rhine

Genuine Friendship

And it came to pass, when he had made an end of speaking unto Saul, that the soul of Jonathan was knit with the soul of David, and Jonathan loved him as his own soul.
1 Sam.18:1.

SATAN'S GREATEST JOY is to divide God's children on the basis of such issues as race, social status, language, nationality, culture, color, education, and more. We have to determine in our hearts not to allow this to happen. We all need to be loved, and we need friends with whom to share this joy. Jesus calls us His friends. From childhood, every person on earth needs to establish friendships for healthy living. Parents have the responsibility to guide their children in the importance of choosing their friends wisely.

God knows that we need friends. In fact, He created the first human friend for Adam in the person of Eve, and then He gave them children. No person is an island, nor should they want to be. Many times my friends have come through for me and made a great difference in my life.

Jonathan became a sincere friend to David. David was a young shepherd, while Jonathan was the son of King Saul. Yet David experienced genuine friendship from Jonathan. The fact that King Saul hated David did not change their relationship, for the Bible says that David's soul was "knitted" to that of Jonathan's. An eternal godly bond was formed and led to David taking lifelong total care of Jonathan's crippled son, Mephibosheth. David also restored the lands of Mephibosheth's father and grandfather to him after Jonathan's death.

In this relationship we see the key qualities for a truly lasting friendship. These include genuine love, mutual respect, and esteeming the other person better than oneself. Even more was unselfishness, the willingness to risk one's life for someone else, and a sense of justice, humility, patience, and forgiveness. This was the basis on which Jonathan and David made a pact which united them and their children in life and in death.

The world is longing for friendships and relationships like this. The qualities Jonathan and David exemplified—love in word, deed, and action—transcended all barriers. Let us examine afresh this kind of friendship and seek to imitate the qualities displayed. We need these in our quest to form lasting friendships and relationships. These are the basis for the ties that bind eternally, and by God's grace we can all experience it.

Shirnet Wellington

Conversation at the Sink

God is faithful, who will not suffer you to be tempted above that ye are able;
but will with the temptation also make a way to escape, that ye may be able to bear it.
1 Cor. 10:13.

WE INVITED FRIENDS HOME for a meal after some meetings. I looked forward to a chat with the young woman, a busy gal whom I loved but didn't often get to be with. When the lively conversation continued after the meal, I suggested everyone relax in the living room.

With scarcely a glance around, all exited. I began clearing the table, hearing bits of their talk. It interested me, but someone had to clean up and after all, it was my home. I was upset. Didn't anyone care that I would like to be enjoying their company? It seemed so unfair. Wasn't I tired and in need of refreshing, too? And my greatest hurt was that my friend whom I loved didn't offer to help. She seemed oblivious to my needs. I was filled with self pity and banged a few pans and dishes louder than needed—hoping someone would notice. (They didn't.)

As my upset feelings grew, I knew I needed help. I didn't like the way I felt. In silent prayer I poured out my disappointment to God: *Why doesn't she give me any help?* I asked.

"She doesn't have it to give!"

I was startled. God was listening—He answered! And His answer stopped my self-pitying thoughts. She needed to be in there to have her spiritual and physical needs recharged. My love won out—briefly—over my self-filled thoughts. But soon more self-pity bombarded my mind: *Don't I have needs? Who cares? I'm tired, too. Who's going to meet my needs?*

"I will!"

Oh! He was still listening! I shivered, realizing what was happening. I was not alone in the kitchen. God was there with me—and aware and ready to meet my needs. Suddenly I was glad no other human was in the kitchen with me. God was there! He was meeting my needs. I thought about Him. I trembled a little as I asked, *What do You need?*

"Someone to do dishes!"

I laughed with delight. I was washing dishes for Him. What a sense of humor He has! He knew just what I needed—I needed Him. Wow! What a God!

Doing dishes has never been the same since.

Juanita Kretschmar

When Forgiveness Seems Impossible

And when ye stand praying, forgive, if ye have ought against any: that your Father also which is in heaven may forgive you your trespasses. But if ye do not forgive, neither will your Father which is in heaven forgive your trespasses.
Mark 11:25, 26.

I HAD NOT REALIZED how bitter I had become, nor did I realize that the cure for this is forgiveness that comes from God. Instead, I used the old adage "I will forgive but not forget."

When I started going to the church regularly, I did not know—or even imagine—that some church members would not like me. I was kind, compassionate, willing to help when and where needed, and could generally make friends with anyone. However, I was not liked by all, and I was not shown the love of God. My outstretched hand was refused. Groups disbursed as I approached. Did I have some contagious disease?

You see, my attitude had to change as well. My attitude had become *I will show the offender. I will outlast them.* And so I did. The offender finally left the church to fellowship elsewhere, and I could be myself again. I had won—or so I thought. Years went by and life was nice. Then one day the offender and his family showed up again. I was crushed. He spoke to me, and I snarled back. I was still bitter. I was angry at everyone—even God—for allowing the offender to come back and mess up my life. I did not realize that Satan had caused my pain and suffering and God was attempting to restore me from what Satan had done to harm me.

This went on for months. Then one day I was approached by the offender, asking to meet with me to discuss our problem. Not acting like a Christian but still wearing the Christian title, I set up the meeting. *It's not going to change a thing.* But with God all things are possible. Today we have nice conversations. We can mingle in the same congregation. Our families attend social events outside of the church, and there are no snarled or harsh remarks. I have forgiven.

I want you to know that no matter how you feel you've been treated, God is still in charge. Continue to pray and believe on Him who is able to keep us. God is so good. He took me to it to bring me *through* it. I had never experienced forgiveness like this before. He took the hurt out of my heart and the anger out of my voice. I will praise Him until the end of time.

My prayer: that we examine ourselves to make sure we both forgive and forget.

Anna Williams

Lessons From the DMV

Consider it a sheer gift, friends, when tests and challenges come at you from all sides. You know that under pressure, your faith-life is forced into the open and shows its true colors. So don't try to get out of anything prematurely. Let it do its work so you become mature and well-developed, not deficient in any way.
James 1:2-4, Message.

IN THE NOON 113°F HEAT a traffic camera clicked, but I didn't hear it. I didn't see the flash either, but weeks later I received a nice little letter from my friends at the Department of Motor Vehicles. Ripping open the envelope with trembling hands, I found inside a flattering picture of myself behind the wheel. The citation read, "Red light violation." It included a hyperlink to an actual video record of my indiscretion.

Ugh. In my quest to get a break from the sterile atmosphere in my husband's hospital room, I had taken a fast trip to the drugstore by way of an intersection armed with traffic cameras. Being in a hurry to return, and figuring I had the usual time for the orange light, I followed the other cars into the intersection. Well, obviously, I misjudged the time. I had not been paying good attention either. Now I didn't have much choice. Even after my on-the-spot confession and traffic school enrollment, the fine was steep. In the end the only thing I could do was to hand a few hundred dollar bills to the DMV.

Looking for some comfort or heavenly advice, I looked for a verse to soothe my angry soul, and I found it. "Consider it a sheer gift, friends, when tests and challenges come at you from all sides. You know that under pressure, your faith-life is forced into the open and shows its true colors. . . ."

Pondering the possibility of a mug photo if I fought the case, I realized that patience is the key to sharing anything in God's kingdom, including praising God in song. The act of nursing my brake at a traffic signal is similar to learning to praise God under pressure. It's easy to laugh and smile, even be sweet to those who treat you right, but facing an unfair situation, becoming a mere number to a government clerk, requires divine help. I am His patience, His kindness, His joy . . . His voice.

Dear Lord, Let me sing through You!

Nancy Ann Neuharth Troyer

She Knows My Voice

His sheep follow him because they know his voice.
John 10:4, NIV.

THE PHONE RANG EARLY on a crisp fall morning as I dressed for church. "Hi, Mom," the sleepy voice said. "Happy birthday!"

"I'm surprised you remembered as busy as you've been lately."

"This is going to be a special birthday," my son continued. "Extra special. We're at the hospital and you're going to have a grandbaby today."

"Wow! That's wonderful!" I gasped, unable to contain my excitement. "But I thought she wasn't due for three more weeks."

"I guess she wanted to make the day special for her Nana."

With a flurry of activity we hurried to the hospital instead of to church to find the young mom in active labor. And so it happened that on the same day of the week, at the same time of day as I was born many years earlier, I greeted my first grandchild. What a delightful gift!

My son held his baby girl as we looked at her together. "Oh, Mom, isn't she beautiful!"

I knew these words were coming from a new dad because at that moment I saw a pointed head and a red, wrinkled face. But how great that God looks at us like a loving Father and sees not the outside but knows what we are on the inside and sees us as His beautiful daughters.

After the baby had been passed around a bit she started to whimper. New daddy came to the rescue. "Oh, let me have her," he said. "I can get her settled down. She knows my voice."

Wow! What a concept! But it's not a new idea. More than 2,000 years ago Jesus talked about how the sheep know the voice of their shepherd. He called Himself the Good Shepherd who even gave His life for His sheep. They listen to Him; He quiets them. He leads them.

How can I recognize the voice of the Good Shepherd when so many voices clamor for my attention? Jesus' voice won't be the loudest, but it's the most kind and consistent and easy to listen to. As I study His word I am training my ears to pick up His gentle tone. I can then feel secure and know that He will quiet my fears. I want the Good Shepherd to look at me and say, "My beautiful daughter, I can settle the chaos in your life. You can trust Me because you know My voice."

Roxy Hoehn

A Wheelchair Full of Blessings

Your marvelous doings are headline news; I could write a
book full of the details of your greatness.
Ps. 145:6, Message.

I MOVED TO FLORIDA as my new church family was in the throes of putting out their church directory. Since I had been through the process before, I volunteered to help. My job was simple: call each member and set up an appointment for the photo shoot. At my first call, Sister A was delighted to be reminded. So it went for the next four calls. Then I called Sister Q. I identified myself. "Who?" the bewildered voice inquired. I repeated my introduction. "Who?" The grate in her voice suggested that my answer did not help to clarify her problem. Finally I identified myself as the daughter of parents who had been long-time members of the church. Still Sister Q was clueless. I tried again: "I'm the one in the wheelchair."

I could almost hear the light dawn. "Oh, yes, my dear. Now what were you saying?"

I realized that though I may be identified as a wheelchair person, I would not define myself as disabled. I would select my own designation and gild it by counting my blessings—ones that were unique to me. Wheelchair blessings, I'd call them.

Eugene Peterson's version in today's text says it all. I could write a book when I think about the blessings God has given me. For instance, now I have easy access to services and buildings. Flying anywhere, I find that my travel agent automatically orders a wheelchair for me. At the airport, a helpful porter collects my documents and wheels me directly to the gate. And it doesn't stop there. One Sabbath our church was packed. No seats were available, but I had one: my wheelchair. And it got better. My little niece, finding no seat of her own, came to stand beside me. Her eloquent, dark eyes flashed a message, *May I sit on your lap?* I was charmed. So apparently are the little children who now run up to me each week with greetings and kisses.

God taught me His closeness as I prayed my way through the book of Psalms. When my right hand became too weak and shaky to write or even curl my hair, I had to learn to use the left. Somehow I heard His voice from the pages of my Bible. "Nevertheless, I am continually with you; you hold my right hand" (Ps. 73:23, NRSV).

Yes, I'm the one in the wheelchair—the one powered by His mighty arm.

Glenda-mae Greene

Just Put Him to the Test

If you ask anything in My name, I will do it.
John 14:14, NKJV.

IN ORDER FOR US TO GRASP God's answers to our prayers, we must build a relationship with Him. It is not automatic. I've heard and read about many other people's experiences with God, and I finally realized that all I had to do was to put God to the test. I actually did. When I prayed to God, it was a natural part of my relationship with Him. I felt very comfortable coming to God with my needs, my concerns, and whatever issues were current in my life.

I asked the Lord for many things and He delivered. For example, if I desired to awake early in the morning, for whatever reason, I would pray before I retired: "Dear God, You know what my program is for tomorrow. Please wake me at an appropriate time whereby I can prepare myself for this appointment." Amazingly, I would be awake at just the right time to make preparations according to my assignment for the day. God is wonderful, and we must exhibit confidence in His word when approaching Him. The Bible says that if we ask anything according to His will, He hears us.

I teach a class for the School of Behavioral Sciences at the University of the Southern Caribbean, and I told my students that if they prayed before they began studying for a quiz, the Lord would lead them to focus on the exact areas the quiz would cover. By the end of the semester, some of the students testified that it did work for them.

The story is told of a man who asked God for a flower and a butterfly, but God gave him a cactus and a caterpillar instead. The man didn't understand. After some time, he went to check on his forgotten request, and to his surprise on the dull, thorny cactus was a bright, beautiful flower, and the unsightly caterpillar had been transformed into a beautiful butterfly.

God always does things right. His way is always the best way, even if it seems all wrong. You can be sure that He will always give you what you need at the appropriate time. What you want is not always what you need. God never fails to grant our petitions, so keep on going to Him without doubting or murmuring. Today's thorn is tomorrow's flower. God gives the best to those who leave the choices up to Him, for He makes everything beautiful in its time (see Eccl. 3:11, NKJV).

Carol J. Daniel

Scar Tissue

*Beloved, I wish above all things that thou mayest prosper
and be in health, even as thy soul prospereth.*
3 John 2.

SOME YEARS AGO, when an elderly friend or relative would announce with an air of finality that it would rain the following day, I would look up into the clear, blue sky and smile rather patronizingly. Rain? Impossible! I'd think. But to my surprise—not to say chagrin—it invariably did rain. And today I myself have reached the stage—or should I say age—that I no longer need a barometer, for my own body warns me that bad weather is on its way.

Over the years we all suffer various physical injuries, and it is pain in some of these old wounds which often reminds us that the barometric pressure is dropping. I can't explain this phenomenon, but it is one of the facts of life. However, our progress through life doesn't leave in its wake only physical scar tissue, but emotional and spiritual wounds too. These scars tend to cause us pain, especially when our spiritual barometer is dropping.

Every experience through which we pass creates a memory. Some of them are fresh and joyous even after many years. When we recall the event, our hearts beat faster as a wave of happiness sweeps over us, engulfing us in a veritable tsunami of exhilaration. Other events are "scar tissue" memories which still hurt badly every time they come to mind. Our eyes fill with tears and our hearts are like lead as we relive vivid scenes which we wish had never happened.

As there are skillful plastic surgeons who can remove painful, debilitating scar tissue from our bodies, so there is One, and only One, who can excise the deepest scars in our emotional or spiritual memories. The operation is free of charge to all. Our Surgeon asks only that we entrust ourselves fully to His care and cooperate with Him as far as is humanly possible.

Why do we hesitate? Our Savior is the only one who can remove the excruciatingly painful results of sin and recreate us in His unblemished image. There is a bonus too, for as He works on suffering minds and hearts, His scalpel deftly removes some physical scars as well, and we begin to enjoy a degree of physical health we would never have dreamed possible.

Jesus came to save us wholly, and His healing touch slowly restores every aspect of our sin-sick, battered lives.

Revel Papaioannou

Before They Call, I Will Answer

And it shall come to pass, that before they call, I will answer;
and while they are yet speaking, I will hear.
Isa. 65:24.

EXPERIENCE HAS TAUGHT ME that one of the most important things a Christian can do is to attend prayer meeting on a regular basis. Herein lies power and a constant source of encouragement and strength. It is sheer joy to drink in the rich fellowship shared with other Spirit-led believers.

On one such prayer meeting night, I rushed to get ready so I would not miss the bus. As I hurried to cross the street to the bus stop, the bus whizzed toward me. Confident that the driver saw me, I ran across the street, waving to attract his attention, knowing that I would not be able to get all the way across in time. Still confident that he saw me, I fully expected him to pull to a stop and let me on. He did not. He didn't even slow down.

I could not believe it! Why would the Lord let this happen to me? He knew my purpose in going to prayer meeting, and He knew that if I missed that particular bus I'd also miss the connecting bus that would get me to church on time. How I hurt! I felt the Lord had forsaken me. But why? Had He not said I should go to prayer meeting?

I sulked as I waited impatiently for the next bus, my thoughts running wildly in the net of doubt. God seemed far away. Then a strange thing happened. A car approached and pulled to the curb near where I was standing. A friend poked his head out of the window and asked if I wanted a ride. I gladly got into the car and he took me directly to the church door. Not only did I arrive on time, I was early!

How chagrined I felt for having chided the Lord. Had He not said, "And we know that all things work together for good to them that love God, to them who are the called according to his purpose" (Rom. 8:28)?

He had anticipated my situation and by His all-wise providence, provided what I needed and longed for in my heart. True to His promise, He reminded me, "Before they call, I will answer" (Isa. 65:24).

Lord, give us each faith to know that You hear, that You love, and that You care.

Audre B. Taylor

In His Time

But I trust in you, O Lord; I say, "You are my God." My times are in your hands.
Ps. 31:14, 15, NIV.

LORD, GET ME THERE SAFELY; *Lord, get me there on time.* My twin prayers reverberated in the confines of the small car. Ahead, a dusty blue Volvo hogged the one-way road, doing less than 20 miles per hour in a 30-mile-per-hour zone. There were no turns off the road, and I had no choice but to crawl along behind.

It was a typical Wednesday afternoon. The school traffic had died down and the rush hour had yet to put in an appearance. I'd foolishly left handing in my assignment to the last possible moment, and it was now uncomfortably close to the 5:00 deadline. Still more than a mile from the university campus, I was impatient both with myself and the driver in front. The winding side road was wide enough to accommodate two lanes of traffic. But there he was, slap bang in the middle, taking a "Sunday afternoon" stroll.

Because of the way the road twisted and turned, I was unable to see more than a few meters ahead and found myself driving in his tracks as if we were joined with a tow-bar. After muttering my desperate prayer, I fixed my attention on the Volvo's rear bumper and chided myself for being presumptuous. I'd had six weeks to finish and submit my work. But here I was, at the last minute, as usual, rushing to get it in on time. How could I expect God's help when the truth was I didn't deserve it?

Suddenly, the Volvo swerved left. I did too. Just in time to miss a small car with overseas plates driving in the wrong direction and headed straight toward us.

Thank God for that Volvo with its slow, steady pace hogging the road in such a way that I was held back from trying to overtake it. That car wasn't the obstacle I'd imagined it to be—it was in fact a protecting shield.

Now, whenever I'm in a hurry and a slow vehicle lodges itself in front of me, my first instinct is still to hurry him along, but then I'm reminded of that day and breathe a quiet *Thank You* to God for whatever harm He's protecting me from. *Not because I am good, oh God, but because You are good—in Your time.*

Avery Davis

Sticks 'n' Stones

Death and life are in the power of the tongue: and they
that love it shall eat the fruit thereof.
Prov. 18:21.

AS A CHILD GROWING UP in the southern part of the United States, I was familiar with the saying "Sticks 'n' stones may break my bones, but words will never hurt me," and I believed it. That is, until I was older and realized how far it is from the truth. My mother, who was forced into the single parenting of six children after my father abandoned us, always made me feel and believe that I could do anything I put my mind to. Even though I have yet to realize some of my dreams, there is something inside me that repeats again and again, "I can, I can." Recently, I completed graduate school, getting my MBA. With that behind me, I continue to work on other projects in the hope of realizing still other dreams.

I have known children whose parents or relatives have told them "You'll never be anything; you'll never amount to much." Even though those awful words have never been directed at me or my siblings, I can imagine how they cut and hurt to the core. Words can never be taken back, even when apologies are made. They cut deeply and wound far more than those who ignorantly and carelessly throw them out realize. I'm sure some children would rather receive a thrashing for misbehaving than hear those terrible words hurled at them. A spanking stings for a while, but the words "You'll never amount to anything," if allowed to play over and over in the mind, greatly increase the probability of their ending in truth.

It is far better to instill in children and to encourage adults with the idea that with hard work and determination anything can be achieved. After all, God has great stock in us and has equipped each of us with brainpower. Despite what we are told, we must dream and envision ourselves as accomplishers, victors, overcomers, winners, champions of our dreams and goals. Yes, like sticks and stones, words can hurt terribly, but we can decide whether or not we will let the "tapes" play out in our heads and lives. We can override them with positive thoughts, beliefs, and actions.

Lord, we know that You desire only good for us, and that You are ready and able to help us make our lives fruitful. May we always be mindful that You will complete that good thing in us.

Gloria Stella Felder

A Matter of Respect

Then make my joy complete by being like-minded, having the same love,
being one in spirit and purpose. Do nothing out of selfish ambition or vain conceit,
but in humility consider others better than yourselves.
Phil. 2:2, 3, NIV.

A FEW MONTHS AGO I heard a man in the city say, "We who have a college education think we are better than farmers." You will be proud of me—I held my tongue and didn't give the reply I wanted to give. (He had no idea who we were.) However, since then I have thoughtfully considered how we respect people who have chosen a different way of life than ours.

We've all heard comments such as: "dumb farmers," "he's just a grease monkey," "she's an airhead waitress," and on and on. Not only are business people and people in the service industries denigrated by these types of comments, but so are people in other professions. Most of us can remember statements made by others about the careers some have chosen. Why do otherwise sensible humans feel the need to elevate themselves by putting others down?

I think of how thankful I am for the professional mechanics who willingly help me when I suddenly need a new alternator while miles away from home. Weary and hungry, going to a restaurant looking for both physical rest and good food, I am always glad there are people who have learned the gracious art of serving. The dentist, who fits me in between already scheduled appointments and deals with my aching tooth, is loved. I am so appreciative of my hairdresser's abilities to make me presentable again. The list could go on and on.

We never raise our children all by ourselves, and I appreciate those along the way who have taken the time to show them respect and given of their time and love. Grandparents—yes, even those who haven't had the advantage of a college education—are often the ones who are able to instill a real sense of values in a young child.

I want to go back to the man who thought he was above farmers and ask, "Did you eat breakfast this morning? If you did, thank a farmer." I respect those who are ever conscious of the value of every person and who show respect to them. They appreciate what each one contributes to society. They will be more like Jesus who had a deep respect for all of His people and demonstrated this during His earthly ministry.

Evelyn Glass

Cracking the Compassion Code

When Jesus landed and saw a large crowd,
he had compassion on them and healed their sick.
Matt. 14:14, NIV.

MY NEW YEAR'S RESOLUTION consisted of a single prayer that God would enable me to show more compassion for individuals around me who may be in distress. This simple, trivial, and unassuming prayer has led to a series of unpredictable events which have taught me some extremely invaluable lessons.

Last Monday night I went to a Mexican restaurant with my friend Brittany. When we arrived at Lamson Hall, the women's dormitory at Andrews University, we were approached by a female in distress. A complete stranger, I must add. She explained that her vehicle had stalled, and she was looking for someone to give her a jumpstart. My friend, immediately "moved with compassion" and without a hint of reluctance, offered her assistance. I must insert here that it was an extremely cold, winter night, and Brittany was not dressed suitably for the weather.

After this incident, I was struck with flashbacks from sermons I'd heard that centered on the biblical narrative of the good Samaritan. The most important character in this story acknowledged the life-threatening danger of helping a stranger. Yet, as a friend, he was moved with compassion and offered assistance.

I have learned that compassion occurs when our hearts are stirred by the Holy Spirit. This allows us to be moved, sometimes to the point of tears, because of the misfortunes of another. Compassion is not only an emotional or internal, passive acknowledgement of the need of another but is also an external, active response.

Compassion demands that we offer assistance even when it is not convenient. It also means that we must be willing to ignore factors such as gender, race, class, or religious affiliation, and reach out to individuals in need because we are all children of God.

Compassion could mean simply acknowledging that someone is in a difficult position and offering a word of prayer. Jesus may be asking you to say to someone today, "Don't give up; you can make it!" God might be calling you or me to be there for someone who needs a listening ear, an encouraging word, a loaf of bread, a jumpstart—for their hopes may have been stalled by the challenges of life.

Fay White

A Spitting Image

If you knew me, you would know my Father also.
John 8:20, NIV.

NO DOUBT you have heard it several times—it might even have been said about you. I have heard it said numerous times: "You are the spitting image of your dad." Now it was my daughter's turn to hear, "You look so much like your dad."

I pondered the statement. Was it just another cliché? Something people say as a conversation piece? But I'll tell you, I must agree with the comments. My daughter, Kadia, closely resembles her dad. Her physique, her complexion, her walk, and the way she stands are all like her dad. She even holds her cup the same way he does, with her little finger protruding. Her toes are shaped like her dad's. She has similar birthmarks. With all these and more she resembles her father. Indeed the statement is true: she really reflects her dad in more ways than I thought. She reflects her father, but not by choice. It is just in her genes.

Pondering this, a sobering thought overpowered me. Do I reflect my Father, my heavenly Father? How much do I reflect Him daily? Do I reflect Him in what I eat and drink? What do my mannerisms say of Him? Do I walk and talk like He does? When we come to really know God, we begin to reflect Him.

As I continued to think about this resemblance, I made a conscious effort to reassess myself. I resolved that day to review the character of my Father and I made a determination to be like Him.

When I reflect Him, others will see Him more clearly; they will see the reflection of my Father in me. They will come to know Him because of my love for others, the kindness that I show to those in need, my compassion for those who are struggling with harmful habits.

When Jesus Christ is everything to us—the first, the last, the best in everything—His Spirit and His character will color everything we are and do. We cannot then center our thoughts on self. It is no more we that live, but Christ that lives in us. Matthew 10:37 tells us that it is not family that is important, but Jesus Christ! Then we can truly declare that we are sons and daughters of our heavenly Father and King. We are the true image of our Father.

Gloria Gregory

No More Hidden Hands

Who may ascend the hill of the Lord? Who may stand in his holy place?
He who has clean hands and a pure heart.
Ps. 24:3, 4, NIV.

I'M NOT SURE WHEN IT STARTED, but every time I drew a picture of a person I would hide the hands behind the back. Whenever I did draw the hands, they would be popcorn-looking bubbles. As the mother of a small girl, I found myself drawing more and more often, and every time it came to the hands I got a little frustrated with my inability or unwillingness to portray them in a realistic way. Don't get me wrong—I'm no Leonardo da Vinci—but I'm very sure that in times gone by, I had been able to draw human hands.

The excuse I gave myself was that fingers were too complicated and took up too much time. But deep inside I knew the real reason: guilt. Like a child caught stealing cookies from the pantry, I hid my hands in shame. I was terrified that others might find out about the things I had done. Although I had confessed all the big and little sins and had stayed away from most of them, I still chose to hold onto the feelings of remorse in a vain attempt to earn God's forgiveness.

And so I sat myself down for a deep heart-to-heart talk, and I decided that it was about time I stopped hiding my hands because God had removed my sins from me and thrown them into the depths of the ocean. By hiding my hands in guilt, I was inadvertently telling God that I didn't believe that His forgiveness was real. I asked God to help me realize that this amazing gift of mercy and grace was free, and that no punishment I could give myself would ever make me worthy of His love.

So the next time my little girl asked me to draw pictures with her, I forced myself to draw human-looking hands with the correct shape and the right number of fingers.

No matter how grave your sins might have been, if you confess them to God, He will forgive them, and He won't expose your dirt to others. He will wash you clean, hands and all, so that you too can stand before Him faultless. As it says in Isaiah 1:18 (NKJV), "Though your sins are like scarlet, they shall be as white as snow; though they are red as crimson, they shall be like wool." I no longer hide my hands in drawings because Jesus' blood set me free from guilt. He can do the same for you.

Dinorah Blackman

Beware of the Tiny Spoilers

Catch us the foxes, the little foxes that spoil the vines, for our vines have tender grapes.
S. of Sol. 2:15, NKJV.

MY HUSBAND AND I were asked to work on the big island of Hawaii. When we arrived there we discovered that groceries and produce were very expensive. We shouldn't have been surprised because Hawaii is a tourist island and almost everything is shipped from the mainland.

Since we loved gardening, we decided to start a vegetable garden. My dream was to plant corn, okra, beans, cilantro, and several kinds of greens. If we succeeded, we could defray some of our grocery expenses. We were very blessed because a friend loaned us a tiller and even helped us make the plots. I was delighted that in a short time we had a huge garden with many kinds of vegetables. God was so generous to send the rains at nighttime and the sun during the day. But while the young plants were sprouting, we noticed that the tender leaves were disappearing. The culprits? Huge, ugly, giant slugs. I was so upset that I started killing them with a hoe. Every morning found me out in the garden killing those pesky slugs—comparatively little, but spoilers. At times I thought perhaps the Lord was unhappy with me for killing them, but I couldn't help declaring war against them.

Soon the garden looked lush and healthy because the enemies had been wiped away. I felt victorious and happy. The plants were robust and growing fast. The Lord was gracious in blessing our garden and when harvest time came, we had much to share with others in the area. In spite of those annoying slugs, we saw the fruits of our labor. But it wasn't only a one-day fight. It was a continuous, daily battle until the enemies were annihilated.

When I recall that experience of daily struggle against those giant slugs, I can't help but think of our struggles against the enemy of our souls. Ephesians 6:12 says, "For we do not wrestle against flesh and blood, but against principalities, against powers, against the rulers of the darkness of this age" (NKJV). Daily we need to fight against our weaknesses, too—our neglect of reading the Word, our lack of effective communion with God, wasting precious time in senseless TV watching, and other useless activities. Such weaknesses are the "slugs" we need to fight against so that our spiritual life may function in harmony with our heavenly Father's will.

Ofelia A. Pangan

Even Before I Asked

Delight yourself in the Lord and he will give you the desires of your heart.
Ps. 37:4, NIV.

BEATRICE CALLED ME at my home in England from Virginia in the United States. I was so happy to hear from her. We had visited for about an hour when I suddenly realized that my den was full of smoke. I rushed to the kitchen to discover that the microwave had not automatically shut off after a minute as was expected, but had been on for the entire hour. The pies were in flames and thick smoke filled the kitchen so that I could hardly breathe. I shut off the microwave and opened all the windows even though it was winter. Later I tried to clean the microwave, but it no longer worked. All the same, I was very grateful because God took care of the fire before it could turn into something disastrous. Our kind and able Father never fails us.

I did not forget to give a testimony about the incident the next day at Sabbath school. Though I would now be eating cold foods as I could not afford a new microwave, I did not complain. I left my heart's desire in God's able hands and forgot about it.

The sound of my doorbell awakened me the next morning. When I opened the door I saw one of the student pastors from Newbold College and his wife, Yohanna. With broad smiles, they held a brand new microwave! I was so confused with joy that I shut the door in their faces. When I finally invited them in, the pastor apologized for dropping in unexpectedly. Then he said that my testimony gave them the opportunity to help me. Ever since I'd been ill he and his wife had been wanting to help me in some way, but they could not think of what to do. So they were happy to realize that I needed a microwave. They quickly bought me one before someone else might think to do it. Dumbfounded, I watched as they assembled it for me, and I even managed to thank them. Thanks to God—no more cold food!

This is our faithful God who never fails His own. Sometimes He does not even wait for us to ask before He grants us our heart's desire or meets our needs. I was convinced that day that I belong to the great family of God. They fear Him and are ready to obey His voice when He speaks or sends them to help someone else. That gave me a glimpse of heaven where everyone will be one another's keeper. I thank the Lord for His grace which abounds for all.

May glory and adoration be unto Your holy Name.

Mabel Kwei

Depending on the Clock

The Lord is good unto them that wait for him, to the soul that seeketh him.
Lam. 3:25.

MY HUSBAND AND I are very reliant on our alarm clock. Each night after our prayers are said, we set the alarm for 5:45 a.m. Then the lights are turned off. We have gone as far as to check up on each other to make sure that the clock is set for the next day. We have grown so accustomed to having the alarm sound at 5:45 every morning that on those days when we don't need the alarm—because we're sleeping later—the resounding beep still sings in our minds and ears.

One night my husband and I were sure that we had set the alarm. We had gone through the routine—prayers, clock, and lights—and confidently went to bed. But the alarm did not ring the next morning and we both overslept. What had happened? Frustrated and annoyed, we tried to recoup the time lost by rushing to get ready and quickly heading out the door. We had no time then to figure out what had gone wrong.

That evening, my husband discovered what went wrong. The night before, the clock's plug had been pulled from the socket and its backup battery had not been replaced. Just then the realization hit me. I depended on this tangible object to wake me up in the mornings, but it had failed me. Yet, I often struggle to truly depend on the great I AM. I thought of the many times I depended on the bus to arrive on time and was disappointed when it arrived late. Nevertheless, I went back the following day fully expecting that the bus would show up on time. I depended on my car to run, even though it left me stranded on the road. I knew once I got the engine checked, the transmission serviced, or new spark plugs, that my car would be reliable. Yet it was hard for me to rely on God.

Today's text states, "The Lord is good unto them that wait for him." God has given us His word that He is available every second, every minute, and every hour of every day. He will not fail or disappoint.

The prophet Jeremiah says that it is only by God's grace and compassion that we are still alive. God has proved that we can rely on Him. We don't have to turn Him on, plug Him in, or do anything else to be sure He is ready. His grace and compassion are new every morning (Lam. 3:22, 23). Rely on God today. You will not be disappointed.

Diantha Hall-Smith

Friendship

Therefore, since we have been justified through faith, we have peace with God through our Lord Jesus Christ, through whom we have gained access by faith into this grace in which we now stand. And we rejoice in the hope of the glory of God. Not only so, but we also rejoice in our sufferings, because we know that suffering produces perseverance; perseverance, character; and character, hope. And hope does not disappoint us, because God has poured out his love into our hearts by the Holy Spirit, whom he has given us.
Rom. 5:1-5, NIV.

FRIENDSHIPS COME IN ALL SIZES and shapes. They may be casual or deep and trusting. Sometimes we are separated from our friends by betrayal or death, or simply because one moved away. Interests, too, may change. Whatever the reason, friendships change or do not always last.

Jesus wants a friendship with you and with me—the long lasting kind. One we can always depend on. What will that kind of friendship do for us? Our relationships with others will change because we will start looking at life differently. We will have peace with God through Jesus Christ (Ps. 29:11). We will have faith. We will no longer live with hostility, fear, or rejection because we are in God's presence.

We will have joy as we face the hard times, as well as the happy times, that come into our lives. We know that God has a purpose and plan for our lives. He can take the bad times and make good out of them. We are on the path to heaven. God wants us ready. So our joy is real now and in our future as we share our lives with God and others.

Our resources from God will never run dry. He has an abundant supply. He will give us more than we need or could want. His love overflows for us. He gives us the Holy Spirit to change our thinking and to show us how real God's love and friendship really are. The proof of that love is Jesus dying on Calvary for you and me.

The door to our friendship with Jesus is always open. We don't have to stay on the outside. We are always welcome on the inside no matter who we are or what our lives have been. His friendship is always there for the asking. You will not be denied.

I am most grateful for Jesus' friendship and what that friendship has done for me. He tells me that my friendship with Him is deep and abiding. He gives me the invitation to "Come, I'll always be here waiting for you."

Carolyn Voss

Every Little Thing

In all your ways acknowledge Him, and He shall direct your paths.
Prov. 3:6, NKJV.

IT WAS ONE OF THOSE DAYS when there seemed no end to the errands I needed to run. I had gone to pick up material for a sewing project, to get paper, envelopes, and card stock for my office, and to try to find a suitable toy for my newest grandchild. Add this to grocery shopping, going to the post office and the bank, and—well, I'm sure you get the idea.

As I was coming out of the office supply store I toyed with the idea of going to a neighboring mall just across the river from where we live. We had been gone all winter, and I wondered what new stores might have come in. I thought I would just go and check it out.

As I got into the car, the radio came on with the news. It was mostly just background sound until I heard the name of the shopping mall where I was planning to go. It seems there was a big traffic problem there and many police cars were on the scene. They were asking drivers to avoid that area of the freeway. As I sat there in shock, I thought how interesting that God was, in His way, telling me not to go there.

You see, I am one of those people who just cannot start my day without giving it all to God. I know that His plans for me are much better than my own. I do make plans, but if I don't get everything done, I figure there is a reason for it, and it's OK. God has many ways of speaking to us, but never before had He spoken to me through a news item on my car radio. I hardly ever have the radio on—it was just at the right time to inform me, and I could not believe what a mess it would have been had I gone without knowing. It would not have been a sinful thing to do; it was just one of those instances where God knew how frustrating it would be for me, and He "spoke" to me before I ever went.

Once again, it was brought to my attention that God truly does care about every little thing that concerns our peace. He wants us to be happy, and how better to insure that I have a good day than to turn it over to Him? Even if something goes wrong, I know He will be right there with me, giving me peace. See how close His salvation is to those who fear Him? As Jesus said, "Peace I leave with you; my peace I give you. I do not give to you as the world gives. Do not let your hearts be troubled and do not be afraid" (John 14:27, NIV).

Anna May Radke Waters

The Glory of the Lord

To the Israelites the glory of the Lord looked like a consuming fire on top of the mountain.
Ex. 24:17, NIV.

WE WERE TRAVELING IN ISRAEL with a tour group. A trip to the Sinai Peninsula and an ascent of Mount Sinai were also included in the program. It was still dark when we set out after a short night's rest, and we intended to be back for breakfast. It would have been too hot to climb the mountain under the midday sun as there are no trees or bushes to provide shade.

Some had flashlights and others followed step by step behind the lights. Some camels accompanied us. We could have ridden them to make the ascent less strenuous, but those who tried it soon got down again as they grew almost seasick from the rolling movements of the camel. Slowly the day began to dawn. We were still climbing upwards over stone slab-like steps. It was such an effort, and sometimes we stumbled over stones in the darkness.

At last we arrived at the mountaintop where Moses is said to have received from God the Ten Commandments written on tablets of stone. There we saw a wonderful spectacle. The whole of Sinai, the desert and the mountains, began to shine, reflecting the rising sun. The landscape glowed in hues of red, from a brilliant dark red to orange and, finally, a lighter pink. It was as we read in Exodus 24: "the glory of the Lord looked like a consuming fire on top of the mountain."

Awed by this wonderful experience, we got our Bibles out of our backpacks and read the words the Lord spoke to Moses: "Come up to me on the mountain and stay here, and I will give you the tablets of stone, with the law and commands I have written for their instruction" (Ex. 24:12, NIV).

All too soon we had to start our descent to flee the burning sun which was already making the stones hot. On that memorable morning the Lord let me, once more, see His glory and love for us. He gave Moses His commandments, written with His own finger. In these commands given on Mount Sinai God placed the family, men and women, under His protection. His law is the record of the respect and esteem we should have one for the other.

Traveling to biblical places has always been a source of joy and strength for me. It reminds me of God's greatness and omnipotence and how much I need His guidance every day.

Ingrid Naumann

Faith on the Menu

When he looked up and saw a large crowd coming toward him, Jesus said to Philip,
"Where are we to buy bread for these people to eat?" He said this to test him,
for he himself knew what he was going to do. Philip answered him, "Six months'
wages would not buy enough bread for each of them to get a little."
John 6:5-7, NRSV.

I AM PART OF THE HOSPITALITY MINISTRY TEAM at our church. Whenever we have a fellowship meal, regardless of how much the team has cooked the previous day, it always appears to me that the crowd of people lined up to eat will need double the amount of food we have in the kitchen. Usually I make mental rapid calculations and think about making an urgent trip home to raid my freezer. But just before we go out and serve, the team gathers in the kitchen for fervent prayer. Then we go out and serve in faith.

When faced with a crowd of hungry people who'd been following Him, Jesus saw an opportunity to test Philip's faith. Philip, however, unaware that he was being tested, started some panic calculations. By any reckoning, six months' wages is a lot of money to expect one person to carry around just in case it is needed for groceries. Worse still, as far as Philip was concerned, even if he had that much money it would buy just a small portion for each person there. It was hardly worth organizing the seating arrangements and taking the lunch of one small boy. Or was it? John 6:6 says that this was a test, because Jesus already knew what He would do. He wanted to teach Philip a lesson about faith, not about planning a meal on a tight budget.

When we face situations which seem overwhelming, Jesus already knows what He will do. Equally, when we worry about what to feed extra guests, Jesus already knows what He will do. Jesus is asking us to step away from the daily concerns which can demoralize us. He is waiting for us to recognize that the kingdom of God is not about eating and drinking, but rather about righteousness, peace, and joy in the Holy Spirit (Rom. 14:17, NRSV).

There's always enough to feed our guests at the fellowship lunches, yet I become concerned every time I see a crowd. Seeking God's peace and a place in His kingdom, each day my prayer is, *Lord, help me to entrust my every care to You. When I exercise faith, I know exactly what You will do.*

Judith Purkiss

Holy, Healing Band-aids

Get rid of all bitterness, rage, anger, harsh words, and slander,
as well as all types of evil behavior.
Eph. 4:31, NLT.

I FELT DRAINED AND LIMP and my legs balked at walking. My thoughts were muddled and tears trailed cold as I struggled to focus on Mom's pale cheeks against the white sheets on the gurney. The heart catheterization, scheduled for a brief 45 minutes, had taken a terrible eight hours. Then the doctor spewed a torrent of words on my dad and me. We listened intently but all I could make out was, "I put a Band-Aid on your mom's heart. There is little we can do." I'm a nurse, but I felt as helpless as a tiny child and understood very little of what the doctor said. His manner did not invite questions.

Mom was transferred to the coronary ICU and my dad and I were ushered to an L-shaped waiting room. Troubled faces lined its walls. Voices quivered. Dad sat silent and numb beside me as I sobbed and trembled, my heart stunned by the harsh, abrupt news.

In the midst of the crowded room of chattering, tear-blurred faces, a soft female voice broke into the noise and a warm hand squeezed mine. "Honey, can I pray with you?" The room fell into a reverent silence. I don't recall a word of the prayer she uttered, but I will never forget the presence of God in the room as she knelt boldly before Him and humbly before us.

Eleven years have passed since that day when the quick-fix bandage on Mom's heart was blessed by prayer, hallowed and holy. Its strength lies in the Lord.

We touch and are touched countless times as we live our story. Moments like finding a soul mate, rocking our babies and grandbabies, a wink, a smile, the words "I love you"—these "forever" moments change us forever.

Pharmacy shelves display an array of adhesive bandages: Strawberry Shortcake, Dora, Mickey Mouse, and more—all designed to help heal small hearts while healing tiny wounds. But broken, wounded hearts change us too. Wounds like death and sickness that pierce the heart may be clearly visible, but wounds inflicted by thoughtless, cruel words can be hidden deep inside. Yet they sting and slowly crush our bodies and our spirits.

You could change a life forever, maybe your own. Share a holy, healing strip of compassion and forgiveness that has been blessed by God.

Judy Good Silver

God Knows All

Indeed, the very hairs of your head are all numbered. Don't be afraid.
Luke 12:7, NIV.

WE NEVER LIKED FRIDAYS in the office. Things could be left unattended other week-days, but on the last working day there was no choice but to deal with the logistics and shipping. Everything had to be sent out. One certain Friday I was already hungry at 9.00 a.m., and that was unusual for me. Time flew as I worked, but by noon hunger gnawed at my stomach.

It was not possible to take a lunch break—I had to forget it. I consoled myself with the thought that I'd have a good supper that evening. The work didn't let up. The telephone rang constantly. Suddenly my husband was on the phone. He said he'd be picking me up from work an hour later than usual. He had to see to something in the hospital. It was urgent.

I was exasperated. My hunger was almost killing me, and now I had to wait another hour. The phone was ringing when we finally arrived home. It was someone from the hospital asking my husband to come back because they'd forgotten to have some papers signed. Not back there again! What about food? For some reason I accompanied my husband, but I was mad at the incompetent hospital personnel. My hunger really hurt by now.

At the hospital ward, a nurse told us that the doctor who had the papers to be signed had been called to an emergency surgery. We were asked to wait. My husband was the official caretaker of the affairs of an elderly woman who was to have surgery the next morning. I decided to spend the waiting time at her bedside. I found her despondent, crying, and trembling. For two hours I tried to comfort her and encourage her. Slowly she calmed down and placed her life in God's hands. Just at this moment the doctor arrived and my husband signed the papers.

On my way home I realized why the doctor had forgotten to get the signature in the first place. It was God's plan! Jesus, our Savior, had seen the need of the elderly woman and sent me to console her so that she could face the surgery with hope.

Nothing happens—not a single hair falls from our heads—that God doesn't register. God knows all. He knew where I was needed. And I was hungry no more. Praise the Lord of the heavens who sees and directs everything

Ursula Ziegler

The Gift of My Time

Hear, O Israel: The Lord our God, the Lord is one. Love the Lord your God with all your heart and with all your soul and with all your strength. These commandments I give you today are to be upon your hearts. Impress them on your children. Talk about them when you sit at home and when you walk along the road, when you lie down and when you get up.
Deut. 6:4-7, NIV.

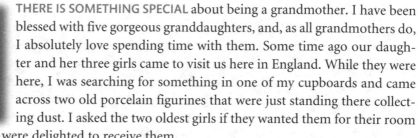

THERE IS SOMETHING SPECIAL about being a grandmother. I have been blessed with five gorgeous granddaughters, and, as all grandmothers do, I absolutely love spending time with them. Some time ago our daughter and her three girls came to visit us here in England. While they were here, I was searching for something in one of my cupboards and came across two old porcelain figurines that were just standing there collecting dust. I asked the two oldest girls if they wanted them for their room and they were delighted to receive them.

The 4-year-old who was playing on the floor looked up at what was happening but then continued to play. A few minutes passed. Then she got up and came and stood in front of me. Holding her two chubby little empty hands toward me, she said, "Here is nothing you have given me."

Since that day, I have often thought of her words: "Here is nothing you have given me." Have I only filled her little hands with material gifts, things that will break, go out of fashion, fade, and loose value as time goes by? Or have I also given her gifts of the heart, gifts of eternal value?

The older I get the more I realize how important it is for me to not only give these little ones gifts in their hands, but to give them the gift of my time. I want to spend more time listening to their concerns, more time talking about things of eternal value, more time praying with them, telling them of Jesus' love for them, and giving them the opportunity to express their love for Jesus. We greatly undervalue the precious gift of time. God has shown me a model in Deuteronomy 6:4-9 of how I should spend my time with my grandchildren: I am to talk about God and what He has done for us at all times and in all the ways I can. As an example it even says, "Write them on the doorframes of your houses and on your gates" (verse 9). I pray that I will remember this model the next time I get to spend time with my granddaughters. I want not only to give them material gifts, but also to give them the gift of my time.

Anne-May Wollan

God Sees Me

So God created humankind in his image, in the image of God he created them.
Gen 1:27, NRSV.

I'VE OFTEN WONDERED about this God who created me in His image. Who is He? I guess that's a question many of us have asked at different times in our lives. One day, not too long ago, I decided to search the Bible to find out just who God really is. I found that the best way to answer this question was to look at the character of God through names people gave Him because of something He did for them or because of how they saw Him act in a given situation. From my readings I'll share with you a different name of God that has given me strength and joy.

I've been through trials, and once the question came to mind: Where is God? Does He see me? Does He know I'm suffering? Then in Genesis 16 I found the name that Hagar, an Egyptian slave, gave to God. Hagar ran away from her mistress Sarai who was treating her harshly. You know the story: disobedience on Abraham's and Sarah's part gave birth to a situation that should never have been. But in her distress and pain, God did not forsake Hagar. He met her near a desert spring and gave her a promise for the future of the child she carried. Overjoyed that the God of Abraham came to her and gave her a promise, she called him *El Roi*—"The God who sees me."

Amazing! Hagar was not one of God's chosen. She was a pagan. Yet He saw her distress and visited her and gave her comfort and hope. He saw her. Does God see me in my distress? Oh, yes He does. He sees me and loves me and promises me that He who made me in His image will never forsake me (Heb. 13:5).

An old hymn says, "His eye is on the sparrow, and I know He watches me." Today I praise God for His watch care. No matter what my situation, He sees me. He is my *El Roi*. And He sees you too. In times of discouragement and distress, you are not alone. There is One who watches over you. Remember, "The Lord looks down from heaven; he sees all humankind. From where he sits enthroned he watches all the inhabitants of the earth—he who fashions the hearts of them all, and observes all their deeds. . . . Truly the eye of the Lord is on those who fear him . . . to deliver their soul from death" (Ps 33:13-19 [NRSV]).

Heather-Dawn Small

The Robe of Righteousness

I will greatly rejoice in the Lord, my soul shall be joyful in my God; for he hath clothed me with the garments of salvation, he hath covered me with the robe of righteousness.
Isa. 61:10.

ONE EVENING we sat in the waiting room of a hospital in Mongolia while a friend visited a patient. Hospitals in Mongolia allow only one visitor at a time and they are very strict about it. The Mongolians do their best to keep their hospitals and clinics clean as they are inspected from time to time by the health department. My husband and I were watching people go in and out of the hospital when suddenly we heard bloodcurdling screams coming from upstairs. Hospital personnel began running here and there. The police arrived a short time later, and we became a bit fearful. Later our friend told us that a man who had come to see a relative refused to wear the hospital gown over his own clothes. There is a rule in Mongolia that every one who visits a patient must wear a gown provided by the hospital. The man was drunk and insisted that his own clothes were cleaner and better than the hospital gown and flatly refused to wear it. When a nurse took his arm to stop him from going in the room, he hit her. She screamed for help. Police arrived on the scene, seized the drunk, handcuffed him, and locked him in one of the empty rooms. The offender was left in the locked room all night.

This incident reminded me of Jesus' parable of the man who refused to wear the wedding garment that the groom had provided for the invitees. The man without the garment was bound and thrown into outer darkness.

How important it is for every one of us to keep the rules. Those who keep them do not get into trouble. And how much more important it is that we who are followers of Christ accept the robe of righteousness offered by our Lord Jesus Christ. Those who are not covered by the robe will not enter heaven and will not have a part in the wedding reception in heaven. Like the drunk, many of us think that our righteousness is good enough, but Isaiah 64:6 says that "all our righteousnesses are as filthy rags."

"Look away from yourself to the perfection of Christ. We cannot manufacture a righteousness for ourselves. Christ has in His hands the pure robes of righteousness, and He will put them upon us" (*That I May Know Him*, p. 241).

Birol Charlotte Christo

The Hiding Place

Rescue me from my enemies, O Lord, for I hide myself in you.
Ps. 143:9, NIV.

THE HIGHLIGHT OF A RECENT TRIP to Holland was a visit to the Ten Boom home in Haarlem. This house became a refuge, a literal "hiding place" for fugitives and people sought by the Nazis during World War II. By protecting them, the Ten Booms put themselves in real danger. Their nonviolent resistance against the Nazi-oppressor was an act of faith. This faith led them to hide Jews, students who refused to cooperate with the enemy, and members of the Dutch underground resistance movement. Their home became a center of underground activity with a network of contacts.

In the living room we listened to the moving history of this family of faith and then embarked on a tour through the home. Of special interest was Corrie ten Boom's bedroom for it contained "the hiding place." The fugitives removed a box from the bottom shelf of a cupboard, lifted a door big enough to crawl through, and hid behind a false wall. As I studied this small opening, I knew I could never make it with my back problems. Those sheltered in the house practiced until they all could be hidden in only 70 seconds.

On February 28, 1944, the family was betrayed, and the Gestapo raided the house. Six members of the family were arrested, plus another 30 friends who visited, unaware of the betrayal. But the Gestapo did not discover the four Jews and two resistance members safe in their "hiding place." The Gestapo stayed in the house a number of days, convinced that Jews were hidden there, hoping to starve them out.

Though Corrie's father soon died in prison and her sister Betsie died in Ravensbrück, a notorious women's concentration camp located in Germany where they were interned, Corrie survived. After the war she traveled the world for 30 years testifying of the power of God's love and forgiveness. She encouraged all she met with the message that Jesus Christ is victor over everything, even the violent, hopeless misery of a concentration camp.

The Ten Boom museum is more than just a museum. It reflects in a powerful way the spiritual strength and active life in faith of this family.

Lord, may I be a faithful witness for You in everything that I do today. We all need the kind of faith shown by this family who opposed the enemy in the face of death.

Nancy L. Van Pelt

Forgive as Christ Forgives

Forgive us our sins, for we also forgive everyone who sins against us.
Luke 11:4, NIV.

THE MAN WHO SAID he would marry my sister left her instead with a broken heart, a baby, and a beautiful wedding gown she didn't use. His action caused my sister untold pain and my family and me great sadness and hurt. The mention of his name—even the very thought of him—reminded us of his despicable behavior and the unspeakable grief it placed on everyone involved. Until about two years after his disappearance his name was seldom mentioned. Forgiveness is hard.

Talking casually, my sister hinted that he wanted to come back and marry her. My first thought screamed, *No way!* But as I heard her words, and knowing her so well, I detected a softness that indicated she had already forgiven him. So I prayed that the Lord would set my heart aright and that I would be a support for my sister and not a stumbling block.

A few months later she phoned to ask if I would forgive him and give them a chance to be a family. Obviously, she didn't need my permission, but the thought of doing something that I would not be a part of didn't sit well with her. I quickly responded, "Of course, I'll support you." She knew that this was not easy for me and said so.

Behind my enthusiasm to be supportive was a heart transplant wrought by the spirit of the living God. As I grumbled against that man, the Spirit reminded me that we have all sinned, and that no sin, however grievous, is greater or lesser than the other. We all stand in need of a Savior—a man called Jesus—who stands at the right side of the Father and constantly pleads our cases. We are forgiven, not because of what we do, but because of what Jesus did on the cross and continues to do on our behalf.

"But if we confess our sins, he will forgive our sins, because we can trust God to do what is right. He will cleanse us from all the wrongs we have done" (1 John 1:9, NCV). What Jesus does for me in the cleansing and the forgiveness of my many sins propels me to forgive others whether they hurt me, my precious sister, or anyone else.

Dear Lord, it is not easy to forgive with a heart of flesh. Please give us the heart of Jesus and the mind of the Holy Spirit so we can forgive as You have willingly forgiven us.

Rose Thomas

If God Can Use a Donkey

*Being confident of this, that he who began a good work in you
will carry it on to completion until the day of Christ Jesus.*
Phil. 1:6, NIV.

WHEN WE LIVED IN SOUTHERN CALIFORNIA, I had the special job of traveling six days a week to three area hospitals to distribute questionnaires and gather data for a university study on the effects of alcohol on the fetus during pregnancy. During the almost three years I did this, I became acquainted with many wonderful people who worked and served in those hospitals.

My husband, who'd been taking graduate studies at the university, accepted a teaching position in Ohio. Before we moved, I wanted to give a token of appreciation to the many people who had enabled my work and touched my life.

I'd recently rediscovered the joy of writing. With the help of friends, I self-published a thin volume of poetry and prose titled *First Draft* and gave it away as a farewell remembrance. One recipient, a senior chaplain, invited me to his office. After thanking me for the book, he leaned back and said, "When I was a young pastor I wanted to become a great preacher. It felt good when people shook my hand and said, 'Good sermon today!' I thought I could improve on my sermons by asking, 'What do you remember most about the sermon?' Do you know what? Not one person remembered a single line. What they told me had little or nothing to do with what I'd preached. My words had only triggered memories or other thoughts in their minds.

"It made me terribly depressed. I thought of giving up the ministry—until I remembered Balaam's donkey [Numbers 22]. God had instructed Balaam, but in his greed for money and power he tuned God out. So God made the donkey speak."

He chuckled. "It taught me not to take myself too seriously. I realized if God could use a donkey, He could use me, too, in any way He chooses. If people hear something different from what I say, it is God speaking to their needs, not me. I decided to just do my best and leave the rest with God."

What a nice way of telling me that I hadn't written a best seller but still it would bless. But it's also a priceless lesson for me in every aspect of my life: Do my best by His power and grace and leave the rest with God.

Lois Rittenhouse Pecce

Saved From the Lion's Den

The Lord himself goes before you and will be with you;
he will never leave you nor forsake you.
Deut. 31:8, NIV.

THE PATIENT WAS A YOUNG, influential newspaper reporter on hemodialysis as a result of chronic kidney disease. He subsequently contracted hepatitis. According to the protocol followed on the hemodialysis unit at that time, persons with hepatitis were not permitted in the program, since the nature of the procedure could put other patients at risk. As coordinator of the Nosocomial Infection Control Commission, I worked closely with the hemodialysis team, and it was clear that the patient in question should be removed from the program.

Notwithstanding clear directives, it was decided to hold a special meeting of the hemodialysis team, the medical director of the hospital, and myself. At this meeting, the protocol was rehearsed, discussed, and discussed yet again. All present offered opinions. I could not understand why there was all this talk when we all were well aware of the directives. I was tempted to say, "Be done with it! This patient must be removed from hemodialysis." But I held my peace. After about two hours of deliberations the meeting ended with no decision made or action taken.

I thought and thought about the matter and could make no sense of it. I am a person of strong character, clear ideas, and knowledge regarding my areas of expertise, and quite ready to state my views and offer recommendations. But on this occasion, although participating, I—strangely for me—refrained from making a definite recommendation. Then it dawned on me. All were waiting for me to pronounce the death sentence!

My career would have probably come to a screeching halt. The newspaper headlines flashed on the screen of my mind's eye: "Heartless Woman Doctor Dooms Newspaperman to Die!" "Doctor Places Procedures Above Patient's Life," and so on.

I was in a den of lions, and, as the youngest, was being set up to unwittingly make the call that those older and wiser in medical politics were skillfully avoiding. Yes, all agreed, tacitly, that the patient should not continue on hemodialysis, but who would make the decision? My God delivered me. He intervened and saved me from the lion's mouth when I was too innocent to even begin to comprehend the issues at stake. What a mighty God we serve!

Marion V. Clarke Martin

Touched by the Sun

Great is his faithfulness; his lovingkindness begins afresh each day.
Lam. 3:23, TLB.

I MUST ADMIT I'm not often awake to greet the dawn of a new day. However, when I am, it's a wondrous joy to watch the sun dispel the darkness and flood the earth with God's gift of light and color.

When my husband and I go camping, we enjoy the quieter spots where we can appreciate nature at its best. By the river a chorus of various birds awaken us early in the morning. Kookaburras laugh, magpies warble, cockatoos screech, and the butcher birds' clear dulcet call is one of my favorites. Likewise, by the sea the flocks of gulls and terns squawk and pelicans grunt. No matter where they are, come daybreak each bird sings its happy song without complaint. In complete faith that dawn will break, they often begin their chatter while it's still dark.

How quickly the darkness is dissolved as the world comes alight with the rising sun. The landscape can look dull and changed when clouds rush over, and this makes so much difference when endeavoring to capture photos. Recently this became very important when we visited central Australia.

My father, an active 88-year-old, joined us on our travels. One of the great attractions of this part of Australia is Ayers Rock (Uluru), and he was anxious to see this in all its glory at sunrise. This rock can change progressively from gray to purple, brown, orange, yellow, and bright red—but only if there is sun. Every day hundreds of tourists line the roadway at sunrise and sunset to capture the colors the sun brings to this rock. We were not disappointed, and we took many pictures. However, the sunlight did not last. Clouds came in and Uluru became a very ordinary color.

Most of the rock formations in outback Australia turn brilliant colors when the sun shines. We visited a place called Rainbow Valley, and I can only liken its color to the red and yellow embers of a camp fire. Once again, without the sun its attraction vanishes.

As Jesus' light touches our lives with the sunshine of His love, may we reflect Him and His beauty. He has given life and salvation. Without the Son of God our lives would have vanished too, just like the color of the rocks without sunshine.

Lyn Welk-Sandy

God Cares About Little Things

Before they call I will answer.
Isa. 65:24, NIV.

GOOD YARD WORKERS are hard to come by, and I was getting a bit desperate as our yard— back, front, and sides—needed someone to dig out the weeds, trim the shrubs and the bottlebrush tree, mow the lawn, remove the tall grass growing between and among the plants, rake the leaves, and prune some of the fruit trees. With a recent injury to his foot, my husband was unable to tend to the yard chores. Besides, he didn't relish weeding and climbing a ladder to cut and shape the tree in the front yard. It was shaped like a disc and trimming it was a no-no for a senior. After some thought, I found a card that I had received from a yardman about a year before. I called the number and made an appointment for him to come and give me an estimate—which he did. After explaining all the things that needed to be done, we agreed on a price and he and a helper set to work.

After filling our trash can and several plastic bags with leaves and cuttings, they declared that they had finished the job. But when I inspected their work I discovered that much of the grass between the shrubs wasn't cut, the weeds had been plucked, not dug out, and the branches I wanted cut still remained. To add to my disappointment and frustration, one of the sprinkler heads was broken and the TV cable which was draped on one of the shrubs in the backyard was severed. They denied cutting the cable with their weed whacker but did replace the broken sprinkler head. After much discussion, I made out a check minus a small amount to pay for mending the cable.

The next day I went outside to look at the cable. To my surprise it had been taped together in a professional manner—and the TV was working again. I immediately inspected the two gates and the garage door. All were securely locked. No one could have come into the backyard to repair that cable. It was a mystery to my husband also. Could an angel have repaired it? Anything is possible with the Lord. I was overwhelmed with awe and thanked Him that He was not too busy to perform a miracle.

I have shared this story with some of my friends. Some are skeptical, but I know that I didn't ask God, and that He acted before I asked. How is it with you, dear readers? How has the Lord met your needs even before you asked?

Aileen L. Young

Your Hand in My Life

You hem me in—behind and before; you have laid your hand upon me.
Ps. 139:5, NIV.

HER VOICE WAS SO FULL of emotion that my friend Nadine could hardly share her experience of a few days before. She had read from Psalm 139 that morning for her devotions, little realizing how much verse 5 would come alive for her that day.

As she left for town she had several important errands to attend to. First she dropped the letters into a curbside mailbox and then went to the bank. Nadine and her husband were building their dream home, and she had a bank bag of money to deposit to pay for materials. But when she got to the bank the money bag was missing. Her heart sank. Now what? Retracing her steps she checked around the mailbox, even asking the postal clerk to open the box to see if she had accidently dropped the money in with the mail, but it wasn't there. When she reported her loss to the police they didn't give her much hope as there had been several thefts in that area recently.

Although she dreaded the next step, Nadine told her husband what had happened. His first question was, "Have you prayed about it?" Of course she assured him she had been praying all along. And she had told of her trust in God to everyone she talked to.

As Beverly walked to work that morning, she discovered a bank bag on the street near the curbside mailbox. Upon opening it she saw quite a sum of money. Her first thought was how much that would help in paying some upcoming bills. But her next thought was that the money wasn't hers and the only thing to do was look for the owner. When she got to work she discussed the matter with her boss and he offered to help her find the owner. In the bag he noticed the name of an area lab technician whom he recognized, and soon the money was returned to Nadine and her husband.

Although Nadine didn't care about publicity for herself, she thought that Beverly should be rewarded for her honesty. Also she wanted people to know how God had answered her prayers. Two days later, on February 14, the day that love is traditionally honored, the local newspaper gave the story front page coverage, and the area radio station featured the incident.

Thank You, Father God, for laying Your hand on Nadine's life and rewarding her faithfulness by answering her prayers.

Betty J. Adams

Serving as Instruments for God

Blessed are those who mourn, for they will be comforted.
Matt. 5:4, NIV.

I LOVE TO TRAVEL and since I usually travel alone this gives me the opportunity to meet very interesting people. But on one specific trip I had decided that I would not engage in conversation with any other passengers. I was so tired from all the usual preparation it takes for a trip that I just wanted to relax and sleep.

After going through the long lines at check-in counters and the routines at security checkpoints, I finally boarded the plane and made myself comfortable, relaxing just as I had planned. Next to me sat a middle-aged woman. She seemed a little distraught and was dressed in black. I discreetly looked at her and thought that it would not be difficult to keep to my plan of resting and not talking to anybody in the plane.

After four hours of flying the plane was ready to land. I was content that the flight was over and I would see my family soon. As the airplane taxied on the tarmac I looked at my seatmate again and decided to ask her why she was making her trip.

With a quivering voice and with a lot of sadness on her face she told me that her sister and her family of six had been in an accident the day before, and all six were killed. She was going to the funeral. How awful and guilty I felt! How selfish I was. How many comforting words could I have said to her in four hours? How could I have missed the opportunity to tell her about our loving God and His love for the sufferer? I tried to say some comforting words but I was not very successful. I immediately elevated a prayer to God asking for help for this desperate soul who was suffering. I also prayed for forgiveness—I had miserably failed God. He had put me there as a means to console her in her grief.

We are God's instruments to reach and help others in any possible way. He puts people in our way for a purpose. Let's allow the Lord to do His work through us. Perhaps we all should think about Colossians 3:12, 13, which says in part: "Therefore, as God's chosen people, holy and dearly loved, clothe yourselves with compassion, kindness, humility, gentleness and patience" (NIV).

Dear God, I want to be Your instrument. Please use me to be a blessing to others—and help me to be ready and willing.

Hannelore Gomez

Waiting Lines

But they that wait upon the Lord shall renew their strength; they shall mount up with wings
as eagles; they shall run, and not be weary; and they shall walk, and not faint.
Isa. 40:31.

THE OTHER DAY I had a painful one-hour-and-forty-five-minute waiting experience. My husband and I were among hundreds of passengers from five aircraft that
landed in quick succession. A deluge of passengers formed into long, snakelike lines
in the immigration room.

I occupied myself by people watching. A procession of wheelchair passengers
were also waiting during that time. A baby protested so loudly that Mom hastily
took him out of the stroller and started dancing with him in their restricted space.
A 4-year-old boy entertained himself by playing hide-and-seek with his noncom-
pliant mom. Some complainers completed the picture.

What did I do? I dreamed up innovative ways to make the wait more bearable.
I pictured that a popcorn vendor, a marimba player, or a large TV screen with
comic cartoons would be pleasant additions to the otherwise stressful waiting
room. I even wished that an invisible agent would whisk us away from our Number
325 place in the line and land us right in front of an immigration officer.

Waiting slows us down, makes us captives, and deprives us of control.
However, waiting is not always bad. Today's text enumerates some benefits of waiting: renewed strength, mounting up like eagles, running and not being weary, walking and not fainting. Waiting does not have to mean useless inactivity. We can still
continue our journey and fulfill God's purpose for us while we wait. "Wait on the
Lord: be of good courage, and he shall strengthen thine heart: wait, I say, on the
Lord" (Ps. 27:14).

Perhaps you, too, are in a waiting room. Pray, "Show me Your ways, O Lord;
teach me Your paths. Lead me in Your truth and teach me; for You are the God of
my salvation; on You I wait all the day" (Ps. 25:4, 5, NKJV).

And guess what? An agent actually whisked us out of the line and directed us
to an immigration officer. That is how our God works. He comes in His own time
and delivers us out of the waiting line or room. Our challenge is to wait patiently,
to be of good courage, and to look for His presence as we continue to wait.

Gloria Lindsey Trotman

Florida Adventure

The Lord preserveth the simple: I was brought low, and he helped me.
Ps. 116:6.

MY DAUGHTER WAS TEACHING at a Christian school in Florida and during her spring break she had planned a wonderful vacation for her family. I flew to Orlando and my other daughter, her husband, and my two grandsons traveled to Florida in her in-law's RV.

We journeyed as far south as Key West, camping all along the way, with each new place providing an exciting adventure. One of my favorite excursions was collecting shells on the beaches.

Both the boys had head colds but managed to shake off their infections after a few days.

As my vacation drew to an end, I felt poorly but thought I had just caught a cold from being in close quarters in the RV. I tried to ignore the situation but it continued to worsen. My daughter's friend (who later became her husband) is a doctor, and he told her that he thought I had pneumonia. Still, until I was quite weak, I refused to even consider that I was extremely ill. I didn't want to be a burden to my busy daughter and I wanted to return to my home as my roundtrip ticket would soon expire.

Finally, I consented to let my daughter and her friend search for a clinic that would be open that evening, but to no avail. So they took me to the emergency room at the Florida Hospital. Test after test was arranged, and indeed I did have pneumonia in both lungs. A pulmonary specialist and a cardiologist were assigned to my case as they found atrial fibrillation, which is an irregular heart beat.

I was restricted to the ICU of the hospital for a few days until a room opened up on another floor. When a chaplain came to pray with me, reality sunk in. I was in trouble and in need of healing prayer. Many friends, family, and church people provided that strength.

The burden fell on my daughter to make all necessary phone calls to my employment manager, church, and the airlines to reschedule my departure time. I was confined to the hospital for nine days, and the cardiologist tactlessly told me, "You could have died." I prayed to the Lord with a thankful heart because He delivered me from death's door when I procrastinated getting treatment. *Father, forgive us for waiting to come to You for ultimate healing. We come today.*

Retha McCarty

Living Examples

*If a brother or sister is naked and destitute of daily food, and one of you says to them,
"Depart in peace, be warmed and filled," but you do not give them the things
which are needed for the body, what does it profit?*
James 2:15, 16, NKJV.

THIS IS AN ALL TOO FAMILIAR TEXT that usually goes by the wayside. I hear people tell others in situations like those in our text, "I'll pray for you." But many times in His Word Jesus tells us to take care of the less fortunate.

At the present time my family has the unfortunate/fortunate opportunity to apply these verses to our lives, as we are the ones in need. My husband's job came to an untimely end, and he is still in the process of finding another. I'm concerned because we have a toddler son still in Pampers and a daughter in private school. Not to mention bills that must be paid, and other basic necessities to be met. I have worried, gotten frustrated, maybe even been a tad depressed. When I feel that way I pray. My prayers of stress are usually simple. *Lord, You know!* I really don't have to say much because He does know. He knows that I need milk, working vehicles, utilities, and other things. I call this time in my Christian experience my "Job experience." I wonder what else could go wrong? I don't have to wait long to find out. The IRS is auditing us for taxes incurred two years ago!

I shared some of these challenges with which God has presented me—to help me trust Him more—with people who seemed concerned and with others whom I thought were just being nosy. But did I simply pray for God's intervention? *Oh, me of little faith.*

God has allowed people whom I least expected to do so, to help and show kindness to us. On several occasions a coworker bought cases of milk. Another friend paid for a mechanic to fix my car. Another paid bills. Another told me where I could get help with my utility bill, and I did! I was even able to find all necessary documentation for the IRS!

Now I am going to say it to you, "You know!" You know that God is a God of His word (Num. 23:19). His children do not have to beg for bread (Ps. 37:25). God never ceases to provide for His family (Matt. 7:11). I want to say Thank you to all those who are living out their faith. I invite you to trust God with me as we face together the challenges He allows us to have. These trials can help to make us all living examples of faith.

Trudy Duncan

Mistaken Identity

And thine ears shall hear a word behind thee, saying, This is the way, walk ye in it.
Isa. 30:21.

CULINARY ARTISTS rightly experience a lovely feeling of success when foods they bake rise—the breads, the cakes, the muffins. But action in none of these can match what I once witnessed issuing out of a saucepan on the top of my stove.

A relative of mine was visiting. She is an excellent cook, and I was convinced that she could produce a gourmet meal from the most mundane menu, so I gave her my kitchen. Needing some oil for a dish she was about to prepare, she picked up what looked like the appropriate container and poured a generous amount of its contents into a saucepan. As she stirred it just kept frothing and frizzing. She was just about to call me when I entered the kitchen to find the "volcanic" eruption of a miniature Vesuvius.

The cook was in a quandary. Her expression depicted frustration and surprise. She could not understand the extreme effervescence of the frothy, bubbly, golden substance rising out of the pan. She had never seen any kind of oil react so vigorously under any circumstance.

We discovered that instead of cooking oil, the liquid in the pan was Joy© dishwashing detergent. The container had unfortunately been placed on the shelf with the soy sauce, olive oil, liquid amino acids, and other liquids.

There was nothing wrong with the dishwashing liquid. In its proper place, selected and used appropriately, it serves its proper function very well. My failure to put it where it belonged caused much anxiety and distress. I entered the kitchen at a crucial moment, just when my sister needed my help. My sincere apology and provision of the proper liquid—the olive oil—resolved the matter.

How significant the truth that the more we associate with any person or group and the more we communicate, the more we grow to look like them and the more we begin to blend in.

Sometimes the choices we make, innocently or otherwise, produce tragic circumstances and result in bitter consequences for ourselves and others. But God is willing to come to our rescue. He says, "This is the way, walk ye in it." And when we make mistakes, we are assured, "Before they call, I will answer; and while they are yet speaking, I will hear" (Isa. 65:24).

Quilvie G. Mills

What I Learned From My Teddy Bear

Therefore if any man be in Christ, he is a new creature: old things
are passed away; behold, all things are become new.
2 Cor. 5:17.

A PHOTO taken on my first birthday shows me sitting on a table surrounded by vases filled with roses. My first teddy bear, Tobby, my first birthday present, sits beside me.

This teddy was made of pale yellow lamb's skin and had beautiful button-like eyes. It could turn its head. Tobby has stayed with me my whole life, but I have not always dealt kindly with it. I remember a fight with my beloved big brother, when I hit him with my teddy. I hit him so hard that Tobby's head remained in my hands while the body flew. I took Tobby to my mother who sewed the head in place. Now it had a stiff head. I also discovered my parents' small nail scissors and cut all the fur off one arm. Nobody had told me it would not grow back.

Then one day my father brought me a large teddy bear. I fell in love with this new teddy. Poor Tobby was too old-fashioned compared to him.

I can't remember when I gave away the new teddy, but I still have Tobby. He spent many years in a box in the basement, but I recovered him, washed and brushed him, and now realize that he doesn't look so bad after all. He has a sweet face even though he is old-fashioned.

I have learned three things from my Tobby. First, like Tobby, God has not always had the first priority in my life. He has almost been ousted out of my heart, too. I have to decide every day: Do I want to live this day with God? Do I want to love Him with all my heart? Is He so close to me that I can trust Him, here and now? God wants to be close to us. It is my decision to either put Him somewhere in the corner of my life or to live each day with Him.

Second, God, like a poor teddy bear with a shaved arm and stiff head, loves me and has never let go of me. He has never thrown me in the dump, although sometimes I probably deserved it. Last, in our daily lives we meet many Tobbys who have been hurt, who have scars on their souls. Often they have been treated unkindly and put into a corner somewhere. But they are important to God. To love God means to love all the people who are important to Him.

Jesus wants to change us Teddys and Tobbys so that we become more like Him. That is the secret of God's love which transforms us into new people. Will we let Him?

Hannele Ottschofski

On Wings of Joy

For the Lord himself shall descend from heaven with a shout, with the voice of the archangel, and with the trump of God: and the dead in Christ shall rise first: Then we which are alive and remain shall be caught up together with them in the clouds, to meet the Lord in the air: and so shall we ever be with the Lord.
1 Thess. 4:16, 17.

NIGHT AFTER NIGHT Pastor Holley spoke words of faith, hope, courage, and the assurance of God's love, and I wrote down many of the precious phrases—promises such as, "all war and sin will cease," "we receive healing," "caught up to meet Him in the air," and "rescued from sin." Some of the phrases seemed to come to my ears in a rhyming way, going around and around in my head 'til I was sure that a poem was there, somewhere, waiting to be composed.

A wonderful closeness grew among those who came to the meetings each night, and we were especially pleased to see people who did not belong to our church attending too.

About halfway through the series of meetings we were surprised to hear that Rachel, a lovely woman, perhaps in her seventies, had suffered a stroke and possibly even a heart attack. Many prayers were offered for her recovery and well being. For a short time she seemed to improve somewhat, but within a few weeks she passed away. All of us were saddened by the loss of a friend, but we were joyful for our hope in the resurrection. I gathered the thoughts Pastor Holley had given about Christ's coming and the resurrection and finished writing a poem I called, "On Wings of Joy."

I gave one of the first copies to Rachel's grieving husband, Frank, who was very grateful for the thought. I sent another copy to Pastor and Mrs. Holley who had gone on to their next appointment.

Many times during the past years I have sent or taken a copy of the poem to families who have lost—or who would soon lose—a loved one. It has always been well received and appreciated. In a time of loss it is hard to think of joy, but we can have joy and hope through Jesus Christ.

What joy it will be to be reunited with Rachel and all the others to whom we have temporarily said goodbye. I look forward to that exciting day! When we've all been rescued from sin and with the sound of trumpets Jesus will say, "Enter in." And we will—on wings of joy!

Lillian Musgrave

Who Gets It?

Delight yourself also in the Lord, and He shall give you the desires of your heart. Commit your way to the Lord, trust also in Him, and He shall bring it to pass. Ps. 37:4, 5, NKJV.

MY HUSBAND DRIVES our two grandsons, Alex, age 6, and Austin, age 9, home from school each afternoon. Rather than going straight home, both boys like to stop by Grandma and Poppa's house to play with their cousin, Riley. One afternoon Alex asked, "Poppa, can we please go play at your house before you take us home?" My husband replied, "We'll go past your house and if your daddy is home early, you'll have to go straight inside."

Then from the back seat Alex loudly announced, "I'm gonna' pray." Before Poppa could respond Alex bowed his head, folded his hands, and said, "Dear Jesus, help us to get to go to Poppa's house right now and play. Amen." But a few minutes later they saw their daddy's car in the driveway. He had, indeed, come home early.

"God didn't answer my prayer!" Alex said indignantly. My husband smiled and said, "Well, maybe your daddy was praying too. Maybe *he* was praying that you'd get home quickly so he could see you."

Puzzled, with furrowed eyebrows of concern, Austin asked, "Poppa, how does the prayer thing work? Does the first one who asks God get it?"

Many of us, like Alex, want God to grant our immediate desires—and when the desire is not granted we, too, cry, "God didn't answer my prayer!" And many of us, like Austin, are puzzled by how God answers the prayers of two people who are requesting diametrically opposed desires. Does the first one who asks God get his wish?

No. Rather, those who delight in the Lord each day get the desires of their hearts. Is that because somebody got to their knees faster than we did and beat us to Him? No! As we delight in Him and learn to surrender to His will, an amazing transformation takes place—our desires begin to change. As we draw closer to Him, He is able to mold us by the power of the Holy Spirit into His likeness. Our prayers will no longer have elements of manipulation, selfishness, bargaining, murmuring or complaining, but will reflect God's desires for our lives. God's will and our desires will merge. When that happens, we will experience the thrill of having every prayer answered.

Ellie Green

My Peace I Give You

My peace I give to you; not as the world gives do I give to you.
Let not your heart be troubled, neither let it be afraid.
John 14:27, NKJV.

I WAS AWAKE ONE NIGHT but trying to get back to sleep. To try to relax, I decided to mentally sing the hymns that I knew that speak of peace. The first to come to mind was "When peace like a river attendeth my way." That seemed restful, but the next line says, "When sorrows like sea billows roll." I began to go over some of the sorrows that had attended my soul of late, and that didn't help at all.

The next hymn I remembered was "Peace, peace, wonderful peace." But then the end of the chorus requests that this peace sweep over my spirit forever "like fathomless billows of love," and the word billows started a train of thought about the sea billows that caused terrible floods in places like New Orleans, and I didn't feel at all rested over that thought.

"Peace, Perfect Peace" was the next hymn that came to mind. However, the next phrase is, "In this dark world of sin" and it goes on to say that "the blood of Jesus whispers peace within," which is a true but disturbing thought—that only through Christ's death on Calvary can we obtain peace. I gave up on trying to get to sleep singing these hymns in my mind.

A few days later we were studying the book of Philippians in our small group Bible study. We read in chapter 4, verse 7, that "the peace of God, which surpasses all understanding, will guard your hearts and minds through Christ Jesus" (NKJV). I looked up the word "peace" in the concordance at the back of my Bible and found today's verse. "Let not your heart be troubled, *neither let it be afraid.*" This last phrase was just the assurance I needed. We don't need to be afraid of anything because God will give us, by His grace, peace. If we don't have peace in this world, we will surely have it in the world to come. In the same chapter of John's gospel, verses 2, 3, we read the reason why we should not be troubled: "In My Father's house are many mansions; if it were not so, I would have told you. I go to prepare a place for you," Jesus says, finishing with the promise, "and if I go and prepare a place for you, I will come again and receive you to Myself; that where I am, there you may be also" (NKJV). Surely this is the great hope of Christians, and with this thought I can sleep peacefully.

Yes, God is good, and His Word is sufficient for us in all crises.

Ruth Lennox

Refuse Disposal

Blessed is he whose transgressions are forgiven, whose sins are covered. Blessed is the man whose sin the Lord does not count against him and in whose spirit is no deceit. When I kept silent, my bones wasted away through my groaning all day long. . . . Then I acknowledged my sin to you and did not cover up my iniquity. I said, "I will confess my transgressions to the Lord"—and you forgave the guilt of my sin.
Ps. 32:1-5, NIV.

THE REFUSE DISPOSAL TRUCK comes once a week. We gather our rubbish in the dustbin, push it out onto the street in front of our gate, and the truck comes and empties the bin with a big noise. Our refuse is taken to the rubbish dump and our dustbin is once more empty. We gather our rubbish for another week and then the same process starts all over again.

As I watched the disposal truck, I discovered a spiritual dimension to rubbish disposal by comparing it with the forgiveness of our sins. We gather our "rubbish," push it onto the street in front of our gate, and ask God to forgive us. God picks it up and throws it into the depths of the sea (see Micah 7:19). For us this means that our sins are gone, and we can forget about them!

If we do not accept God's offer of "rubbish disposal," the dustbin starts smelling bad and the refuse will turn poisonous. The spiritual meaning? If our soul is filled with grime we get sick and sometimes even infect others with our "poisonous refuse."

We should consider the effects of sins we do not confess. For God, no sin is too big to be forgiven. He offers us complete forgiveness. Through Jesus' sacrifice on the cross God can dispose of the rubbish of sin and Satan can no longer blame us. At the rubbish dump the refuse is burned. Likewise, all the garbage of this world will be burned up at the end (see 2 Peter 3:10).

God will create a new earth without sin, even though we cannot yet imagine such a life. We would be the greatest fools if we did not accept this offer—and it's free. It doesn't cost us anything. We pay a monthly fee for our earthly rubbish disposal. But Jesus paid for the forgiveness of our sins with His life on the cross of Calvary.

Our gratitude and joy will last a whole eternity! Yes, "You are forgiving and good, O Lord, abounding in love to all who call to you" (Ps. 86:5, NIV). God forgives us if we confess our sins! That's a promise.

Ingrid Berker

New Glasses, By Faith

Before they call, I will answer; and while they are yet speaking, I will hear.
Isa. 65:24.

THE TIME HAD COME when I needed progressive lenses in my glasses. However, old age doesn't come alone. My other problem was that finances were worse than tight. Nevertheless, I went ahead—by faith—and ordered the glasses. I had 10 days to come up with money to pay the remainder of my bill.

I picked up the mail on my way home from ordering my glasses by faith, and there was a letter from our dentist. I had been paying off our dental bill little by little since we moved. I opened the letter and I couldn't believe what I saw. An anonymous person had paid off our dental bill. The dentist was returning $115 to us, and wished us well.

I was in tears as I shared with my little family what I had just read. I showed them the check, and in my other hand they saw the bill showing what I still owed for my glasses—that I had ordered by faith. You guessed it: $115! It was literally the exact amount of money that I owed.

Here was a miracle that only God could have configured. So many details had to happen to have this all come together on that day. First of all, the dentist had to decide to send us this check and then have someone write it and send it. He even apologized for forgetting to send it sooner. But God is in control—even of the Canadian post—for He had that letter and check arrive three days after it was sent. I received it just minutes after I took a step of faith. If it had arrived earlier or later it never would have had the impact that it did. God is amazing and loves to surprise His kids.

It was living proof that God was at work, and it was a gentle reminder, in our situation, that He was caring for our every need. Now it is more than nine years later. The other day I was cleaning out some of my files and there was the photocopy of my bill and the check. As I showed it to my husband the tears came again as I relived the miracle of God's care. My husband said "There is a story waiting to be written." So here it is. I pray it will encourage you to trust the Lord, for He is able, and it is safe to trust Him.

As Pastor Brian Jones said, "God is always at work upstream in our lives."

Gay Mentes

God Is So Good

The angel of the Lord encamps around those who fear him, and he delivers them.
Ps. 34:7, NIV.

I WAS SO EXCITED to be going home for a visit after being away for almost two-and-a-half years serving as a missionary in Korea. I had planned my trip well—or so I thought.

I decided to spend the night before I left with my daughter. She lived near the airport and I had an early flight, making it difficult to get to the airport on time from my home. Before going to bed, I once more checked for my passport, traveler's checks, and other documents. My traveler's checks were nowhere to be found! I then remembered cleaning out my purse and throwing things into the garbage before leaving my apartment. I called my neighbor who obligingly went through the garbage without success. When my daughter bade me farewell, she said, "Mom, I hope this is the worst thing that will happen to you on your trip." I was hoping and praying the same. With that we said our goodbyes.

Upon arriving in the Philippines to spend nine days with my son, I was ecstatic to be greeted with tropical, sunny weather. My son could not come to meet me as he was taking a final exam, so he arranged for me to be picked up at the airport. As we drove to our destination, I took in the scenery and asked if there were poisonous snakes in the Philippines. The reply came fast: "No, no poisonous snakes." At the guesthouse I took a shower and nap, leaving the door open and the screen door closed.

The next morning I felt impressed to get up, move my suitcase, and unpack. So I prayed, got up, and moved my suitcase. When I looked down, I saw a snake coiled in the spot where the suitcase had been. I screamed and screamed, but the snake didn't move. I ran to the door and called for help, but none came, so I went to the garage, found a short-handled broom, and tried to sweep the snake out. It woke up and escaped under my bed. Now I was really frightened. Once more I ran to the door and called for help. This time a man who was cutting the grass came running. He found and killed the snake. I asked what kind of snake it was and he said, "A deadly cobra." God is so good. At any time I could have been bitten, especially when I got up to use the bathroom during the night without turning on the lights. All God wants is to use us for His glory. Let Him use you today and every day. Has He saved you to serve Him as well?

Bessie Haynes

A Family Affair

*Excuse me, sir. Would you believe that I'm the very woman
who was standing before you at this very spot, praying to God?
1 Sam. 1:26, Message.*

A WOMAN, surrounded by her sons and daughters was being served a feast by her husband, the children's father, Elkanah. Yet her stony glare across the table at the sad woman sitting alone and childless said that all was not happy. Was the husband oblivious to the evil undertones? In modern parlance, did he get it?

First wives, second wives, spouses who take lovers, broken hearts, spoiled children, jealousy, and hatefulness—Hannah bore the brunt of it all. No babies comforted her lonely heart. Year after year she endured her rival and every year a squall heralded another baby added to Peninnah's tally of superiority.

Hannah had promised herself she wouldn't cry this year. But when Penny stealthily hissed across the table that it was clear who God favored and who displeased Him, the tears came unbidden. She fled. Her husband followed. "Why don't you eat? Why are you downhearted? Don't I mean more to you than 10 sons?" (see 1 Sam. 1:8). It didn't help.

Hannah found a corner in the temple to sob. Only her lips moved as she prayed. She cried and cried. Priest Eli, watchful for problems during the feasting days at Shiloh, strode over and told her to come back when she was sober. Could we say he was being insensitive?

Dear Hannah mopped her eyes and told her story. With fatherly concern, he entered into her sorrow. "Go in peace," he said, "and may the God of Israel grant what you have asked."

Hannah gave birth to a son. Oh the joy! She named him Samuel. But can you imagine the strength it took the day she told her darling boy, "This is Priest Eli whom I have told you about. You are going to live with him now" (see verses 24-28).

Hannah's joy, and the relief that she had kept her promise even as God had kept His, pours out in prophetic praise. She points us forward to all earthly and eternal happy endings. From an obscure woman in an impossible situation, Hannah became the mother of one of the greatest prophets in Israel's history. Read and ponder Hannah's story in 1 Samuel 1–2:11. Pour out your heart longings to God. He won't fail to understand. Wrapped in His arms you will find comfort and answers.

Marilyn Joyce Applegate

The Object Lesson Cake

Now may the God of peace Himself sanctify you completely; and may your whole spirit, soul, and body be preserved blameless at the coming of our Lord Jesus Christ. He who calls you is faithful, who also will do it.
1 Thess. 5:23, 24, NKJV.

IT WAS MID AFTERNOON when my husband remembered that he was in charge of the sound system at church that week, and that we had a guest speaker. The speaker was also doing an afternoon and evening program so we should stay for potluck. Suddenly I needed to make enough food to share.

With two appointments scheduled that afternoon, I rushed about trying to get things done. I quickly mixed a cake. But when I went to pour the batter in the usual rectangular cake pan, I couldn't find the pan. Rushed for time, I quickly decided to use two round pans and then rushed off to my first appointment. I returned to find both cakes cooling on the counter. I was relieved. Now all I had to do was frost them and head off to my next appointment. I went to get my round cake carrier and couldn't find it. All I could find was my rectangular cake carrier. What to do?

With time running out, I grabbed a knife and cut one of the cakes into four sections, positioned the uncut cake in the center of the rectangular carrier and put the pieces around it. It just fit. Quickly I put a thin layer of frosting on and dashed out the door to my last appointment.

In the back of my mind I wondered, *How am I going to decorate this cake so it looks appropriate for potluck?* Realizing the time, I knew that it would have to be a very fast something, and I started discussing ideas with the Lord. Sprinkles, colored frosting, and such seemed either too childlike or too time-consuming. Then I thought of writing something on it—but what? Then the Lord brought words to my mind and showed me how to make them fit on the strangely-arranged cake. On the top left corner in pink icing I wrote, "No matter." On the top right I wrote, "how many." On the bottom left "pieces" and in the bottom right I wrote, "you're in . . . " Then on the center cake I wrote in a teal green, "God makes you whole."

There are many things in our lives that can shatter, rip, or shred us, but the answer to all is the same: in God we are whole. Open your heart and life to Him today. Let Him make you whole.

Juli Blood

Fear Not

For God hath not given us the spirit of fear;
but of power, and of love, and of a sound mind.
2 Tim. 1:7.

I HAD BEEN STRUGGLING with what I thought was a particularly diffi-cult assignment and was definitely becoming discouraged—so I pro-crastinated. Time went by and it seemed that I made little progress. Thanks to modern technology, my mother and I video-chat almost every day though we are thousands of miles apart, she in Texas and I in St. Lucia. At first when my mother inquired about the assignment, I'd say, "Things are coming along," and quickly change the subject.

However, my mother loves details so she would press further. Her inquiries continued for a while until some days I didn't even feel like talking to her because one of the first things she'd ask was, "Brenda, how is the assignment coming?"

My response would be a quick, "Coming along," or "Little by little."

One day it was too much for me so I finally broke down and told her how dif-ficult it was for me, that the deadline was quickly approaching, and I didn't seem to be making any progress. She skipped out of friend mode and immediately went into Christian-parent mode. She reminded me to exercise faith in God and ask for wisdom, believing that He would grant it to me. She informed me that she would also be praying for me in this regard.

While I accepted her counsel in word, I still felt discouraged at my slow progress—there were times when I wanted to just give up. My husband also kept encouraging me, but one day I felt overwhelmed as I sat at my desk meditating be-fore starting on my assignment. I opened the Bible and came upon John 20:19: "Jesus came and stood in the midst, and said to them, 'Peace be with you'" (NKJV). At that point I felt that peace and knew it would be all right. With renewed energy I began working on my assignment and saw it through to completion. I knew that God had taken away my spirit of fear and given me a spirit of peace and confidence.

It may not be a written assignment that you have to complete but something else that is paralyzing you with fear of failure. God has given us the assurance of His peace. As His beloved children, we should willingly accept it.

Brenda D. (Hardy) Ottley

Deeper Faith

Whoever calls on the name of Lord shall be saved.
Rom. 10:13, NKJV.

I LIVED AT MY UNCLE MADRID'S while in primary school. He played an important role in a company and this granted me good living conditions at home. But worries arose with a physician's bad news that my uncle had an incurable disease. Deep changes in his way of life began that day: hopelessness, lack of self-esteem, and disinterest in earning a living.

A few months later he was notified that the company he worked for would terminate his contract, complying with all legal matters in connection with his departure. Later on, he was issued some papers, including a check. The following days were bad. Living conditions became more and more unsustainable, mainly due to scarcity of resources at home. Sometimes, late at night, one could hear him complaining loudly as if he were going crazy.

Even though this family was shocked and fearful, we did find the strength to start praying intentionally. In such heavy circumstances, all you can do is pray from morning to night, no matter where you are—and leave the rest in God's hands.

My uncle saw the sadness in our eyes and admired all the effort we made to get him healthy through our prayers. He joined us every morning and night in the living room to praise the Lord. Some weeks later, Uncle Madrid began recovering from his illness. Even the look of his face changed. This was mainly due to his fighting spirit and the considerable love and affection we showed him. Both helped to sustain his faith and trust in God. He began attending church again, and also began a little jogging to help him relax and relieve anxiety and stress. We kept encouraging him and taking care of him as usual. Day by day, he became more like the uncle we knew: kind, calm, and very affectionate.

Actually, the illness did change him—for the better. What I drew from that experience was that if you have trust and faith in God, He will make your life a marvelous journey even here on this earth! Like it says in Proverbs 3:5, a deeper faith means trusting only God and not your cleverness. He will then make a smooth path for you.

Julienne Lumière Ngo Massock

Being Different: A Present From God

We have different gifts, according to the grace given us. If a man's gift is prophesying, let him use it in proportion to his faith.
Rom.12:6, NIV.

I HAVE OBSERVED that differences are not a challenge to live with but a privilege granted by God. Variations are present not only among humans but also in the color, form, and glow of nature. The animal kingdom is not far behind. Examples of differences include charming giraffes, dainty cats, friendly dogs, the slow moving sloth, busy ants, colorful butterflies, singing birds, and the lions with their fuzzy headdress. These differences can teach us the great love of God. In the midst of so many ideas, personalities, and creativeness, He cares for, protects, and loves all creation.

It would be no fun to spend hours fixing myself up to go out and discover others exactly like me, nor would it be fun to talk to someone whose thoughts were exactly like mine. I'd feel like a robot if I went to choose clothing and found everything the same—no difference in styles, colors, prints, or types of cloth. Shopping wouldn't be any fun. Imagine all babies just alike. And the divorce statistics would rise even higher. Spouses would not need to share ideas since their partner would think the same. Things would be complicated.

Yet our different gifts are our greatest challenges. For some of us they seem complicated, and for others they are easier. Children, too, feel the weight of being different, whether it's because of age, skin color, cleverness, or friends. These characteristics follow us throughout life and should be improved and multiplied.

I am happy to be different and to learn from the differences of those around me. Loving and respecting others transforms differences from burdens into something light and easy to live with. It also helps us mature and grow.

Remember, God is the Creator of everything and He used His holy creativity to transform this world, filling it with beautiful differences. As a present, He offers us one sun that shines for all and rain that moistens the earth. In thanksgiving they give us the diversified nourishment of each season. We have the opportunity to go through life overcoming the obstacles. If we feel that being different is an obstacle, we must make the change within ourselves, and in this manner be happy. As our text says, we each have different gifts.

Luciana Barbosa Freitas da Silva

God's Perfect Way

As for God, His way is perfect.
Ps. 18:30.

TWO OF OUR FRIENDS had invited my husband and me out to dinner on a Wednesday evening. We did not like to miss prayer meeting, but decided it would be OK this special time. However, while I was visiting in their home that Tuesday the husband discovered he could not keep the appointment because of a previous engagement he'd forgotten. I told them that was fine and that we could go another time, so we set it up for the following Monday evening.

Wednesday afternoon a neighbor called to ask if we could take her to the doctor that afternoon. She had had a stroke a few months earlier and was under strict instructions not to drive. The stroke had been serious, and now she occasionally blacked out. When she came to, she would find herself on the floor, too weak to get up. The last fall had resulted in a black eye. Her appointment was at 4:15, so we told her we would pick her up at 3:45, which we did.

At the doctor's office, I asked if she would like for me to accompany her into the examining room. "Oh, yes!" she said happily. It was not long before a pleasant young nurse ushered us back, took her necessary information, and then assured us that the doctor would be in soon. Unfortunately, we waited for more than an hour before the doctor arrived. Our neighbor was so happy she did not have to wait alone. I told her I would make notes on all that the doctor said—and did—so we could let her daughter know what was happening. This seemed important to her since her memory fails her sometimes.

When the doctor finally entered the room he casually listened to her complaints, did a little testing, and then said that she should not live alone anymore. He also said that she must never drive again. He also gave her a prescription for a walker to use at all times.

Prayer meeting was over by the time we returned home, but how we thanked the Lord that the dinner appointment had been canceled so we were available to help our dear neighbor. God knew before we did how much she would need us that very day. His plans are always best. Have you too found times when God's way was perfect? I pray that it will increase your faith and the faith of those with whom you share.

Anna May Radke Waters

Facing Parkinson's With Humor

A merry heart does good, like medicine, but a broken spirit dries the bones.
Prov. 17:22, NKJV.

IT'S EASY TO BE HAPPY when your life is running smoothly, but it's a greater challenge to be happy when problems arise or your health fails.

Several years ago, when my brother-in-law, Clarence, was diagnosed with Parkinson's disease, he had to give up farming and move to a condo in another town. It took some stamina to remain cheerful while making three adjustments at the same time, but he faced his challenges with humor. Soon after leaving the farm Clarence told people he couldn't milk cows anymore because they'd have too many milkshakes.

The one constant he enjoyed for a few more years was spending the winter in Arizona, playing shuffleboard and bowling. Eventually, he couldn't play anymore, but he still took an interest in the games as others played. One day as he kept score for shuffleboard, a woman nearby watched him make a zero with a very shaky hand. Seeing her pitying look, Clarence broke the tension, saying, "I bet you can't make a flower like that!" They had a good laugh.

Another time a concerned friend asked how he was doing. With a serious look on his face, Clarence replied, "My marriage is shaky." His friend looked at him, aghast. When Clarence held up his trembling hands, his friend immediately got the joke.

Clarence never found his niche in the kitchen, but he told people he could now get the lumps out of the gravy. One day his wife came home late for dinner and jokingly asked, "Do you have dinner ready?" He replied, "No, I didn't think you wanted scrambled eggs."

In spite of his limitations, he maintains a positive attitude and puts people at ease with humor and by acknowledging he has Parkinson's. By doing this, people are more solicitous of his well being.

Whatever our challenges, we are not the only ones who are carrying burdens. Difficult as it may be, let us follow King Solomon's advice and maintain a merry heart today and every day. Let us anticipate the day when "God shall wipe away all tears from [our] eyes; and there shall be no more death, neither sorrow, nor crying, neither shall there be any more pain: for the former things are passed away" (Rev. 21:4).

Edith Fitch

Blackout

God is light, and in him is no darkness at all.
1 John 1:5.

IT WAS SABBATH MORNING and my husband and I were just getting up. He turned on the radio to listen to southern gospel music. When I called my prayer partner for our morning devotion, she said she would call me right back. About a second later the music stopped and we were in total darkness. The power was out—not only to our house but the entire neighborhood.

This was a disaster as I needed to get ready for church. My husband was singing at a sister church for Sabbath school and the plan was for me to get a ride. Miguel would meet me at our home church for the worship service. The phones were not working either so I used my cell phone to call my daughter who lives in the same community and left a message on her cell phone, asking her for a ride.

I had no way of getting hold of Mazie as I could not remember her cell phone number, so I took a shower before the water got cold, and then got dressed by candle-light. I decided to make a fashion statement by wearing a hat to cover up my bad hair.

I woke my other daughter and filled her in on the situation. She found solace by jumping into my bed and pulling up the covers to counteract the cold. Eventually she got dressed and we headed to the kitchen for something to eat. I settled for warm apple cider, raisin bread, and cheese. Cassandra and I got a good laugh after she stood patiently waiting for her bread to toast. No power meant no toast!

My husband fetched a flashlight but it went dim after about five minutes as the battery died. My prayer partner and I had our devotion via my cell phone and the aid of a candle.   Our normal Sabbath morning routine was thrown off because we had no light, and it struck me that we were helpless without the power. This made me think of the Greater Light that we all need in our lives every moment of every day. He is the Light of the world. If I struggled to get through a morning without the power source, imagine going through life without God. Our lives would be filled with chaos and confusion.

Lord, help us to recognize our need of You and to keep connected to You by faith, for with You there is no darkness.

Sharon Long (Brown)

Blessed Assurance

Blessed be the God and Father of our Lord Jesus Christ, the Father of mercies and God of all comfort, who comforts us in all our tribulation, that we may be able to comfort those who are in any trouble, with the comfort with which we ourselves are comforted by God.
2 Cor. 1:3, 4, NKJV.

IN MY NEIGHBORHOOD is a widow who holds Bible studies in her home for some friends from her church, and she invites her neighbors to join the group. Even though I do not attend her church, when she invited me to the study I felt compelled to go. I prayed that I could be a witness to my neighbors in the group in some way. We meet once a week. We pray for any in the group who have a need: when any are ill, or have family or other neighbors who are ill, or have any other special needs. It is comforting to each of us to belong to this group of Christian women who pray for each other.

After prayer we usually read a chapter from one of the Gospels which the hostess has chosen for our study. We take turns going around the circle, each of us reading a passage. Then the hostess reads from a commentary she has on that Gospel which has scriptural references for us to look up. She has those references written on little slips of paper for us to read when called upon. It is very enlightening and I, for one, learn much.

Even though we don't all come from the same denominational background, we find our common ground in the Gospels. I try to carefully bring out my views on a subject when I have the opportunity, and they are usually accepted in kindness.

I read in Luke 10 about the lawyer who asked Jesus what he should do to inherit eternal life. Jesus asked him, "What is written in the law? What is your reading of it?" The lawyer answered, "You shall love the Lord your God with all your heart, with all your soul, with all your strength, and with all your mind, and your neighbor as yourself."

"You have answered rightly; do this and you will live," Jesus said (Luke 10:25-28, NKJV).

Where bitterness of feeling exists because of differences in religion, we can make a difference by loving and caring for each other. It can help to remove prejudice as well. I continually pray that I can do that.

Bessie Siemens Lobsien

Expectations

Trust God all the time. . . . Because God is our protection.
Ps. 62:8, NCV.

VACATIONS. Traveling to new places. I love to plan it all and learn what I can about the area's history and attractions. Because we were taking the Martin Luther tour in Germany, I thought we would first tag on a week in Europe. So it was with excitement that we flew into Napoli, Italy. I had read online what to do and not to do in Napoli, as well as read Rick Steves book on that area. But as we left the airport we mistakenly boarded the city bus—a mistake, according to my research! After arriving at the piazza we weren't supposed to be in as tourists, we found the Alibus and continued to the port for the ferry to the island.

Once at our villa, my enthusiasm disappeared. It was *not* what we expected. It was winter and weather was unpredictable at best. And most things were closed as it wasn't tourist season.

The day before our flight from Napoli to Berlin we went online to check in, but couldn't. Finally a man called Italia Airlines for us only to discover the flight had left that morning. Not good news! After a long phone call to the United States, we were told we had new tickets for the next day—which was the date on our ticket.

The next morning we went to the closest port and waited for an hour for the ferry, only to discover it wasn't leaving from there because of stormy weather. We hurried to the other side of the island where we caught the ferry in time. I was praying! And getting from the port to the airport was worse than it had been coming in, but God faithfully protected us. By putting the right people in our path and surrounding us with His angels, we arrived at the airport safely, thinking our stress was over. But no. After two hours of trying to convince the airlines we had new tickets, we had to purchase two new tickets on site—in Euros! To say I was anxious would be putting it mildly. But the good news was we were able to purchase new tickets, get to Berlin in time to meet up with our tour group, *and* we had a wonderful time visiting the Luther sites!

Our week in Italy wasn't what we had expected, and wasn't at all what the colorful brochure promised. However, we were reminded that we can always trust God to give His protection and provision for our every need. *Father God, thank You for Your watch care over us when we travel miles from home—even when it doesn't meet our expectations.*

Louise Driver

In His Time, God Answers

Is any among you afflicted? let him pray. Is any merry? let him sing psalms. Is any sick among you? let him call for the elders of the church; and let them pray over him, anointing him with oil in the name of the Lord: and the prayer of faith shall save the sick, and the Lord shall raise him up; and if he have committed sins, they shall be forgiven him.
James 5:13-15.

I WAS ILL for more than two years with congestive heart failure, swollen legs and body. Then I developed a heart arrhythmia. At times I felt weak and dizzy, and didn't dare to drive the car. The cardiologist tried various medicines for me but nothing worked—or if it did I was allergic to it. Finally I talked with our church youth pastor and asked about special prayer and anointing. But I was not healed immediately—instead, I became more ill. I started questioning God but received no answers. I asked Him if there was something I was hiding in my heart, but found nothing that would impede any answer to my prayer. Two weeks later I was diagnosed with double pneumonia. My whole body was swollen. Unable to breathe, I went to the ER and was admitted to the hospital. When my cardiologist came in he said, "I have you right where I need you!" He said that he wanted to start me on a new medicine that he could give only if I were in the hospital for something else. So he started the medicine. That very day my heart went into a regular rhythm and has stayed in rhythm for six months now. I feel better than I have in about three years. I had the medication for five days in the hospital and have not had to have any since I came home.

We all want to be healed instantly, but sometimes God has other ways to do just that. As you see, I needed to get worse before I could get better, but I praise His holy name every day for the healing hand He extended in my behalf. I am more than 80 years of age and He has been good to me all my life. We need to trust and believe, and yes, even question God sometimes. But we must also keep the faith and not let go because, as our text tells us, "and the prayer of faith shall save the sick, and the Lord shall raise him up." It happens as He desires it to come to us, according to His timing, not ours.

Lord, I know that today many who read this page are suffering from many challenges. May they have the faith to know that You love them and will do what is best for them.

Virginia Eggert Pearson

Two Interventions

And call upon me in the day of trouble; I will deliver you, and you will honor me.
Ps. 50:15, NIV.

ONE LATE AFTERNOON I was feeling sad and discouraged with my work. I had classes to teach that night. It is my habit to begin class by reading a Bible text on which the students can reflect, and then I offer prayer. But today I didn't feel like doing that. I was concerned with the number of classes I was teaching and the fact that the class was not reacting well to the material and extra activities. *How can I pray? How can I talk of God, if I have such a negative spirit?*

A pathway runs between my house and the class building, with trees and grass on both sides. I like to walk this slowly, and always go through this area praying that God will place the right feelings within me and that He will give me the capacity to speak of Him in the appropriate manner with the students. On this day, I placed my discouragement before the Lord and even my doubts regarding His will for my life. *Am I in the right place? Is this really what You want for me?* I wondered in a prayer.

I entered the classroom and greeted the students, and just then someone knocked at the door. It was a Christian university student team. They asked me to allow them to present worship for the class and, thankful, I immediately agreed. They spoke about the God who performs miracles. They sang and prayed for the class and for me. Their activities were like rain to my soul, washing away my sadness and my discouragement. I felt renewed.

Two weeks later, the situation was similar. I'd had a busy, stressful day. I considered what I would read to my students and how I could pray when I was so exhausted. Once again, the university group knocked at the door. They spoke, sang, and prayed, as well as complimented someone who was having a birthday. My eyes filled with tears because the message met my need to feel that God was near. At the end, when we were all talking, I felt joy return to my life, and I could give the classes with renewed vitality. At the right time, God sent help through human instruments who allowed themselves to be used by the Holy Spirit.

Blessed are these people who concern themselves with talking of God, and who promote moments of union with Him!

Iani Dias Lauer-Leite

Finding the Right Terminal

Blessed is every one who fears the Lord, who walks in His ways.
Ps. 128:1, NKJV.

IT WAS MY FIRST TIME TO TRAVEL by domestic flights inside the United States. My plane left at 6:20 a.m., so I left at 3:00 a.m. to drive to Los Angeles. My uncle and cousin came with me to help, and I'm so glad they did! A long queue waited at Terminal 1, and I lined up with it. After some time my uncle left us to go to the restroom. While he was on his way he discovered that we were at the wrong terminal. American Airlines was at Terminal 5. We ran to our vehicle as it was parked on the third floor and Terminal 5 was a long way from Terminal 1. Jumping into the car, we drove as quickly as possible to Terminal 5. We saw the American Airlines sign, but when we went inside and showed my ticket to another attendant she told us that plane was leaving from Terminal 4. Now we were in a real rush! It was already 5:45. To further complicate matters, I was six months pregnant and was getting very tired. When we arrived at Terminal 4, my uncle showed the ticket to a luggage carrier. I asked my uncle, "If everyone in charge has given us wrong information, how could this luggage carrier give us the right information?" But you know what? The information of that luggage carrier was exactly right—finally.

He told us to go to Terminal 3—also American Airlines but operated by Alaska Airlines. Now we had to move very fast. But I couldn't walk fast anymore. My uncle and cousin were far ahead of me with my luggage, while I trailed behind, alone. I thought I'd miss my plane and then miss my connecting flight for the next leg of my trip, but I could walk no faster.

Have you thought about how many times you've tried to find a solution to a problem in your life but found that you were knocking on the wrong doors? In our human wisdom we try to get solutions from worldly-wise sources, answers from financial advisors, advice from the experts, but we don't follow the simple instructions found in our Bible. The Bible alone will make it easy to find the heavenly terminal the first time and on time. God has instructed us, "Seek ye first the kingdom of God, and his righteousness; and all these things shall be added unto you" (Matt. 6:33). Do you do the opposite as I did? Let's try to find His council and solution from the real source.

And I did make my flight and connections.

Sweetie Ritchil

Conquer All

My help cometh from the Lord, which made heaven and earth.
Ps. 121:2.

OUTSIDE MY FRONT DOOR is a plant I treasure. To my amazement it is growing from under the brick border of the garden onto the cement and stone driveway. Despite having had no watering or nutrients it continues to grow and produces clusters of flowers while my cared-for seedlings struggle along.

Every time I walk out my front door this special plant reminds of my near neighbor Colleen. She and her husband, retired workers for the church, were returning from volunteer ministry at Lightning Ridge in Australia and were about to check into a motel. As Graham turned to check the car he glanced back and saw Colleen lying on the ground, unconscious. No one saw or heard what had happened to her and, later, she had no recollection of what took place. It was a holiday weekend so obtaining help quickly was difficult.

She was put on life support and airlifted to Brisbane for X-rays and specialist treatment. Unfortunately, she had broken her neck and was too weak for surgery. Colleen and her husband were devastated when told that she would have to be on a ventilator for the rest of her life and would never walk again.

Many earnest prayers ascended to the Master Physician for healing and direction. God blessed, and eventually Colleen could speak, her mind was clear, and she had movement in one arm. After seven months in the hospital medical experts said that no more could be done to improve her condition, and it would never improve if she returned home. Her strong faith sustained her, and with the support of a devoted husband and daily community support, she defied the verdict and went home without a ventilator. She refused to wallow in self pity.

Now wheelchair-bound, Colleen set about making a new life and to enjoy the very limited ability she had. Never a word of complaint passes her lips, and her life is an inspiration to all who visit. She conducts Scrabble afternoons for the lonely, perseveres with jigsaws puzzles, supervises the home cooking, visits people in the hostel, and gives abundant encouragement to all. Like the flower at my front door, despite extremely difficult circumstances, she radiates happiness to all, and particularly enjoys serving her Lord.

Joy Dustow

My Sheep Know My Voice

And his sheep follow him because they know his voice.
John 10:4, NIV.

I ATTENDED CAMP MEETING at Auburn, Washington, and heard a speaker from New Zealand named Gerald Minchin. He had a distinctive accent, and I loved it and his message. When I returned home I picked up the *Adventist Review* and scanned the table of contents. There was an article by Pastor Minchin! I quickly read the piece and as I read, I could hear his voice speaking the words he'd written!

Now I know what Jesus meant when He said, "My sheep hear My voice." As I read the Bible I get more familiar with the voice of God. Then when He chooses to speak to me audibly or in a still, small voice I recognize my God.

I have heard God's voice at other times. We had been Christmas caroling in an apartment building one evening. A young woman, holding her tiny baby, came to the door and listened with tears streaming down her face. I wondered why she was crying and told myself to come back soon to find out.

A few weeks later I was heading for home after a long day's work at the newspaper office when God spoke, telling me to turn around and go back to the apartment house and visit the young woman. I argued with God, saying, "Oh God, I am tired and don't want to do it tonight," but He kept urging me, so I turned around and went there.

The young mother shared her story with me. Her husband, who was in the Merchant Marines, was away over the holidays, and she was so alone—just she and the baby. I started to visit her each week, studying the Bible with her and leading her to Jesus. I wondered about her smoking and prayed a lot about it. That was when I found out that the Holy Spirit takes care of these problems Himself. She stopped smoking on her own, under God's influence, not anything I said.

When she moved about 20 miles away, I still continued visiting and studying with her. When her husband returned home, he took his family and they left. I felt sad that I never knew where they moved, but was confident God continued to watch over her and her salvation.

I want always to be in tune with the Spirit of God, listening to His voice and following His directions, don't you?

Betty A. Pearson

Bring You What?

*Now this is the confidence that we have in Him, that if
we ask anything according to His will, He hears us.
1 John 5:14, NKJV.*

OUR YEARS OF MISSION SERVICE had been enjoyable and rewarding, but now it was time for a furlough, and we looked forward eagerly to seeing our family again. Andrew was a faithful national coworker with my husband, and as we prepared to leave he met us with an earnest request: Would we be able to bring him some books by Ellen White? Of course we could. But his next request presented a real problem. Andrew played an accordion and provided the only music for his little village church. Someone had stolen his accordion, and it was impossible to replace it locally. Could we please bring him an accordion? This overwhelmed us. The price of the instrument itself would be substantial and the duty required to bring it into the country could be prohibitive. "Andrew, there isn't a chance in this world that we can bring you an accordion" we told him. We did not want him to count on something we simply could not provide.

"Well," he said, "I will be praying about it."

To be perfectly honest, we forgot about the accordion in the rush of furlough activities—until we stopped by a school where we had served for several years. In the course of a visit with a dear friend and teacher she asked if I knew of anyone who might use an accordion. Did I! A chill went up my spine. I thought to myself, *Oh ye of little faith!* It seems someone had given her a good accordion, but she had one of her own and did not need this one. Andrew had been praying—no doubt about it. Of course the accordion could be added to our luggage. As for the duty fees, God could take care of that, too, and He did. The officer waved us on through customs with no trouble at all. Andrew was pleased but not too surprised when we presented him with the accordion. He believed in God's ability to answer his prayer.

What a strengthening of our faith! What a reminder that God cares about the little things! So, if some days our faith begins to waver for whatever reason, when there seems to be no clear answer to one of life's problems, let's remember Andrew and his accordion. We can always depend on God's answer being the right one at just the right time, whether it is yes, no, or later. "Ask, and you will receive, that your joy may be full" (John 16:24, NKJV). What a promise!

Martha Spaulding

Just As I Am

*For by grace are ye saved through faith; and that not of yourselves:
it is the gift of God: Not of works, lest any man should boast.
Eph. 2:8, 9.*

IN MY FIRST YEAR of medical school I had difficulty with a particular class. I just could not get a good grasp of the material. All of my efforts seemed in vain. Another set of exams was approaching and I had other courses to prepare for, yet I did everything I could think of to get ready for this particular exam. I studied alone and then with a group. I met with the professor to discuss my questions. Last, I began to panic. I had to pass this test!

On D-day I prayed with my mother and went into the exam, still panicking, but hopeful. Overall nothing on the test was foreign to me, but I continued to worry and pray. Exam results were available as early as the next day but I refused to look at them until the entire exam week had passed. Then some time toward the end of the week, I had an epiphany. I caught myself trying to win God's favor by doing "good" things. Somewhere in my mind I must have figured that God would help me do well in school if I were good.

It all came to a head the day before the last two exams. Although I was reading my Bible and praying more than usual, I realized that my motives were wrong. My attempts to be closer to Jesus were not motivated by a deeper desire to know Him. Rather, I hoped that God would be flattered by all my extra attention, and give me an extra blessing. It's not as if God didn't see past my façade. He could see and know my motives—and loved me anyway. I had to confess my wretchedness and pray for His forgiveness. The next day, with sweaty palms, I checked my grade on this worrisome test. I was prepared for anything, but God had blessed me above my expectations. I got only two questions wrong!

From childhood, we learn that few things are just handed to us with no strings attached. Perhaps that explains why we have such a difficult time accepting God's grace. After all, we haven't earned it. It just seems too good to be true, but God really is that good. He gives us His unmerited favor, and all that He asks is that we let Him take care of our every need. There are no hidden fees or disclaimers hidden in fine print. Now there's an offer that is much too good to pass up.

Kimone Powell

For the Good of God's Children

And we know that in all things God works for the good of those who
love him, who have been called according to his purpose.
Rom. 8:28, NIV.

I SAT IN A HOSPITAL ROOM not understanding how this should be for my good as a child of God. When I learned I was pregnant I'd been convinced it was for my good. But in the eleventh week of my pregnancy, when my husband and I went for my routine checkup, after repeatedly checking the monitor the doctor told us that the baby's heart had stopped beating. It took a few panic-filled seconds for us to realize what he'd said.

I knew an obstetrician in my church and I asked to be transferred to her hospital. We called her and told her we were coming. She came and took a lot of time to examine me and gently explain everything . She even wanted to operate herself and that was a consolation for me.

My husband stayed with me a long time, but in the evening I was alone in my hospital room and unable to sleep. How fortunate that the hospital nurses were from a Protestant nursing order called Sisters of Aidlingen. Thus there were no television sets in the rooms, but just across from my room was a little library of Christian literature. I picked up a stack of Christian women's magazines and found in them articles about women who had experienced tragedies— things I could identify with. One woman told about a miscarriage, another about the death of her child at birth. Every article shared how the women had managed to cope, and how God had helped them. I realized that I was not the only one of God's children who had to experience such pain. As I read peace came into my heart.

I was still scared of the surgery—and I asked God to give me an encouraging Bible text. Normally I don't open my Bible at random and point at a text, expecting it to fit my situation. This time, however, I was convinced that the special situation necessitated a special sign. And so, after praying, I opened my Bible and landed at Daniel 6. Yes, that was exactly how I felt, like someone destined to be thrown into a lions' den. But God showed me that He would also get me out of it safely as he had saved Daniel. And that is what happened.

I clung to today's text in Romans, and God did not disappoint me. Ten months later I was overjoyed when I held our newborn daughter, God's greatest gift to my husband and me, in my arms.

Undine Binder-Farr

Heaven Is a Home

If anyone loves me, he will obey my teaching. My Father will love him,
and we will come to him and make our home with him.
John 14:23, NIV.

HOME: WARMTH, COMFORT, ACCEPTANCE. These are words that come to mind when I think of the word home. The dictionary defines it as "a place of residence." But that definition sounds cold and sterile. For most of us, the word home conjures up sweet images of parents and siblings. It brings to mind holiday dinners, warm conversations, and lots of hugs and kisses. It also carries within its letters a full range of emotions: everything from the celebration of birth to the desolation of death, and all that lies between. And love. Certainly, and always, love. It's the root of all good things. It nourishes and strengthens, grounds and frees us. It is the thing that makes a house a home.

There is, I'm happy to say, a second definition for the word home, found in my dictionary: "the place in which one's domestic affections are centered." Now that's more like it. It's part of the dream to have the perfect home and family. We've all wanted that at some time or another. But since we live in an imperfect world I would like to add another definition: a place where life, love, and mistakes happen.

Most of us weren't raised in a Norman Rockwell painting, and we feel we lack the ability to create a picture-perfect home. Those with small children hope and pray that their home is all that it should be, and those of us with empty nests hope and pray that it was all it should have been. But that's not to say we cannot experience, here, all that the word home implies. We can. God has promised to help us. He promises to move right in and to furnish each room with compassion, sympathy, and love. He is the ultimate arranger and decorator.

So whether our nest is full, not so full, or even empty, whether we have happy, healthy memories, or carry sad and painful pictures of our past, it really shouldn't matter. Today and always there is a place where we can continue to build, where we can experience a little bit of heaven here on earth even as we look forward to our heavenly home—permanent, perfect, and complete. A home where acceptance lives and love reigns supreme. A home whose builder and maker is God.

Emily Felts Jones

Up the Golden Stairs

Come to me, all you who are weary and burdened, and I will give you rest.
Take my yoke upon you and learn from me, for I am gentle and humble in heart,
and you will find rest for your souls. For my yoke is easy and my burden is light.
Matt. 11:28-30, NIV.

MY GRANDMOTHER LOVED CHILDREN. I guess that is why I enjoy them so much. They are a source of fun as well as an inspiration to me. One day I was going up the stairs to the worship service after teaching my preteen class. I was following a little slowpoke, about knee-high to a grasshopper, who trudged up the mountain of a stairway. It must have indeed felt like a mountain to him, for his steps were weary and arduous.

He was encumbered about by his very favorite possession in all of his little world—his blankey. It was wrapped all around him from neck to stair, winding between his little legs and very nearly toppling him down the precipice with each step. It was tattered and stained, bearing testimony of a long and soothing friendship.

The grandmother in me at once offered to carry it for him until he reached the top. Oh, no! He let me know with a determined hug of his blanket that he thought the offer tantamount to some sort of invasion. There was no way that he would even negotiate letting go of this familiar "huggy" even though help getting it up the stairs would ensure an easier and safer trip for him. He was thinking of the immediate, and he was not about to let someone take his blanket.

How much am I like that little child, Lord? What is it that I cling to as I struggle onward through life? What is the thing that means comfort to me—even security—that You long to carry for me to help me make it up those hills and mountains in my life? Could it be finances in these uncertain times? Maybe it's health. Perhaps it is even family and friends. I hope it's not pride in some way, even in my church duties and ministries. Do I cling way too much to food? Lord, help me to want more of You and less of what I think is vital.

Every evening at bedtime my beloved grandfather would say, "It's time to go up those golden stairs." My heavenly Father wants to help me get up those "golden stairs" to His heaven. Even more, He wants me to make the trip with added ease and safety. If only I'll allow Him to carry the load for me!

Ann Northwood

Betrothed in Faithfulness

I will allure her, will bring her into the wilderness, and speak
comfort to her. I will give her . . . the Valley of Achor [suffering] as a door of hope.
I will betroth you to Me . . . in righteousness.
Hosea 2:14, 15, 19, NKJV.

I WAS IN A WILDERNESS of agony. For 30 years my husband, John, had suffered devastating paralysis from multiple sclerosis (MS). Then it attacked his mind, causing a form of mania. John became verbally abusive though he had no idea what he was doing. Every second was agony for me. John had been a wonderful husband. But this monster wasn't John.

In the wee hours of one horrific day, the Lord said to me, "Mark this date. One year from now you'll be rejoicing." I immediately underlined the date, March 19, on my perpetual calendar. My heart leapt with hope.

In a few days the MS attacks subsided, and John returned to his gentle self. Then he became feverish. His breathing was labored. John had developed pneumonia. After a few days in the hospital he passed away.

The loss of John shook my world. As I struggled to make sense of life, Jesus rushed in like a flood. He became my husband. He encouraged me to rest and trust Him while He miraculously provided for every need. Thirty years as a caregiver had left me exhausted and riddled with pain. But under Jesus' care I healed; my strength and hope returned.

The following year, as I flipped my perpetual calendar to March 19, I was surprised to see the date underlined. Then I remembered the horrors of the previous March and recalled the Spirit telling me, "Mark this date." I rejoiced that John and I were both free from our wilderness of agony. By the next year when I flipped my calendar to March 19, the Lord had swept me into a whole new life with new interests and possibilities. Once again, I rejoiced!

God alone knows what every March 19 will bring, but it will be good because He promised rejoicing. As time moves on, I ponder why I have no scars from the traumas of hard days in the wilderness. Instead, I have greater faith—faith born of trials. And I've found my "door of hope"—the very arms of Christ—opened wide for me. Sometimes He allows us time in a wilderness of suffering to establish us in faithfulness.

Laura L. Bradford

Sitting at the Feet of Jesus

Then the scribes and Pharisees brought to Him a woman caught in adultery.
And when they had set her in the midst, they said to Him, "Teacher, this woman
was caught in adultery, in the very act. Now Moses, in the law, commanded
us that such should be stoned. But what do You say?"
John 8:3-5, NKJV.

ALTHOUGH MANY BIBLICAL SCHOLARS do not agree with me, I personally believe that Mary Magdalene was the woman caught in adultery. When the Pharisees brought her to Jesus they didn't know that at the feet of Jesus was the best place they could have brought her. They presented her as a prostitute worthy to be stoned. Instead of agreeing with them, Jesus planted the seed of His love in her soul: "Neither do I condemn you; go and sin no more."

Jesus knew that the Pharisees wanted to trick Him, presenting the law of Moses and daring Him to agree with it. But Jesus saw beyond their trickery. He cared about the Pharisees also, and tried to plant the seed of His love in their hearts so He could show them how to love. But they refused to learn.

The Bible says that seven times Mary came back, falling at His feet in confession. Seven times Jesus was faithful to forgive and cleanse her until at last Mary knew the only safe place for her was at Jesus' feet. He understood that and when Martha, her sister, complained to Jesus that He should make Mary get up and help her, Jesus defended her choice to stay at His feet.

At Simon's feast, Mary anointed Jesus' feet with perfume, bathed them with her tears of gratitude, and wiped His feet with her hair. Mary was at the foot of Jesus' cross. She saw His blood dripping down for her. She saw love rejoicing at the victory that had taken root and born fruit in her life. At His resurrection, when Mary recognized Jesus, she again fell at His feet in worship. *Father, help me realize the only safe place for me, too, is at Jesus' feet.*

Today I sing the words of the great old hymn: "Sitting at the feet of Jesus, Oh, what words I hear Him say! Happy place! so near, so precious! May it find me there each day; Sitting at the feet of Jesus, I would look upon the past; for His love has been so gracious, it has won my heart at last. Sitting at the feet of Jesus, where can mortal be more blest?"

Won't you too join me there?

Lana Fletcher

Are We Deaf?

But he said, Yea rather, blessed are they that hear the word of God, and keep it.
Luke 11:28.

ON A SUNDAY AFTERNOON I arrived once again in one of my favorite cities: New York! As soon as I dropped my bags at my girlfriend's apartment I went out again. Just walking the streets of New York makes me happy and energetic. I had a lovely time walking through a street fair and going in and out of shops. And I enjoyed more of the same the next day.

By Monday afternoon I was exhausted but so happy! When I returned to my friend's place I decided to organize my handbag. To my surprise, I couldn't find my passport. My air ticket was there but no passport! Panic. I looked some more. Nothing. I called every shop that I'd been in. Nothing. I called the Brazilian Consulate and realized that it was going to take some time to issue a new passport and that I was going to have to cancel my upcoming trip to Toronto where I planned to meet another girlfriend. It was to be our once a year meeting!

I was devastated and confused. Suddenly I understood how one feels with no identity. I was fortunate, I knew, as I still had my money, I still had my credit cards, and I had a place to stay. I thanked God for all those blessings for I realized how lucky I was.

However, I am still human and I worried. I was sad. I was insecure. Result? I hardly slept that night. I woke up very early and got ready to prove who I was to the Consulate.

I took the bus. As we rode toward uptown we passed Eighteenth Street and three shops where I had spent part of my Monday. I'd called them the night before and each one told me that they'd found no passport. But as the bus went on, I heard a very clear voice saying, "Get out of the bus!" Recognizing our Lord's voice, I said, *No. I already tried. It's no use.* The voice continued, "Get down." I remained stubborn as we sped through Twenty-fifth, Twenty-sixth, Thirtieth Streets. I finally got off at Thirty-fourth Street, stubbornly deciding to—reluctantly—obey His voice.

There was no passport in the first or second shop. Walking into the third shop, almost giving up hope, there it was. My passport!

I jumped with joy. I hugged the sales clerks. I hugged the shop guard. And I walked out talking to God, thanking Him profusely for persisting with a person as deaf as myself. I promised to listen to Him, to be more obedient, for He knows what is best for us—always!

Joelcira F. Cavedon

Being Fully Human

Then Jesus was led by the Spirit into the desert to be tempted by the devil. After fasting forty days and forty nights, he was hungry. The tempter came to him and said, "If you are the Son of God, tell these stones to become bread." Jesus answered, "It is written: 'Man does not live on bread alone, but on every word that comes from the mouth of God.'"
Matt. 4:1-4, NIV.

"WELL, YOU CAN'T EAT FLOWERS," she retorted to Dr. Ellah Kamwendo who was visiting Solusi University and admiring the beautiful landscaping. Dr. Kamwendo had taught at Solusi University before she left to become the director of education for about a dozen countries in southern Africa. Already the economy was deteriorating in Zimbabwe, and it was increasingly difficult to buy necessary food items and even petrol. But now the shelves in shops had only a few odd items: several bottles of vinegar, a handful of spices, a baby rattle, some washcloths.

The campus struggled to obtain enough food for students, staff, and faculty. The farm grew some greens, peanuts, and oranges, and vehicles were sent to Botswana to buy cornmeal, beans, and flour for the occasional treat of a loaf of bread. But there wasn't enough flour for the bakery to operate, and many days the students went hungry with only one—though sometimes two—meals a day. It's hard to concentrate on studies or work when the tummy is growling for food. And after days and years of chronic hunger and no sign of hope for the future, life begins to feel mean and meaningless.

It is when we are in such situations that we need to be reminded of what it means to be human. When one is facing surgery or the loss of a loved one, flowers remind us that to be truly human is to know beauty and the love of others. To be human is more than food, or to be hemmed in by adversity, or even caught by death.

When created as human by God, we were meant to live forever and were given the ability to create beauty and new life. To be human was to live in relationship, as man and woman and families. To be human was to be in relationship to God.

So when gripped with the hunger and thirst of 40 days and nights, Jesus could retort to the Tempter, "Man does not live on bread alone, but on every word that comes from the mouth of God."

Lisa M. Beardsley

Moving Mountains and Trees

If you have faith as small as a mustard seed, you can say to this mountain,
"Move from here to there" and it will move. Nothing will be impossible for you.
Matt. 17:20, NIV.

I HAVE READ today's text many times and always wondered if God really meant we could move a mountain or was this just a rhetorical way of referring to how He can solve the problems we meet in life? But I now know that God can move a mountain, or in my case, a tree.

It was the last official day of winter. The Michigan day was dreary with some freezing rain. My daughter, Katie, and I were on our way to see my mother with a full day planned. We had traveled most of the 40 miles to my mother's house when I hit a patch of black ice and my car went into a spin. I did a complete 360-degree turn in the road and then started sliding sideways—rushing toward a tree. It was inevitable. The car was going to slam broadside into the tree. In a heartbeat, at this potentially life-threatening situation, I sent up a silent prayer for protection. It was all happening so fast. When the car came to a stop Katie and I both looked out the window. "Where is the tree?" Katie asked. She emphatically asked again: "We were headed straight for the tree. Where is it?" I had seen the tree, too. I knew we were going to hit it, but now we didn't even see it. I couldn't get my car out of the ditch, but I was able to get out of the car to look around. I saw the tree about 20 feet from the car. Did the angels push the car forward so we wouldn't hit the tree? *Thank You, Lord, for saving us.*

We had much to be thankful for as we went about the day. A man with a pickup truck and a chain pulled us out of the ditch. Even though the car sustained heavy damage, I could still drive it. We did all of the things we had planned to do. Our hearts were full of thanks and praise.

On the way home, Katie and I had to pass the site of the accident. The evidence of our accident was plainly visible. You couldn't miss the tire tracks through weeds and mud. When I stopped so we could get a better look, I was too shocked to speak. Silent, I turned toward Katie. Her mouth was open in disbelief and her face was pale. When she could speak again she said, "Mom, the tree is there again—right by the tire tracks." Indeed, it was. The angels hadn't pushed the car out of the way of the tree. They had moved the tree and then moved it back again.

The God of the Bible that promised to move mountains still moves them.

Susan Drieberg

The Empty Shelves

*And this gospel of the kingdom shall be preached in all the world
for a witness unto all nations; and then shall the end come.
Matt. 24:14.*

I PULLED INTO THE PARKING LOT of the library in the area where I live, thinking about how I could share my faith with others. I was feeling anxious and eager to do something so that someone could learn about Jesus or learn to know Him better. I'd had some *Steps to Christ* books in my car for a long time and said quietly to myself, "These books are just sitting in my car. I need to give them away." So taking them out, I headed toward the library. I was determined to share the love of Christ with others.

I approached the librarian and asked if she would kindly accept some free books for the library. She then pointed to a table where I could put them. I prayed that the books I placed there would be read and would touch the lives of all those who read them. The Lord always provides different ways for us to share the goods news of salvation with others.

My visit to the library was not over. I needed books to read to my students and I also needed a few DVDs for myself. After selecting a few books and DVDs for my students, I proceeded to the adult section where it said Religion and Musical. I saw the Religion sign but the shelves were empty. I kept looking but realized that all the DVDs and videos were gone. I was disappointed, but then felt happy when I realized what the empty shelves meant. It meant that people are becoming interested in religion. People are eager and anxious to know more about God. It also reminded me that Christ is coming soon. This was the first time I have ever visited a library and found the religion shelves empty. I returned a few days later and all the books I had left were gone, and when I returned to the empty shelves I found two videos.

The empty shelves have lingered in my mind ever since, and have touched my life also. Each time I think of them I am reminded that Jesus is coming soon. The Bible says that in the last days people will be eager to learn about Christ. And as the songwriter wrote, "Jesus is coming again! Coming again, coming again, Jesus is coming again!" My heart is so happy, and my soul is so glad because the empty shelves continue to remind me that Jesus is coming soon.

Two important questions for you: Are you ready for Jesus to come? And are you sharing the good news of His coming with others?

Patricia Hines

My God Shall Supply All Your Need

But my God shall supply all your need according to his riches in glory by Christ Jesus.
Phil. 4:19.

IT WAS A BALMY, BREEZY AFTERNOON in March. A perfect introduction to spring! Having an unusually busy schedule that day, I had coordinated my activities for the most efficient use possible of my time—or so I thought. Then, as I finished my last errand before heading home, I made a startling discovery. I could not find my keys. The most diligent searching did not produce them.

I stood by my car and searched the bottom of my purse. No, the keys were not there. Surely I had not locked them in the car. I looked through the car window and didn't see them, so I went back into the bank where I'd last been. The keys were not there. Now, what must I do?

I just stood there in stark disbelief! How could I do such a thing on such a hectic day! Again I searched my purse, hoping against hope I'd find them nestled some place in the bottom. No, they just weren't there.

Walking toward the car, wondering what to do next, I heard a familiar voice. I turned to look directly into the face of one of the elders from my church. He was standing in line before one of the automated teller machines and just "happened" to turn around at that time. I explained that I couldn't find my car keys. His transaction finished, he bent down and peered into my car. To my amazement, he discovered the keys hanging in the ignition. From my vantage point, when I had checked before, the keys were not visible. He offered to take me to pick up my spare keys. On the way back he mentioned the promise that "My God shall supply all your need." He went on to explain that he'd had no intention of going to the bank that day. Then while waiting to use the automatic teller, he'd turned around just in time to see me pass by. I had not seen him.

The Lord knew how carefully I had laid my plans to use my time as judiciously as possible. He cared that, in my humanity, I had erred. How grateful I am that He foresees our needs and plans ahead to meet them. He sees the little sparrows fall, and He sees you and me.

He cares for us in tangible ways, and His Word is true today, and will be tomorrow, and always. Friend, He will supply all your needs.

Audre B. Taylor

It Could Happen to My Children

*I tell you the truth, whatever you did for one of the least of these
brothers of mine, you did for me.*
Matt. 25:40, NIV.

ONE EVENING as I walked home from the radiotherapists I was tired, depressed, hungry, lonely, and cold. Then I saw them. Three young boys stood in the cold near the main bus station. I could tell that they were tired and desperate. The eldest ran to me and said, "Mum, can you please top up our bus fare with 50 pence for us to go home?"

"No!" I replied and walked away. But as I sat at my bus stop waiting, a voice said to me, *It could happen to your child or grandchildren.* I just bowed my head in shame and with a big lump in my throat, whispered, "Father, please forgive me."

I quickly went back to where the boys were and gave them a pound, even though I had only two pounds left on me. They jumped about happily, then rushed over and entered their bus. They waved at me with joy.

Why did I refuse them at first? Maybe I was thinking about other boys who use their bus fares for candies or cigarettes. But whatever they would have used their money for should not be my concern. After all, did Jesus not tell us in Luke 6:37, not to judge others? Rather, He said that we should give and help one another and the needy.

How could I be telling the children's stories at Sabbath school, trying to advise children to help one another and strangers while I ignored needy children on the street? Suppose I had not helped those boys. Who then was I expecting to help them instead of me? I had been praying to God to provide for my children and the needy everyday. How could I ignore some children who were in real need?

I am glad in the end that I helped those young men. I know that the good Lord has forgiven me for my bad attitude toward them as they, too, are among His precious jewels. I know that they appreciated my help that evening, and I hope they learned a good lesson from it and will do the same for someone else someday.

Thank You, Jesus, for Your reminder. Please keep on tapping me on my shoulder when I go wrong and teach me to love and help the needy always, especially Your precious jewels.

Mabel Kwei

Positive, Positive, Only Positive

I will praise You, O Lord, with my whole heart; I will tell of all Your marvelous works. I will be glad and rejoice in You; I will sing praise to Your name, O Most High.
Ps. 9:1, 2, NKJV.

HOW MANY OF US, when things go wrong, think positive thoughts? Do you shout for joy? Sing and praise God? Are you full of joy?

I know that in my life, if I am truthful, I have a hard time doing what God has asked us to do. And yet one of my favorite Bible texts is, "All things work together for good to them that love God, to them who are the called according to his purpose" (Rom. 8:28).

I have asked God to help me to sing for joy, to shout, and to praise His name when I am down. This is not always easy to do. But God has a sense of humor. Maybe it's because I am a first–grade teacher that He has given me a game to play. Here is how it goes. When you say or think anything that is negative, stop! Now how many negative thoughts did you have? Was it one or five? For me it is sometimes even more. When that happens I must think of all the good and positive things I have in my life: I am alive; I am healthy; it is a wonderful day; God loves me and has promised to save me. But the hard part is to actually play the game. I have to think of three times more blessings then negative things in my life.

I also collect songs that help me be more thankful and joyful and positive. Here is one of them: "Count your blessings, name them one by one, count your blessings, see what God hath done! Count your blessings, name them one by one, and it will surprise you what the Lord hath done."

When I think only about the things that worry me—and there are a lot of them, I can get very negative and stressed. But when I start counting my blessings and exercising my will to be happy in Jesus, He will, and has, changed me from the inside out. I like that way much better than outside in.

So when you are lonely, sad, or anything that is not what God has promised, please try my game, and I hope that it will bless you and your family today. Remember with me that Paul says, "But godliness with contentment is great gain" (1 Tim. 6:6).

Praise to You, God and Creator of me.

Susen Mattison Mole'

The Examination Day

I can do all things through Christ, because he gives me strength.
Phil. 4:13, NCV.

THERE ARE NOT MANY THINGS I FEAR in life, but one of my greatest fears is taking a final examination. Ironically, a significant part of my work involves administering examinations and I enjoy this part of my job immensely! But when the shoe gets on the other foot, when I must do the writing, it is a totally different matter. I tremble with fear.

By now, most of us have discovered that adequate preparation is the secret to minimizing or eliminating this kind of fear. Recently I faced a final examination that I had spent years dreading. It was the comprehensives for my doctoral studies. There was no getting away from it—I had to face it. During the many months prior to the 15 hour examination I was supported by my Christian study group members, praying family members and friends, and godly facilitating professors. However, in spite of all this support, I had to do my part by studying diligently, praying constantly, and applying myself. I am pleased to report that the process worked because I was successful. To God be the glory!

There is another examination we all must take, and it is coming soon. It is far more important than the Ph.D. comprehensives, and to eliminate fear we must adequately prepare. We need the support of family and friends, but we must faithfully do our part to get ready. I have found the words of the following song by William Longstaff to be perfectly instructive in helping us prepare for this great examination day, the day when we will meet face to face with Jesus our Lord, Savior, and King.

"Take time to be holy, speak oft with thy Lord; abide in Him always, and feed on His Word, Make friends of God's children, help those who are weak, forgetting in nothing His blessing to seek. Take time to be holy, the world rushes on; spend much time in secret, with Jesus alone; By looking to Jesus, like Him thou shalt be; Thy friends in thy conduct His likeness shall see. Take time to be holy, let Him be thy Guide; and run not before Him, whatever betide; In joy or in sorrow, still follow thy Lord, and, looking to Jesus, Still trust in His word. Take time to be holy, be calm in thy soul."

I can face this examination without fear if I have placed my future in the hands of the One who will help me to prepare. I invite you to do the same.

Jacqueline Hope HoShing-Clarke

The Currency of Heaven

Show me the coin used for paying the tax.
Matt. 22:19, NIV.

COUNTING OUT THE CURRENCY to pay my bills, I remembered something I had read in my devotions: "But God's servants are to be representatives of Him. He desires them to deal only in the currency of heaven, the truth that bears His own image and superscription" (*The Desire of Ages,* p. 352). Looking at the $10 bill in my hand, I thought, *Who do you represent?* The United States of America. *And whose image do your bear?* Alexander Hamilton's. *What is your superscription?* The one I like best is: We the People.

A servant serves her master. She is obedient, applying her skills for him. *God, is that what I am doing for You? Do others see me as Your servant, using my skills for You? Am I rightly representing You like the $10 bill represents the United States of America?*

Representatives are agents, spokespersons, ambassadors. Am I an agent God can send to represent Him? Will I look after His business in a way that will increase His kingdom? As His spokesperson, do others hear Him or me? Do they hear the sweet music of heaven calling them to come up higher? Am I a fit ambassador for the kingdom of heaven? Do those I encounter see the splendor of God's kingdom and want to become part of it?

What is the currency of heaven? The dictionary defines currency as: money, coins, legal tender, notes, coinage, exchange, cash. I can't imagine these in heaven. Yet God says He want us to "deal only in the currency of heaven." Currency is money I use to pay my bills, buy the necessities I need and some luxuries. Society uses money to generate power, fame, and social status. Money is important to us, the controlling force behind much we do.

I ask God, *What in Your kingdom has this kind of power?* The truth about God found in His Word and His people has power. That's the currency of heaven, isn't it? A truth that bears God's image will be like God. When anyone examines that truth they will discover God.

A superscription is written or engraved on the surface, outside, or above something. *I want Your truth written and engraved on me and in me; then I will be part of the currency of heaven. People will recognize me as Your servant because they see Your image superscripted all over me.*

Joan Beck

Spring Cleaning

And forgive us our sins; for we also forgive every one that is indebted to us.
And lead us not into temptation; but deliver us from evil.
Luke 11:4.

IS THERE ANY WOMAN who has not, at some time or the other, deeply cleaned her home? Why is it necessary to "spring clean" anyway? Because day after day, little bits of dirt and dust accumulate. It is those little bits of dust that get left behind in daily cleaning.

A new house is normally a clean house. It's bright and shiny. It even smells clean. But when we move in little bits of dirt and dust move in with us. Every time we go out and return, we bring in a bit more dust. At last a good "spring cleaning" is necessary. We can never get away from this need to clean.

The same is true in our relationships. It's important to do spring cleaning from time to time. Through time we all accumulate attitudes, words, encounters with our parents, husband, friends, and relatives that were filed in the folders of our mind. Of course, we have many positive and happy memories. It is good to keep and review these files from time to time. They are sources of joy and contentment. But bad and hurtful things may be there too, and they only serve to take up space. Situations where your mind created a negative record and filed it in your memory.

So cleaning your house and heart is in order. But perhaps you are thinking, *I don't have anything to forgive. I don't have anything against anyone.* However, each time someone hurts you with words, gestures, looks, or any other action that causes anger or pain, these events are filed within your mind. It's time for a good spring cleaning of the mind.

This type of cleaning is done through forgiveness—genuine forgiving with your whole heart. Forgiveness burns all the records that have been filed against those who have offended you. And then, the house can be impeccably clean and pleasant. I am certain that you will notice a difference in your heart and your mind after you forgive.

Today if you have to forgive someone, do not hesitate. The more you forgive—do spring cleaning—the closer you come to the state that human beings were when created by God: beautiful and wonderful. I am certain every woman wants those results.

Susana Faria

God's Plan

But Hannah answered and said, "No, my lord, I am a woman of sorrowful spirit. I have drunk neither wine nor intoxicating drink, but have poured out my soul before the Lord. . . ." Then Eli answered and said, "Go in peace, and the God of Israel grant your petition which you have asked of Him."
1 Sam. 1:15, 17, NKJV.

I WAS BLESSED to receive a college scholarship. My mother and I were both so grateful. My experience reminds me of Hannah, recorded in the Bible. Though married to Elkanah, Hannah had no children because the Lord had closed her womb. Penninah had children, and at the yearly sacrifice Elkanah gave her and her children meat to sacrifice, but to Hannah he gave a double portion. Yet Hannah was in bitterness of soul, and praying to the Lord, she wept in anguish and made a vow that if God gave her a male child she would give him to the Lord for all the days of his life.

The high priest was worried because of the way Hannah prayed and he thought she was drunk. But God heard her prayers and answered her request. A few years later she fulfilled her vow by taking the child, Samuel, to the Lord.

This Bible story is an inspiration to me; it tells me we should be persistent. Whatever we ask for should be for the glory of God. For instance, as I study at the University of Eastern Africa Baraton, it has always been my heartfelt desire that God would help provide my school fees. I want to complete my school program and find the ways and means to help the needy, especially orphans. And He has done that for me through the scholarship program.

May we as Christians emulate Hannah in the way she prayed. If we make vows to God through prayer, and He fulfills them, we must keep our vow as Hannah did. Surely, as God did for Hannah, He will also bless us.

In Jeremiah 29:11 the Bible tells us that the Lord has good plans for each one of us, plans for good and not of evil, to give us a future and a hope. Our journey may not always be smooth, but God has a good plan for us. What a wonderful and joyful experience it is to live with and expect blessings from the Lord by faith. Our Lord is so faithful to us, His beloved daughters.

Agnes Chepkorir Rotich

Another Paradise

In my Father's house are many mansions: if it were not so, I would have told you.
I go to prepare a place for you. And if I go and prepare a place for you, I will come again,
and receive you unto myself; that where I am, there ye may be also.
John 14:2, 3.

IN MY CHRISTIAN CHILDHOOD, I was not accustomed to hearing much about a new earth and living with Christ. As a consequence, here in this fallen world, I felt a need to seek a special place to live. Unfortunately, the place I have chosen to relax in is a condominium; by coincidence, it is called Paradise. In it are beautiful houses and an enchanting path along the beach for walking and reflecting. It is truly a special place for me and my family. I can rest, listen to the birds and the sound of the ocean, and recharge my batteries for the challenges that await me in the daily labor as I return to my house.

The peace, the silence, and the habit of people greeting each other along the pathways have made for pleasant outings filled with "Good morning" or "Good afternoon" greetings.

As I write this, it is April, the Easter period, and I am back at my private paradise. However, my quiet time this year has not worked out as I planned, for my paradise has been invaded by strangers. The people next door and those behind us decided to hold a party. It was not pleasant for their neighbors as the sounds and deafening music began in the late night hours and extended through the early morning hours. When I go for a walk, I see dozens of unfamiliar people who do not belong to this condominium complex. They do not know the habits of peaceful and quiet living so I do not hear the customary phrases of greetings.

I am beginning to become irritated and feel penalized because I can't relax. I think that my paradise isn't to be found in this place and I need to have patience and wait a little longer until Jesus returns. My eyes fill with tears of longing for a place that I do not yet know. I love to think about a beautiful enchanted land, a place where joy is complete, and has been chosen for all of us.

I want to take advantage of this opportunity to ask God to prepare my eternal home. I want Him to help me overcome in the battle with evil. I want to work to hasten the soon return of His beloved Son Jesus. Let us remember to keep the faith.

Andrea de Almeida Santos

Keeping My Words

Let the words of my mouth, and the meditation of my heart,
be acceptable in thy sight, O Lord, my strength, and my redeemer.
Ps. 19:14.

I DON'T ALWAYS keep my word. In fact, I've let myself and others down countless times because I've failed to keep my word.

A few years ago, a precious young friend and I had gone to do sign language interpretation at an afternoon service. We interpreted together and after the service she led me to the entrance of the interstate I needed to go home. Later that month she came to my mind and I promised myself that I'd call her very soon. I wanted to thank her for being so gracious and kind during our interpreting together and during our years of friendship. I postponed the call. And then she died suddenly. The personal guilt and shame I've carried have only been relieved by God's mercy, but the remorse lingers to remind me to keep my word.

I've also failed others when I didn't keep my word. My husband depended on me to purchase our car registration since I've done it willingly over the years. One year, I simply postponed the renewing and purchasing of my husband's car registration even after he reminded and warned me that he would run into trouble. He would have gladly taken charge of the matter, but I reassured him that I would take care of it since it still was not due—I had time, or so I told myself. But I didn't get it done.

As he feared, my husband was stopped and fined for the past-due registration. Again, God's grace and my husband's kindness have sheltered me even while I continue to despise my sins. When was I going to learn? In Matthew 5:37, Jesus says, "Let your word be 'Yes, Yes' or 'No, No'; anything more than this comes from the evil one" (NRSV). The lesson to me is, Don't say you are going to do something unless you are really going to do it.

More and more, I feel the sweet voice of the Spirit calling me to keep my word to others and to myself. The small things that I neglect to do often result in deadly or horrible guilt, shame, inconvenience to others, or worse. So I pray today and always, *Dear God, let the words of my mouth and the meditation of my heart be acceptable in thy sight. For You, my Redeemer, will give me the strength to honor them.*

Rose Thomas

Is There Hope at Last?

In hope of eternal life, which God, that cannot lie, promised before the world began.
Titus 1:2.

IT WAS ON FRIDAY, April 11, that we made the 90-minute trip to Birmingham to see the specialist, Dr. Oh. After the nerve conduction test and a needle EMG, the doctor deemed it necessary to do a muscle biopsy instead of a nerve biopsy. When all the tests were finished we were instructed to wait at least three weeks to hear from the doctor before we called in ourselves to find out the diagnosis. On Friday of the third week we contacted both doctors' offices and were told that we would receive a call on Monday.

On Monday, we were informed that the specialist felt there were some conflicting test results and he was unable to make a definite diagnosis. Some of the tests must be repeated. So on Friday, May 23, we once again set out for Birmingham, hoping that this time we would receive a diagnosis.

After the tests were repeated and I was allowed to return to the examining room, the doctor gave us the diagnosis: inclusion body myopathy. There is no cure for this progressive muscle disease. For a short time I could hear nothing else. My mind reeled. My worst fear had become a reality. This diagnosis left us with no hope. James would continue to have muscle depletion and one day would become bedridden and eventually succumb to this disease. In private I asked the doctor how long he thought that James would have before he became unable to care for himself. The doctor said that I could get a good idea by how the disease had already progressed. It had been only about four months, and James had lost most of the use of his right arm, and already was starting to have trouble with his left arm. I felt helpless and alone. How could this be? Could I care for my ailing husband and five young children by myself?

With much thought—and even more prayer—I came to the realization that I was not alone: God would see us through. I would soon have to stop working anywhere and my family would become my only job, and a full–time job it is. Although there is not any hope for my husband's life to be extended on this earth, there is always the hope of life everlasting with our Lord and Savior Jesus Christ. Psalm 31:24 says, "Be of good courage, and he shall strengthen your heart, all ye that hope in the Lord."

Theodora V. Sanders

Sunshine

But if we walk in the light, as he is in the light, we have fellowship with one another, and the blood of Jesus, his Son, purifies us from all sin.
1 John 1:7, NIV.

THE DARK WINTER MONTHS are over—at least in the Northern Hemisphere. The days are getting longer, the sun's rays are becoming stronger, the earth is warming up, many things are awakening to new life. Nature has begun to change. All this is wonderful, but there is another side to consider. The clear, golden rays of the sun which cause such beautiful changes in nature also have a negative side. We homemakers suddenly see smudges and dust throughout the house, and so we begin spring cleaning. The more the sun shines into our houses the more dirty corners we discover to be cleaned. It can seem that we fight a losing battle against grime. The light shows us new dust.

God is like the light. God's nature is light and in Him there is no darkness (see 1 John 1:5). He or she who comes to God's light will be surprised to realize how smudged and dirty they are. The longer we live with God in His light, the more and more things we discover in us that are out of order; the more we see things in our lives that are not good.

It's the same in our human relationships. If I am looking for a friend and am ready to open up my life, things will be uncovered that must be cleaned away for the friendship to have a chance to develop. I can't stay like I am—nor can my friend—even if we often hear that a good friendship can overcome anything.

Our relationship with God has to develop too. But isn't it humiliating to confess things before people and before God? What should I do with the dirt? Of course, God knows everything already. He knows in what condition I am because He knows me thoroughly. He also has the solution for my problem. Today's text says it clearly: "But if we walk in the light . . . we have fellowship with one another, and the blood of Jesus, his Son, purifies us from all sin."

Only if we are prepared to confess our sins and faults will we experience the healing effect of forgiveness—in our dealings with people or with God. Then we will not be afraid of the sunlight which makes everything visible. We can enjoy its blessed rays. This light—God's light—will be a blessing for our human relationships as well.

Regina Fackler

Changing Directions

The Lord will guide you continually, and satisfy your soul in drought,
and strengthen your bones; you shall be like a watered garden,
and like a spring of water, whose waters do not fail.
Isa. 58:11, NKJV.

HOW EASY IS IT for you to change your mind? Or your vocation? Or your home address? Or your character? We know that God wants us to change our characters and promises to enable us to do just that. All we have to do is cooperate with Him, and not oppose His efforts to change us. But how easy is that? Sometimes it's not easy at all.

I used to think that old age would come gradually, but old age grabbed me one day with a totally unpredicted heart attack. I was a strong wilderness hiker and backpacker on mountain trails. But, like Paul, one surprising day I was stopped and redirected. Now I can do only simple walks at low elevations, or one-day hikes without a pack. Admonitions of "Don't go alone" haunt every walk I take out of town. Paul spent a time in Arabia emptying his total being of his previous life of crime. As I write this I've spent nearly two years trying to comprehend and cope with the new me and to get moving in a more appropriate direction. But it's hard!

Suppose you were born into and grew up in a loving, expressive, generous, socially active family. And after you'd been married a while you realized your husband inherited the opposite traits. He keeps his troubles to himself, prefers staying home to going out, doesn't spend any more money than absolutely necessary—you get the picture. How easy is it for either of you to change? Have you accepted the fact that you must not only practice Christian love yourself but perhaps teach it to your spouse? No matter the issues, Jesus' love reached to the lowest depths, and you are His disciple.

The answer is the same in all change challenges: "Lo, I am with you always, even unto the end of the world" (Matt. 28:20). It is important to stay close to God: "The Lord of hosts is with us" (Ps. 46:11, NKJV). We need faith in His help: "Hope in God; for I shall yet praise Him, the help of my countenance and my God" (Ps. 42:11, NKJV). Then we need to speak up! "In the great assembly; indeed, I do not restrain my lips, O Lord, You Yourself know" (Ps. 40:9, NKJV).

And last, there is today's promise. With Him you can change directions as needed.

Louise Rea

Kindness and PMS

I can do everything through him who gives me strength.
Phil. 4:13, NIV.

KINDNESS IS NOT EASY for me during a certain time of the month. My hormones seem to be furious at me, leaving my nerves on edge. Aware of this, for several years I avoided resolving controversial matters and attempted to reduce my communication with people during this time for I become extremely objective and arid with my words.

On one of these crucial days a friend came to my house to exchange ideas about a master's degree program she wanted to enroll in. My patience, which normally is not great, was almost nonexistent. I questioned her in a direct manner and harshly offered my opinion.

"Objective like a man," stated my sister after the incident. At the end of the afternoon when one of my sisters came to my home she commented that I was treating her very matter-of-factly; not rude, just matter-of-factly. I shared my feelings as I struggled to control my unprovoked irritation. My other sister, who had witnessed the conversation with my friend, confessed that she thought I had exaggerated with the objectivity. "I'm afraid that your friend could have been frightened by your attitude," she observed. My sisters agreed that I should talk to my friend and explain the situation.

I prayed about this before going to bed and God helped me remember His purpose in allowing me access to knowledge through graduate studies. One of the reasons was so that I could help people who came to me. I also remembered a text which explained that what knowledge we have beyond what others have, makes it our obligation to share. No matter what it may be, notions regarding manners, cutting the grass, foreign languages, writing a project—they are gifts we should share. After reading this I made a pact with myself to share the knowledge that I acquired. Now it was time to correct the situation.

The next morning, I recorded some examples of graduate projects on a diskette and I went to my friend's home. She welcomed me with joy. I gave her the material and explained what had happened the previous day and promised to help her as much as possible.

As I left, I felt better, knowing that I was sharing a small part of the objective that God had for me. This purpose made all the difference in my day.

Iani Dias Lauer-Leite

My Very Own GPS

I guide you in the way of wisdom and lead you along straight paths.
Prov. 4:11, NIV.

IT'S THE STORY OF MY LIFE: I was late again. I needed to get to the airport—quickly. My husband was returning from meetings in London. Now, I must tell you that since I was a little girl, I have loved airports and the crowds of people waiting to see loved ones. I love watching them smiling, laughing, hugging, crying, and the jibber-jabber of interaction. My favorite thing: the doors open and your loved one walks through—their eyes scan the crowd, then the face breaks out in a smile and you hurry to get to each other. It is always worth the wait—but I digress.

You see, we live in Korea, and the speed limit is 56 mph (90 km/h), a far cry from the 75 mph (120 km/h) in my native South Africa—especially when one is late. So, I got creative. It appears that every car in Korea has a GPS that announces the next hidden speed camera—every car, that is, except ours. We do not have one of these gadgets. So I decided to get smart and follow another car. As we whizzed along the highway toward the airport I felt quite proud of myself for this magnificent idea. I was now pretty sure that I would be on time. I imagined the doors opening, our eyes meeting, and my husband's infectious smile.

Suddenly other thoughts intruded my daydreams. Questions popped into my head: *Does the car I am following so blindly have a GPS? Is his GPS working? Will he respond to it in the way I hope he will? Does he care about getting a ticket?* Judging by his car, he could probably afford one. I considered my options for a minute and decided that I should slow down. I sighed at the thought of being late but resigned myself to the fact.

I arrived at the airport a few minutes late to find my husband's flight delayed. My three-hour-wait gave me plenty of time to contemplate some realities. I realized that in life I am prone to run after a GPS of my own choosing when, in fact, Jesus is—or should be—my GPS. I can always rely on that GPS as He is always working. He knows where I'm going. He also knows the speed limit. If I want to run ahead of Him, He helps me to slow down. He knows where the hidden cameras are along the road of my life and points them out. He is my guide. Following another's GPS blindly comes at a price that I simply cannot afford. I thanked the Lord for this wonderful lesson.

Maike Stepanek

Farming Faith

The Kingdom of God is like a man who scatters seed upon the ground,
and then continues sleeping and rising night and day while the seed sprouts
and grows and increases—he knows not how.
Mark 4:26, 27, Amplified.

RECENTLY I HEARD A PASTOR SAY, "We have to farm faith." However, a farmer must be patient, and we can be so impatient. We want the right results right now, but Mark 4 tells us that God doesn't work that way. I love the seed principle and the mystery of how God brings things together at just the right time. Our job is to scatter the seeds and keep ourselves watered and rooted in His Word—that is what grows our faith. We can rest in the fact that the seed sprouts and grows, ready for harvest in God's perfect time.

I have seen this principle of growth in my children. Our older daughter, Allison, is in her third year of college. It's taken years of hard work and dedication for her to get to this point. If she continues doing her part, I believe God will bring opportunities at just the right time, and she will see some fruitful results. You might say she's had a favorable season and so we're predicting a good crop.

Our younger daughter, Morgan, has autism and has had challenges from the time she was small. Over the years she has spent countless hours in speech, occupational, and behavioral therapies. She is now 14 years old, and at times still struggles to communicate her basic needs. All this time I have known that hidden within Morgan are some very capable seeds. I continue doing what God has given me to do, never giving up, just as I know He doesn't give up on me. I fully trust the results to Him. I trust in the "mystery of the kingdom of God" (Mark 4:11), just as a farmer must trust what is going on beneath the soil. My only responsibility is to see that the conditions for growth are as favorable as possible.

Dear Father, today I plan only to do what You've given me to do. I will rest in Your promises because I believe in Your Word. The mustard seed "is the smallest of all seeds upon the earth, yet after it is sown, it grows up and becomes the greatest of all garden herbs and puts out large branches, so that the birds of the air are able to make nests and dwell in its shade" (Mark 4:31, 32).

Tammy Vice

Lessons From a Palm Tree

*Blessed is the man who walks not in the counsel of the ungodly, nor stands
in the path of sinners, nor sits in the seat of the scornful; but his delight is in
the law of the Lord, and in His law he meditates day and night. He shall be
like a tree planted by the rivers of water, that brings forth its fruit in its season,
whose leaf also shall not wither; and whatever he does shall prosper.*
Ps. 1:1-3, NKJV.

SEVERAL YEARS AGO we retired and moved to Florida. Through the years since then
we have noted an interesting feature of Christmas in Florida. Palm trees are often
decorated for Christmas with strings of brightly colored lights wrapped around
their trunks. One year I noticed two palm trees completely decorated, trunk and
fronds. One of them stood in front of the Palms of Sebring, a facility that included
a nursing home, assisted living quarters, and independent living quarters. I believe
the lessons that my palm trees taught are suitable throughout the year.

When we first moved to Florida we brought a few medjool dates with us from
Maryland. As we used them, I saved four of the pits and planted them in small pots on
our patio. Two of the four sprouted and grew. Those I replanted as needed into larger
and still larger pots. Later I gave one of them away and the other I planted in our own
front yard. It grew to be quite large, reaching higher then the roof of our house.

However, my neighbor planted their palm between two large palms. "I am
afraid," I told the neighbor, "that your little date palm will not grow well. It does-
n't have enough room."

Several years went by and the palm never grew more than about two or three
feet high. It remained a diminutive tree between two giant palms. Some people in
our development had trouble keeping their palms trimmed—they were so tall.
When a company came through offering to buy our big palms and replace them
with smaller ones, several accepted the offer. Among those to go was that cluster of
three palms—two giants and one stunted in growth.

Like that little date palm, we Christians need room to grow spiritually. We need
to make time each day to drink long at the fountain of living water and to nourish
our souls with the bread of life. If we do not have room in our lives to spread out
our spiritual fronds, like that little date palm, we will find that we have become spiritual dwarfs.

Naomi Zalabak

A Star for Christ

A man's heart plans his way, but the Lord directs his steps.
Prov. 16:9, NKJV.

LOS ANGELES, CALIFORNIA, *bright–eyed, bushy–tailed, and ready to turn the world on with a smile.* I was anxious, excited, and smiling from ear to ear. I took my baseball cap off my head and threw it in the air. Little did I know that this adventure would be a turning point in my life. I was raised a staunch Christian. I grew up in the church, worked in the local Christian school, and had a Bible scripture for every occasion. Even so, I had the bug! The itch! That star-glazed passion! I had entertainment flowing through my veins and I just couldn't shake it. I wanted to be a stand-up comedian and the only place for me was Hollywood. Lights! Cameras! Action!

Reality hit quickly as I stepped off the Greyhound bus with only the clothes on my back. Who knew where my luggage went? I realized that I had no money, no job, and no place to stay. I thought I'd secured living arrangements before I left Florida, but as was my habit, I leaped before I looked. I was directed to the local YWCA, and upon my arrival, there was some kind of mix-up, or should I say "spiritual set-up." Everyone seemed to think I was there for a job. Guess what? I got the job! After securing the job, I was directed to a local women's shelter.

It was at the shelter that I realized my true calling. Most of the women there were drug users who were trying to stay clean and off the streets. As I mingled with my newly found sisters, I discovered that I had a heart for service. I assisted women in obtaining medical attention, finding rehabilitation facilities, and yes, even finding housing. My assistance was so greatly appreciated that I was used as a shelter volunteer. I attended a seminar titled, "Completing Your Goal Within 24 Hours." The presenter stated that if a person identifies a goal and follows through within 24 hours, there is a 95 percent chance that they will complete the goal. That night, I set a goal of attending college. And yes, I registered for classes within 24 hours.

I never became a Hollywood star, but I am a star for Christ. Today I have a master's degree in social work, and I continue to help women in need. As for the bug—well, I'm a Christian comedian, sharing the gift of humor through workshops, children's stories, and motivational speaking. The Lord will direct our steps if we allow Him to do so.

Charlotte S. Grant

Keep Looking Up.

I lift up my eyes to you, to you whose throne is in heaven. As the eyes of slaves
look to the hand of their master, as the eyes of a maid look to the hand of her mistress,
so our eyes look to the Lord our God, till he shows us his mercy.
Ps. 123:1, 2, NIV.

WE WERE ENJOYING the house that we bought, buying new furniture, hanging up pictures, and doing other decorating. My husband was happy that he didn't need to get up early to drive to his work—now it was a five-minute walk down the road. I was excited because our house had many rooms. At last I could store our stuff. We felt so comfortable. Life was good!

Then Martin came home from work and announced he'd been terminated. He was one of the workers to be laid off. I was so shocked my stomach hurt. As usual we prayed, knowing that only God could give us peace and hope. He had done it before. Martin had been jobless before, and it had taken only two weeks before he found work. So we trusted in the Lord that this time He would do the same. But God wants us to learn to be more patient. We need to keep on trusting Him even when we don't know what will happen next. Martin filled out application after application, hoping it would take only a short time to find a new job. Every day the mailbox held letters of rejection or his letter being returned with a wish for good luck in the future.

We worried about our finances because of the additional payment for our mortgage. Martin took odd jobs, not all of them connected to his line of work. He continued to apply for work—sending out more than 400 applications, but still no job. Months passed, and he began to grow impatient and discouraged. Though I kept on encouraging him through the promises of God, I myself began to doubt. But I didn't say a word or show any negative feelings; I just burst into tears when talking to God while driving and playing religious music in my car. And God answered all my questions in my heart. One song gave me hope and kept me going: "Thy God is still the same today, keep looking up, He will not fail thee come what may; keep looking up; the darkest cloud will roll away. So do not doubt, but keep looking up!"

We were almost at the end of our rope when God answered our prayers. Now we know that if we encounter trials and problems again we can say, "Just look back at how God has helped us in the past and keep on looking up!"

Loida Gulaja Lehmann

Lightning Struck Twice

O Lord, thou art my God; I will exalt thee, I will praise thy name; for thou hast done wonderful things . . . For thou hast been a strength to the poor, a strength to the needy in his distress, a refuge from the storm. . . . And it shall be said in that day, Lo, this is our God; we have waited for him, and he will save us: . . . we will be glad and rejoice in his salvation.
Isa. 25:1, 4, 9.

ONE EVENING I was enjoying time with two of my granddaughters while my husband sat nearby working at his computer. The girls had wanted to go outside but it was lightly raining so they were confined to indoor play. The drizzle turned to a steady rain, then a heavy downpour. Fresh in my mind were previous experiences with severe storms and power outages—the instant darkness and the girls screaming at the top of their lungs—so I had a hurricane lamp next to me, ready to light if needed.

We were laughing and talking until a terrific boom, crackle, and pop cut into our fun. It sounded like it was right outside our door. A bit frightened, I went to look outside but saw nothing but torrents of rain. I returned to the kitchen and the girls, but within minutes we all jumped in fear at a horrific boom, crackle, pop—much louder than before. It, too, sounded like it was right outside our door. I prayed silently for the storm to pass quickly, and soon the rain subsided. The peaceful atmosphere was a welcome relief, and at bedtime it was easy to settle in. I went to bed, never thinking to look outside again.

I awoke at 2:15 a.m. Wondering what the street looked liked, I peered through my bedroom window and there, on the right side of the house, it looked like a large tree had fallen across our property. *Oh, no, no, no!* I thought. I got back in bed but tossed and turned until daybreak, then anxiously went outside. To my dismay, not only was that tree down but a tree limb laden with leaves had fallen on the left side of the yard and was jutting into the street. No trees or limbs were down anywhere else on the street. I quickly ran to tell my husband.

Throughout the day my mind wandered to thoughts of how fortunate we were that the lightning had struck only the trees! We had been very close to danger because the kitchen was barely 25 feet from both trees that were struck. Yet God protected us during that storm, just as He does during the many storms—spiritual, physical, emotional—that assail us in life.

Iris L. Kitching

Faith Legacy

Now faith is the substance of things hoped for, the evidence of things not seen.
Heb.11:1, NKJV.

For God did not send His Son into the world to condemn the world,
but that the world through Him might be saved.
John 3:17, NKJV.

For by grace you have been saved through faith, and that not of yourselves;
it is the gift of God, not of works, lest anyone should boast.
Eph. 2:8, 9, NKJV.

FAITH IS PART OF THE CHRISTIAN LIFE from beginning to end. As the instrument by which the gift of salvation is received, faith is distinct from the basis of salvation which is grace, and from the outworking of salvation which is good works. Ephesians 2:8, 9, confirms my belief in salvation. For this reason I bow my knees to the Father of our Lord Jesus Christ.

All of that leads me to the gift of a faith legacy that we leave to our following generations. Our family, through five generations, has received this faith legacy from our parents—and what a gift, what an inheritance to leave to our children and their children. We are so blessed. Would you leave this gift to your children and generations to come?

It is through our faith in Jesus and our belief that He was born of a virgin, lived as an example, and died on the cross that our sins are forgiven. He paid the price for our sin once and for all. Hebrews 11:6 says, "But without faith it is impossible to please Him, for he who comes to God must believe that He is, and that He is a rewarder of those who diligently seek Him" (NKJV) What is faith? It is a belief in or confident attitude toward God, involving commitment to His will for one's life. Hebrews 11:3 tells us "By faith we understand that the worlds were framed by the word of God, so that the things which are seen were not made of things which are visible" (NKJV). I believe when God created us, He planted faith within us so that we would love and trust Him in all things. We know that God is the only one that we can trust. People fall short, just because they're human, and we cannot put total trust in humans for we will be disappointed.

Again and again—when given the chance—Jesus proves to us that He never fails us no matter what our circumstances may be. We find in John 3:17, "For God did not send His Son into the world to condemn the world, but that the world through Him might be saved" (NKJV). That is a legacy that anyone should be happy to receive. To God be all the glory!

Margaret Duran

Destination: Heaven

Hold tightly to what is good. Love each other with genuine affection,
and take delight in honoring each other.
Rom. 12:9, 10, NLT.

SONNY (AGE 21), was sick with a nasty cold. I never know how long we'll be house-bound during his times of illness so I decided it would be a good idea to make "Sonny Art Valentines" for us to work on over the holidays. On Christmas Eve day we took our paperwork to Staples to be photocopied. Sonny used Kyla's pen to sign his name on the master copy. Then with a radiant smile Kyla proceeded to make us 525 Valentines. Just a week before Sonny had given Kyla a copy of *Heaven's Whisper* for Christmas. "I'll treasure this book forever," she said proudly while blessing me with a hug!

Kyla made it easy for people to love her. She overflowed with genuine respect and kindness toward everyone, and spiritually I saw her as another little saint in training. During the past 10 months she had helped make 400 copies of "Our Journey Through Time With Sonny." From the get-go, Kyla knew that Sonny's book was going to some very influential people: politicians and policy makers, who in our society determine the fate and quality of life for the majority of people with developmental disabilities. She, too, desired our book to be perfect, and it is perfect enough for the Lord to use as He wills. The truth be known, this book is documented evidence of how my life is being lived out in faith and obedience to Jesus for His glory and the expansion of His kingdom. On my last order, Kyla apologized because she had lost count and made several extra books. I said, "Honey, we know Who we are working for and this was no mistake. Jesus knows these books will go to some very special people."

On January 3, the second of Sonny's Valentines was ready for photocopying, but Kyla wasn't at her work station. We found out that Kyla, age 21, had gotten sick on the last day of the year and passed away two days later of a tubal pregnancy. You cannot imagine the grief that pierced our hearts and the hearts of everyone who knew and loved her. I sent a copy of Sonny's book to Kyla's parents. And in the spirit of lovingkindness I'm confidently looking forward to introducing you to Kyla and her family in Paradise. No matter what happens in your life, be ready to share God's love with someone.

Deborah Sanders

Every Family Is Precious

But as for me and my family, we will serve the Lord.
Joshua 24:15, NLT.

IN THE ACCOUNTS of family life recorded in the Bible, we see a representation of Jesus and His love for us, His children. It's so sad how sin destroyed happiness right from the very beginning. No doubt Adam and Eve loved each other and the children they were blessed with. How tragic that one son became bitter enough against his brother to kill him. The Bible account tells of Cain first turning from God and allowing anger and bitterness into his mind. God desired to help him. "You must subdue it and be its master" (Gen. 4:7, NLT). This he rejected.

Sin always drives wedges between people—including, sadly, families. These barriers can be jealousy, hatred, blame, or an infinite list of other problems. Satan targets families to divide and weaken what God intended to be strong. You may know homes in the community and church, or sadly your own family, where love and forgiveness have come unstuck.

Like Adam and Eve, some parents have raised their children to know Jesus, only to watch them later in life turn against church life and lose hold of faith in God's Word. They often change their approach to life and to others, and this may affect how they spiritually instruct their own children.

Have you had a spiritual burden for others weighing upon your heart? Most times these are circumstances out of your control, yet it has the power to overshadow and sap energy and happiness in your own life. Because our children and grandchildren are very precious to us, more than anything else we desire that they all be ready to meet Jesus. Be encouraged and comforted by God's promises for He said, "I will never fail you. I will never abandon you" (Heb. 13:5, NLT). This means we need to include Jesus in every anxious thought and moment we have concerning precious family members.

Our heavenly Father understands a parent's aching heart. Pray diligently that the Holy Spirit will strive in your children's lives, that they find peace in accepting Jesus as their Savior, the only one who can end bitterness, nurture forgiveness, and restore damaged relationships and hurting hearts.

Live as an example, and never stop loving them.

Lyn Welk-Sandy

Calico, the Cat

Call upon me and come and pray to me, and I will hear you.
Jer. 29:12, ESV.

I CALL HER CALICO because she is a colorful cat, speckled grey, black, white, and orange.

She meets me whenever I come home. She rubs against my legs. She rolls over and exposes her furry stomach with her four paws lifted. She is submitting to me, showing me respect.

"That's a good cat!" I tell her as I scratch her tummy. "You know who's boss around here, don't you!"

She runs ahead of me when I go for a walk, back and forth in front of my feet. If I scold her for trying to slow me down, she rolls over in submission. I laugh every time I see her do it. Often I hear Calico's squeaky voice at the front door or one of the windows. "I hear you, Calico," I call in answer to her meow.

The other day I found a small card my daughter had tucked into a journal she gave me for a gift. It has a picture of a yellow kitten that has rolled over on its back with its paws in the air. Beside it are the words, "God hears even the smallest voice." I pasted the card in my journal that day, a day that had been long and frustrating. Under the card I wrote these words: "Oh, my God, I feel as helpless tonight as this little kitten. Now, like the kitten I 'roll over' and submit myself to You as my Master. I'm calling on You now. You can hear my weak voice. You know my pain, sorrow, and care just now. You have promised to hear when I call. Thank You, Lord!" Then I copied the following from *Steps to Christ*, p. 102: "Keep your wants, your joys, your sorrows, your cares, and your fears before God. You cannot burden Him; You cannot weary Him. He who numbers the hairs of your head is not indifferent to the wants of His children. . . . His heart of love is touched by our sorrows and even by our utterances of them. Take to Him everything that perplexes the mind. Nothing is too great for Him to bear, for He holds up worlds, He rules over all the affairs of the universe. Nothing that in any way concerns our peace is too small for Him to notice. There is no chapter in our experience too dark for Him to read; there is no perplexity too difficult for him to unravel. No calamity can befall the least of His children, no anxiety harass the soul, no joy cheer, no sincere prayer escape the lips, of which our heavenly Father is unobservant, or in which He takes no immediate interest."

Dorothy Eaton Watts

God's Compensation

God is faithful, who will not suffer you to be tempted above that ye are able;
but will with the temptation also make a way to escape, that ye may be able to bear it.
1 Cor. 10:13.

AS HUMAN BEINGS, we probably fear pain even more than we fear death, especially excruciating pain over an extended period of time. This is natural, and pain is certainly not an experience that anyone would choose to pass through. However, for one who loves God there are some hidden blessings in such an experience. I like to call them "God's compensation."

A long time in bed without any kind of exercise soon causes sleep problems. I often nap during the day, but the nights are endless and pain always seems worse in the dark. Job said that God "giveth songs in the night" (Job 35:10), and Paul and Silas certainly found relief from the torture of their lacerated backs as they sang at midnight in the Philippi prison. However, it is not always possible to sing, especially if others are sleeping in the house. Fortunately, there are other, quieter ways of engaging the mind and so soften the pain.

I used to keep a notepad and pencil by my bed and spent many a night hour writing articles for the women's devotional and composing poems and occasional notes of encouragement to friends who were passing through difficult times. Not everyone enjoys writing, but God has other ways of shortening long night hours.

Often He brings to mind inspiring and comforting texts from the Bible and encouraging quotations from favorite devotional books, both of which give me hope and a deeper trust in God's leading in my life. The resulting peace of mind brings physical relief as well.

And what conversations God and I have had! He stays so close and listens so patiently. Though I never hear an audible voice, my heart resonates with His answers to my endless questions. There are no deadlines to meet, and this unhurried communion is sweeter than any I have ever experienced before in my frenzied, hectic life.

Perhaps the most lasting result of this bittersweet experience has been a closer walk with my Savior and a renewed hope in His soon coming to take us home. I praise God for "songs in the night," for gentle promptings to write down thoughts which might help others, for precious promises from His Word, and sweet, unhurried communion with Him. The resulting peace of mind is compensation indeed!

Revel Papaioannou

A Face That Shines With His Glory

The Lord bless thee, and keep thee: the Lord make his face shine upon thee, and be gracious unto thee: the Lord lift up his countenance upon thee, and give thee peace.
Num. 6:24-26.

IT WAS JUST A BRIEF, SACRED TIME with her husband, her son, and her daughter-in-law before she was taken to the operating room for surgery. In the quietness of that morning, she spoke words of counsel and comfort to her family. To her son and his wife, she encouraged them to live in peace and faithfulness with each other. To her husband she spoke words of love and comfort. She made things right with each one of them and they did the same with her. With forgiveness and love for each other, they kissed each other, embraced, and prayed together.

Then her husband, noticing the glow on her face, declared, "Honey, you look beautiful." Later, he told us that in spite of all the suffering she had gone through, she looked beautiful. I told him that God's peace was on her face and in her heart.

You see, my beloved sister lived only four hours after her surgery, and that was in a coma. Those beautiful moments she spent with her family were the last time for each of them, but they were peaceful and beautiful moments with God's blessing promised in today's text.

I love to watch people, to learn who they are, and to make new friends. There are different faces with different expressions and different body languages. I love to see the innocent faces of babies in their mothers' arms and to study whom they resemble. I love to meet friends from my school days and to search for familiar faces which may have changed over the years.

It is interesting to note that as babies grow older, changes take place on their faces; their expressions reflect what they have learned. It is sad that for many, innocence disappears and fear, insecurity, hatred, and pride appear in its place. I have discovered faces that radiate a glow that expresses peace, security, gentleness, love, and humility. They happily mix with others, treating all as brothers and sisters. They are ready to give a helping hand. Their very presence invites harmony and goodwill.

As we look at the mirror each morning, do we see a face that is washed by the blood of Jesus? Do we see a glow of peace, the presence of God who forgives and saves us? May today's promised blessing be yours each day.

Birdie Poddar

My Gethsemane Experience

But my God shall supply all your need according to his riches in glory by Christ Jesus.
Phil. 4:19.

MY MARRIAGE OF 18 YEARS was crumbling. One Sabbath evening at church, where Yvette, my daughter, was reciting an essay on temperance, I felt a wrenching feeling in my abdomen. When we arrived home, my worst fears were confirmed. My husband had left for good. A tumultuous year later the divorce was final and I was awarded the house in North Carolina. At the time, we lived in Fort Leavenworth, Kansas. Thus began my Gethsemane experience.

I rented a big U-Haul truck to move the family of five. My two eldest daughters were at Union College in Lincoln, Nebraska, so I hired two men to load the truck and drive it to Lincoln where we stayed a few days. I dreaded the trip to North Carolina. My state of mind was so fragile that I had convinced myself I could make the journey with $350, an expired driver's license, expired tags, and no spare tire for the car. Mario, my 16-year-old son, had only two years of driving experience but he convinced me he could help drive.

The following morning, I opened my Bible to the promise of Romans 8:28: "And we know that all things work together for good to them that love God." After breakfast and a season of prayer, we loaded up—Mario, Claudia, and Nicolette in the truck and Linda and I in the car. We said goodbye to Sonia and Yvette and were on our way.

Because of a bad tire on the truck, we drove to the U-Haul garage in Liberty, Missouri, for repairs. By doing so, we bypassed Kansas City. When we stopped for the night we learned that the area where we would have otherwise traveled had been flooded. In West Virginia, we were stopped by a state trooper, but he didn't ask for my license.

Each morning and evening I opened the Bible at random to a new promise. We thanked God for traveling mercies and He faithfully reassured me of His unfailing love and protection. During the day we ate sandwiches, fruit, chips, and juice, and stopped each night at a motel for hot meals and rest. We traveled five days and four nights.

When we arrived, only one dollar of the $350 remained. We had traveled 1,268 miles (2040 kilometers) without incident. We were so thankful to be home. Our God is awe-inspiring.

Wilma C. Jardine

Moment of Reflection

The Lord gave, and now he has taken away. May his name be praised.
Job 1:21, TEV.

TODAY I AM IN A REFLECTIVE MODE, the result of a series of experiences I have faced in recent days.

My dear friend, who is terminally ill, appears to be on the last leg of his journey. He was a brilliant doctor who had a lot more to offer the medical field. Now he lies in bed, waiting, as medical knowledge has apparently failed him. I can only pray for him.

Last week four young adults from the university that my son attends, died; three burned beyond recognition in a car crash. The fourth succumbed to a variety of sickle cell disease, again an apparent failure of medical knowledge. I am sure that each of these students had plans to make big footprints on the world, and their parents must have been awaiting graduation with expectancy to reap the rewards of their labor. I dare not say that I understand how the parents feel, because I cannot. I can only empathize and say a prayer for them.

Last night I received an e-mail that a cousin three years my senior who lives in Canada and had retired earlier this year, had died of a massive heart attack. She was alone in her home and was discovered some days after her death. The irony is that I had sent e-mails to her after she died. We had talked a few months before, and she told me of the wonderful send-off and many accolades that she had received at her office. She probably made as many plans for retirement as I did.

Does any of this make sense? Turning to the Bible for comfort and answers, I found comfort. In 1 Corinthians 15:53 I read, "For our dying bodies must be transformed into bodies that will never die; our mortal bodies must be transformed into immortal bodies" (NLT). Isaiah 41:10 reads, "Don't be afraid, for I am with you. Don't be discouraged, for I am your God. I will strengthen you and help you. I will hold you up with my victorious right hand" (NLT). And here is Isaiah 43:2, my favorite: "When you go through deep waters, I will be with you. When you go through rivers of difficulty, you will not drown" (NLT).

Answers we may never get in this life, but may we so live that some day we will be able to talk with God face to face. If you are experiencing one or more stressful or crisis situations, may He give you the strength you need to endure and the faith not to question His wisdom.

Cecelia Grant

The Call to Gethsemane

They went to a place called Gethsemane, and Jesus said to his disciples, "Sit here while I pray." He took Peter, James and John along with him. . . . "Stay here and keep watch."
Mark 14:32-34, NIV.

I QUITE LIKE MARK'S DESCRIPTION of Jesus' desperate need for prayer as well as prayer support which He entrusted to His disciples. He said to them, "Sit here while I pray."

Then Jesus took Peter, James, and John, His three prayer warriors, a little further. He asked them to, "Stay here and keep watch." Jesus Himself went a little further on to pray. He was deeply distressed and troubled. His soul was overwhelmed with sorrow to the point of death (Mark 14:32-42). Many things had prompted this journey to Gethsemane. Jesus needed to be alone with His disciples; He wanted to share with them openly about who He was, and He needed to talk with His Father about the great burden of the cross.

The women of our university chose to go away from their daily routines and dedicate a weekend to prayer. The theme of the weekend encouraged them to claim God's promise that if we humble ourselves and pray, if we seek His face, and turn from our wicked ways, He will hear us, forgive, and heal our land (see 2 Chron. 7:14).

The coordinators challenged each other, "Let us make this retreat our Gethsemane where we can come to be alone with each other and the Lord. Where we can study God's Word and know who our God is, where we can talk and communicate with our heavenly Father. This is our Gethsemane; therefore, sisters, keep watch with Jesus. Let's pray like we have never prayed before and plead with the Holy Spirit to make our lives and our spiritual gifts acceptable for God's service."

It is my prayer that each day we will humble ourselves, go to our chosen Gethsemane, and pray. It will take us to a special height in our experience with God. Our churches need our prayer support. Our families need us, our nations need us, to pray and watch for Jesus' return. Do not slumber and sleep. Keep watch. Jesus said to His disciples, "The hour has come. . . . Rise! Let us go! Here comes my betrayer!" (Mark 14:41, 42, NIV). We live in enemy territory. Let us be awake and pray unceasingly in Gethsemane.

Fulori Bola

Me First

She said, "Give your word that these two sons of mine will be awarded the highest places of honor in your kingdom, one at your right hand, one at your left hand."
Matt. 20:21, Message.

SALOME IS NOT THE MOST FAMILIAR WOMAN of the Bible, but she is an important figure. We first read about her in today's text. From other biblical references we can infer that Zebedee, her husband, was well to do as he owned a fishing business with multiple boats and employees. We also find Salome as one of the women who brought spices to anoint Jesus' body following His crucifixion. Mark 15:41 says that she was among the women of Galilee who "had followed him and cared for his needs" (NIV). Luke 8:3 says these women were "helping to support them [Jesus and the disciples] out of their own means" (NIV). This indicates that she was a woman of means and influence. And she and her husband had at least two boys, James and John.

Most of us are familiar with the story of Salome going to Jesus and requesting that her sons be given positions of influence and importance in His kingdom—one to be seated on the right hand and one on the left. No doubt James and John had put their mother up to this as Matthew says she came to Jesus with her sons. As you may guess, it was not received favorably by the other disciples. Why should those two receive preferential treatment just because of their mother's money and her willingness to make such an audacious request?

"You don't know what you are asking," Jesus tells Salome. When Jesus asks James and John if they are able to handle what such a request might involve, they are certain they can.

Both Matthew and Mark place this incident just before the crucifixion week. So what do you suppose Salome and James and John felt a week later when they saw Jesus on the cross with someone on His right and someone on His left? Did they remember Jesus' saying, "Can you drink the cup I am going to drink?" (Matt. 20:22, NIV). And Jesus had further added, "You will indeed drink from my cup" (verse 23). Did they now want to be first?

Sometimes we ask for things, positions, or relationships without a clue what we are asking for. We don't think of the possible consequences of saying, "Me first." This would be a good time to read the rest of the passage where Jesus says, "Whoever wants to become great among you must be your servant, and whoever wants to be first must be your slave" (Matt. 20:26, 27, NIV).

Ardis Dick Stenbakken

Hatted

But we see Jesus, who was made a little lower than the angels,
now crowned with glory and honor because he suffered death, so that by
the grace of God he might taste death for everyone.
Heb. 2:9, NIV.

ONCE UPON A SPRINGTIME, there was a smart little quintet of friends who made plans to make Easter Sabbath special for their friend Diane. It was a wonderful day at the Melbourne church. Not only because it was Easter, but because Diane was coming to church. She'd been through several grueling weeks of chemo and radiation therapy. There was one problem, as she saw it, however—the well-known side effect of chemotherapy. The therapy, though very effective, had stolen her beautiful, red-gold hair. "Wear a hat," someone suggested.

And so began a special e-mail chain. All Diane's close friends were urged to wear a hat that Sabbath. The plot thickened when those friends asked other members to do the same. And so it was that when a hatted Diane arrived at church, at least 25 other similarly attired women greeted her with welcoming smiles. They were indeed a sisterhood. There were new hats and borrowed hats, felt hats and straw hats, cowboy hats and party hats, outrageous hats and simple hats. But they all had one common theme: loving support for a courageous sister.

That faith-affirming incident reminded me of a similar story of a young high school football player stricken with cancer. He too lost his hair. When he went back to school, he was welcomed by his entire football team, all wearing caps. When they doffed their caps, every one had a clean-shaven head! The young man couldn't help grinning.

Both heartwarming stories are testimonies of the courage and strong support we all need, regardless of our age or gender. And, as my sister-in-law Jan often says, "You can't have a testimony without a test." Thank God for the wonderful side effects of His tests.

But there is a third story of courage, and its powerful "side effects" far surpass these stories. While the first two had undertones of love, this one is the epitome of love. It happened more than 2,000 years ago and goes far beyond mirroring the effects of a suffering soul. It is a story that cost our heavenly Brother the pain and disgrace of suffering for sins that we committed. It's a story that cost Him His life. Now, because of Him, we get to enjoy the "side effects" of His shame-laden sacrifice. We have the promise of eternal life with Him.

Glenda-mae Greene

Is Anything Too Hard for God?

He who dwells in the shelter of the Most High will rest in the shadow of the Almighty.
Ps. 91:1, NIV.

OVER THE YEARS I've developed a habit of keeping spiritual journals. One journal is for my prayers and devotional time with God. Then there's my Blessing Book. It's here my family and I write our prayer requests, date them, pray over them, and then date and write God's answers. And then I have my Joy Book. I promise myself that each evening at bedtime I will list at least five things that I can thank God for. You may wonder why I spend time chronicling my journey with God. One reason is something the author Ellen White wrote: "We have nothing to fear for the future, except as we shall forget the way the Lord has led us, and His teaching in our past history" (*Life Sketches,* p. 196).

So many times when trials come my way I can forget that I serve a mighty God, the God whom Abraham called *El Shaddai,* the mighty God: "I am the Almighty God; walk before me, and be thou perfect" (Gen. 17:1). And it is at times when trials seem more than I can bear that I need to run to the shelter of the mighty God. But more than this, I need to *dwell* in His shelter. Each day of my life I need to take time to spend with God, for it is in my time of sheltering that I find Him and His strength. Then when trials come my way I stand secure in God who is my strength.

I have a little "thing" I do when I face trials. I look at my trial from all angles and ask myself, "Can I fix it?" Most times the answer is no. It's too big, too complicated. I just can't fix it. So rather than spend days and weeks worrying about my problem, trying with all my might to fix it, I say to God, "Lord, this problem came to me, but I can't fix it. It came to the wrong address. It's all yours." That's how I give my problems to the mighty God, the *El Shaddai,* the God who is able to do more than I can ask or think.

And that's why I keep my journals. I want to remember the way God has lead in my life. The mighty God who said, "Those who sow in tears will reap with songs of joy. [She] who goes out weeping, carrying seed to sow, will return with songs of joy, carrying sheaves with [her]" (Ps. 126:5, 6, NIV). I don't ever want to forget His goodness and faithfulness to me. For when I remember, my courage is strong. He did it before. He'll do it again.

Heather-Dawn Small

Probation Closed

*Multitudes, multitudes in the valley of decision! For the
day of the Lord is near in the valley of decision.
Joel 3:14, NIV.*

"HAVE YOU VISITED THE GRAND CANYON, HEPZI?" my friends asked. When I said no, they said, "It's worth visiting. You will love it." I had longed to visit the canyon ever since I heard about its grandeur, and my dream was fulfilled when my brother-in-law took us there. From 9,000 feet (2,743 meters) above sea level we enjoyed the magnificence of the Grand Canyon and glimpses of the Colorado River flowing below. We used the shuttle between different spots and spent as much time as possible admiring God's great handiwork.

At one point, though we wanted to stop a little longer, we decided to move on when the shuttle arrived. A group behind us could not decide what to do. The vehicle waited for 15 minutes with the door wide open. We watched as they struggled to make a decision. Finally, the door shut. Surprisingly, the group then rushed to the shuttle. Some banged on the side. The passengers seated inside asked the driver to open the door. Instead he started the engine and drove off.

I pitied the group that had to wait until the next vehicle came along. But when I regained my senses I realized that the door had been wide open for them to enter leisurely. They were slow to decide. The consequence—they missed the shuttle.

This incident reminds me of the people who lived while Noah built the ark. For 120 years this godly man warned everyone that a flood was coming. He invited them all to enter the ark and be saved. But none outside his family heeded the warning. When the rains came the frightened people banged at the ark pleading with Noah to open the door. Alas! It was too late.

This incident also reminds me of what Jesus said. Before He comes people will be like those that lived during Noah's time, unable to make the right decision.

On several occasions, I have faltered in making the right decision. But my heavenly Father still waits for me with the heavenly portals wide open and with outstretched arms. He gives me several opportunities. I know too well that it will not go on forever. The time for me to decide is now, for I do not know when my life will come to an end nor when my probation will close. *Dear Lord, help me to make the right decision now to enter Your heavenly gates.*

Hepzibah Kore

God Is in Control

I will bless the Lord at all times, His praise shall continually be in my mouth.
Ps. 34:1, NKJV.

THE DATE HAD BEEN set for my hip surgery. I had a doctor of whom everyone said, "He has done so many hips that he could do them in his sleep." Of course, I preferred he stay awake during mine. I had an anesthetist, Eric, from our church, who I knew, and in whom I had confidence.

The surgery went very well. The next day Terry and Nancy came. The first thing Nancy asked was, "How's your hip pain?" I said, "I don't have any." She said, "Praise the Lord!" She explained that she and Terry had been praying that God would take away any pain, and He did.

After my stay in the hospital, I was sent to a rehab center. It was a very nice place and everyone was great. Every day I had three hours of physical therapy (PT) and occupational therapy. One day the PT nurse, Jena, and I were talking about God's miracles. I had told her the answer to prayer regarding no pain in my hip. Jena said she had a story of a miracle that had happened to her husband.

Collin works for the Forestry Department. Usually he worked by himself, but this day he had been assigned two Grand Valley University students to work with him. One of the students was taking nursing plus Aeromed training. When they heard thunder Collin decided to pack up so they wouldn't get caught in a storm. But he was still in a tree when a bolt of lightning hit a tree across from him. The lightning shot down the trunk and across to the roots of the tree he was in, up through the tree and into his body, burning him and knocking him out of the tree. The two young men rushed over to him. One started CPR and the other dialed 911. Collin had stopped breathing but thanks to their quick action they saved his life. The air ambulance came and flew him to the burn unit at the hospital and someone there called Jena. When she got to the hospital Collin hung between life and death. But through medical care, prayer, and trust in God he completely recovered. Jena had been afraid she might end up as a single parent for she had an 18-month-old daughter and was pregnant with their son.

Jena and Collin just couldn't get over how God provided the right help to be there at just the right time. God is good and still in control of each situation in our lives.

Anne Elaine Nelson

My Favorite Profession

Show me Your ways, O Lord; teach me Your paths.
Ps. 25:4, NKJV.

ALL MY LIFE I have been a creative person who likes to play. I loved small children and so I knew early in my childhood what profession I preferred: to work in a kindergarten. Therefore my parents chose a school suited to my plans. I enrolled in the social line and to the amazement of my teacher I even graduated with an A in social work! But it was in creative things that I was at my best. I think back on the embellishment of the school building, drawing, crafts, and realizing ideas. Yes, indeed, this was my world!

However, my life took a different turn. After high school I did not attend the special training school for becoming an early-childhood worker. Why? It was obligatory to play a musical instrument there. And this I didn't like at all.

When I was a child my parents urged me to play the piano, and I detested it. Still, my parents insisted that I play. This gave me a distaste for all musical education. But without attending this special academy I could not become a kindergarten or nursery school teacher. However, I found a profession related to my skills even though it was not working with children. I worked in the advertising field, using my manual skills and graphic gifts. But I'm still dreaming of my favorite profession. The reason why things turned out like this is still on my mind.

However, God has now given me an answer. He has helped me to realize my dream a little bit. For 20 years I have had an active part in the children's care and ministry in my local church. I have not regretted a single day. I am responsible for all the children's groups in my church. I have loads of ideas, and even singing makes me feel good!

So what about the profession I was not able to achieve? I guess God gave me the talent to work with children in order to help in His church. God needs me more in His church than does the kindergarten in my town.

I enjoy the work God provided for me. God's intention often differs from what we imagine. But God does not make any mistakes.

Even if we cannot understand it, we can trust in Him.

Sandra Widulle

Confessions of a Modern-day Martha

Pride goes before destruction, and a haughty spirit before a fall.
Prov.16:18, NKJV.

WIVES, MOTHERS, AND OTHERS often try to ease their hectic schedules by multitasking. I worked part time and took care of our house and children and two of my husband's elderly relatives. With little help from others I became the Little Red Hen, trying to do everything myself.

I became quite proud of how well organized I was until one day's events took me down a peg or two. I was baking a cake, cooking beans, boiling potatoes, filling the laundry tub of my Speed Queen with water, spinning wash in the other tub, and drying clothes in my dryer. As I swept the floor I was answering one of our two children's questions.

Just then my husband came in and asked, "What happened? I was working on the truck and suddenly water splashed down on my head and shoulders and filled up the wheelbarrow next to me!"

"Oh no!" I rushed to the flooded laundry room. Turning off the faucet, I said, "You know how with this semi-automatic machine the spigot has to be turned off manually?" He nodded.

"Well, I was so busy that I forgot to check back, so the tub overflowed. Sorry!" He accepted my apology. I concluded, "Sometimes it's possible to multitask too much."

Martha is probably the Bible character that I'm most like. Being earnest, hard-working, and attending closely to details is good. But even Christ didn't work every moment. He told His disciples, "Come aside . . . and rest a while" (Mark 6:31, NKJV).

Occasional work breaks would refresh me. Breaks would help me be more productive than I am when I keep going until total exhaustion sets in. And some of the breaks should involve Bible study, prayer, or simply sitting quietly, thinking. "Be still, and know that I am God" (Ps. 46:10). God could thus give me strength to go on and I'd feel less rushed and strained.

Yes, I still multitask some. But I don't go about it as hard and fast as I did the day the washing machine overflowed. Life is so much better if we take some time to smell the roses.

God can help us find the balance in our lives that we need. All we have to do is ask.

Bonnie Moyers

Don't Need That Kind of Stress

For he shall give his angels charge over thee, to keep thee in all thy ways.
Ps. 91:11.

MY ONLY SISTER, JACKLYN, was conversing with me on her cellular phone while she exercised at a gym in Indianapolis. It was after 10:00 p.m., but this was normal for her. After a while I asked, "Are you on your way home now?"

"I'm through with my exercises and trying to get my key into this lock," she said. "I already tried a few times with my phone in one hand. Please hold on while I put down the phone."

I waited. Finally my telephone went off. I tried to redial her cell several times but there was no response. Here I was, in St. Croix, Virgin Islands, trying to imagine why my sister in Indianapolis had suddenly "disappeared"! Was she trying to unlock the door of a car that was similar to hers and did not recognize her error?

About 20 minutes later I called her home. No response! *Do I call my son who lives in the same city to get help?* I thought. *What if she was attacked? Could she have suddenly fallen ill and was unable to respond?* Those questions and more kept racing through my mind. Finally my husband suggested we pray about the matter.

At that I recalled a similar stressful experience. On that particular evening, before the invention of cell phones, I had been awaiting the return of my husband and two other ministers from a trip through the treacherous Dominican countryside. At 1:00 a.m. I finally called the police. A catastrophic landslide had occurred in the part of the country where they were, closing the road and disrupting telephone connections. Thankfully, God had intervened!

Jackie's key problem turned out to be with the gym locker, not her car. However, as we'd talked, the battery of her phone died without warning. But she was safe.

Why was I so fearful? What precious reassurances God gives! We know Psalm 23, yet we sometimes forget the promise, "I will fear no evil: for thou art with me" (Ps. 23:4). And Psalm 91 has actually taken me through a severe hurricane.

I want to learn to lean on God unreservedly and trust His promises of protection. It must be possible to have enough faith to avoid some of these stresses.

Lord, grant us such faith so we can be courageous and always peacefully depend on You.

Gloria Josiah

A Family Legacy

And all thy children shall be taught of the Lord; and great shall be the peace of thy children.
Isa. 54:13.

DURING THE EARLY 1930s and 1940s my grandmother was a vibrant young woman. Although she had only a third-grade education she had an aptitude for learning and studying. Grandmother loved her Bible and read it every day. Further, she had the ability to commit to memory whatever she studied. She even gave most of her children biblical names.

Grandmother lived with her family on one of the beautiful islands in the Atlantic Ocean. At that time, on this island, her church was still classed as a mission. This meant they did not have a pastor. Rather, pastors were sent to the island to minister as needed, traveling by seaplane from the United States.

My mother told me this story about Grandmother. One particular week the minister did not arrive. At the last minute, the church needed someone to speak that Sabbath morning. So my grandmother stood up to speak. Her name was Ellen, and, like another Ellen—Ellen White—whom she looked up to, God used her. She recited Psalm 119, all 176 verses! It took her two hours to do so. The congregation became upset that she was taking too long, but she kept on until she finished. What a feat!

I somehow got a bit of that ability. In early elementary school I was given the longest poems to recite and was able to put to memory the things I studied during the school year. During exams I could look back in my mind and recall all that I had studied, thus earning 100 per cent for the various subjects most of the time. I thank God for all my abilities in life because I do believe they come from Him. Let the world see Jesus in each of us. What has He asked you to do?

Now I've passed on my legacy to my children. "Only be careful, and watch yourselves closely so that you do not forget the things your eyes have seen or let them slip from your heart as long as you live. Teach them to your children and to their children after them" (Deut. 4:9, NIV). That is a responsibility we each have in some way. Let us be faithful to use God's gifts.

Alice K. Binns

The Mothers of Israel

Many women do noble things, but you surpass them all.
Prov. 31:29, NIV.

THROUGH MY MOTHER, I learned to give love and receive love. In her loving embrace, she taught me that God is love.

With my mother, I learned the stories of the great Bible heroes that still influence my life. She was my first teacher. Mother taught me to love the Bible, to participate in church activities, to pray, and to sing praises to God. All of these have helped to make my life a blessing. When I was still a little girl I went with her on her missionary visits, and this taught me that God expects us to offer solidarity and love.

My mother's example makes me remember the mothers of Israel—the women who exercised a strong influence for the good of God's people. My mother's faith makes me think of Jochebed, whose love saved her son Moses from the hands of Pharaoh, preparing him to be the deliverer of his people. It also reminds me of Hannah, who every year went to the temple to take a coat to Samuel, the son whom she had offered to God because of her grateful heart. Mother's example reminds me of Dorcas, the protector of the poor. It also reminds me of Eunice, the mother of Timothy, who taught him the Holy Scriptures when he was young. These women's children became powerful instruments in the hands of God. They were a blessing to the world.

My mother is one of the modern mothers of Israel. She represents the mothers who pray to God for wisdom to educate their children in the paths of good. I know that I have overcome many trials in life, in spite of numerous battles, because my mother prayed for me. The prayers of a Christian mother can have a great result. God is pleased to answer them.

We need more mothers like this: women who fear God and are dedicated to the service of the Master. The influence of such mothers can never be measured in human terms. Only heaven and eternity will reveal their real value. The Bible affirms, "A woman who fears the Lord is to be praised" (Prov. 31:30).

Mother taught me to love all mothers. And today I offer this recognition, not only to my mother but to all mothers of Israel. I pray to God in their behalf so that they may always continue to be faithful in the work of the Lord.

Valquiria Teixeira dos Santos

The Birds

Look at the birds of the air, that they do not sow, nor reap nor gather into barns,
and yet your heavenly Father feeds them. Are you not worth much more than they?
Matt. 6:26, NASB.

IT IS STILL DARK in my bedroom as I wake up. My cat, Sasha, is stretched out full length on top of me. She gets very heavy after a while, and I will wake up from her weight or from a nightmare about cement blocks or some other weighty matter resting on me. I gently push her off and relax as the early dawn hours approach.

I feel the gentle breeze on my face from the open window. And I hear the first little chirp of a bird also awakening to the dawn. I am delighted to just rest and listen as one by one more chirps are added. The birds are awakening, too, and now there is a choir of chirps.

There are two theories as to what this chirping is all about. For many years I believed the birds were chirping or singing because they were happy. They were happy for companionship, food, and their trees. Just recently I have read the second theory that it is a time of commands, orders, and plans for their group.

I like both ideas. First, isn't it wonderful to be happy and to able to sing about it? Let us think of that for ourselves. No, I can't sing well, but I can be happy and show it by smiles and cheerfulness. I am happy when there are red Bing cherries at the market, or when someone compliments me on a church program, or things like that. I am happy for my house—my home—and I could chirp loudly about it. I have lived in it a long time. It bespeaks of me and my family's life: the family photos, the children's art work, the artifacts from our trips, and even the comfortably worn chairs. Having the children return home for visits is one of our greatest joys.

But I also was thinking, as I lay listening to the birds, that they were planning their day. I see them in my mind, sitting on the branches of the big maple tree sorting out the duties for the day. Maybe they are even voicing opinions as to who wants to do what. And after a while the choir of chirps becomes little single ones as they fly off for the day.

What is the bird's song? We wish we could understand what it is all about. This we do know: the Lord sees even a sparrow's fall. Think of how much more He cares for you. Now we too need to make plans and be about our day's work. With our Lord's blessings, let us sing too.

Dessa Weisz Hardin

Take Care of My Friend, Lord

Howbeit Jesus suffered him not, but saith unto him, Go home to thy friends, and tell them how great things the Lord hath done for thee, and hath had compassion on thee.
Mark 5:19.

THE PHONE IS RINGING, a familiar ring I have preprogrammed for Celeste's calls. I run excitedly to answer, and say hello. No response. My heart sinks. I know the answer must be that the test came back positive. A few moments later her tearful response confirms it. She has breast cancer. How can one moment change a person's life? While still waiting in the doctor's office she gives me the details, the facts she knows just now. I am in shock.

I hang up the phone and sit there, soaking in the information. She had been checking on a lump she found in her breast. Every time she went to have it checked out I would have her call me with the results, never thinking it would turn out as it has.

I look back to when I moved to Tennessee. I knew it was where I was to be, for God's leading was clear. But it was a sad moment leaving my friends, especially Shellie. We are practically related and I know that Sprint developed its Friends and Family Plan just for us!

When I got to Tennessee I prayed for a bosom buddy, a kindred spirit, not dreaming the Lord would ever answer such a silly prayer. I didn't think about it until I met Celeste. She was similar to Shellie but in many ways different. She has been a great supporter, friend, and confidante. That is why this has hit me so hard. She is like a sister to me and it hurts me that she has to face this battle.

She and I have a lot of fun together, whether it's taking walks, serving at potlucks, or my telling her about my adventures while she laughs at my crazy antics. Together we may plan some special event. She backs me in whatever activity I take on, even when she's not directly a part of it. So here I am on this end of the phone, feeling inadequate as a friend to meet the task. She would have been better on this side of it.

Lord, You know I love Celeste, but I know You love her more. Please be with her and comfort her, and if it is Your will, heal her. Please guide my actions and help me to be the friend she has been to me. Thank You so much for the many, many friends You have given to me. Do not let me take any one of them for granted. Amen.

Mary M. J. Wagoner-Angelin

Peace for the Hurried

And the work of righteousness shall be peace; and the effect of
righteousness quietness and assurance for ever.
Isa. 32:17.

FRIDAY WAS ONE OF THOSE DAYS. I love to cook and bake, and people tell me I'm good at both. I planned to make some of my favorite pumpkin apple streusel muffins. Because my stove in the basement bakes better than my main kitchen stove, I ran downstairs to turn on the oven then back up the stairs to mix the muffin batter. Within a few short minutes a heavenly aroma wafted up the stairs—reminding me that I'd forgotten to remove the granola I'd made a couple of days earlier. I ran downstairs and took the granola out of the oven. Fortunately, it hadn't burned to smithereens like it did on another occasion when I tried the same trick.

I left the granola to cool and went back to mixing the muffin batter. After putting the muffins into the oven, I began working on another project. Oh, no! I'd forgotten to put the streusel topping on the muffins. Dashing downstairs again, I reasoned that the muffin pans hadn't been in the oven long enough to be hot. I opened the oven door and grabbed the pans with my bare hands. Big mistake! As I jerked my hands away from the hot pans, one of the pans turned upside down and emptied its contents all over the oven door, the inside of the oven, and in all the cracks and crannies in between. What a mess! I turned the oven off to let it cool a bit so I could spend the next 20 minutes getting it all cleaned up.

After replacing the muffin batter, and this time remembering to add the topping, I put them in the oven to bake. Thirty minutes later when my timer rang I went downstairs only to find unbaked muffins. I'd forgotten to turn the oven back on after I'd cleaned it!

I was beginning to think someone was trying to tell me I wasn't supposed to make muffins that day. Then the entire ridiculous situation became funny and my husband and I enjoyed a good laugh. And the muffins (eventually) turned out well.

Perhaps I should slow down and order my life in a less stressful vein. Perhaps humor and peace can be found in the worst of situations. God is good. By keeping my focus on Him and allowing Him to work out His plans in my life, He and I together can be conquerors. And through His guidance I can experience the quiet peace He has waiting for my soul.

Barbara Horst Reinholtz

Oregon Junco Nest

Therefore I say to you, do not worry about your life. . . . Look at the birds of the air,
for they neither sow nor reap nor gather into barns; yet your heavenly Father feeds them.
Matt. 6:25, 26, NKJV.

SINCE BIRDS DON'T WORRY about themselves maybe we shouldn't worry about them either, but last Mother's Day I did. I had flowers to plant, and when I walked out on the deck, a bird swiftly flew away from somewhere. But I planted marigolds, petunias, and alyssum in the first barrel.

The next planter was full of pansies that had grown back from the year before. I'd just stopped to admire them when I saw a bird's nest holding three eggs. That's where that bird flew from! And that's when I became anxious. I was afraid I might have scared the mother bird away for good or maybe the eggs had gotten cold as she stayed away from the nest the whole time I was planting. Quickly I left. Peeking through the kitchen window I saw an Oregon junco come sit on the edge of the planter, look around nonchalantly, and disappear in the pansies.

Right away I worried that she hadn't picked a good spot, for our cats lounge around on that deck. When it rained, I worried that mama bird would get too wet or the nest would fill up with water so my husband slanted a board over the planter to keep the rain off the nest. Now we felt better. Later when I sneaked out on the deck to look, I saw three tiny baby birds. Through the window I watched the mom and dad busily feeding them. But I still worried that the cats would find the babies until we noticed that the babies didn't make a peep. The cats walked back and forth and never knew the secret.

One sunny Sunday just three weeks after I first saw the eggs, I tried to do some weeding a little way away, but the mommy and daddy kept scolding me. That was the only time I wondered if the birds worried. The baby birds were much bigger, overfilling the nest. However, because they were in the planter, it was fine because they just sat protected under the pansies.

Ed saw a baby fly to the ground. He picked it up and put it back thinking, *You're too young to fly.* Early the next morning they were all gone. They were old enough to fly.

Where did they go? Now I could worry about that, but I decided it was time for me to trust God like the mommy and daddy bird did all along.

Lana Fletcher

The Mother Who Prays

Her children rise up and call her blessed; her husband also, and he praises her: "Many daughters have done well, but you excel them all." Charm is deceitful and beauty is passing, but a woman who fears the Lord, she shall be praised. Prov. 31:28-30.

EARLY IN THE MORNING I placed my luggage in the trunk of my car, and with a prayer I headed out on the three-hour trip to the airport. I was tired, but had a great book on tape that would keep me awake for the journey.

Two hours into the trip I saw the most beautiful buck deer. The problem was that it was right in front of my car! I tried to stop. I honked the horn—all to no avail. Unfortunately, this massive creature was killed instantly. I was scared, but thankful I was still alive. My car told of its injuries as the dashboard lit up with various lights and smoke poured out from under the hood.

Within minutes the lights of the Pennsylvania state police came up behind me. A kind officer distracted me as he took my information. Shortly after, the tow truck driver informed me that I had totaled my car.

I was two hours from home and an hour from the airport. It was 3:15 in the morning—or should I say night—and I didn't know where I was nor anyone who would be awake at this hour to help me. I waited until 6:00, then called my mother. I didn't tell her about the accident but casually asked if she had just awakened. As is her habit, she told me that she arose in the middle of the night to pray for me. I again inquired as to what time she may have gotten up. It was at the time of my accident! When I told her I had totaled my car at that exact time, it solidified what I already knew: it was my mother's prayers that kept me alive.

I am so blessed to be the daughter of this amazing woman who lives on her knees. I arise and call her blessed. Yes, Jesus still hears the prayers of mothers. Even now in 2011, or beyond. As the Spirit calls, pray for those whom you love. I believe we are living in the last days of this battered world, and our prayers are needed now more than at any other time. It is important that mothers pray, but it is even more vital that all women, regardless of age, spend time in prayer. Don't ever think it does not make a difference!

Sharon Michael

Look Up

But when these things begin to happen, look up, hold your heads high, for you will soon be free. Luke 21:28, Phillips.

IT IS THE FIRST WEEK OF MAY and I can't help but reminisce. Three years ago I was lying in a major trauma hospital after a near-fatal car accident. I couldn't turn from side to side because of the numerous tubes coming out of my body. All I could do was look up—up beyond the sterile white ceiling to a merciful, caring, loving heavenly Father whom I could trust implicitly with my future. It gave me incredible peace.

I couldn't read, but I could listen to classical as well as heavenly music a good share of the day. Ear phones delivered uplifting songs of that heaven and homeland that would ultimately be mine whatever my immediate future held.

As I contemplated God's loving care in preserving my life, I couldn't help but wonder about the future. Would I ever again watch the birds on my daily two-mile walk? Would I be able to continue playing the piano for a number of churches and community organizations? Would I be able to travel, especially to visit my far-flung family? Would I be healed, or left with physical handicaps?

I knew that initially, God had miraculously spared my life, but I could never have dreamed how marvelously He has healed me. When my grandsons made a cross-country visit three months later we were able to walk slowly down the mile-long trail and back.

During the four months my broken neck was encased in a brace, my husband would share the good news that my condition was definitely improving (because I couldn't look down). I could only look up and see a bright future. When the brace was removed the doctor was amazed that my range of motion was so normal. I didn't even need physical therapy!

There will be struggles ahead for all of us before Jesus comes, but they will give us precious opportunities to gaze upward and feel our Father's presence. In the meantime, during any time of trial, we can look up, hold our heads high, and know that some day soon we will be freed from this sin-cursed earth.

Sister of mine, no matter what today brings, don't forget to look up!

Donna Lee Sharp

Mother's / Mothers' Day

Guide older women into lives of reverence so they end up as neither gossips nor drunks, but models of goodness. By looking at them, the younger women will know . . .
Titus 2:3, 4, Message.

"I'M GOING SHOPPING for Mother's Day cards," I commented aloud as I prepared to go to lunch.

"How long will it take you to pick one card?" my coworker chuckled. "How slow do you read?"

I chuckled too as I continued getting my things together to leave. "No, I need a few more cards than that—closer to 35 or 40," I said teasingly as I poked his shoulder while passing by.

His jaw dropped. "What? Were you raised by a village?"

I thought about his comment as I waited for the elevator to arrive. Mother's Day is celebrated to some degree in many nations around the world. Some have a specific date, such as in Greece, February 2; Azerbaijan and Romania, March 8; El Salvador, May 10; and Panama, December 8. Other countries designate a time frame such as the second Sunday in May, as in Australia, Belize, Brazil, New Zealand, the United States, and Zimbabwe, to name a few. To a large degree it is noted as a time to give tribute to the "mother" in one's life, whoever that may be. With each year I look back and recall with both wonder and appreciation the many women the Lord has allowed to cross my path just when I needed them. Theirs were words of wisdom, or they offered deeper insight into a situation, a calm, level head providing foresight, or a degree of objectivity. Others simply expressed personal regrets, hoping I would heed their advice and avoid their pain.

Did I always appreciate and understand? No, but as always, the Lord knew just what I needed and just when I needed it, and He provided it just then—through a vessel willing to be used of Him. Some of these women were just passing through my life, while some became a permanent fixture, claiming a part of my heart. But for each I am now grateful and honored to have met and known her.

Lord, thank You for providing Mothers in Zion. They are Your voice when we cannot hear, and Your arms, to shake us, if necessary, but always to hug and nurture.

Maxine Williams Allen

And Now She Is Eight

*In You, O Lord, I put my trust. Ps. 71:1, NKJV. For You are my hope, O Lord God.
Ps. 71:5, NKJV.*

SIX A.M. LONDON TIME. The flight from Washington-Dulles to London Heathrow was behind me. Now I stood in another long security line waiting to walk through a metal detector while my carry-on crept through the X-ray. I passed. My carry-on didn't.

A guard asked if he could search the suitcase, and I gave the only reasonable answer. When I lifted the lid he murmured, "This is a very *busy* suitcase." Packed tightly with clothing, books, and small, wrapped gifts for two different occasions, it was truly "busy." A long time later I cleared security. Two more hours and I boarded a flight to Nairobi. Only nine-and-a-half hours to go. I read. Ate lunch. Watched a movie on a four-inch screen. I slept, awoke, and read some more. Trading my aisle seat for one by a window, I stared at the orange sands of the Sahara Desert 35,000 feet below. It grew dark. We were getting close.

In Nairobi, I stood in another line. A long, sweaty hour later my passport was stamped and I had my visa. Thirty more minutes . . . where were my suitcases? At last—the final checkpoint. To make this long trip, you *really* must want to go to Kenya, and I *really* did.

Only four months before my daughter and her family had spent three weeks in the States. I'd gone to camp meeting with them and taken yet more vacation time to spend with our grandchildren. And one day Larissa had looked up from where she was chiseling a tiny dinosaur from a plaster egg and asked, "Will you come to my birthday party?"

What a question! I'd love to come—if only it weren't 8,000 miles away.

Now my son-in-law turned into their driveway. And now I saw my daughter and granddaughter through the living room window. I turned the doorknob, pushed open the door. Larissa began laughing, jumping up and down, and running around the room. I grabbed her up in a big hug. Her arms squeezed my neck; her legs clasped my waist.

Two months before, her mother had e-mailed, "She thinks you're coming. She asked you, so she thinks you will." My simple reply: "I *am* coming. She asked me to."

I don't like far–fetched spiritual lessons, but I'll risk making one here. There are many good reasons to long for heaven. One is very important to me: God asks us to come. And heaven will be worth a lot more inconvenience than what I experienced on this trip.

Penny Estes Wheeler

Sleeping Through the Storm

He shall cover thee with his feathers, and under his wings shalt thou trust.
Ps. 91:4.

MAY 10, 2008, was sunny and warm, a typical spring day in Atlanta, Georgia. Sabbath services had gone well, and at the end of the day my husband and I returned home exhausted and ready for bed. I was excitedly anticipating Ellie's arrival. My friend of more than 30 years, she would be visiting from California the following Monday. I had scheduled time off from work, and we would relax and just have a good time. One special arrangement I had made was a surprise full-body massage for Ellie, a belated birthday gift.

Saturday night, all was calm when we retired. Little did we know, however, an un-forecast hurricane was headed our way, the worst in more than 50 years. My husband woke me up at about 2 a.m. He had been awakened by the sound of heavy rain and wind that sounded "like a freight train," as he described it. I could not hear the wind, and because I had grown accustomed to Georgia's heavy downpours, I turned over and went back to sleep. We both did. All was calm when we woke up Sunday morning, but when we looked out the window, to our horror, shingles from roofs, broken glass, huge slabs of wood, and all sorts of debris were scattered all over the neighborhood. Quickly getting dressed, we checked our house inside and out for damage. We soon realized that we had no electrical power. We went out to join our neighbors picking up debris.

Fortunately, there was minimal damage to our home compared to uprooted trees, fallen fences, and major damage to other homes in our neighborhood. Several had been demolished. Emergency vehicles arrived and helicopters flew overhead. We soon realized our area had extensive damage. The police department set up mobile headquarters in an effort to keep out spectators. Looking around, we could only shake our heads and thank God—not just for protecting our home—but for sparing our lives. No fatalities were reported.

As for Ellie, we called her that night to tell her what had happened, and she decided to keep her plan to arrive on Monday. Despite the devastation of the storm, we had a most pleasant visit. My husband and I continue to praise God for His goodness and protection.

Lord, You are truly awesome. Thank You for Your protection of us even when we don't realize the danger that swarms around us.

Gloria Stella Felder

Vivid Memories

*Assuredly I say to you, inasmuch as you did it to one of the least
of these My brethren, you did it to Me.
Matt. 25:40, NKJV.*

IT WAS A VERY OLD SECTION OF TOWN. I remember that day, so long ago, when I was a child of about 5 years old. My mom and dad took me to that part of town because that's where my mother's father lived. As we entered the faded building, I saw several men lying on pallets with what looked like foot-long pipes in their hands. I had never seen anything like it before. As I looked closer I saw that the men blew into one end of the pipe and water in the pipe gurgled. I later learned that this was a hookah, a smoking apparatus in which the smoke is drawn through a container of water and cooled before reaching the mouth. This was a form of relaxation for Grandpa who was always lonely after Grandma went to China, never to be heard from again after China was invaded by Japan.

Since there weren't any chairs, my parents and I just stood around while they talked to Grandpa who only spoke Chinese. Soon I got tired of standing and my mother gave me an orange and told me I could go outside to the sidewalk to eat my fruit. There wasn't anyone around as I peeled my orange, and since there weren't any trash cans around, I simply threw the peels on the sidewalk. However, out of nowhere, there appeared a street urchin who looked dirty and disheveled in clothes that surely needed washing. To my amazement this person—who resembled a girl—quickly picked up my orange peels and began to eat them hungrily. I stared dumbfounded because I had never seen anyone eat orange rinds and I knew they tasted bitter. This girl ate them all, and when she finished she quickly slipped away.

On my way home, I told my mother what I had seen, and she said, "Yes, there are some people who are so poor they never get enough to eat."

Today's media brings us tragic scenes of starving children with distended stomachs and even flies crawling over their faces, and I am glad for the opportunity to give of my means to help, not only the hungry, but the sick and lonely like my old grandpa. Jesus has told us in His Word that whatever we do to help others we have done it unto Him.

Aileen L. Young

More Tests

I can do everything through him who gives me strength.
Phil. 4:13, NIV.

"NEVER GIVE IN, never give in, never, never, never, never." Those are the words of the famous commencement speech delivered by Sir Winston Churchill. It was my mantra as I struggled to earn my graduate degree.

"Momma, I don't understand why you're struggling to get a degree just because you want to be a writer. All you really need is a creative imagination in order to be a writer," my teenage son said.

"Well, if I study and earn a degree, publishers might give me more credibility as a writer who has studied the craft." That was my defensive statement to support my endeavor.

At age 50, I had earned a Bachelor of Arts in Journalism and the degree opened up a door for a new career. I changed career paths from an administrative support person to a family service worker. Reimbursement for college tuition was a fringe benefit of the job.

I applied for graduate school, was accepted, and started working on a Master of Arts degree in English. I breezed through the program. However, after completing the course of study I had another hurdle. I had to take a comprehensive exam and pass it.

During the testing session I lost my answer to one of the essay questions because of a faulty diskette and had an anxiety attack about my ability to complete the remainder of the exam in the time allotted.

Several weeks later I got back my results and learned I had failed the exam. I was devastated. I was given a second opportunity to take the test so I restudied the material and felt confident that I'd do much better than before. Despite my feeling that I'd done much better this time, I failed it again. Special permission from my academic advisor was required for me to retake the exam. Permission was denied. So I filed an appeal by writing a letter to the university president requesting permission to retake the exam. Permission was granted.

I prayed a lot and took the exam again. I passed! I had followed Churchill's mantra, "Never give in." Weeks later I proudly marched across the stage and received my graduate degree. It was my faith that sustained me; I knew that God gave me the patience and wisdom to prevail. Never give up! Never.

Fartema M. Fagin

The Interpreter

When you are in trouble, call out to me. I will answer and be there to protect and honor you.
Ps. 91:15, CEV.

MY DAUGHTER AND I shared the privilege of going on a mission trip to the Philippines where we spent time in a remote, primitive mountain village. The people there spoke Tagalog, a local Philippine language. We communicated mainly through interpreters.

To reach our destination we travelled as far as the local jeepney (a kind of bus) could take us, and from there it was a two-hour mountain hike to our village. The hike was on narrow, steep trails. We crossed various bamboo bridges and waded through rivers, occasionally stepping aside into the brush to allow local villagers to pass on their horses or caribou, sometimes called water buffalo. It was a wonderful experience.

After a few days of living in our bamboo hut and adapting to primitive mountain life with some beautiful people, it was time for my daughter and me to return to the main town at the base of the mountains. A local couple was asked to escort us to the "road" where we were to be met by the pastor and his friend who would take us back to town by motorcycle. This couple spoke only Tagalog and my daughter and I spoke English, knowing only a few words of their language. When we reached the end of the trail we saw no one we recognized to meet us. Two rough looking individuals rode up on motorbikes and gestured to us to get on, all the while trying to take our backpacks. My daughter and I looked at each other and for the first time during our trip we both felt uneasy.

We were having quite a challenge trying to communicate with an ever-increasing gathering of the village men when my daughter said to me, "We need to pray right now!" With that we held hands and bowed our heads while I shared our dilemma and concern with our heavenly Father and asked Him to lead us. As we opened our eyes a young man was standing in front of us, very flushed and panting. His English was quite limited but he was able to tell us the pastor had been delayed. The village captain graciously invited us in and fed us while we waited.

This experience reminded me of the ever-present nature of our loving heavenly Father who knows our needs and never fails to prepare a way of escape if we simply call on Him.

Beverly D. Hazzard

Remember!

I will remember the deeds of the Lord; yes, I will remember your miracles of long ago.
Ps. 77:11, NIV.

THE BIBLE ADMONISHES US to recall history, remember God's dealings, and teach our children the lessons thereof. We know God better when we see His work throughout a period of time, and we can build on the past wisdom and avoid pitfalls.

I'm writing from Sahmyook University in South Korea, where my husband has come to teach for one semester—50 years after we first came here as missionaries. At that time this was a two-year institution for pastoral training, with 150 students. Before we left, it became a four-year college. Now it is a doctorate-granting university with nearly 6,000 students and many departments. Few countries have changed so much. Students today have little idea of how their parents lived, how their families were forever split by the Korean War. The college was so poor that twice the president came to the two other missionary families and asked for a loan so the cafeteria could buy rice for lunch that day. Now the university is prospering.

Back then, missionaries were almost the only ones with cars. We'd pick up anyone waiting for a bus as we drove on errands, heading past rice paddies on the one-lane dirt road into Seoul. Today, there's a six-lane highway surrounded by high-rise apartments, businesses, and universities. Sahmyook's 10 shuttle buses steadily traverse to nearby subway stations, part of an efficient seven-line system. Space for parking student and faculty cars on campus is tight.

We had an old crank-handled army telephone, connecting only within campus. Korea today has wireless Internet access everywhere, more cell phones per capita than any other country, and most people on the subways wear ear buds.

Growth on campus has necessitated many new large buildings. Leadership is Korean, with foreigners mostly teaching English. Required to accept some non-Christian students, the university hires one chaplain for every 20 students. Each year many are baptized. The Korean church sends missionaries to Japan, China, Taiwan, Mongolia, and elsewhere.

"We have nothing to fear for the future, except as we shall forget the way the Lord has led us, and His teaching in our past history" (*Christian Experience and Teachings,* Ellen G. White, p. 204).

Madeline Steele Johnston

Unexpected Meeting

*For we are to God the aroma of Christ among those
who are being saved and those who are perishing.
2 Cor. 2:15, NIV.*

OUR MEETING WAS TOTALLY CASUAL on that wonderful afternoon. The breeze blew slightly. I first saw her as I admired the branches of the acerola tree covered with little red shiny fruit. Even before seeing her, however, I was conscious of her presence. But now she stood there in front of me—impossible to ignore. In truth, I did not want her near because I never liked her type. It was not because of her appearance—of course not. Actually, she was even elegant and lively. But it was because of a peculiarity, a characteristic that belonged specifically to her: her manner of greeting whomever might be nearby. The impression that I have is that she reacts as though everyone is her enemy, and therefore she tries to scare them away. This does not please me. Certainly not! It is impossible to think that someone could be captivated by a creature of her type. However, I should admit that on seeing her inside the container of fruit, a new feeling bloomed in my mind.

Oh! I have forgotten to introduce you to her. This little green creature that I am talking about is a . . . a . . . forgive me, I do not know her true name, that is, her scientific name. The name she's commonly known by and called is stink bug. (Stinky Maria, in Portuguese). That's right. It's because of the strong smell she emits when something comes into contact with her that I dislike her.

Do not ask me why she's been given the name "Maria," because certainly the species includes males. Actually, on that day I do not know if I met a little Maria or perhaps a little Mario. However, it does not matter. The most interesting part is that I discovered at least three valuable lessons. First, we are all different and should learn to respect each other in spite of our differences. God made us this way. Second, rather than dwelling on our appearance, we should pay special attention to our words, gestures, and the manner in which we relate to others. May our motto always be to be the perfume of Christ.

And finally, may we be alert to rapidly repel the enemy—the worst of all, Satan. The stink bug reacts through instinct. We, however, have the capacity to think and choose.

Edileuza de Souza Meira

Thy Will Be Done

Our Father in heaven, hallowed be your name, your kingdom come,
your will be done on earth as it is in heaven.
Matt. 6:9, 10, NIV.

I WAS ACTIVELY INVOLVED in caring for people who were seeking asylum in our country. On a Friday afternoon I received a desperate phone call. Mr. E., a refugee from Africa, had been taken away from his family in handcuffs. The police were taking him to the airport from where he would be deported to his home country.

Accompanied by a friend from our refugee group, I at once drove to see the family. The pregnant wife was desperate and in shock. Their two little girls were crying and could not understand why the police had taken their father away. Everything had happened so suddenly that he was only able to take a little money and his Bible with him.

Many African friends had gathered in the little room of this family. They were also afraid of deportation. The atmosphere was depressed. My friend and I were ashamed of how our authorities treat people who seek asylum in our country.

Mr. E. was permitted to call his family from the airport. After speaking with his weeping wife, he asked to talk to me. What could I say? I said, "Mr. E., all we can do now is pray." Was that a small consolation? Then the phone connection was cut.

I had no more words left so I suggested that we pray the Lord's Prayer together. I will never forget this prayer in the little room filled with asylum-seekers. Some prayed in their native African tongues, others in French, and my friend and I in German. It is difficult to describe the situation with words.

The next morning we heard nothing from Mr. E., but Sunday we received the incredible information that we could go and pick up him up at the airport. What had happened? When the plane landed in Kinshasa one of the Congolese police officers said to Mr. E., "When you come into the country we'll cut your head off!" One of the German officers understood French and realizing the great danger Mr. E. was in, said to him, "We will take you back to your family."

The joy in our community was great! Ever since this time the Lord's Prayer has been a special prayer. How do you value this prayer? It is addressed to the God of power.

Edith Haberzeth-Grau

The Weeds Are Gone

But thanks be to God! He gives us the victory through our Lord Jesus Christ.
1 Cor. 15:57, NIV.

MOVING TO A NEW HOUSE I encountered some new weeds. Never before had I dealt with the dollar weed and the wild shamrock. Both were persistent and proved to be a great challenge for me.

The dollar weed has a long white, thread-like root with many tendrils that travel just below the surface of the ground. The shamrock has a small bulbous root. Unless you get the entire root system these two weeds keep growing back. Again and again I sought to get rid of them. I dug and I worked and dug some more. Each time I saw no more visible evidence of their presence, so I thought I'd finally won the battle, only to see them appear again. I finally learned of a product designed to kill weeds without harming the flowers. After diligently striving to remove every weed, root and all, I used this product. It worked very well.

Bad habits are like weeds in the garden of our characters. Their strong roots go deep, making it hard to eliminate them. Acknowledgment of their existence comes first. Then must come a desire to be rid of them. After that, we must put forth real effort to get them out of our lives. This isn't an easy task. It is said that it takes 21 days to form a habit—some experts say 40. If it takes that long to form a habit, it probably takes at least that long to be rid of it. Often we get discouraged and give up, continuing with the same bad habit day after day.

Like my effort with the weeds, we must have another agent enter the picture. God is always willing, through the Holy Spirit, to give us victory. We need only to come to Him, acknowledging our helplessness and the need for His grace that we might overcome. He can turn every failure into victory when we allow Him to change our hearts and minds to become like that of Christ Jesus. It is the only guaranteed solution.

Even then, victory may not be instantaneous, but we must not despair. Many verses in the Bible tell us to endure to the end and we will be saved. That principle applies to getting rid of all our undesirable, un-Christlike habits too. With complete surrender victory will come!

Aren't you glad we serve a God who is powerful enough, when we place our hand in His, to give us victory over every onerous habit!

Marian M. Hart

Caught in the Hidden Bog

Call upon me in the day of trouble; I will deliver you, and you will honor me.
Ps. 50:15, NIV.

WE WERE ON A CAMPING VACATION in the Richard B. Russell State Park in northern Georgia when we decided to take a hike on a trail through the woods. As we hiked we could hear the squirrels jumping from tree to tree and the birds sending a warning call that we were in their territory. We walked for miles and finally came out by the lake. We took the path as it wound to the left and followed the lake. We kept walking until we arrived at a small beach and rested on a bench for a while.

When we looked at our watches we were surprised how quickly the afternoon had slipped away, so we started back to our camper. We decided to take what we thought was a short cut along the river's edge so we could get back before dark. My grandson Luke led the way. All went well until he came to a place covered with tall grass. Suddenly we heard him scream. He'd fallen into a bog and found himself waist deep in thick mud. My husband ran ahead of me to help Luke, but when he tried to get him out, my husband fell in too. When I reached them and realized what had happened, I stretched my arm out toward them, but the ground was too soft so I backed away.

My husband was able to grab hold of a tree root. He told Luke to grab onto his belt and hold on. As they tried to climb out they discovered that the thick mud didn't want to release them. It was quite a struggle, but at last they were free. They were covered with mud from head to toe, so we decided to turn and go back to a place by the lake where the ground was firm so they could wash off the mud. By the time we got back to the camper it was dusk, but we were very glad to be "home."

Life is full of hidden bogs, traps that Satan sets to catch us. Some are physical and some are spiritual. It may be a situation where someone is spreading lies about us. All of these situations are hard to get out of on our own, and it is hard to know what to do. It's important to be on our guard, especially in this day when we are so close to Jesus' coming. When we do find ourselves in a bog, whether spiritual or physical, we can always call upon the Lord for help. He will help us find a solution or a way out. If our "hidden bog" is caused by people, we must remember to pray for them and their salvation as well as our own deliverance.

Celia Mejia Cruz

Right Place at the Right Time

Ye thought evil against me; but God meant it unto good.
Gen. 50:20.

IT WAS NEARLY 10:00 O'CLOCK that Friday night and I was very tired as I negotiated the nearly six miles of a dark, winding road on my way home from choir rehearsal. Though the road had no streetlights or shoulders, I often took this shortcut. I always thanked God for traveling mercies as He guided my faithful car along this dangerous stretch with one lane in each direction. For several days my 10-year-old car had been making strange noises and I had planned to take it to the mechanic, but had not. I made it safely home and immediately went to bed since I had to get up early the next morning to go to church.

Sabbath dawned bright and sunny and as I drove, I thought about my part in the worship service for prison ministry later that day. Halfway through the twists and turns of this same roadway, I looked in my rearview mirror and saw a police officer following me. Though I wasn't speeding, I still felt anxious. The thought crossed my mind that I would have to drive several more miles with him behind me because double yellow lines indicating no passing were painted the length of the road. Almost immediately upon thinking that I felt uncomfortable with the officer driving behind me, my car stopped dead in its tracks. It would not move. As the traffic began backing up, the officer got out and walked to my side to ask what was the problem. When I told him my car would neither go forward nor reverse, he started directing the traffic around me.

It happened that that same morning a group of construction men were at the same place preparing an area where more houses were going to be built. The police officer had the men push my car to the only possible spot where a car could sit safely off the road in the entire six-mile stretch.

As I waved and thanked the police officer and the other men, I prayed a prayer of thanks for God's mercy. I can't begin to imagine what would have happened on that dark, lonely road the night before when I was driving alone. During the numerous times I have traveled that road I had never been followed by the police, nor had there been a place to pull off. Although I expected something negative when my car stopped, God knew what I needed and sent help just in time!

Charlene M. Wright

A Dog as a Gospel Messenger

*If I . . . can fathom all mysteries and all knowledge, and if I have
a faith that can move mountains, but have not love, I am nothing.*
1 Cor. 13:2, NIV.

ABOUT 10 YEARS AGO a dog called Ragdai came with its master to a lake in Paijauri, in the utmost northwestern part of Russia, an area that Finland had to cede to the Soviet Union after World War II. When Ragdai noticed something unusual on the other side of the lake, he went to look. Thus the noble dog met a group of nature researchers led by my husband, Heikki, and stayed there with them. And so the dog's master had no alternative but to come and fetch his dog. The researchers thus made the acquaintance of the artist Anatol Shevnin. The research project was planned to last seven years, so the researchers visited the artist each summer in his wilderness camp. This was the beginning of a lasting friendship.

"No matter when you come, or with whom, or even if you come alone, you are always welcome. Our cabin is yours and we will help you," Anatol said to Heikki. My husband and his assistant dreamed of a vacation with their wives in this wilderness. When the project came to an end Anatol and his wife Raisa were sad because they would miss the yearly visits. That provided the occasion for Heikki and his assistant to tell them about their dream vacation. Two years later the dream came true.

In the meantime, our husbands organized an art exhibition of Anatol's work in a church of our home town in Finland. In this church Anatol found a Russian copy of *Steps to Christ* and asked if he could have it. On our vacation we took a Russian Bible and *The Great Controversy* to give to Anatol and his wife.

We set off on an adventurous hike through uninhabited forests, swamps, lakes, and rivers. At the end of an exhausting hike we finally reached the camp where Raisa welcomed us with a warm hug and a meal and showed us our comfortable beds. We absolutely wanted to see the place where the dog Ragdai had met the researchers. Ragdai has passed away, but he had been God's messenger. He helped his master Anatol get to know the Lord as a personal Saviour. Here on the lakeside Anatol has erected a huge wooden cross with the inscription, "Jesus Christ, King of the Jews; Faithful Lord" as a memorial of salvation. If God can use a dog to carry the message of His love, how much more will He use us if we let Him.

Aila Rehumäki Kauhanen

There Is a Way That Seems Right

There is a way that seems right to a man, but in the end it leads to death.
Prov. 14:12, NIV.

OUR DAY BEGAN BRIGHT AND EARLY because we had a 14-hour road trip ahead of us. We were returning home after visiting our son and his children for a week.

However, the return trip was going to be different as we would have two extra passengers and a dog. Our son and his 8-year-old daughter were riding with us. Meagan was particularly excited because she would soon see her 3-year-old cousin, Jasmine. It wasn't often that they got to be together, so this was going to be fun for both of them. Meagan entertained herself in the car by playing guessing games with Papa, solving mazes in a book, or just cuddling one of her many Webkinz® stuffed toys. Occasionally she would ask, "Are we almost there?" One of our stops was in a rest area near a rushing, mountain stream. It felt good to be able to stretch our legs. But all too soon it was time to leave.

After a few more hours, Meagan asked again, "Are we almost there?"

"Just three more hours," I was happy to tell her.

Her dad was driving now. It had gotten dark but we felt relatively safe traveling on a four-lane highway. However, we were aware of the danger of deer and other wildlife on the road. Suddenly our son saw lights coming toward us in our lane. Quickly checking over his shoulder, he was able to move to the right lane just as a truck pulling a trailer sped past us at top speed. We asked each other, What was that driver thinking? Didn't he realize this was not a two-lane highway? Immediately my husband called 911 and we made a U-turn at the next crossroad. Being a doctor, our son intended to be on the scene and available to assist in case of an accident. Then we noticed the taillights of the truck had come to a halt. Had he realized that he was heading the wrong direction?

Once again we turned around and continued heading in the right direction. I shuddered as I thought of how tragically our trip might have ended. Indeed, God had heard our prayer earlier that day and sent His angels to protect us.

On the road of life, we—or someone else—may be heading in the wrong direction spiritually. We must ask God to send His help there too so that neither we nor they meet a fatal accident.

Vera Wiebe

My Miracle Trip

Trust in the Lord with all your heart and lean not on your own understanding;
in all your ways acknowledge him, and he will make your paths straight.
Prov. 3:5, 6, NIV.

RECENTLY I HAD TO MAKE A TRIP to a church elders' meeting. The problem was that the meeting was in Ottawa and I was not familiar with the route as my husband usually does the driving on our city trips. However, I headed out on the freeway. Traffic was light and the miles slipped by as I sang along with my tapes. I had no problem getting close to the city, but I was suddenly fearful that I would lose my way.

I had prayed for guidance before I left, so when an impression to turn off onto Exit 417 came to me, I turned off onto that exchange and headed into the city. God's prompting was correct. That highway became the Queensway. Now all I had to do was to turn off on the correct exit and my trip would be a success.

My husband had told me to turn off on Greenbank. I did, but I quickly realized that he had been mistaken. I pulled off on the side of the street and lifted up my situation to the Lord. As I turned off on Carling, I began looking for a gas station. I was hoping that the attendant would be able to direct me. And then I saw a station. Prayerfully, I entered the little store. "Could you tell me where Benjamin Street is?" I asked.

"No, never heard of it," the attendant replied.

I was just beginning to turn away when I heard a softer voice speaking. "Go to the next stop light, not this one, the next one. Turn right, drive along and you will soon see the street name on your right," said an older gentleman.

I followed the directions with hope in my heart. But as I turned into residential area streets, I began to worry. Had he been right? I remembered that I had prayed for help and now the shreds of doubt were creeping in. *Help my unbelief,* I asked my Lord. Then suddenly right before me was Benjamin Street. It was a simple matter then to turn into the church parking lot. I had made my meeting on time.

How I rejoiced. God had directed me in spite of my doubting. Too many times we get impatient and forget that God has the future all planned out. We just need to listen for His voice.

Patricia Cove

Taking Care of Mom

Before they call I will answer; while they are still speaking I will hear.
Isa. 65:24, NIV.

EVERY DAY THINGS HAPPEN in our lives where we can see God's leading, but on some days we can see it better than on others.

Several years after my father passed away, my mother lost her center vision due to macular degeneration. Darlene, a friend of hers, had just lost her husband to death. Upon hearing about Mom's vision loss, Darlene decided to move in with Mom to keep her company. This arrangement helped them both. Darlene didn't want to live alone, and Mom could no longer enjoy her hobbies of reading and quilting so Darlene read to her, and they enjoyed each other's company. This was the first miracle for both of them.

Eight months later, a friend of mine, Krystal, who was going through a divorce, came by my office to tell me that she wanted to move back to the metro area and go to school to become a massage therapist. However, she did not have the resources to do it. After discussing it for a while, I thought perhaps Krystal could move into the downstairs apartment of my mom's house and be the caretaker for both Mom and Darlene, whose health was deteriorating. But I needed to talk to Mom and my brothers about it first. Krystal and I had prayer together, and she was just about ready to leave when the phone rang. I asked her to wait as it was one of my brothers. He was at our mom's house, and Darlene had just announced that she was moving into an assisted living facility. "What are we going to do for Mom?" he asked me. "She cannot live alone." I told him that someone was in my office who needed a place to live. She might be able to live in Mom's basement apartment for free plus earn a living wage in exchange for being a caregiver!

This was the second and third miracle! Someone to take care of Mom in her home, and a place for Krystal to live to get her education. The fourth miracle was that Darlene moved out the same day Krystal moved in—neither of them knew the other's schedule.

All of these miracles for my mother took place *before* we prayed about it! God knew the needs and supplied the answers to three wonderful women who put all their trust and faith in the mighty God we serve. What an amazing God! It increased my faith, and I know that "all things work together for good to them that love God!" (Rom. 8:28).

Ginger Bell

What Shines Through?

Let your light so shine before men, that they may see your good works,
and glorify your Father which is in heaven.
Matt. 5:16.

I ONCE BELONGED to a writers' group known as The Ink. We were about a dozen individuals from various walks of life: newspaper reporter, teacher, preacher, radio ham, nurse, farmer's wife, gift shop owner, college student, etc. We were also of diverse personalities with multi-styles of writing and topic selections. I found this diversity an education in establishing my writing style—always in nonfiction. Although I couldn't relate to all the themes the club members wrote about, I often found the constructive criticisms they offered after each oral reading applicable to my own writing.

One woman in the group wrote "homespun" stories and poems that I appreciated. I sensed her love for her aging husband in a poem, "My Hero." She wrote of her gratitude for God's beautiful creation. Then there was her humor. Her son's team became distracted and lost every hockey game when his "maw" was in the bleachers screaming, "Go, Denny, go!" Finally the son escorted his mother to the car, saying, "Go, Mommy, go!"

She and I often did editing for each other and developed a closer bond than with the other members. I eventually dropped out of the group because of the driving distance and lack of time. Sometime later I heard that my writing friend had published a book, *Dear to the Heart*. It sounded like a good book so I placed an order. When she received my order, she phoned me. After some informal chatting, she got to the purpose of her call. "Edith, I don't think you want to buy my book," she said.

"Why not?" I asked in surprise.

She didn't want to go into details but added, "It is not the kind of book you would read."

I found it interesting that she sensed my moral convictions and didn't want to jeopardize our friendship by letting me read her novel. Apparently she had been selective in what she had shared with me at previous meetings. I thanked her for respecting my values.

This experience provoked a sobering thought. People are always watching and evaluating those they meet. Are my words and actions a true portrayal of my beliefs and character?

Edith Fitch

Pity —or Censure?

He took pity on him.
Luke 10:33, NIV.

ONE SUNDAY AFTERNOON my husband and I drove 140 miles to hear a choir. The host church, however, was deserted: the concert had been cancelled. Before leaving town, we decided to make a phone call to make sure we didn't have the time wrong. (This was before nearly everyone had a cell phone.) We approached an intersection that had a gas station on each corner, each with a phone booth on the lot. At the nearest set of phones, the phone books were missing. Across the street, also no books. We went to a third station—success!

As we were about to drive away, we watched a young woman approach the phones. She went to one phone to make a call, then pounded the phone in frustration and kicked the base for good measure. She tried the second phone and again slammed her hand against the telephone. Then, with shoulders slumped and bleeding fingers, she started back toward her car. All I saw was a woman having a childish tantrum. My husband, however, heeded an inner nudge and drove up alongside her. "Can we help you?" he asked kindly.

Through tears she blurted, "My car broke down, and I don't know anyone here, and when I tried to call my husband my phone card wouldn't work!"

"Let me try," said Vic, and we returned to the phones.

Vic produced a handful of change, dialed the number for the distraught woman, and handed over the phone when her husband answered. Vic also managed to get her car to run intermittently, enough so she could follow us to where her husband would come to meet her.

"You're the answer to my prayers!" she said as we parted.

"God sure has some devious ways of putting people where He's going to need them," I joked to my husband.

Although this experience did speak to me of God's provision, it also convicted my heart. All I had seen was a woman having a childish tantrum. I could easily have *tsk-tsk-ed* and driven off. But Vic saw beyond her behavior. He sensed her panic and desperation and reached out to her with compassion. By his example, the good Samaritan I'm married to reminded me to look beyond the obvious and not harden my heart. Pity, not censure. Maybe a good lesson for all of us!

Dolores Klinsky Walker

Its Shame and Reproach Gladly Bear

And let us not grow weary while doing good,
for in due season we shall reap if we do not lose heart.
Gal. 6:9, NKJV.

WHEN I READ IN MY BIBLE about how important it is to witness and share the Gospel with others, I want so much to share the truth of God's Word with my neighbors. I've been taking small tracts and pamphlets to our community library in our clubhouse. I made a box for free literature and labeled it as such. I pray for my neighbors and ask God to help them see and take the free papers. From time to time I look to see if anyone has taken anything from the box, but it always has the same amount of literature. It seems that no one is taking the material.

Most of the books found in the clubhouse library are cheap pulp novels and mysteries which are constantly being read and returned by many of these retired people. As I try to share my Christian faith with them, I pray they will read the Gospel truth in the free literature box and magazine racks I put there. Like today's verse says, I must not grow weary doing well, for in due time the reaping will come. I sow the seed and God reaps the harvest, right? *I may never know the results of my labors until the judgment day*, I remind myself.

Ellen White wrote, "Since the time when the Son of God breasted the haughty prejudices and unbelief of mankind, there has been no change in the attitude of the world toward the religion of Jesus. The servants of Christ must meet the same spirit of opposition and reproach, and must go 'without the camp bearing His reproach'" (*Review and Herald*, Feb. 7, 1888). That is why I must not become discouraged.

In 1913 George Bennard wrote in the song we all sing, "To that old rugged cross I will ever be true, its shame and reproach gladly bear." It calls me to more bravely present God's amazing love to my neighbors.

Then I realize that in addition to Christian literature, the most important way to show kindness and love is to live out the Gospel. What matters most is what they see in my life—that Jesus is the most important thing to me.

Dear Lord, please give me the spirit of faith not to be weary in well-doing. May I do my sharing with Christian love. Please help me to keep my hope focused on the season of reaping that will come in due time.

Bessie Siemens Lobsien

Why Do You Love Me?

The Lord has appeared of old to me, saying: "Yes, I have loved you with an everlasting love; Therefore with lovingkindness I have drawn you."
Jer. 31:3, NKJV.

IT'S AN AMAZING NIGHT. The breeze is cool, the stars are shining bright, and the moon is as big as a hot air balloon. The universe seems immense. My mind is racing with thoughts of God. Have you ever wondered why the Lord loved us enough to give His life for us? How can it be that the king of the universe cares about the little things in our lives?

Why does He love me? I am a sinner—not worth much in my eyes. I'm not famous nor do I have lots of degrees. But my Lord loves me so much anyway. I can't even begin to tell you of the quantity of that love. He takes care of me. He gives me my heart's desires and takes care of my life even when I think I know what I'm doing.

I ask myself, and I ask Him: *Lord, what can I do for You? How can I tell the world how much You love them? How can I show them Your love or what You have done and are still doing for me?*

Well, I can start by saying, "He's my everything." I'll tell everyone how much I love Him and why I serve Him: it's because He loves me unconditionally. Did you hear me? He loves me—us—unconditionally. I want to shout it from the rooftops so everyone will hear me. He is here by my side when I need Him, whether it is day or night. And I need my Jesus every day of my life. Oh, how He loves me, and heaven is where I long to be, giving Him my praise, showing Him all my love because He cares about everything in my life. He's my hero.

I can breathe easier as long as I keep my eyes on Jesus, testifying of His love, keeping His commandments and testimonies, showing Him that I believe in Him, and showing others how much He loves them. He waits on each of us to truly want what He wants for our lives: time with each of us in heaven. Imagine me and my Jesus for all eternity. Won't you make that same plan today?

Remember, no matter what you have done, no matter how much you think you have sinned, God is there to pick up the pieces of your life and forgive your sins. All you have to do is ask. Don't make Him wait any longer.

Tammy Barnes-Taylor

My Nest Is Empty— Now What?

Jabez cried out to the God of Israel, "Oh, that you would bless me and enlarge my territory! Let your hand be with me, and keep me from harm so that I will be free from pain." And God granted his request.
1 Chron. 4:10, NIV.

I GREW UP with eight brothers and sisters. My aunts and uncles also had many children, so I was accustomed to a great deal of social interaction, and I developed a love for always having the house full of people. God granted me the privilege of raising three children: two girls and one boy, and the pleasure of participating in the development and education of an adopted daughter. I involved myself completely with those four children for almost three decades. When they were high school age, they went to a boarding school, and later three of them lived at home during their university studies. It was a difficult period—I cannot deny it— but it was extremely gratifying to be able to see them developing professionally, making life-shaping decisions, and little by little becoming independent adults.

Yesterday, the last one left! I went from empty bedroom to empty bedroom with tears filling my eyes, verifying each detail that had been left behind: books, photos, CDs, dolls, stuffed animals, bottles of perfume, collections of stamps, coins, medals. Although marriage may seem "outdated" these days, God gave us the pleasure of seeing our four children married, and now they are distributed throughout the world.

Thank You, Lord, for giving me the pleasure of their company. The days were unforgettable, filled with lights on at all hours, loud music, music group practices, young people and friends coming and going at all hours! And it all went by so fast!

I look for the positive side of this new reality and without much effort I find it. Now I have more time for the father of my children, my companion. But more than this, now I can take care of my "Father's business" with more dedication. I am now closer to my church family. I ask my Father to train me for His work, to strengthen me, to provide me with love and humility toward my brothers and sisters so that I can learn from them as I learned from my children.

My prayer is the prayer of Jabez: that God may broaden my family horizon and that I may soon be able to be a part of the heavenly family where separation shall never again exist.

Nair Costa Lessa

God Is God

*Surely goodness and mercy shall follow me all the days of my life:
and I will dwell in the house of the Lord for ever.
Ps. 23:6.*

WHEN WE WALK WITH THE LORD and recognize His blessings of goodness and love, there's much to be thankful for.

My friend, whom I met at a women's retreat, taught me much by her example of simple trust in God. When I traveled with her in the car I noted how she talked aloud to Jesus for safety and direction. She negotiated traffic problems with patience and calm, and I could not help but feel the presence of Jesus with us. I should not have been amazed at this because the Bible tells us, "Draw nigh to God, and he will draw nigh to you" (James 4:8). Maybe we sometimes forget these things, and it's good to have a friend—or to be the friend—who encourages another in our daily walk with Jesus.

There are countless times when God's goodness surrounds us, even in the struggles of life. Some years ago our youngest son was left a single parent with two boys aged 7 and 8. Having full responsibility for the care of them presented some difficult times. The nature of his employment meant that he was regularly called out of state to manage the business affairs of a large company. On these occasions, my husband and I would go to look after the boys in Adelaide, a couple of hours from where we live. As all parents do, we longed for the happiness and stability of our family, so this situation became a matter of prayer.

We don't know how God works in answering our petitions, but we can rest knowing He hears, cares, and does what is best for our specific needs. I was impressed at a women's ministries camp to put our son's name in a prayer journal: "The effectual fervent prayer of a righteous man availed much" (James 5:16). The Lord saw fit to answer by sending a lovely woman to our son, and in due time they married. We praise God for this goodness, for the two boys then had opportunity to grow up in a Christian family environment.

Looking back at the evidence of God's leading in my life, and that of my family, I firmly believe that it's only by practicing the presence of Christ in our lives that we can endure. May I witness this to others just as my friend showed by her example to me—because God *is* good!

Joan D. L. Jaensch

Body, Mind, and God's Way

And so, dear brothers and sisters, I plead with you to give your bodies to God because of all he has done for you. Let them be a living and holy sacrifice—the kind he will find acceptable. This is truly the way to worship him. Don't copy the behavior and customs of this world, but let God transform you into a new person by changing the way you think.
Rom. 12:1, 2, NLT.

WE WERE CRUISING from Alaska to Vancouver. The weather was horrid—cold, wet, foggy. Outdoor activities were impossible. Indoors? My mind clearly said that the casino and shows were not for me. Yet the dining room was a different story. With uniformed servers offering and even urging delectable tidbits, eating appealed to me. The desserts were especially attractive. Yes, I knew that the sugar overload was bad for me; I knew, in fact, that I'd eaten more than enough even before dessert.

In the midst of this situation, I read Romans 12 and chewed on it. Was Paul telling me that God wanted my body but not necessarily my mind? Am I not one, made of body, mind, and spirit? I wondered, yet the command is categorical: Because God has done so much for me, I need to sacrifice my body and its desires. In fact, the sacrifice of my body is the "logical" (as it is in the Greek) way to worship Him.

Then, in verse 2, I found the mind part! God makes me "into a new person by changing the way" I think. I am not to conform to the schemes of this world. I am to allow my thinking, my mind, to be changed. That is a passive voice—not something I do, but something God does.

The last part of verse 2 completes the picture, showing me the result of allowing God to transform my mind so that I am willing to sacrifice my body: "Then you will learn to know God's will for you, which is good and pleasing and perfect."

The desserts were beautiful, mouth watering. But saying no to them—my sacrifice to God—was made possible because He gave me a new way of thinking, a new way to understand God's will for me. He wants me to have control over my appetite as well as perfect health of mind and body.

Thank You, Lord, for helping me to understand that my body and its desires must be subject to a new way of thinking that You are giving me. I want to do Your perfect will.

Nancy Jean Vyhmeister

The Water Into Wine Wedding Miracle

If you . . . know how to give good gifts to your children, how much more
will your Father in heaven give good gifts to those who ask him!
Matt. 7:11, NIV.

WE WERE EATING PASTA in my daughter's student house. Her boyfriend, Tim, had come over for lunch, and we were trying to catch the last elusive ribbons of tagliatelle when he said, "We've been wondering about getting married next summer." We weren't surprised.

We celebrated with a bottle of elderflower drink, but as we drove away I wondered how we'd ever manage to pay for a wedding. Both Beth and Tim had large student loans to repay, and we worked for a church organization. Even though I worked almost full–time, I was paid as a half-time worker. We never had any money to spare at the end of a month, and even a simple British wedding could cost around $30,000.

Bernie and I run couples marriage weekends called "Turning Water into Wine." As I prepared the publicity for the next retreat I thought about Jesus' first miracle, at a wedding, blessing the couple with a totally generous and completely unnecessary gift just to make the occasion extra special. So I sat down at my kitchen table with a glass of water and read the story in the second chapter of John all over again. *Father God*, I said, *Remember the wine miracle? Well, we could really use another one now. Beth and Tim want their wedding to be a celebration of the love You've shared with them. They want their marriage to be focused on Your desire for their lives. Financially, all we have is a little water. But we believe You can take that water, that almost non-existent amount of money, multiply it, bless it, and transform it into a beautiful wedding. I believe You can do this for us, for Beth and Tim.*

I made Beth's dress, Tim's uncle made an amazing cake, friends made bouquets and provided music. Beth's youngest brother spent the summer making table decorations from tree branches, stripped bare and painted white. He spent many hours working, carefully attaching tea-light holders so they would scatter twinkling light over the banquet.

God worked miracles with our fragile finances. For a whole year there was money left over at the end of each month. We had everything we needed to pay for their elegant celebration and everything else we needed as well. Our watery finances were transformed into the sparkling wine of their wonderful wedding.

Karen Holford

Red Letter Day

Hezekiah received the letter from the messengers and read it. Then he went up to the temple of the Lord and spread it out before the Lord. And Hezekiah prayed to the Lord. Isa. 37:14, 15, NIV.

IN THESE DAYS of e-mail, instant messaging, and text messages, I find it nice to receive letters. So nice, in fact, that on the occasions when I am at home during the day, I look forward to seeing the postman walking up the drive. One particular day, the thud in the letterbox was promising. I had just graduated and had applied for several jobs—perhaps there was a letter inviting me to an interview—or better still, there might be a job offer. But no. All I found was rejection letter after rejection letter, junk mail, and—bills. It was demoralizing and I needed to talk to God about my situation.

God knew that I needed a job; He knew about the evenings spent scouring newspapers for jobs, followed by hours of painstakingly filling in application forms and writing personal statements. He knew that I, as a new graduate with no experience, would find it challenging to find work quickly. He knew that I needed to make a good impression in my interview. He knew too about the pressing matter of the student loan and the utility bills. He knew all about it, including parts I didn't even know about.

Like Hezekiah, I took the bills and the letters of rejection and spread them on my bed. Then I knelt to pray. I told God about my disappointment and acknowledged the fierce competition in the job market. I told Him that I knew He was going to find a good job for me where I could witness for Him. Just that day I had read from 2 Corinthians 3 as part of my morning devotion. I read it again. Then I understood; I was not only to expect good news by post, I was to be good news to others. As the Apostle Paul wrote, "You yourselves are our letter, written on our hearts, known and read by everybody. You show that you are a letter from Christ, the result of our ministry, written not with ink but with the Spirit of the living God, not on tablets of stone but on tablets of human hearts" (2 Cor. 3:2, 3, NIV).

I rose from my knees at peace, giving thanks that my good news would be coming shortly, and the letter offering me my first job did come soon afterward. My personal letter of testimony to God's goodness and grace lives on in my life.

Judith Purkiss

Hold On

As an eagle stirs up its nest, hovers over its young, spreading out its wings,
taking them up, carrying them on its wings, so the Lord alone led him.
Deut. 32:11, 12, NKJV.

WHEN OUR FATHER DIED, we were a young family of five children, left alone in that bereaved and cold moment. All other family members and relatives abandoned us. No one seemed to care if we existed. At one point, all hope was lost, and we thought we would never make it. Our widowed mother battled and struggled, doing all she could without any regular work to see that all her children survived. We held on.

My secondary school years were extremely difficult. Each month we had to spend two weeks working on the farm in order to earn a small amount of money. Needless to say, after secondary school I had no hope of furthering my education. I got a job for which I was paid a meager 300 naira per month. After a while, I decided to get married. I asked God to look into my situation and give me a caring, understanding husband.

I held on, and God heard my prayer and gave me such a husband. He encouraged me to enroll for the West African examination, which I did. I passed, and was then admitted to study information resources management while still holding on for a miracle. Because things were still tight and difficult for the family, I applied for a women's ministries scholarship, hoping it would come when I needed it. Time passed. I continued praying and holding on to God. And God did it. Today I am a graduate, happily married, with two sons.

Yes, at different times in life we are faced with some difficulties which come in different ways. It may also look as if the whole world is turning against us. Whatever the case may be, hold on to God. Put your trust in Him. He is the author and finisher of our faith. He says, "Can a woman forget her sucking child, that she should not have compassion on the son of her womb? yea, [she] may forget, yet I will not forget thee. Behold, I have graven thee upon the palms of my hands; thy walls are continually before me" (Isa. 49:15, 16). When I was going through all the difficulties, I never knew that one day my story would change for good. So I've learned that God's promises are ever sure. Claim them. Hold on to them by faith, and He will never let you down. He has promised.

Ezinwanyi Madukoma

The Touch of His Love

Filled with compassion, Jesus reached out his hand and touched the man.
Mark 1:41, NIV.

WITH THE WARM SUNLIGHT on my face, that spring Sabbath should have been a welcome reprieve from the winter's cold. But it served only to mock the gloom in my heart. I stood alone, clutching my 2-year-old son close, while people swarmed around us. I held tight to the hand of my once successful pastor-husband. Every fiber of my being wanted to run from the patio of that large institutional church. Somehow, I stood planted, hoping that no one would notice me, yet wishing that just one person would stop and say, "Good morning. I'm glad you came."

Shortly after entering the ministry, through a series of political moves we did not understand and over which we had no control, we found ourselves unemployed, living with my parents in a large city, wondering, praying if we should return to ministry or stumble along searching, praying for God's new path. The pain ran deep. The "church" had turned against us. And now in a different city here we were at church. We had come to worship, instinctively knowing we needed to be part of a faith community, yet afraid to try. Now we stood there, alone.

And then, out of the crowd of thousands she appeared, elegant, well-dressed, smiling, her little daughters close behind. She stretched out her hand. "Good morning," she said warmly. "My name is Elizabeth. I saw you in Sabbath school. I'm glad you have come." I reached for her outstretched hand. In the warmth of her hand, the gesture of friendship, a simple kindness, a sister among the throng of well-dressed worshippers, I felt His touch, His grace, His care.

Sabbaths came and went. We worshipped there regularly. The uncertainty of our ministry and finances tested our faith that long summer. Elizabeth was there each Sabbath, smiling, caring, inviting us to her home, but not probing.

Every week, on other patios, other foyers, they stand there—young mothers recently divorced and returning to church; others with tobacco smoke still clinging to their clothes; fathers who have come alone, their children scared and hiding; the elderly, struggling into the sanctuary, every step a chore. I notice them, alone. Do I stop, step out of my group, and offer my hand? The now distant, yet gentle memory of Elizabeth's smile flickers across my mind. Who knows why they have come? Could my touch, my words be His only words to them today? And so I stop, I reach out my hand—really His hand—and His grace flows through.

Cinda Lea Sitler

When the Church Prays

Do you see what I've done? I've refined you, but not without fire.
I've tested you like silver in the furnace of affliction.
Isa. 48:10, Message.

WE ARE TOLD that one of the best ways to tell others of Jesus is to tell what He has done for us. I am so happy to tell you how I have come from the furnace of affliction. It has been wonderful, watching the expressions on people's faces as I have shared my experience.

For the past few years my husband and I have taken a winter birding trip to somewhere warm. This year we decided to go to Ecuador. Looking at a Christian birding site, we found a group trip going just where and when we wanted to go.

After two weeks of birding the east slope of the Andes and the Amazon rain forest, we traveled by bus to several cities. We enjoyed the city of Cuenca with its very old churches and buildings, and then we moved on to Quayaquil, and then Salinas on the Pacific Ocean. We enjoyed the country and its beautiful scenery so very much. It was in Salinas that I had what I thought was just the "traveler's bug," and that it would soon pass. But I did not feel well for the next few days—and one of those days we traveled by bus eleven and a half hours from Manta to Quito. I had Cipro, an antibiotic, with us which I started taking.

We had left our car in Phoenix, Arizona. By the time we arrived back in Phoenix my symptoms just exploded. I felt so ill and weak. Although we'd planned to stay in Arizona for a few weeks to enjoy the warmth and more birding, I told my husband I just had to go home.

Once home, numerous medical tests and a visit to the ER for intravenous fluids and another consultation still did not provide the answer: What was this disease?

We now believe I had typhoid fever. For a couple of weeks my temperature ranged from 102° to 104° F. I could not tolerate food. The abdominal symptoms just did not go away, and I lost weight. Each day I had the chills, and my whole body would shake.

One Sabbath my husband called a friend and asked that they pray for me at church. What an answer to prayer! After that morning I had no more abdominal symptoms or a fever. None! The corporate prayer of the church brought the answer that I so needed. God has not promised that there will be no afflictions, but He has promised to carry us through.

Carol Stickle

The Difference

*Forty days later Noah opened a window to send out a raven, but it kept flying
around until the water had dried up. Noah wanted to find out if the water had
gone down, and he sent out a dove. Deep water was still everywhere,
and the dove could not find a place to land. So it flew back to the boat.
Noah held out his hand and helped it back in.*
Gen. 8:6-9, CEV.

DOVES AND RAVENS don't look alike and their other differences are significant too. Birds may look alike, but the purpose for which they were created can be vastly different. Ravens are scavengers and belong to the crow family. The Bible classifies them as unclean. Doves and pigeons belong to the same family and are classified as clean. Ravens are associated with death and dying while doves are a symbol of hope, peace, and healing.

Noah sent both a raven and a dove out of the ark following the flood. Both came back to the ark, but Noah did not take the raven back inside the ark. The raven kept going back and forth until it found a place to nest. "At the end of forty days Noah opened the window of the ark that he had made and sent forth a raven. It went to and fro until the waters were dried up from the earth" (ESV). But when the dove returned, Noah reached out and brought it back inside. A week later he sent the dove out again and it returned with an olive branch in its beak, a sign to Noah that the waters were receding and vegetation was growing once again. The raven never returned to Noah with anything.

At first reading of this story, I felt sorry for the raven until I realized that the raven was no longer needed inside the ark. Its reason for being saved from the flood was accomplished; now its purpose lay outside the ark. The raven was a scavenging bird, the dead carcasses were outside of the ark. Noah was allowing the raven to fulfill its God-given purpose by letting it go.

Likewise, God will give us instructions which He expects us to follow until He tells us otherwise. When a divine purpose is accomplished He will let us know when to let go or abandon a particular course of action. It makes no sense to try to change or alter a divine purpose for which a creature was created. Know the difference between what belongs inside your ark and what belongs outside. When God says open the window, do so. Take the dove back, but let the raven go. Your deliverance depends on it.

Desrene L. Vernon

My First Flight

Where can I go from your Spirit? Where can I flee from your presence? If I go up to the heavens, you are there; if I make my bed in the depths, you are there. If I rise on the wings of the dawn, if I settle on the far side of the sea, even there your hand will guide me, your right hand will hold me fast. If I say, "Surely the darkness will hide me and the light become night around me," even the darkness will not be dark to you; the night will shine like the day, for darkness is as light to you.
Ps. 139:7-12, NIV.

FOR MY SEVENTIETH BIRTHDAY my children presented me with a gift of an air ticket to South America to stay with my daughter who lives in Paraguay. Before this trip I had never flown on an airplane. I could not even imagine anything like it. The flight was simply wonderful. I am convinced that God prepared everything to give me the wonderful feeling of flying over the clouds without experiencing any agitation or fright. I cannot explain it otherwise.

We started in Frankfurt/Main in Germany at 11:00 p.m. An hour later I dozed off in the midst of clouds. I must have continued to hear the noise of the engines because I woke up again after a few minutes when the sound changed. Through the window all I could see was snow, and the plane seemed to be standing still. When I told my daughter, who was traveling with me, she was greatly amused—we were above the clouds. Overwhelming!

The heavens were full of stars and the bright moon shone close to us, making everything light as the day. During the night while everyone else was sleeping, I wandered around in the plane, raising my arms and bending my head. I was careful not to disturb other passengers or stumble over objects lying about. As we approached Sao Paulo, I saw the sun coming up like a huge, majestic ball, rising in only nine minutes with elegance and ease. What splendor!

I stood still and looked at the sleeping people and realized that they had complete confidence in the skill of the pilot. That was good. When the pilot had greeted the passengers over the cabin monitors, I had seen a really trustworthy looking gentleman of middle age. But the question came to my mind: Are these people aware who is really the Pilot in the cockpit? It was the One who accompanied me on my first flight in such a wonderful way. We can trust our Pilot without reservation. He knows what is good for us and loves us above all.

Maria Lamprecht-Schmid

My (and Your) Mission Field

Therefore go and make disciples of all nations, baptizing them in the name of the Father and of the Son and of the Holy Spirit. Matt. 28:19, NIV.

WHEN OUR GIRLS were around 3 and 5 years old, we had the privilege of being sent as missionaries to a far off place. Although we were excited about what the Lord had in store for us, we also found ourselves fearful. I still remember saying goodbye to our families, not knowing whether we would ever meet again. There were tears in our eyes, tears of joy and of separation.

As we boarded the plane—our first international flight ever—we felt excitement and fear at the same time. I remember praying, *Lord, I am afraid. Where will You take us?* I cried deep inside, fearful of the unknown. However, as I looked at my little girls, content, happy, and with no cares at all, I told myself, *Jemima, if you have given everything to God for this mission, then there's no need to worry. Just follow His leading.* With this thought, I was comforted.

We'll never forget our African mission adventure. We made beautiful friends. Our lives, simple and humble, were full of joy and contentment. Joy from serving the Master 24/7, and contentment from the love from the people we worked with.

Then a few years after we moved back to America, I asked my husband, "Danny, can we go back to the mission field?" He wanted to know why, of course. I told him that I missed the activities we had in Africa, the simplicity and life of service I felt we led. After giving it some thought, Danny told me that America was now our mission field because our mission field was wherever God placed us. He reminded me that people here need us just like people in Africa had.

That thought stuck with me, and instead of wishing I was back in the "mission field," I began living the life of service I used to live. God told me that we are missionaries wherever we are. Our families, our friends, our fellow church members, people we meet in the supermarket, in the train or bus station, at our work place, everybody—they are our mission field. We must love them, put them first in our lives. Forget about our comfort zones.

Now I am happy and content with life. I have realized that I don't have to be somewhere far from home to be a missionary. I don't have to be in Africa, Asia, or any other continent to live a simple life. I don't have to be thousands of miles from home to experience the joy of service.

Jemima Dollosa Orillosa

Daddy Issues

The Lord appeared to us in the past, saying: "I have loved you with an everlasting love; I have drawn you with loving-kindness." Jer. 31:3, NIV.

AS I SETTLED DOWN on my couch after a long day teaching needy third graders, I turned on the television to watch the Tyra Banks' show. Tonight the program featured sex workers—those who wanted to get out of the profession and others who sought to prove the glamour of their job.

One young woman hated her adoptive father for introducing her to the world of prostitution. He showed her "secrets" of the trade and how to keep men "happy." Another girl loved her pimp because he had "discovered" her in a mall as she was fleeing her abusive boyfriend. He told her she was beautiful, and promised to take care of her. Tyra was infuriated! She stated vehemently that such a man preyed upon young, attractive girls who had self-esteem issues. Then an ex-prostitute pleaded with the girls to get out of the prostitution lifestyle while they still could. She shared that she'd been attracted to the cars, nice clothes, and the apartment overlooking the city, but there was a terrible downside to it all, and she had almost been killed nine times.

I thought, *Why would these girls do this to themselves? Why would they sell their priceless bodies so cheap? Really, was any price worth what they were doing to themselves?* I thought that these girls must have one thing in common: daddy issues. And indeed, each one admitted they had lacked a positive male role model in their lives. They longed for a father to hold them and tell them how beautiful they were. They longed to feel secure, safe, and special. These young women were like little girls inside.

I wish I could have told them that they do have a Father who loves them dearly, one who would never sell them to man after man for a whopping $125 each. I wish I were in the audience yelling at the top of my lungs that they are princesses who are infinitely invaluable. They have a "Daddy" who has no hidden agenda in caring for them or in loving them. He was the only One who had their best interest at heart. Oh, how I wished *I* had known this when I was a teen and looking for the next boy to tell me how beautiful I was! It seems at that time in my life my heart was a bottomless pit. I needed attention every second. But my heavenly Daddy filled that hole in my heart. If I keep close to Him, He will draw even closer to me. I am spoken for—and always will be.

Raschelle Mclean-Jones

Baxter Gets a Ride

Love is patient.
1 Cor. 13:4, NIV.

SEVERAL WEEKS AGO I saw a Cocker Spaniel dog wandering on our street. I continued with what I was doing, and then as I once again glanced out the window I realized that seeing this particular dog was strange. Rarely, if ever, do I see a dog without an owner attached to it. So it dawned on me that this indeed was a runaway dog. Then it sunk in that it was our mechanic's dog—the mechanic who lives a few blocks away.

I looked up his number and called him. Sure enough, Baxter was missing. I told Wilf where I'd seen his dog and he said he would be right up. I soon saw the car pulling up to the field across from our house, so I quickly went out and told Wilf the direction that I had seen the dog heading.

A few minutes later I was again on the phone when Wilf waved as he drove past my window. He was no doubt happy to have found Baxter, the escapee, and the sight I saw was priceless. Baxter was sitting tall on the passenger seat looking proud as punch, chauffeured by his owner—who was patiently driving him home.

What a great object lesson! It made me think how much like Baxter we are. We all have a wonderful Master who loves us, feeds us, protects us, and cares for our every need day in and day out. But we get a notion that we want to follow our noses, and that sometimes leads us to places where we don't belong or just don't need to be. We happily sniff around, probably not even realizing that we have wandered far from home and, in fact, are in danger. But our faithful, patient, kind, loving Master comes to our rescue, perhaps answering our previous prayers or the prayers of friends or family. He gently reminds us that we are lost and have wandered from His side. He tenderly and gently leads us back to Himself.

We wander in many ways. We get too busy to spend daily time with our Master, but He waits and helps us recognize our need of Him. When we come back, He shows us His love: unending, unconditional, and unchanging. God is a wonderful Master.

When will I ever learn? I'm so thankful God continues to patiently teach me. He wants to lead you and me, to be by our side today. Let Him be your Master today.

Gay Mentes

Thy Maker Is Thine Husband

For thy Maker is thine husband; the Lord of hosts is his name; and thy Redeemer the Holy One of Israel; the God of the whole earth shall he be called.
Isa. 54:5.

I WAS IN MY EARLY TWENTIES and a relatively new Christian. After a rather unfavorable relationship with a young man, I had a desire to build friendships with Christian men and women all over the world. I was definitely not looking for a new boyfriend, but I thought it could inspire and help in my walk with the Lord if I got in touch with other like-minded people. So I found an advertisement for a catalog which was supposed to help people find "contacts worldwide." This sounded good to me, and so I posted a picture of myself with a little note saying, "I am looking for contacts with Christians all over the world"—not realizing that this was actually a catalog for people who were looking for a spouse. During the next few months, I received letters from men of all ages, from all over the world, not necessarily Christians, who wanted to marry me! This really turned me off. At some point I didn't even want to open these letters anymore as I knew it could be another marriage invitation.

But what about the marriage invitation of the Lord? Had I really invited Him to take full control over my life? How often had I hardened my heart to His voice, even after I had been converted. Yet He truly wanted to have this close, intimate relationship with me which resembles the earthly husband-wife relationship.

It was only after another unfavorable relationship that I decided to fully give my life to God and be baptized. Ever since—and that was more than a decade ago—I have been single. During this time, the Lord has taught me many valuable lessons. In fact, I am now married to Jesus Christ—yet I do not rule out being married to an earthly husband some day. Undoubtedly, the Lord has instilled in us a desire to be united in matrimonial union here on earth, and I've often asked Him why He has not yet provided me with my "other half." Nevertheless, I've been truly blessed in this "incompleteness," which has been completed by Him.

"And you are complete in Him, who is the head of all principality and power" (Col. 2:10, NKJV). He will never fail me and He knows exactly what is best for me, and when.

Thank You, Jesus, for the gift of singleness!

Daniela Weichhold

Paradise Lost—Paradise Found

When you walk through fire you shall not be burned, and the flame will not consume you.
Isa. 43:2, NRSV.

PARADISE WAS ALMOST LOST, but God found—or saved—it! In June, 2008, lightning from thunderstorms caused fires all around our area. Paradise, California, is located on a ridge with canyons surrounding the town. If a fire starts in the canyon the winds quickly cause the flames to rush up either side of the canyon. We thought the smoky, overcast air would clear up, but instead it thickened with smoke, and we faced several mandatory evacuations from our homes. All the schools and offices in the area were closed because of the threat. We stayed glued to the TV to learn if we'd have to evacuate.

The fires were named according to the street or area in which they started. The first main fire, the Humboldt, started nine miles south of us. The firefighters thought they had it contained, then the winds began to change directions. That meant the fires were racing toward the south side of Paradise. We live on the west side of the ridge, two streets over from the canyon.

My husband, Ben, and I decided to wait for the phone call for the mandatory evacuation. However, when our electricity went out and we didn't know what was going on, we packed our things, including Sheba, the cat, and Buster, our miniature red dachshund, and evacuated. We'd already been told to stay prepared to leave at a moment's notice. Deciding what to take gave us a weird feeling. We were scheduled to soon speak at the Minnesota camp meeting, and we left our home not knowing whether or not our house would be standing when we returned a week later. It took us more than three hours to travel what normally took 20 to 25 minutes.

Fires so engulfed our area that we had to wear masks most of July and August. The Humboldt fires had almost subsided when fires on the east side began to soar. The challenge was the Adventist-owned Feather River Hospital. The fires came so close to the hospital that it had to be evacuated for at least 10 days. The fire chief reported that there was no way those fires should not have consumed the hospital, yet it was safe. God answered our prayers for the Paradise community. God still controls the fires, the weather, and our lives. He is worth worshipping! Paradise was almost lost, but God saved it.

Mary L. Maxson

The Nature of God

For God so loved the world that He gave His only begotten Son, that whoever believes in Him should not perish but have everlasting life.
John 3:16, NKJV.

A FEW YEARS AGO when my husband and I were returning home from the Jasper National Park where the annual Jasper Dental Congress had been held, we decided to spend the Sabbath in the park. We had such a wonderful time admiring God's creation! The mountain view was breathtaking. The wildflowers were beautiful, and I really appreciated seeing so many wild animals. In addition to the usual robins, magpies, and squirrels, we saw a bald eagle, mountain goats, big horn sheep, coyote, and many deer.

Every time my mom visited the Rockies she had high hopes of seeing bears. It was the highlight of her day when she saw one, and she'd say that God answered her prayer. I always shared Mom's excitement as there are no bears in our home country of Brazil. And knowing that the Jasper National Park area is bear country, I expected we'd see at least one that Sabbath. But now that we were going home the chances were getting smaller by the mile.

As I drove, I silently prayed, *Thank You, dear God, for all the blessings we've received this weekend. It was awesome. Lord, I know I don't deserve it, but in my heart I also want to see a bear. I know! I should be content with what I have. Yes, thank You, Father.* And thus, feeling content, I kept admiring the Rocky Mountains as we continued the drive.

The views were simply spectacular, and it was easy to get distracted. Then after a curve I saw many cars stopped on both sides of the road. I knew what that meant: wild animal on site. Excited, I slowed down but continued going because I didn't know where the animal would be. I passed a couple of cars and there he was: a black bear cub just seven feet from our car!

Joy and amazement filled my heart. After we started driving once more, I prayed again: *Thank You, thank You so very much. I know I didn't deserve this, but I'm so happy.* The Lord answered, "I know. I didn't do this because of you, but because of Me! I am loving, merciful, and gracious, and I delight to see you happy. I did this because I love you and wanted you to know that; I didn't do it because you deserved it. I smiled and thought, *You gave Your Son, not because I deserve it, but because You love me.* That made the trip unforgettable. I saw a bear because God loves me. Always remember: He loves you, too.

Eunice Passos Molina Berger

Voices From the Heavens

The heavens declare the glory of God; the skies proclaim the work of his hands.
Ps. 19:1, NIV.

I AM TRULY AMAZED at the beauty of the heavens. What an awesome experience to view the Milky Way, the Big Dipper, Orion in its regal commanding splendor, and even the Southern Cross. And then, of course, there is the morning star. Each planet, star, and constellation visible to the human eye declares a wonderful message of God's grace to His children on earth. One particular morning, upon waking and going to my usual place of praise, I was arrested by the observable phenomenon of being able to view the Southern Cross directly in front of me. What a sight!

Immediately I was propelled to Calvary and what Jesus had accomplished there for me. My mind was captivated by the fact that the heavens declare His everlasting love to all the inhabitants of planet earth.

My gazing into the heavens revealed another striking heavenly body, the morning star. This planet, Venus, continually reminds me of the faithfulness of God. When I gaze into the skies in the morning there is Venus, and when in wonder I look at the evening sky, Venus is still there—the evening star. I am encouraged today for my Father is faithful. He will keep His word. I can depend on Him morning and evening and all through the day. He is always there. "For great is your love, higher than the heavens; your faithfulness reaches to the skies" (Ps. 108:4, NIV).

I looked a little longer and noticed the constellation Orion in all its magnificence. A burst of gratitude and hope flooded my mind, for I remembered that it is through the opening in the belt of Orion that Jesus will make His second entrance back to earth. Life, as we experience it, will not continue forever. Glory to God! The heavens declare that soon and very soon Jesus will come and rescue all His children.

Thank You, Lord, for speaking to me from the heavens! Thank You that because of Your sacrifice on Calvary's cross, I can be assured of Your faithfulness to me. Thank You for the living hope in Your return to take me to live with You forever and ever in the new heavens and new earth. I love You!

Claudette Joy Andrews

The Invisible Help

And God blessed the seventh day and made it holy, because on it he rested from all the work of creating that he had done.
Gen. 2:3, NIV.

IT IS 7:00 FRIDAY MORNING. The children have left the house and I am thinking about the coming day. There is so much to be done. I will never be able to manage everything; I need help. In my devotions I feel peace flood my heart, and I can begin my day.

I quickly prepare the bread dough. I want my family to have a good supper tonight. Before I go out with the dog I manage to clean the bathroom. Now I can go out with the dog. Just then, the telephone rings. Should I pick it up? I don't have the time! But my hand is already on the receiver. "Hi. I just had to call and tell you all I have on my heart. Do you have time?" *Oh Lord, please give me time!*

Finally, half an hour later the dog gets out. Never mind, it will just be a short walk. But an hour passes before I return, held up by a neighbor who tells me he has been diagnosed with cancer.

I make a cake, prepare tomorrow's meal, and set potatoes to boil for today's lunch. The children come home from school. They give me their sandwich boxes and water bottles, information notes for parents, and tests to sign. After lunch the children do their homework. Later I'll need to check on that as well. In spite of all this, the kitchen is finally clean.

My husband arrives home from work: "Darling, I'll vacuum the upper floor." Wonderful—I only need to vacuum downstairs and mop the floors. When I finish, the children have already taken their baths. I look at my watch. Has time stood still? I still have an hour until sundown. I can prepare a nice supper and mentally prepare myself for Sabbath.

How often I don't manage to finish my work and get at the important things until late in the night. But again and again I notice that my work gets done more quickly on Fridays, particularly when I take time to listen to the cares of other people. In the desert wilderness God helped His people prepare for the Sabbath; a double portion of manna fell from heaven on Fridays, and it was preserved for twice as long as on other days. I experience this today. I receive a Sabbath blessing already on Friday because God helps me with my preparation. Thus I can celebrate the Sabbath with a thankful heart.

Heike Steinebach

Not Meant to Be

The Lord directs the steps of the godly. He delights in every detail of their lives.
Ps. 37:23, NLT.

A BLAST OF CRISP, early morning air energized me as I packed my suit-cases into the car. It was 3:00 a.m., and I was on my way to a national conference where I would present a paper and attend several breakout sessions. Several former classmates would be there, and the whole experience held great potential for lasting memories.

Getting to the airport was uneventful. At the terminal there were few attendants, but several self-check-in stations. But when I typed in my travel information the computer screen flashed a warning message: *Error. Use handset and talk with an agent.* I tried again, hoping for a different result—maybe I had mistyped something the first time. The result was the same. Suddenly I saw a uniformed man, someone who represented the airline. "Sir, I am getting an error message when I enter my information. Could you—"

"You need to see a ticket agent, Ma'am," he retorted, and kept on his way.

By now I saw that several others were experiencing a similar problem with the check-in stations and the lines to live agents were very long. With great anxiety and frustration, I joined a line. As the time for my departure drew closer, my anxiety level rose, especially when I realized that I still had to go through security.

I missed the 7:38 a.m. flight, and was graciously confirmed on a 10:40 flight. But the 10:40 a.m. flight was overbooked, so I was bumped to a 1:10 p.m. flight. The 1:10 flight was delayed to 3:02, then to 4:02, and was finally cancelled. A snowstorm hit the city and all outbound flights to New Jersey were cancelled for that night and the following day.

I never made it to my destination, although my luggage did. I finally returned home, after more than 21 hours in the airport terminal, two shuttle rides of 180 miles (290 kilometers), and a 70-mile (113-kilometer) round trip car ride. I pondered why the best laid plans sometimes go wrong without any rhyme or reason. Our plans look good on paper, but unforeseen circumstances turn things upside down. I realized that there are times when life's events are so extreme we have to believe that God has a reason for allowing them. If He truly orders our steps, then we can only take delight in knowing that we are firmly and securely in His care.

Faith-Ann McGarrell

When Being Late Became a Blessing

For he shall give his angels charge over thee, to keep thee in all thy ways.
Ps. 91:11.

I WAS A NEW TEACHER at a costly private school, and as such I constantly did my best to follow every rule and procedure. One strict rule was that all homeroom teachers had to be in their classrooms by 7:05 a.m. to receive the students. I was always on time, and I would sigh as the supervisor walked down the hallway just a few moments before some of the other teachers got to their rooms.

One Monday morning I wanted to get something printed before class. I had enough time to print my papers and rush to my classroom, but the printer refused to budge. I started getting desperate and tried again and again, but to no avail. Two coworkers saw my dilemma and came over to help, but instead of printing my document it kept printing a page somebody else had been trying to print earlier. Now we had about six copies of this other teacher's document, and not one copy of mine. We tried everything we could think of, but the printer refused to print my pages. I glanced at my watch. It was already 7:15! I couldn't believe I had been fighting with this printer for more than 15 minutes. I thanked the women who had tried to help, and half ran to room 7B. I knew I was late.

As soon as I got near the door I heard excited voices and the crunching sound of shoes stepping on glass. One of the long tube-type fluorescent bulbs had fallen out of its fixture and dropped right on my desk. The area was covered in broken glass and dust. It took awhile for the full impact of what had just happened to sink in. If the printer in the teacher's lounge had not started acting up, I would have been seated at that desk. I could not even begin to imagine the consequences of getting hit by that large falling bulb, not to mention the damage that would have been caused by broken glass and mercury inhalation.

Our God is indeed awesome and His protection and mercy have no bounds. The next time you are tempted to complain when unforeseen circumstances keep you from fulfilling your plans, remember that you don't know what's going on behind the scenes. Paul was in no danger of being hit by falling fluorescent bulbs, but he was certainly right when he wrote, "Give thanks in all circumstances, for this is God's will for you in Christ Jesus" (1 Thess. 5:18, NIV).

Dinorah Blackman

The Great Physician

And He said to her, "Daughter, be of good cheer;
your faith has made you well. Go in peace."
Luke 8:48, NKJV.

WHILE SITTING IN THE DOCTOR'S OFFICE, I thought about Jesus as the great physician. He took the ordinary, simple methods and made extraordinary and practical cures. He knew each patient's medical history without having to look through a chart or giving the patient a physical examination. He did not need an office in order to prescribe or determine a patient's illness. He did not belong to or support pharmaceutical companies. His patients had no need of antibiotics or pills with side effects. He had His own salve made of spit and mud. With the touch of His hand, the sound of His voice, the lame could walk, the blind could see, and the dead lived again. There was no psychiatrist's couch—He spoke with authority and the troubled and mentally ill were whole again.

He specialized in humanity, and healed with divinity. His patients did not need medical coverage; each visit came with no charge. In fact, Jesus made house calls. He healed without discrimination. He healed the poor and rich, the farmer and government worker. I'm amazed by the story of the woman with the issue of blood. She had suffered pain and discomfort for 12 years. Sick and weak, she spent time and money going to doctors and every kind of specialist—with no results. She was ritually isolated from her family and community. She had no place else to turn. Then she heard of Jesus and the miracles He performed. This gave her hope. She regained her faith, and while walking through a heavy crowd of people she touched the hem of Jesus' garment. Immediately, she knew she was healed. Jesus, too, knew that healing power had flowed out from Him. Her faith was so great that touching His clothing, tarnished by dust and mud, actually healed her.

Jesus has the healing power we need today. He knows how many hairs we have on our heads, He knew us before we were conceived, and He knows our inner thoughts and feelings. The miracles He did in the past, He is able to do now in our lives—as long as we believe.

Father, today I pray that You heal me with Your loving touch. I believe, and have faith that You can make me whole.

Diantha Hall-Smith

When God Speaks

I will lift up mine eyes unto the hills, from whence cometh my help.
My help cometh from the Lord, which made heaven and earth.
Ps. 121:1, 2.

IT HAD BEEN A LONG FLIGHT. Now we were landing in the little landlocked kingdom of Nepal, home of the mythical snow leopard and the tallest mountain in the world.

In the vehicle taking us to the house that would be home for the next several years, I took in the scenery, and because I didn't want to take the chance of being called an ugly American, leaned in close to my husband and said in a low voice, "I am not going to like this place. Look! The cows are in the middle of the street. The monkeys are eating on the sidewalks oblivious of the people." He just smiled and whispered in my ear, "Just wait. Give it time."

Arriving at the house, I checked out every room. The bedrooms were on the first floor, while the living room, kitchen, and dining room were upstairs. "I told you I wasn't going to like this place," I announced. "This is an upside-down house! Who ever heard of a house with all the bedrooms on the first floor!" Then I walked out on the veranda leading from the living room, and right before my eyes was the incredible, majestic Mount Everest, with its snow-capped peaks standing like a monument in time. I was speechless. Suddenly I saw things from a new perspective. I believe God was telling me to embrace differences.

Soon we joined others trekking around Katmandu. I couldn't believe the beauty of the rolling hills and green valleys filled with yellow mustard fields. Young girls carrying water pots and old men sitting on porches smoking long pipes presented a rich tapestry that would tickle the palette of pen or brush. The beauty and diversity of these gentle people will remain with me always.

Every day I put on my walking shoes and hit the hilly streets; that is, except the days my Nepali language guru came. Even then, I took my daily peep at the tallest mountain in the world. The mountain had a language of its own. It spoke the language of strength, endurance, and timeless being. Then came the morning that I couldn't see the mountain when I looked toward the "hills." Fog and clouds covered it, but I knew it was there. Like Mount Everest, God is always there even though we can't see Him. He has promised He would never leave nor forsake us, and He won't. He is always there.

Gustavia Raymond-Smith

Fathers Are the Best

*Fathers, do not exasperate your children; instead, bring them up in
the training and instruction of the Lord.*
Eph. 6:4, NIV.

I GET A BIT SENTIMENTAL when it comes to thinking about Father's Day.
My memories of my father include sitting on his lap as he read wonderful
stories to me. It was while he read to me that I learned to read. The words
on the page began to take shape for me as I asked him about the letters.
Because of this, I was reading quite fluently before I attended school.

Darrell also read to our children and often told them adventurous
stories about when he was a boy. Rod would settle into his comfortable
position on Dad's lap and say, "Tell me a story about when you were a little boy."
One story was never enough. It was always, "Another please."

Peggy was less than 2 years old when she would go with her Daddy for a day's
adventure. Taking along her little lunchbox with her sandwich and raisins, she
could hardly wait to get to the end of the driveway before she wanted to eat. Those
were special times when she had Daddy all to herself.

More memories were made the times that the kids went to town to go shopping
with their dad. Judy and her dad always had (and still have) a joke between them
that she did not bring her purse so she needed Dad's billfold when she went to buy
something. As soon as each kid got a driver's license their dad would race them to
see who got the backseat and who had to drive. Today he just hands them the keys,
then climbs in the backseat.

Grandfathers have the same warm place in our memory books. Grandpas
didn't tell about the times the kids did something they shouldn't have been doing.
They were loyal allies. Life with our fathers and grandfathers has been delightful as
they made our days interesting and fun.

Our children are now grown, and the memories of working and playing with
them are even more precious to all. After a time, the only thing we have left of our
own fathers is the memories we made with them. Let's spend this week and every
week creating special times and memories with the fathers in our lives. The homes
with fathers who are attentive, kind, and thoughtful, with a good dose of humor
and laughter mixed in, are a little bit of heaven on earth.

Evelyn Glass

Do Not Judge

Do nothing out of selfish ambition or vain conceit, but in humility
consider others better than yourselves.
Phil. 2:3, NIV.

MY HUSBAND AND I were on a summer road trip. One morning we sat in the breakfast room of a hotel, and while I enjoyed my breakfast, I observed the people around me.

There were thick ones and thin ones, younger and older ones, and I started evaluating them all. *The sleeves of his blazer are too long. Her shoes are too big. And that lady is wearing too much jewelry. That person is as stiff as a stick.* I continued in this vein until I stopped and asked myself, *What on earth am I doing? And what is my motive?* My self-analysis showed me that the real reason was to make myself look better. *I am perfect; I'm dressed just right for traveling,* and so on. But am I so insecure that *my* self–esteem is dependent on how other people look? Must I measure my worth against the scale of others? Am I not valuable on my own?

Of course I know that my worth does not depend on anything: not my position, my profession, nor that I'm a particularly good mother or grandmother. And yet it seems that inherent in us is the wish to be better than others. We think we need this affirmation for our self-esteem.

But we don't. We have a Father in heaven who, again and again, tells us through the Bible how valuable we are in His eyes. We are so precious that He died for us and did not want to leave us here on earth alone. It was, and is, His desire to be together with us and to enable us to live in liberty. A part of this freedom is the consciousness of the worth of every person in themselves. Thus we are valuable from the moment we are born, and we keep this worth independently of what we do or don't do.

I often forget that I am of value just because God made me. Maybe I should stick a big note on my mirror: "You are valuable even though you might not like your looks just now."

After breakfast I asked my heavenly Father to forgive me for my arrogance toward the other hotel guests, and I prayed for a new attitude and behavior toward my neighbors and myself.

Dear Lord Jesus, help me to realize that in Your eyes I am always valuable, and forgive me if I try to find my worth at the expense of others.

Claudia DeJong

A World Full of Strangeness

For the Lord shall rise up as in mount Perazim, he shall be wroth as in the valley of Gibeon, that he may do his work, his strange work; and bring to pass his act, his strange act.
Isa. 28:21.

QUITE OFTEN in the evening when I am driving home from work or visiting my daughter, I hear parts of a musical program on the radio. My tape deck does not work and one day I was glad. Anyone can phone in and request a song to be played for someone or dedicate it to their friend or loved one. The host, Delilah, is a spiritual woman, or so I assume. She encourages people to think positively. She says, "Bless your soul," and often talks about God and what He has done for her. She encourages listeners to reach out to the Lord to help them in times of trials, sickness, or indecision. She plays uplifting music—even if sometimes it is on the country rock side.

On this one particular night, on air, a caller told her how he enjoyed listening to her music and her words of hope before he went to bed. He said to her, "You give us encouragement and hope in a world full of strangeness." I thought about what he said for many days.

My husband, at one time, said I was strange. You see, in July, 1995, I went on a vacation and came back a Christian—with "strange" ideas. I did not like his secular movies and western music anymore. But I did not think I was strange. I had simply found a better way of life in following the Lord. But he thought I was different—strange.

Yes, this world is full of "strange" ideas, values, and ways of living. In my Bible concordance I find listed many things after the word strange: apparel, cities, countries, fires, flesh, nations, lips, lands, punishment, language, waters, speech, wives—and more. I looked them all up. They were very interesting.

The Bible says God will perform His strange act of appearing as a warrior to subdue His enemies and all will see Him acting in a role that is vastly different from anything they have ever known before. "And I saw heaven opened, and behold a white horse; and he that sat upon him was called Faithful and True, and in righteousness he doth judge and make war" (Rev. 19:11). He will come as "King of kings, and Lord of lords" (Rev. 19:16). I am looking forward to that strange event. I am sure it will be very beautiful and not at all strange. How do I know? Because the Bible tells me so.

Vidella McClellan

Vacation Anyone?

*Wait on the Lord: be of good courage, and he shall strengthen
thine heart: wait, I say, on the Lord.*
Ps. 27:14.

IN 2008, MY FAMILY had two grand events to celebrate: my sister and brother-in-law's twentieth wedding anniversary and my father's seventieth birthday.

We thought it would be nice to celebrate the two together even though they were in different months. After tossing ideas around, my sister decided that they would make their yearly trip to Nassau, my brother-in-law's home, their celebration. And as my dad had done in the past, he and his wife would go with them.

For several years I'd wanted to go too, but never could afford the trip. But since this was a special year and a special celebration, I decided I'd do it. I booked the hotel and almost fainted at the cost! Only if I could find a "cheap" airfare would I be able to celebrate with them in July.

I checked the airfare daily and prayed that the price would drop. I hadn't had a true vacation since 1994, so I was really looking forward to this trip. You may recall that in 2008, gasoline sold at record highs of almost $4 per gallon, and the cost of food was soaring. Maybe this wouldn't be the year for my vacation after all.

I prayed and talked to the Lord. I told Him that it did not sit well with me to spend that much money on a vacation. He either had to lower the airfare or give me peace about spending the money. For the past 100 days the round trip airfare to Nassau from my hometown had not gone below $450. I wanted a fare under $300 and had faith that God would provide. It did start to go down, but not low enough. At last I gave it two more weeks. After that I'd resign myself to not taking the trip. One day I checked the fare morning and evening—it had gone up $38! Wrong way! Then I checked another website and couldn't believe my eyes when I read $299. Going directly to the airline's website, I put in my dates and was completely floored when the price came up at $288.80!

Once again God had "hugged" me and had given me the desires of my heart. That night the tears flowed as I thanked Him in prayer. So I ask, do you know my heavenly Father? Have you experienced His love? Are you anxiously waiting for His return?

Angèle Peterson

Barn Swallow Eggs

Ye are of more value than many sparrows.
Matt. 10:31.

IT WAS THE SUMMER of 1952. We'd finished our Sabbath dinner. The dishes were done and the dish towels hung across the dish rack to dry. The men were in the living room talking about cattle and hay and the women talked of quilts and canning tomatoes. As I made my way outdoors the screen door slammed behind me. It was discretionary time. All week we had worked in the hayfield, but today was the "Day of Rest and Gladness." The drizzle hit my cheeks and stood in little beads on my long brown braids. The younger kids were playing under foot in the house. What was this 13-year-old from the city to do on a drizzly Sabbath afternoon on a Missouri farm?

The city was always clamoring. Our house, only three doors away from the emergency room of the large hospital in downtown Los Angeles, was haunted constantly by the wail of emergency vehicles. Gangs roamed the streets, and an adolescent girl wasn't even safe on a bicycle in broad daylight. But here it was safe. The doors remained unlocked day and night. The pretentiousness of the city was put aside, and I was free.

I wandered toward the barn. Swallows! They had a nest in the hayloft. I wondered if the eggs had hatched yet. I climbed the ladder to the hayloft and peeked into the nest. The sweet smell of hay was comfortable. The pounding of rain on the barn's tin roof told me there was no use to venture outside. I lifted one little egg into my hand. To my delight I saw that it was cracking. The tiny creature inside was trying to find his way out. I was entranced! Gently holding the fragile egg in my hand, I seated myself in the haymow to watch. Slowly at first, the little creature began to peck and push his way out of the shell. I waited At last the little naked bird lay vulnerable in my hand.

Singing from the nearby house floated softly to the loft. It was peaceful. "His eye is on the sparrow, and I know He watches me." I understood. I knew He was holding me gently in His hand, watching me hatch, too. I carefully placed the baby bird into the nest and climbed back down the ladder. The rain had stopped and the slant of the sun peeking through the clouds beckoned the near close of the Sabbath. I went back into the house and sat on the arm of the big chair and joined my voice with my uncle's. "He's got the whole world in His hand!"

Elizabeth Boyd

Unexpected Help

Delight yourself also in the Lord, and He shall give you the desires of your heart.
Ps. 37:4, NKJV.

I AM THE YOUNGEST of nine children. My father had a mental breakdown when I was a baby, and when I was 9 months old he was admitted to a mental hospital where he remained for eight long years. This was during the great depression of the early 1930s, and obviously, we were poor. The older children quit school and found jobs to help keep the family together.

All my life I wanted to be a nurse. It was the uppermost thought in my mind as far back as I can remember. But there were so many challenges that the goal seemed almost impossible. However, I never gave up working toward it. I had to work to pay my way through Christian schools and then managed to go to college for a year, taking the pre-nursing courses. I worked through the summer to pay off the bill.

Finally, I saw my way clear to apply to nursing school though I didn't know how I would finance it. I worked as a nurse's aide in a small hospital and saved every penny I could. I was accepted at the nursing school of my choice and prepared to go, but still did not have nearly the financing I needed.

I prayed earnestly about this and left it in the hands of the Lord. While on duty one day, I was late getting to the hospital cafeteria for lunch. Only one person was left there, the hospital business manager. I got my food and went and sat at the table with him. I had not spoken to him or anyone else at the hospital about my financial need. But to my surprise he suddenly said, "Delores, the hospital director and I have been talking. We know you need more money to go into nurses training." With that, he pulled out a large piece of paper and handed it to me. He said, "If you agree with this, just sign it, and we will send you money whenever you need it. When you finish your nurses' training, you must come back here to work and pay off the loan with no interest."

Wow! *Thank You, Lord,* I silently prayed. *I knew You would help me.* Of course I signed the paper, and what a blessing it was to me as I drew from the loan to pay my way home for vacations and for my other needs. Psalm 37:4 has always been so dear to my heart. The Lord, indeed, did give me the desire of my heart.

Delores Pohle Master

Weeds of Life

And he shall be like a tree planted by the rivers of water, that bringeth forth his fruit in his season; his leaf also shall not wither; and whatsoever he doeth shall prosper.
Ps.1:3.

AFTER RETURNING from a whirlwind excursion that took me to London, Kenya, Tanzania, and Dubai, then, at last, to France, I found 3-foot-tall weeds awaiting me at home. Wow! How is it possible that these weeds took root and grew so tall in just a month? I'd hoped that the perennials I planted the year before would have resurfaced. But I quickly realized that hope without action is hopeless. It amazes me that weeds grow without any prompting or cultivation and their roots grow deep and wide.

Sometimes in our relationships we find weeds growing where we never planted them. These weeds can cause strife, division, and eventually disaster. It reminds me of Jesus' parable about the man who went out to sow seeds: "And some fell among thorns; and the thorns sprung up, and choked them" (Matt. 13:7). Some of my friends who truly enjoy gardening, speak of the joys of weeding, of uprooting those sprawling critters before they take over. They describe the experience as cathartic! There is nothing else they enjoy more. Somehow, I could never relate as I prefer to work indoors. But good stewards must work where needed and not necessarily where they want.

This object lesson has taught me to be intentional in what I want in my life. If I want peace, I must plant seeds of peace. If I want love, I must plant seeds of love. If I want joy, unspeakable joy, I must plant seeds of joy. If I want sound friendships, I must plant seeds that beget friends. If I want financial solvency, I must plant seeds of wise stewardship. If I want wisdom, I must plant seeds of wisdom. If I want transforming, positive changes in this world, I must be the change I want to see. Whatever the desire, it requires that I be intentional in my actions. Otherwise, weeds of doubt, despair, lack, loneliness, and folly will overtake the good. Today I am intentional in my desire to plant seeds of love, joy, peace, meekness, kindness, friendship, good stewardship, and knowledge. And so I do preventative care, pulling up the weeds that hide and choke these qualities of life. Ugh!

Be blessed. I intentionally choose to be.

Lady Dana Austin

My Own King Asa

Asa did good and right in the sight of the Lord his God.
2 Chron. 14:2, NASB.

I STARED WITH A SENSE OF GUILT at the contact card sitting on the hutch shelf in my dining room. It had been sitting there for weeks, maybe months. I am busy with two young daughters, I excused myself. All right, the truth was I was scared to call someone I didn't know. I had accepted the card one Sabbath afternoon after church with good intentions, but being a new Christian my heart was a little ahead of my courage.

Finally one day the Holy Spirit won, and I made the call. A gentleman answered, and through the course of our conversation I learned he was the dad of the man named on the card I held. When I hung up I had an appointment to meet and bring him some literature. I was so glad I had made the contact.

Asa was a sickly-looking man in his mid-sixties. He was very thin and had to use oxygen to aid his breathing. His appearance was rough, but I saw him as a gentle man who loved his Lord. This was the beginning of a precious friendship that lasted several years. I would tease him and call him King Asa after good King Asa in the Bible.

After my children were in bed, Asa would call and say, "Joanie, talk to me about Jesus!"

We would laugh, cry, encourage each other, and pray together. He was a tremendous blessing in my life, and I was grateful to God for such a precious friend.

I visited him and had Bible studies as often as possible. But as life seems to have it, things changed. Asa was sick with emphysema, and the prognosis was not good. He eventually became more ill. One day he told me that just three days before my first call, he had prayed that God would send someone to teach him about God and the Bible. Remember how long that card sat on the shelf because of my fear and immature faith? It was very humbling to be the answer to someone's prayer!

Not long after this, Asa went to sleep in Jesus. Oh, he never joined my church or accepted all of what I shared with him, but I believe that when Asa awakens one day, the first thing he will see is the face of his Savior. He, and what I learned from him, will always remain in my heart and memory as a precious gift from God.

Joan Green

My Final Home

In my Father's house. John 14:2.

An house not made with hands. 2 Cor. 5:1.

Whose builder and maker is God. Heb. 11:10, NKJV.

WHEN I WAS A LITTLE GIRL our family lived in a bamboo and nipa house by the seashore in the Philippines. One day when my siblings and I came home from school we saw big waves crashing over the beach. Worse than that—our house was not there. Other homes had also disappeared. A tidal wave had washed away all the homes around the area. We were homeless, but my big brothers quickly helped build a new home for us.

When I was about 10 years old we moved into a bigger, wooden house. It had four big posts in concrete foundations.

I have lived in many more houses as family changes and jobs necessitated. We had no choice. We stayed in apartments, mobile homes, and substandard houses.

The birth of our last baby made six of us. For a while we lived in a one-bedroom home among the pines in Tucson. We eventually moved into a house with four bedrooms. In California, we rented a three-bedroom apartment and eventually bought a house within walking distance of my job. When we moved to Virginia, our backyard was on a scenic lake and the yard had a gazebo. Friends and neighbors shared fruit and vegetables when available. We were very glad we bought the property. Friends and relatives also enjoyed fishing in the lake.

Now our last home, considered the best, is all concrete. It has two stories overlooking the ocean. On one side there are coconut trees, other fruit trees, and green vegetables. Along another side is a river. The area is landscaped with exotic plants of different colors which blend well with the river rocks. The garden needs no regular sprinklers, but occasionally is watered manually from the well. Rain is frequent and water is abundant.

We consider this property a wonderful blessing from the Lord. So we have dedicated this home, not only to our family, but to missionaries and others who need shelter.

God has a promise for all who believe. We are just temporary residents in these unpredictable dwellings on earth. He has prepared our final home for us in heaven.

Esperanza Aquino Mopera

Journaling Joys

Write this as a memorial in a book.
Ex. 17:14, ESV.

"RITA, WILL YOU SPEAK to the ladies about journaling when we get together for our brunch on Sunday?" Daisy asked me.

I said I'd be glad to, and my mind flashed back to the first time I heard about journaling. My son's first–grade teacher, Mrs. Giem, told me what a blessing and a joy journaling had become to her and suggested that I do it. She didn't realize she was speaking to a new pastor's wife who had not been a church member long enough to understand what journaling entailed—nor would I ask. It sounded like work! I was busy and felt overwhelmed at even the sound of it.

God was patient. He waited about 13 years before suggesting it again, and in an unusual way. While visiting my mom before I moved to Alaska, she said, "Rita, you must start recording your time in Alaska. You're going to experience things that you won't want to forget—but you will unless you record them." It sounded like a good idea. Thus the first journal began as somewhat of a diary. Then at a women's retreat I heard Juanita Kretschmar share the joys and blessings of journaling and claiming promises as part of our daily devotionals. I was starting to get it.

Something else happened. On another visit to Mom's, she showed me a piece of paper that had been left in my great-grandmother's Bible. On it she had written: "Fitchburg, California, Nov. 18, 1910. Have finished reading my Bible through the sixth time and hope, my dear children, you will love to read the Bible. Without Bible reading, you cannot feel you are near God." The entries continued until 1918, the year of her death. I thought this was a great idea. Thus I made my first entry: "June 30, 1996–Anchorage, Alaska. I completed reading my Bible completely through for the first time! Just as my great-grandmother recorded her completions of reading the Bible in her Bible so shall I. What a blessing."

Now 13 years and well over 20 journals later, in June, 2008, I recorded my thirteenth reading of the entire Bible! These journals contain promises, almost-forgotten events that bring encouragement when reread, conversations with God during both good and bad times, miraculous answers to prayers, and prayer requests still on the waiting list. I encourage any of you reading this devotional to ask God to direct you as you begin or continue the journey of journaling.

Rita Kay Stevens

You Are Being Watched

For He shall give His angels charge over you, to keep you in all your ways.
Ps. 92:11, NKJV.

The angel of the Lord encampeth round about them that fear him, and delivereth them.
Ps. 34:7.

ARE YOU BEING WATCHED? And if so, by whom? The concept of being watched is good, as long as we are being watched by the right watchmen: our loving Lord, or our guardian angels. Have you ever been in a community that has an active Neighborhood Watch? You'll likely see a sign posted with these words: "You are being watched." While this sign points us to a temporal watchman, our text points us to a spiritual watchman whose presence is not always visible but tangible nonetheless.

We never know who is watching us. But I know firsthand what it means to be watched by God. Many occasions in my life have given me this experience. I vividly remember something that happened when I was attending school in Canada. One morning, in a split second or two, I was saved from being hit at a pedestrian crossing. Feeling assured that I had looked to my right, and to my left, I began to cross—when I was literally pulled back a few inches. With my head now facing left, I saw a huge van racing down the street. It passed just inches away from me, at full speed. The angels of God guarded me that morning.

When Hagar fled from her mistress to the desert, she became aware of God's watch care over her. "'You are the God who sees me,' for she said, 'I have now seen the One who sees me'" (Gen. 16:13, NIV). Since the very beginning, He has been the God who watches over us.

He tenaciously watches you and me during a variety of times and moments: moments of helplessness and hopelessness, moments of pain and pressure, moments of instability and indecision, moments of fear and failure, moments of sickness and sadness. And that's not all; He also watches over us during moments of success, triumph, peace, joy, happiness, and of course, any other terrific moments in our lives. His jealous guardianship over us is of an intimate nature and should be equally guarded by us.

As we revel in the reality that we are being watched by our omnipresent Father, it gives us the courage we need to keep a stable stance in this world that has so many watchers. *Lord, thanks for watching me.*

Althea Y. Boxx

The Children We Did Not Know

But Jesus said, Suffer little children, and forbid them not, to come unto me:
for of such is the kingdom of heaven.
Matt. 19:14.

WHEN GOOD OPPORTUNITIES ARISE, one cannot help but grasp them if the focus and desires are to serve God. A few years ago encouraging and cheering hundreds of children through outreach ventures was the last thought on my mind, but my path changed and I was afforded the opportunity to organize and coordinate such an activity. Thinking about it now, I wonder, was it a lifesaver, a second chance, destiny, or a gift that I never knew I possessed and was therefore called upon to utilize in a major way? Whatever the answer, the experience, rewards, and benefits far outlived the many questions I had. I say this with confidence because I believe my heavenly Father is in control and has been and is taking care of the needs of all those children I did not know before.

I had the privilege to lead the ladies in my dorm to do a community project of reaching out and touching the lives of some special children. For months we spent time making contact with all the children's homes in the parish where I worked, as well as the children's ward at the town hospital. We collected books and toys from companies, bookstores, and individuals. The project took its toll on us because we had our regular activities to perform as well, and many times we were tired, but we kept on going.

The day came when everyone gathered together for the big event of handing the gifts to these special children. Beautiful songs were sung, readings and poems recited, expressions of thanks were given, and there were smiles on all the faces. It is a day I will always remember. *What better ministry is there than to reach out and touch the lives of those who need our love and care?* I thought to myself. Books are some of the most precious gifts one can give. There is life in books, there is life in reading. And Jesus said, "Suffer little children, and forbid them not, to come unto me: for of such is the kingdom of heaven" (Matt. 19:14).

Dear heavenly Father, as we reach out and touch the lives of others, help us to do so with a pure and loving heart, not concerned about our own comfort and reward, but to bless others as You would. Through Jesus' name I pray and say thanks.

Elizabeth Ida Cain

The Beauty of It All

And the apostles said unto the Lord, Increase our faith.
Luke 17:5.

"WELL, BABY, I'll tell you like this. If you have faith and believe the Lord is all powerful, ask Him, in the name of Jesus, to restore Pete's eyesight. Don't give up," Aunt Annie told me. "Ask Him every day like you believe!" I took her seriously, and made this a part of my daily prayer.

Ten years ago Pete and I sat in the ophthalmologist's office as she examined his eyes. Both the specialist and an intern working with her asked questions as they looked into his eyes. After several tests, the doctor said she wanted Pete to have an ERG (electroretinogram) because she believed he had an eye disease called retinitis pigmentosa; the only way to be sure was to take the test. So Pete had the test, and we prayed until the results came back. The test was positive for RP, a hereditary eye disease that eventually causes blindness. However, because it was diagnosed in the later years of Pete's life, the doctor said chances were he would probably not completely lose his eyesight.

We have been blessed through the years. Pete is legally sightless, but he still cooks, cleans, washes clothes, plants his garden, and takes care of his goats, dogs, and cats! He enjoys having people read the Bible to him. I continue to pray for Pete, and thank God while watching Him act in His time. Pete and I relocated to the southern part of the United States. As the Lord would have it, a year ago my brother said he wanted to get out of the big city when he retired—and he did. We were shocked and elated! He said his main reason for moving to where we live was to help his sister and brother-in-law. What a blessing! It's awesome watching God at work, but this was just the beginning.

I had been wearing glasses since I was 3. Some time ago my ophthalmologist mentioned that I had cataracts and they would need to be removed soon. Well, "soon" came a year later. I had the surgery on my right eye and two weeks later on my left. Guess what? Today I can see 20/20 out of my left eye without my glasses! I use my glasses for reading only—which is constantly—because I love to read. I feel I have received that extra eyesight to make up for the loss of Pete's vision. I am able to truly be his extra set of eyes.

We never know what the Lord has in store for us. I continue to pray for a renewal of our relationship, and Pete's eyesight, physically as well as spiritually.

Elaine J. Johnson

Choices

To learn, you must love discipline.
Prov. 12:1, NLT.

THERE ARE THREE THINGS I've learned concerning accidents. They are never planned (or they wouldn't be called accidents), they come at the worst possible times, and they usually surprise those involved.

My surprise came the Friday before a three-day holiday. While I was driving toward my home the car behind me suddenly stopped—when it hit the back of my car. After proper medical attention and later, physical therapy, I was given permission to resume my normal activities. However, the doctor stressed the importance of maintaining the exercise program the physical therapist had given me. Exercising is not new to me, but the therapist's regime seemed boring.

At home, before beginning my workout, I thought it would be time efficient to first put a load of clothes in the washing machine. So I did. Then, a couple of minutes into my routine I remembered that the garbage needed to be taken out. Since trash pickup was only two days away, the urgency to act was immediate. I emptied all the wastebaskets in the house and garage into the big container the disposal company provides.

The good intentions to restart my workout screeched to a halt when the phone rang. A friend had a question and needed some information. By the time we discussed the situation and finished our conversation, it was almost time for lunch. I felt it best to get a little nourishment before restarting my exercise routine. Deciding that it might not be wise to exercise on a full stomach, I finished eating and postponed my workout awhile longer. You can probably guess what didn't happen that day.

God has graciously given us the power of choice and the gift of time. Although procrastination is tempting when the job may be unpleasant, we eventually need to make a decision. Whatever we elect to do will cost us time. Our choice will often depend on what we want the most. And some choices are harder to make than others.

However, when we do our best to please the Lord, He will, when we ask, equip us with what we need to complete the task at hand. Even with such mundane things as maintaining an exercise program.

Marcia Mollenkopf

Learning to Live With the Old and the New

He said to them, "Therefore every teacher of the law who has been instructed about the kingdom of heaven is like the owner of a house who brings out of his storeroom new treasures as well as old."
Matt. 13:52, NIV.

I LOVE THE COLOR that flowers bring to a room. Although I've never had much ability and time to take care of gardens, after my marriage I promised myself that flowers would never be lacking in my home. I opted for the easiest solution: potted flowering plants, purchased in a flower shop or supermarket, and ready for display. I arranged them in beautiful pots so that when placed in my kitchen they promoted an atmosphere of joy and hope for better days. My great difficulty was to make them last more than two or three weeks. After that I could almost see them dying right before my eyes. It made me sad. I watered the plants, placed them in well-ventilated places where the sun could reach them, trimmed the leaves and dry stems, changed the soil, but nothing seemed to solve the problem. And so I'd buy new flowers and begin a new floral journey—again.

Then my husband and I moved to a pleasant new apartment. He wasn't totally pleased with it because he was accustomed to an enormous house. To improve the atmosphere and bring us in closer contact with nature, I bought flowers to place on the veranda, a beautiful place to read and study. The first week went by OK. The flowers were lovely. But as the second week progressed I noticed the beautiful vase of flowers was beginning to dry. It was time to cut the dry flowers and stems. With scissors in hand, I paused for a moment and thought, *Why not live with the old and new; flowers that are wilting with the flowers that are about to bloom?*

I believe this plan came from God. I was totally pleased living with this duality. I learned to wait for the divine time to be fulfilled without needing to discard my flowers—or other things in my life that I may consider old and am just waiting for something new to arrive. This lesson is especially important with things that God wants me to learn. As I think about my victory with those flowers and what the most important things are for me today, I realize that most of all, I need to hear the voice of God.

Thank You, Lord, because Your lessons from old are for now, and You do not scorn a heart in conflict.

Andrea de Almeida Santos

Riches and Glory

And my God shall supply all your need according
to His riches in glory . . . forever and ever. Amen.
Phil. 4:19, 20, NKJV.

WHEN I ARRIVED HOME from work and opened the front door I was greeted by a blast of stifling heat. Once again the air conditioner wasn't working. For the past several years I'd escaped having to purchase a new air conditioner by adding Freon® to the unit. But this time my usual service call ended with the dreaded words, "Ma'am, it looks like your compressor is going out, and this year adding Freon® isn't going to help."

In case you're not a native Missourian or have never visited Missouri during the summer, let me give you a brief overview of the weather in this Midwestern state. In Missouri, particularly St. Louis, the second week of July is the beginning of a humid, blistering inferno that lasts through the end of September.

As I remembered the estimate I received last year for a new air conditioner, I resigned myself to toughing it out and began planning my strategy for cooling the house. I reasoned that hot and cold air can't occupy the same space without one air mass being forced out, so I opened all the windows and doors and then turned on the ceiling fans. I was certain my plan would create a makeshift front—where two differing air masses would meet, turbulence would occur, and the hot air inside would be pushed out of the house, allowing the cool night air to float in. All night I lay in a pool of sweat waiting for the cool air to rush in. It never did.

After three nights of sweating with no relief, I called my brother to ask for his advice and, if needed, a loan. "Cheryol, I just bought a new unit for one of the houses I'm rehabbing, and last week I got my heating and cooling certification. You can be my third customer; I'll sell you the unit for what I paid for it. Now, it does have a dent in it, but it works fine. If you can pay me what I paid for it, including the cost of the Freon®, you have yourself a new air conditioner."

I was ecstatic! God gave me a new and bigger air conditioner for less than a thousand dollars! The next evening as I lay in bed, reflecting on how God put all the details in place just so He could supply my needs according to His standards—not mine—I wept, and thanked Him for once again taking care of His baby girl.

Cheryol Mitchell

The Little, Fat, Round Sheep

I am the good shepherd.
John 10:11, NIV.

MY DOG RICCO AND I were looking forward to a good long walk. We took a circular route along hedges and luscious fields. A blackbird sang its evening songs and the sun sent its last warming rays. After about 20 minutes the path descended into a valley, and bordering the path was a field surrounded by an electric fence that held a flock of sheep. I had passed these sheep many times, but now saw that one of them was lying on its back, its four legs stretched toward the sky. It didn't move. I knew that a sheep lying on its back cannot get on its legs by itself. This animal was in great danger and needed assistance. I wanted to find out if it was still alive, so said in a soft voice, "Try to get up." It moved its legs but was not able to right itself.

Quickly I took Ricco back home and tried to call the flock's owner. When I couldn't reach him, I went back to the sheep. *What should I do?* How long had this helpless creature been on its back? I didn't know. Then I prayed, "Lord, whom can I ask to help?" Nothing is impossible for God. And then I saw a red car further down the valley and realized that the man who owned the next plot was at his cabin. It was unlikely that he'd seen the plight of this sheep.

I had to call to him several times before he heard me. "What's wrong?" he asked.

"There's a sheep on its back over here. Please come and help," I called.

First we had to turn off the electricity, and I guarded the entrance to prevent the other scared sheep from running away. This neighbor is a strong man and he grabbed the sheep by its legs, pulled it over with a jerk, and the sheep stood on its own legs. It was a little, fat, round sheep. We were happy that it was still able to walk around. A week later the owner told me that this poor sheep had birthed twins. He had worried that the lambs might be born dead as the mother had lain so long on her back, but mom and babies were all in good health.

Thinking about this experience, I remembered the parables Jesus told about shepherds and sheep. Jesus wants to be our good shepherd. Like this sheep we are also in danger. In John 10 Jesus tells of a thief who comes to steal and kill. He also mentions a wolf that attacks the sheep and scatters them. Jesus wanted to remind us that Satan is after us day and night. If a shepherd takes good care of his sheep, how much more does Jesus care for us. This gives me comfort and hope.

Angelika Schöpf

A Child's Plea

Many sorrows shall be to the wicked; but he that trusts in the Lord, mercy shall surround him. Ps. 32:10, NKJV.

CHILDREN ARE A BLESSING, and we can learn so many lessons from them. Many years ago I had the opportunity of teaching science to elementary school children. I still remember their faces each time we did an experiment. For them the wonders of science were like magic. Although they probably did not grasp all the principles I was trying to convey, clearly they understood some, and that was inspiring to me.

But then one day we all learned a lesson. One of my students, a little boy, always found himself in trouble. His mischievous ways seemed to surface at the most inopportune times. Such as the day we were on the playground and the children had lined up to take turns on the swings. My mischievous small friend decided to break the line and jump in front of his classmates. Of course, the children would not have this and quickly retaliated with anger and shouting. As their teacher, I went right into action. "You know that wasn't right!" I told my misbehaving student.

His head now bowed and eyes barely able to look my direction, he muttered, "Teacher, I know I've been bad. Are you going to punish me?"

Before I could answer, one of the other children spoke up. "You're always in trouble, and if you don't stop, you'll grow up to be a bad person."

"I don't want to be a bad person," my mischievous student cried. "I'm sorry. Please forgive me."

What a lesson! Living a wicked life has consequences. We see this every day on the TV and in the newspapers. People commit crimes, and they are punished. Make no mistake: the Bible is very clear that the wages of sin is death (Rom. 6:23). But when we seek God's forgiveness, and trust that He will help us change our ways, His mercy intercedes and surrounds us with love and grace.

For a moment imagine that you're cold, very, very cold. Then someone offers you a warm, cozy blanket. Doesn't it feel good? That's how God's love is. When we trust Him, He puts His blanket of love and mercy around us.

Yvonne Curry Smallwood

The Lifter of My Head

But thou, O Lord, art a shield for me; my glory, and the lifter up of mine head.
Ps. 3:3.

DARK CLOUDS RACED across the sky and collided with each other, emptying buckets of water in a manner typical of that region during the summer. As I drove down the highway in an unfamiliar city my eyes were glued to the tail lights of the car in front of me even as I tried to keep a safe distance between us to avoid a collision should I have to suddenly apply the brakes. My mind was as turbulent as the sky.

I was returning home from the hospital where my husband lay struggling with the complications of a stroke. My sister had died the night before in my island home, and I had just received word that my daughter-in-law was in another area hospital suffering the miscarriage of her first pregnancy. I was filled with despair. The tears flowing down my cheeks rivaled the downpour on my windshield. Then I came to a traffic light and had to stop. When I raised my eyes to look at the signal, I saw it: a dark, angry cloud, but sunlight had formed a bright edge of light behind it. I thought, *Behind each dark cloud is a silver lining.*

Lifting my eyes a little higher I saw a ribbon of the brightest red between the dark clouds and the bright edge of light. Then I realized that the upper part of the car's windshield had a blue tinge. When I looked at the clouds through the untinted section, I saw dark clouds and bright lights. However, when my eyes were drawn upward to look through the blue-tinted section, the light rays revealed the red. A multitude of thoughts tumbled through my mind. The blood of Jesus! Everything seen through the blood is going to be all right! I began to praise God as I drove down the highway shouting at the top of my voice, "Hallelujah! Praise God. Everything is going to be all right."

On several different rainy afternoons in that city I have looked for that red tinge, but I've never seen it again. Truly God knows when to reveal His glory to lift up the head of His children who are bowed down in despair. "Lift your eyes and look to the heavens: Who created all these? He who brings out the starry host one by one, and calls them each by name. Because of his great power and mighty strength, not one of them is missing" (Isa. 40:26, NIV). What an awesome God He is.

Candace Sprauve

When God Answers No

Trust in the Lord with all your heart, and lean not on your own understanding;
in all your ways acknowledge Him, and He shall direct your paths.
Prov. 3:5, 6, NKJV.

ON AUGUST 3 of this year we would have celebrated our twenty-eighth wedding anniversary. How swiftly the years passed! We were married for less than five years when I became a single mother of two young children: a 3½-year-old and a 2-year-old.

Lord, what am I to do? I prayed, fasted, read my Bible daily, and meditated. *Speak to my heart, Lord Jesus, I don't know what to do.* These were often my lamentations to God. *Please fix my marriage. I can't do this alone.*

My prayers were answered God's way. I had to make quite a number of adjustments in my life. The very first was to learn to live on one income and to remain faithful in returning to God what was His. Then came the day when I knew that I must drive. I would no longer continue to have someone driving me and my babies around. I must make every effort to be independent—yet dependent on my Savior. Going to the PTA meetings, Pathfinder club meetings, choir practices, basketball games, after-school tutorials, all became a weekly routine that took some time getting used to. What a new world I'd entered.

Looking back over the years I thank God every day for His response to my request. He has truly been the Provider to me and my darling children. The struggles were enormous but I've learned to live on my knees and not allow the circumstances in my life to keep me down. Instead I've learned to make lemonade from the sour lemons that were thrown at me. This situation has drawn me closer to the Creator. We do serve an awesome God! He is the one who knows our beginnings and ends. He is the one who can rest in the boat while the storm of life rages. He gently carries us through the whirlwind of life's circumstances.

Today my daughters are both professionals in their chosen careers and are holding on to the hands of our God who changes not. When God answers "No" to your prayer request, trust Him with your whole heart. He has bigger plans for you.

My motto has been to let go and let God. Let Him take full control of your life. You will be amazed at what He can do for you.

Naomi J. Penn

The Heavenly Mechanic

*My dear children, I write this to you so that you will not sin. But if anybody does sin,
we have one who speaks to the Father in our defense—Jesus Christ, the Righteous One.
1 John 2:1, NIV.*

ONE SABBATH I responded to an appeal for volunteers who were interested in a visitation program, part of the preparation for an evangelistic
series. Sunday morning we assembled at the church where we prayed
before venturing out in pairs. Then we spent the next two hours going
from home to home. We met people, invited them to the meetings,
prayed with some, and tried to meet their needs. Afterward we re-
assembled at church to report on the contacts we had made.

I took a taxi home. Near a major intersection the vehicle jolted a few times then
came to a stop. What had happened? The driver checked under the hood. He tried
a number of times to restart the vehicle. He even tried to push-start the car, but still
it would not run. He finally called a mechanic, and I took another vehicle home.

I have since reflected on the incident and pondered the problems we can encounter as we travel on the highway to glory. Engine problems, punctures, even
running out of gas should not deter us. Get onto the soft shoulder of God's protective arm where you will be out of danger from other motorists. Then call heaven's
prayer line to the Divine Wrecker Service for assistance. You will be amazed at the
speedy reply from Christ, the chief mechanic. He will send the Holy Spirit and a
host of mechanics to help you. You will learn how many other souls suffered similar defects and how their engines were tuned and their batteries recharged by His
promises. "I will remove from you your heart of stone and give you a heart of flesh"
(Eze. 36:26, NIV).

Punctured tires? Your soul may have been engulfed by all forms of bitterness,
anger, hate, malice, strife, and materialism. Don't worry. You can overcome by sur-
rendering your mind, body, and soul to Jesus. He is your advocate. He will forgive
you of your sins and you will experience rich and full spiritual renewal because of
His marvelous grace.

Running out of gas? Rush to the Divine Gas Station. He has an unlimited supply of the Holy Spirit. He will fill your tank with a double portion of the Comforter.

And credit? Don't be anxious. Remember, Jesus paid it all, way back at Calvary.
The blood will never lose its power.

Bula Rose Haughton Thompson

Priorities First

Therefore I tell you, do not worry about your life, what you will eat or drink;
or about your body, what you will wear. Is not life more important than food,
and the body more important than clothes?
Matt. 6:25, NIV.

I WAS GREATLY BLESSED to have been born into a Christian family with loving parents who were concerned about investing in their three children. Their priorities for us did not include extravagant clothes or fancy non-nutritious food. Rather, they taught us faith in God, promoted good character formation, and provided us with formal education.

I remember my mother praying out loud to God for her children. She taught us Christian principles in our daily worship. My happiest childhood memory is of all of us sitting on our parents' big bed, singing, reciting Bible memory verses, and listening to my mom telling us stories about Jesus. When I had my own family I followed her example. Years later I was very pleased when my own daughter told me that her best childhood memories were the daily worship time and the games we played on the family room rug afterward.

When we were teens, my mother used one particular illustration to teach us to "open our eyes," as she used to say. To deceive God's youth, she told us, the enemy covers sin with an attractive, shiny cloak. He tells teens to try it only once and see how it feels. He suggests that, after all, nobody will see, or even know about it. When youth let themselves be taken in by this seduction and enchantment, the enemy yanks the cloak away. He laughs aloud as he sees their bitter disappointment with themselves and their great affliction at having fallen into his trap. Worst of all, they begin to think that God won't forgive them or accept them back.

To avoid falling into the abominable trap of the enemy, we should not even look at sin, or let ourselves even think that we might be missing out on something good. Instead, we should fix our eyes on Jesus. We should constantly ask Him to shut the windows of our souls to evil and to open them widely toward heaven.

My mother's wise words and prayers provided solid guidance in my life. By the grace of God, my brother, my sister, and I are all happy Christians. My prayer is for God to keep us always faithful to His Word. I thank God for giving my parents the wisdom to recognize the true priorities in life and to act on them.

Vasti S. Viana

His Law Our Protection

How many times have I wanted to put my arms around all your people, just as a hen gathers her chicks under her wings, but you would not let me!
Matt. 23:37, TEV.

MY LITTLE GIRL did not enjoy being confined to the laundry room while I prepared the car and locked the house in preparation for our long drive. She wanted to go outdoors and roam in the garden and the adjoining parks, climb trees, and hunt dragonflies. I felt for her, but could not risk her priority to chase butterflies ahead of her obeying my call. Kelly liked it even less when I put her in her cat carrier on the front seat of my car. As we drove, she squawked, yowled, scratched, and complained. My attempts to pacify her were fruitless. I spoke reassuringly. I coaxed. She persisted with all manner of objections. I turned on some music, to no avail. About three-and-a-half hours later I was ready for a break from driving and from the nagging.

As I took Kelly from her cage, I clipped her lead onto the harness which she wore around her chest. The moment I opened the car door, she eagerly jumped out. Just then a car drove past in the parking lot. Kelly was terrified and tried to run under my car. Fortunately, I had a firm grip on her lead. I spoke reassuringly to her, but her fear was greater than my nurture. She wriggled and squirmed as I picked her up and carried her to a patch of grass. I sat down and stroked her, but she kept pulling on her lead, trying to get away to an area she thought was safer. I felt a little offended that she did not take comfort in my reassurance and my presence.

It was inconvenient, but I cut our break short and put her back in the car to end her distress. Once inside the cage she was content with the safety and assurance that her restriction provided. I was incredulous that she did not meow even once until we arrived at our destination.

I recognized the similarities in our spiritual walk. We may resent the restrictions placed on us until they are adequately explained and the alternatives are considered. Can we be trusted to obey our heavenly Father's call when we are preoccupied with other things? We may be oblivious of His reassurance and trust our own judgment as to what to fear rather than snuggling into His loving protection. I wonder if God becomes offended when we don't trust Him to care for us. Our heavenly Father also inconvenienced Himself when He sympathized with us in our distress and therefore provided our salvation.

Bridgid Kilgour

He Who Watches

My help comes from the Lord, the Maker of heaven and earth. He will not let your foot
slip—he who watches over you will not slumber.
Ps. 121:2, 3, NIV.

I WAS TRAVELING by train in Germany from Upper Bavaria to Baden-Württemberg, an elderly lady and I in the compartment, until two boys entered at Nürnberg. They were rude and disruptive, loud and noisy, banging the windows and seats in time to the rhythm of the music they were listening to.

At first I was scared of them. Only recently the media had reported that an elderly gentleman was brutalized because he had called some youngsters to order. I prayed silently, *Dear God, help that these young people do no harm.* After a while I had had enough of their disturbing behavior so I said to them, "I have the impression that you're bored. Come over and sit next to me. I am bored, too." To my surprise they accepted my invitation.

Soon we were in the middle of an interesting conversation. Then they asked, "And what kind of a lady are you?"

I told them that I am a mom with three sons, and that I am a Christian. "I believe in the living God who made heaven and earth." And then I told them about the love of God, and that He cares for every person and sees and hears everything. I was very much surprised that they listened so attentively. The time passed much too quickly and we had to end our conversation when we reached the boys' destination. Both of them got up and said, "Excuse us, we have to get off the train here. Goodbye."

I reflected on my encounter with these boys, ages 14 and 19, and praised God: *God, it is so wonderful how You are able to control the unruly at any time.* I had felt a difference in them. These teens had entered the compartment like wild animals and left the train like little lambs.

Why am I telling you of this experience? I would like to encourage you, if you should encounter a similar situation, to trust in God. God can change people, even in an instant. We know this because He says, "I am God Almighty" (Gen. 17:1, NIV). We can be sure that He who protects us does not sleep or slumber.

Josefine Wimmer

A Boy and His Dog

A farmer went out to sow his seed.
Matt. 13:3, NIV.

[Some fell] on good soil, where it produced a crop.
Matt. 13:8, NIV.

"NO DOG!" screamed 4-year-old TJ as he hid behind Mrs. H.

My keeshond, Elke, and I were attending a pet therapy session at an inner-city school for children with multiple challenges. Many of them were romping with the dogs. But not TJ. He was afraid.

"Is there a quieter dog for TJ?" Hearing Mrs. H's query, I brought Elke over and placed her so her back faced the trembling child. Slowly the teacher stroked Elke's silver-tipped black fur. "Elke's so soft. Look how quietly she sits," she cooed.

"No dog," TJ whispered, but Mrs. H and I soon noticed one chubby hand reaching around to tentatively poke Elke's fur.

"I go inside now," TJ sighed after about 15 seconds. Yes. Just touching Elke had required a great deal of energy. No doubt he was ready for a soft place to land.

Two weeks later, Elke and I made another visit. And only seconds after we arrived, TJ was standing next to us. "Hi, Elke," he said with a hint of a smile. Then for 15 minutes he and I sat quietly while we stroked Elke from her ears to her tail. Mrs. H took notes from a distance. Then without a word TJ stood up and walked into the school.

At the school for a third session, I wondered what TJ would do. It didn't take long to find out. TJ ran to Elke, knelt beside her, and buried his face in her fur.

"What does Elke feel like, TJ?" Mrs. H asked. We expected him to say things like "furry!" or "fuzzy!" But when TJ lifted his head, he exclaimed, "Elke feels happy!"

Hopefully, with further guidance, TJ will discover how to transfer what he has learned about facing his fear of dogs to other fears he will undoubtedly face in the concrete jungle that is his life. And hopefully someday, facing his fears will lift him out of that jungle.

When I first started doing pet therapy, it was because I enjoy being with children and dogs. But it didn't take long to realize that here was a mission field in its own right. And how delighted I was to discover that the sower was a happy dog named Elke and the fertile field was the heart of a frightened boy named TJ.

Lyndelle Brower Chiomenti

Bubbles

Whereas you do not know what will happen tomorrow. For what is your life?
It is even a vapor that appears for a little time and then vanishes away.
James 4:14, NKJV.

THEY FLOAT THROUGH THE AIR like round, transparent clouds—tiny ones, huge ones, and some in-between. Sometimes they appear as twins or triplets. Often they reflect the iridescent rays of the sun. Bubbles. We loved them as children, and as adults we share the summer joy of blowing bubbles with our children and grandchildren. What a delight to watch the little ones try to catch them in their small hands.

Blowing bubbles is almost as much fun as bursting them, seeing the perfect spheres vanish into the atmosphere, disappearing as if they had never been there, like vapor. And even if we don't burst them, they self-destruct in a few seconds.

According to the Apostle James this is how God looks at our life span, our three score and 10, more or less (see Ps. 90:10). God sees it as bubbles that are here for a few fleeting moments, as a "vapor that appears for a little time and then vanishes away." Our beautiful homes and gardens, our designer clothes and shoes, our careers, our quarrels and misunderstandings, our ambitions are all in the light of eternity, just bubbles!

Yet we put so much emphasis on storing up for the here and now. We work day and night to beautify our little bubbles, making them larger, more magnificent than the neighbors' bubbles. We install expensive security systems to protect our bubbles from thieves, and we pay cleaning services to keep our bubbles gleaming and spotless. Then we fill our bubbles with numerous expensive vaporous spheres. There they float in God's sight like vapor that appears for a short time and then vanishes away.

What about eternity? What preparations are we making for the mansions that Jesus is preparing for us? Do we even remember that we will have another home, an eternal one, when we are taken up to heaven? How sad it would be in that day if we try to hold on to our beautiful bubbles. They will burst and vanish away, and then we lose eternity!

May our prayer be, Lord, *"so teach us to number our days"* [Ps. 90:12] *as God sees them—vapor—that we will make wise decisions about the here and now, and about the hereafter.*

Annette Walwyn Michael

Andy

Let your conduct be worthy of the gospel of Christ.
Phil. 1:27, NKJV.

ANDY WAS THE TYPE of kid who'd slam the door in your face, push over a bike, kick the dog, and karate chop his little brother—all in about 10 seconds. He was big for his years, with a scowling face. My girls were quite afraid of him.

We rented an apartment in Michigan the year my husband finished a graduate degree, and Andy was a problem. He, his mom, and brothers lived in the apartment below us. His single mom struggled to keep her boys corralled, and I'm sure she did the best she could. Most people try. But one evening I heard her calling her 3-year-old in from the backyard with language that would have made a sailor blush. Suddenly I had a little insight into what had made Andy the kid he was. And I looked at him a bit differently after that.

Then one evening Andy's mom called to say she had the items I'd ordered from her through her home party. I told her I'd be right down. Our apartments had the same floor plan. Once inside, two steps to the left took you into the kitchen. After I paid her and visited a few minutes, I peeked into the kitchen. There stood Andy, a large two-pronged fork in his hand, watching a bubbling, sizzling skillet of—something. "Your mom surely is lucky to have you helping her cook supper," I told Andy. "I always appreciate it when my kids help me."

He beamed from ear to ear. Then sticking the fork into the fat, he lifted out a large brown morsel. "Here," he said. "Have some."

I'd been a vegetarian for 25 years but I wasn't about to hurt his feelings. "Wow, that looks good," I said. "You've really got it nice and brown." And it was true. He'd done a good job with it. Taking it from the fork, I carefully put it in my mouth, said my goodbyes, and hurried upstairs. Then I took the hot meat out of my mouth, and that was the end of that. Well, almost.

Andy was at the apartment entrance when I went out the next morning. He gave me a big smile and held the door open for me. I thanked him, and his smile grew even bigger. And after that, you guessed it! Andy and I were friends.

What made the difference? You know, of course. It was because I'd helped him feel good about himself. That's something we all need, isn't it?

Penny Estes Wheeler

Protected

*Deep calls to deep in the roar of your waterfalls; all your waves
and breakers have swept over me.*
Ps. 42:7, NIV.

ON OUR WAY HOME to our little town we saw a thunderstorm on the horizon in front of us. Flashes of lightning leaped from dark clouds and rain poured from the grey sky. We were driving toward a narrow valley which would take us home when we had to take a detour. It took us some time to get back to the valley where we hit a heavy downpour. With only seven miles (12 kilometers) to go, a police car sped past us and immediately blocked the road ahead.

As we took another road up to the hills we passed the fire brigade pumping water out of the basements of houses on the hillside. Reaching the main highway, we discovered that it was closed so we had to take yet another detour to the other side of our town. Here the roads were already flooded and the little peaceful brook by the roadside had become a wide fast-flowing river. Many cars stalled. Fortunately, little by little, we were able to continue. We were happy to reach our home on the hill after two hours of detours.

The next morning I saw the destruction caused by the water in the lower parts of the town. The little river had flooded large areas and everything was covered by mud and debris. The bridges were damaged and blocked by branches and wood. The flood damaged the houses near the riverbank, cars were knocked about and piled on top of each other. The shops were closed.

It was only when I saw the news on television that I realized the extent of the destruction. Three people had drowned; two of them washed away in their car. Then I understood that we, too, could also have been involved. If we'd driven through the narrow valley we would have been caught in the flood. Who knows what would have happened! We had not been happy about the first detour, but maybe it was just what saved us from harm.

Often we do not know why disagreeable things happen to us. Life is like a piece of embroidery where we see only the reverse side with all the knots and ends in disarray. Because we see only one side of the picture we often miss out on the meaning of things we can't explain. But one day we will be able to see the beautiful embroidery of our lives and realize that the purpose of the knots and ends on the reverse were for good.

Hannele Ottschofski

Angels on Duty

My God sent his angel to shut the lions' mouths so that they would not hurt me.
Dan. 6:22, NLT.

CAR TROUBLE AGAIN. My car had quit on me 16 times during the last year and was being held together with hangers, duct tape, and prayer.

Around 9:00 one evening my children and I were on our way home from a church program when the car stopped once again. We were on a dark, hilly road that had very little traffic and few houses in the area. I remembered passing a fruit and vegetable stand about a quarter of a mile back, so I let the car coast back until we were in front of the store. Even though lights were on, the store was closed. Behind the store we could see lights of a house through the trees. My only option was to go back there and telephone for help.

After prayer for protection, 9-year-old David stayed with the car, while 7-year-old daughter Laura and 6-year-old Jeff tried to help me find a path to the house through the trees in the dark. We didn't even have a flashlight. About half way to the house a big dog walked right in front of us. Laura, who loves all animals, reached out to pet him. The dog was slightly out of reach and walked on by us. He didn't even act like he saw us or even heard us talking.

We finally found stairs to the second-floor porch. The man and his wife who opened the door demanded to know how we got there. At that very moment, the dog came up the stairs on the other side and started barking furiously at us. They hurriedly put the dog in the house and closed the door. The man told us that this dog never allowed anyone to come in their yard and it had bitten people who dared to come in, including most of the people who worked in their fruit and vegetable stand. They couldn't understand how I, with two children, had been able to make it all the way to their door without being attacked by their dog.

I know that the same God who sent angels to close the mouths of the lions for Daniel also closed the mouth of the dog that night. What a testimony of God's protection, not only to this man and his wife, but to my children.

Thank You, Lord, for loving and protecting us even when we don't know what danger is lurking in front of us. And thank You for the comfort of my favorite promise found in Psalm 34:7 that says, "The angel of the Lord encampeth round about them that fear him, and delivereth them."

Naomi N. Coleman

Cockroaches

When Adam sinned, sin entered the world. Adam's sin brought death,
so death spread to everyone, for everyone sinned.
Rom. 5:12, NLT.

COCKROACHES!

"How can you dissect a cockroach?" my husband Monroe asked me. We had just moved to Bugema Missionary College in Uganda. He was to be the biology teacher and tomorrow's assignment was for the class to dissect cockroaches. How and where to get them?

"No problem, teacher. We will help you find some," one of the boys spoke up. "Come with us to the kitchen early in the morning and we'll find plenty." Sure enough, the next morning several boys were there to help Monroe. They flipped on the kitchen light as they lifted a large cooking pot from the floor. Hundreds of two-inch cockroaches scudded across the room. With one big swipe the boys gathered a large pan full and walked victoriously out of the room.

That was our first experience with the filthy creatures—but not the last! We covered our kitchen and closet shelves with newspapers to keep them clean. In the night we could hear crunching and knew the horrible creatures were having a feast on our clean newspapers. It was a constant battle trying to get rid of them. At least they were large enough to find. Turning on the light, you never knew when one would hit you as they quickly fluttered to get out of sight. We fought these nasty, dirty creatures almost everywhere we went. We almost got used to having to clean up after them.

In Egypt, cleaning the kitchen of an apartment we were moving into, I reached up to wipe off the top of a dirty, greasy cabinet. To my horror, instantly my hand and arm were covered with tiny crawling creatures. I screamed and jumped off the chair to shake them off. These were the complete opposite of the large critters we fought in Uganda, but there was no question about what they were. I hated them as much as I did the big flying ones in Uganda. We had to learn to put up with them, but we never did learn to appreciate them.

Cockroaches make me think of sin. Both big and little sins exist everywhere. We can't escape them. Some are easier to recognize, but all are sneaky and filthy. They hate light and try to escape into the darkness, and they carry a deadly disease called death. We must stay alert to be able to clean them from our lives.

Frances Osborne Morford

What a Privilege

And he said to Him, "Lord, You know all things;
You know that I love You." Jesus said to him, "Feed My sheep."
John 21:17, NKJV.

DURING THE PROCESS of restoring Peter back into His grace, three times the Lord asked Peter if he loved Him. Each time Peter said that he did, and with each response Jesus gave Peter a directive: feed My lambs, tend My sheep, and feed My sheep. But what exactly does that mean in this era of supersonic living? Can it be something so simple that it overwhelms you with love for such a compassionate God?

The Omega Pathfinder Club was planning to attend the Hispanic Camporee for the first time. The club director had only one more day for preparation, so I offered to take some needed Class-A uniform patches to his house that afternoon. His wife welcomed me. After assisting with how and where to place the patches and putting on citation cords, his wife told me the story of one of the young girls in the club.

The girl's mother, who was not a member of our church, was in the hospital, on government assistance, and couldn't afford the black leather tie shoes that the dress code required. Without them, her daughter couldn't attend the Camporee, yet the mother still offered to provide food for the Camporee.

When the director's wife told me that the girl wanted so desperately to go to the Camporee that she cut up her shoes to try and insert shoe laces, the Holy Spirit moved in my heart. I felt the compassion of Jesus commanding me, "Give your all. Feed My sheep!" I began to silently pray because I knew I had only $10 in my purse and that would not suffice. As I reached for my purse I breathed another prayer, *Lord, let there be a twenty-dollar bill in my wallet instead of a ten.* With tears of gratitude the director's wife accepted the $20 from my hand and together we offered a prayer of thanksgiving.

Later that evening I witnessed the young girl wearing her new shoes. As I drove home, my heart was filled with awe for such a compassionate God. He took my $10 and turned it into $20. I could not help but weep at what a privilege God had placed before me. He expects us to show His love in the most tender of ways. What a privilege!

Evelyn Gertrude Greenwade Boltwood

Blessings, Blessings, Everywhere

My cup overflows with blessings.
Ps. 23:5, NLT.

MY LIFE IS FULL OF SMALL BLESSINGS that I all too often miss. Like the day when we were hoping to find a parking space, any parking space, so that my husband could walk me to class and we found one with 27 minutes still on the meter! A space close to campus and with enough time left that we didn't have to pay for parking. What a blessing! Not to mention the blessing of having the resources to own a car, pay the insurance, and pay for gas. Or that my husband is able to take me to class at all as we have only one car and catching the bus is not really an option. The walk would be 45 minutes, at least. Including a hill. So the ride to class is a huge blessing. Then I thank God that we are able to afford my return to school, and that I was accepted. When you start to think about it, blessings are all around us! Thinking about one usually leads to another and another.

I was busy and nervous that day, not thinking about the large and small blessings God showers down on me all the time. But finding a parking space with money still on the meter suddenly made me aware of God's love and care for me. I realized how important I am to God. Yes, you could argue that finding the spot was a coincidence or that we just lucked out that day. But I see it as a blessing that made my cup overflow. You know, my husband could have dropped me off anywhere. It was a beautiful day, and I'm young, healthy, and strong. I could have walked across campus to my class. However, because my God cares for me, He knew that being able to spend a little more time walking and talking with my husband would turn my day around. My cup really does overflow with blessings, and my heart overflows with thankfulness that the God I serve is so caring, so thoughtful, and so awesome!

I encourage you to look for God's blessings today. You might be surprised at what you discover once you actively start looking for God's abundant blessings in your life. Maybe today is one of those times you'd be hard-pressed to find something that isn't a blessing. On the other hand, maybe today is filled with small trials and hassles enough to drive you crazy. Maybe today you encounter tragedy that shakes you to your core. No matter what your day, or how you feel, God loves you deeply and is pouring out His love for you in blessings of all sizes. May your cup overflow with blessings today.

Julie Bocock-Bliss

He Covered My Nakedness

He shall cover thee with his feathers, and under his wings shalt thou trust.
Ps 91:4.

IT WAS ANOTHER TUESDAY MORNING. I had an 8:00 class, and my daughter was moving all too slowly. I hurried through the morning chores and kindly prodded my little one to hurry. We ran out of the house at 7:55, naked—naked because we did not have our usual family worship that morning; we were not covered with the Word. My year–old nephew who lived next door stretched for me to take him with me as I usually did, but I refused because I'd have to stop and fit his car seat into my vehicle. Time was flying. I had to move on.

My daughter and I drove down the street. A mere 200 yards away we reached the first intersection on our short trip. As I left the minor road onto the major road I suddenly heard a loud crash! My vehicle had been hit and thrown from the left-hand side of the road into the path of the on-coming traffic. All was a-swirl!

My car came to rest no more than two feet from the edge of a small cliff. Other drivers honked their horns; the passengers in the other vehicles stared. Yet a few kind onlookers rushed to the scene. We examined the damage: a broken headlamp, one bumper torn off, water running from the radiator—but not a scratch on my daughter or myself. Mercifully, God had covered us that morning.

Before I could begin to feel nervous, He inspired me to remember the text, "I have loved thee with an everlasting love: therefore with lovingkindness have I drawn thee (Jer. 31:3). Leaving home naked, not covered with the Word, is not visible to the human eye. But even so, that morning God covered me with His grace, His everlasting garment of love and mercy. He provided many words of comfort.

In today's text God promises that He shall cover us with His feathers, and under His wings we can trust. Deuteronomy 33:12 says, "The beloved of the Lord shall dwell in safety by him; and the Lord shall cover him all the day long." No longer naked.

Dear friend, whenever you are tempted to leave your home or office naked, pause and invite your heavenly Father to cover you. He will "cover you with his feathers, and under His wings" you will trust.

Debbie Clarke-Grant

Before We Ask

Before they call I will answer.
Isa. 65:24, NIV.

IT WAS THE SUMMER OF 1995, and my husband, Emil, his brother Pete, Pete's wife, Ruthe, and I were in Bratislava, the capitol of Slovakia to sightsee and visit family.

The young woman who had also been our interpreter in 1993, had spent a couple of days traveling with us. But she could not be with us the day we left to travel by train to east of Bratislava to visit our relatives. She had instructed us how to get to the train station from the hotel and warned us to be sure we bought tickets in first class seating, assuring us the trip would be much more pleasant.

Our taxi dropped us off at the train station Sunday morning. Our husbands chose to remain with the luggage, electing my sister-in-law and me to purchase our tickets. We first went to a window that indicated an available translator. He directed us to a ticket agent across the station where we could purchase our first-class tickets.

We were leaving the ticket window when a young university student we had met at church spotted us and came over to inquire if we were all set for our train ride. When we showed him our tickets, he informed us we had not been sold first-class tickets. So he took our tickets back to the ticket agent. After a few minutes of arguing with her, she finally exchanged our tickets for first-class ones.

This young man told us he had plans to do two things that morning: go to the university library and to the train station. He said he was impressed to go to the train station first. The Lord had directed him to locate us in this rather large and busy station so we could have a more comfortable train ride.

The Lord delights in doing special things for His children, even arranging for more comfortable train rides. Not only does He delight in doing special things for us, He even answers prayers we have not thought to pray. We had asked God's blessings for the day, and He answered when we did not even know what to ask for.

Do we take time at the end of each day to think back and thank the Lord for the special things He does for us each and every day? If not, why not begin today?

Patricia Mulraney Kovalski

In the Service of the King

There are different kinds of service, but the same Lord.
1 Cor. 12:5, NIV.

GOING TO THE BEACH is one of my favorite activities. In addition to enjoying the sun, sand, and surf, I get a real kick out of watching people and seeing the beach umbrellas that dot the beach. While beach umbrellas are structurally very much the same, they vary greatly in size, color, and design. Most boast intriguing patterns integrating various shades of red, orange, blue, yellow, or green. Very seldom do I see two that are alike.

Like beach umbrellas, we humans all have the same structure: usually two arms, two legs, one head, and a trunk. Beyond that there is much variety. The color of our skin, eyes, and hair; the shape of our noses and ears; our height, weight, and body shape differ considerably. Emotions, talents, skills, and abilities are all different too. No two people's DNA or fingerprints are the same. God has made each one of us unique and special. He even knows the number of hairs on our heads (see Matt. 10:30) and has engraved us on the palms of His hands (see Isa. 49:16).

Without the umbrella being opened its beauty can not be fully appreciated. It is most beautiful when it is fully opened, rendering the service of shade from the hot sun.

Our heavenly Father created us for service. If we allow the Holy Spirit into our lives, and if we use the attributes and uniqueness He gives us in service to others, His beauty can be seen through us.

Service to others is a good way to help combat depression, loneliness, and boredom. When guided by sound principles, one cannot give of herself without reaping positive benefits. The Good Book says, "Be generous: Invest in acts of charity. Charity yields high returns" (Eccl. 11:1, Message). In most cases, when I act intentionally or spontaneously in serving others, my experiences have been tremendously rewarding . Blessings have resulted which I never expected. Sometimes I'm not even aware that what I said or did made an impact until I hear about it secondhand. What a joy and privilege it is to be of service to the One who created us. Of course, it may come at a price, as it is often beset with challenges and heartache. But these can be tools to further develop our characters and fashion and mold us to reflect His character more clearly. What a small price to pay to be more like Jesus!

Marian M. Hart

Blackberrying

O Death, where is your sting?
1 Cor. 15:55, NKJV.

WHEN I WAS OUT WALKING with my dog one afternoon, I spied lots of wild blackberries growing not far from where I live. Back home, I soon found an appropriate container to put them in and then spent an enjoyable half hour or so picking as many berries as I could reach. There were enough to add to an apple pie for a special dessert that evening.

But what memories that half hour brought back! How I loved blackberrying as a child. In the late summer months, often on a Sunday morning, our mother would come into the kitchen with her apron full of blackberries. Then armed with small billy-cans, away my two older sisters and I would go.

With the warmth of the summer sun, what had been small hard red fruit had grown into large, scrumptious, juicy blackberries. Mum would bake the most delicious blackberry and apple pies. And of course there would be jars of blackberry jam. How good they tasted!

The farm we lived on had a few patches where the blackberry plants did especially well. One place where they grew prolifically was directly in front of a group of trees that formed a wonderful shelter from any wind. We were always certain to find ripe berries there.

My two older sisters had longer arms than I did, and they were able to pick higher than I could—higher and farther away. But I could get down and look up from under the leaves, and I usually spotted berries that had been missed. One for me, one for the container. More often than not when we returned home there would be that tell-tale purple stain around my mouth!

We were quickly filling our billy-cans one Sunday morning at our favorite blackberry patch when I disturbed a wasp's nest. Those nasty stinging insects flew at me and I dropped the can and ran, spilling my precious blackberries all over the ground. Because of the summer warmth I was wearing a very loose top, and the wasps stung me all over my stomach. I cried all the way home. My mother immediately applied soothing lotion, and both my tears and the pain quickly subsided.

In this world of sin, the death of a loved one always stings us with pain. But thanks be to Jesus and His sacrifice on the cross, we can look forward to that day when death will be no more. No more stings; no more pain; no more death.

Leonie Donald

The Right Thumb

But I rejoiced in the Lord greatly, that now at the last your care of me hath flourished again; wherein ye were also careful, but ye lacked opportunity.
Phil. 4:10.

HAVE YOU EVER BEEN STRESSED, meeting deadlines, multitasking your job, family, and church; planning vacations, tending to the sick? Well, that is exactly what makes up most of my typical day. I'd just returned from work, pulled to a stop in my driveway, grabbed my belongings from the car, and rushed to close the door when suddenly I thought, I'm locking the keys in the car! To prevent this, I hastily stuck out my hand to stop the door. The car door slammed on my thumb. Ouch! I quickly pulled out my finger and stuck it straight into my mouth to provide some soothing. My whole body felt injured and numb.

I hobbled into the house and put the thumb under cold running water until it felt better. By now the fingernail had turned blue-purple and red-black from the accumulation of pooled blood. The nail stayed that way for several months—until it began separating from the quick at the bottom and left side of the thumb. Coupled with the discomfort, tenderness, and ugliness, the problem was compounded with a separating nail that got caught in everything.

I was unable to brush my hair properly, pull on my stockings, do household chores, or write. As I worked particles of dust would lodge between the old and new nails. I decided to cover the nail with an adhesive bandage to decrease discomfort and ugliness and increase finger hygiene. This proved futile. The constant encounter with water and the new nail wanting to push out the old nail made it impossible to keep the cover on for even an hour.

Do you have a small sin that is eating away at you? You try to cover it but it keeps resurfacing? Take the bandage off and let the Living Water cleanse it.

The right thumb is very important to do so many things; I finally left the thumb open, and gradually the old nail died and fell off. A new clean, vibrant, healthy, pink nail replaced it. I did not see the new nail grow, but it did. In the same way the Holy Spirit keeps working on us, perfecting us, making us new again. Just like the old nagging nail that gave way to the new nail, freedom can be achieved from that minute, besetting sin that will separate us from the body of Christ. You, too, can be fully connected again if you cast all your cares upon Him.

Pauline A. Dwyer-Kerr

O Rest in the Lord

Commit everything you do to the Lord. Trust him, and he will help you.
Ps. 37:5, NLT.

TODAY WAS ONE of those topsy-turvy, tail-in-a-knot days. My dear neighbor Sally needed a ride home from her stay in the hospital. Mariana was alone—her daughter and sister-in-law had left after her husband's funeral—and she wanted me to help her make some financial decisions. My husband had trouble with his computer. The correction of my student's paper took much longer than I'd hoped; I practically rewrote one chapter. I invited Deborah to watch Discoveries '08 with us that evening, only to find out that we had to go elsewhere.

In the middle of everything, I heard in my head the serene melody of Mendelssohn's "O Rest in the Lord," and I jumped up and found the music. The melody is restful, but I was especially interested in the words: "O rest in the Lord, wait patiently for Him,/And He shall give thee thy heart's desires. . . ./Commit thy way unto Him, and trust in Him; . . ./And fret not thyself because of evil doers./ O rest in the Lord."

When I saw that these words came, via the German language, from Psalm 37, I became curious to see how close the lyrics might be to the King James Bible, so I pulled my old Bible from the shelf and looked up Psalm 37. There I found verse 5, today's text: "Commit thy way unto the Lord; trust also in him; and he shall bring it to pass." The verse was underlined and had a notation in the margin beside it: "26-7-58"!

It was not hard to remember what had happened on July 26, 1958. On that day Werner and I said goodbye after first meeting and knowing each other for only 10 days during a world church conference. He was leaving for a study tour in the Middle East on his way to his teaching appointment in Chile. I needed to return to my teaching job in California. Obviously, we'd been attracted to each other, but the future was a question mark. Was a romance wise—or even possible?

On that day I committed my future to the Lord, not knowing what would happen. To make a long story short, Werner and I married the following year—and that was more than a half-century ago! It was good, on a tail-in-a-knot day, to remember that I can rest in the Lord, commit myself entirely to Him, and know that all will be well.

Thank You, Lord, for Your promise to guide, help, direct—if only I will commit myself to Your loving care!

Nancy Jean Vyhmeister

Fishing Lures

Watch and pray so that you will not fall into temptation.
Mark 14:38, NIV.

WE WERE ON A FOUR-DAY camping trip in the north Georgia mountains with our grandson, Luke. He had his new fishing pole, tackle box,
and assortment of hooks and lures which we had bought for him on the
way to our campsite.

It was a beautiful day of about 80°F (27°C), with clear skies and a
gentle breeze. Our campsite was on the lake front, just up the hill from
the fishing pier. My husband decided to take a nap after breakfast while
Luke and I went fishing at the pier. We gathered up the sunscreen, folding chair, a
book to read, water bottles, and our sunglasses, and started down the path. We
could see fish jumping in the distance, and as we settled down on the pier we saw
fish swimming under it.

The day before, Luke and Grandpa had come to this same spot and had caught
a 5-inch-long fish. This day would prove different. The fish just were not biting.
They swam around and checked out the lures, then swam away. We stayed on the
pier for several hours, but the fish did not bite regardless of which lure Luke used.
We decided to come back later with live bait.

Satan uses lures to trap us. We usually think of the material lures like ques-
tionable TV shows or movies that bring Satan right into our living rooms, but he
has other lures we sometimes bite. There are lures like someone talking about you
behind your back. Or your husband, children, or coworker trying to provoke you
into an argument. Or maybe your best friend turning against you. All these situations hurt and put us on the defensive.

Do you remember reading that Jesus was falsely accused of things, and the
many times the Pharisees tried luring Him into traps, turning His words around to
get Him into an argument? Jesus was able to remain objective and composed because He spent time—sometimes all night—in prayer and surrendered to His
Father's will. We, too, can overcome Satan's attacks if we spend time with Jesus
every day—for me, morning is best—and live our lives surrendered to His will. He
will help us to always watch and pray, staying on guard for Satan's lures. As it says
in the Message paraphrase of today's text, "Stay alert, be in prayer, so you don't
enter the danger zone without even knowing it. Don't be naive."

Celia Mejia Cruz

No Condemnation

There is therefore now no condemnation to those who are in Christ Jesus,
who do not walk according to the flesh, but according to the Spirit.
Rom. 8:1, NKJV.

REALLY! IT'S TRULY REAL! I think as I lie down next to my orange cat, letting the tears slide freely down my cheeks. I pet his soft fur and he curls into a tight ball. I hear so often the Lord forgives my sins on the spot . . . the second I ask for forgiveness. I've heard it, but have never felt it. So, why was this touching my heart in a different way?

Instead of hearsay, or growing up hearing it said so often that it would dull the brain and mean nothing, God's love and compassionate forgiveness was new to me. And exciting. Today's verse—which seemed to have slipped out of my reach before—I'd just discovered. It was something to relish and revel in. Something to give life and hope.

The tragedy of some of my past actions, the pain and sorrow it still brings to me, feeling as if I didn't live up to my own ideals—after all that, this verse brings hope. God is not condemning me. This means He still wants me.

So often I'm scared someone from my past will come to taunt me and embarrass me. Yet, now I know that the Lord is not judging me for what I've done. No one else, no matter who or where they are from, has the right to condemn me. I can stand in the Lord's strength. Stand in His mercy and His love for me, replenishing my broken spirit with His power.

I sit up and wipe away my tears of regret. There is no more need for them. I have hope. I bend over and kiss my cat's pink nose with newfound feelings of joy and peace. The beautiful heavenly Father has forgiven me! There is no need to dwell on my mistakes, for the Lord is not dwelling on them. He reaches down with His strong and comforting arms; He picks me up, and takes pleasure in giving me His Spirit of healing.

Now that I know this, I can say with confidence to all of my sisters in Christ, "He longs to free you from your closet of skeletons. Why don't you allow Him to do just that? Take Him up on His promise: There is no condemnation to those who are in Christ Jesus. Your slates have been wiped clean. Don't try to pick up the chalk and rewrite what has been erased by Christ Jesus Himself."

Melissa Irene Koeffler

Kitty Lesson

As we have therefore opportunity, let us do good unto all men,
especially unto them who are of the household of faith.
Gal. 6:10.

OUR CAT KITTY is a real opportunist. We have a couple of bird feeders in our yard and Kitty is very observant of the activity going on there. He's tried many different ways to catch a bird. The first was the typical crouch and sneak up tactic, but he did this in full view. Perhaps he thinks he is truly hidden in our inch-high grass. His next attempt was on our front porch that overlooks the yard. Again it was the crouch position, but as soon as he took the leap off the porch, the birds burst into the air. Next he hid under our cars. This was actually a good spot, because, at last, he was hidden. Fortunately the cars were far from the feeders. As soon as Kitty shot out toward them, the birds took off—before he even got close. The next thing we saw him do was to actually sit under the feeders and eat some of the seeds. But those birds know the difference between friend and foe.

One year we had an inflatable pool set up in our yard. Standing by my car, I saw a mourning dove under one of the feeders. All of a sudden the bird walked behind the pool. Kitty, who was by my feet, saw his chance and zoomed like a rocket. I cringed inside, but fortunately the bird flew off before Kitty got there. What an opportunist is Kitty.

At one time we had a goldfish, and again Kitty was very interested. He knew the tank was on our kitchen counter, but due to its height he couldn't get up there to do Flash any harm. One day a chair was placed a little too close to the sink, and boy, he didn't waste any time hopping onto the chair and then onto the counter. He made a beeline to the fish tank. Fortunately I spotted him and quickly got him down. Once again, he saw the opportunity and took it.

Observing Kitty and how he quickly sees opportunities made me wonder if I do the same, not for my own personal advantage, but instead as a servant of the Lord. Do I see the opportunities to serve that come my way? Do I try different methods to reach out and to minister? I believe the only way to truly see opportunities is if I ask the Lord to use me to be a blessing to others. In other words, to let the Lord know I'm available. When he was here on earth, Christ always saw His opportunities to help others. May we also see ours and be led by Christ daily.

Rosemarie Clardy

My Experience of Faith

Now faith is the substance of things hoped for, the evidence of things not seen.
Heb. 11:1.

I HOPE THE PERSONAL experience I'm going to share with you will strengthen the faith of young people—and older ones as well—in their walk with Christ.

I had decided to continue studying in the church university in Cosendai, Cameroon. I had been studying in a public university for three years, but I could not continue there as I faced difficulties because of my religious convictions.

I began selling some natural juices to raise money to solve my financial problems and to have money for school. A week before classes began, I had just 30,000 cfa (Cameroon francs) in my pocket—only five percent of my school fees. But I went on by faith. I told myself that God would provide. I used 20,000 francs of that money for my application, then I kept on praying.

I had a friend, Emilienne. May the Lord bless her because she made my experience of faith stronger. Just like me, her parents had no money for her university studies. So I told her to come with me and I would help her so that we could study together. I said it because I trusted in God.

I asked for help from my local church and friends. They did what they could, enough that I was able to prepare her application too. A few days before classes began, Emilienne asked me where we would stay in Nanga–Eboko, the university town, and how much money I had for her. I just told her God would provide. But Emilienne liked to see before she believed; she told me it was a risk to go there without money. To assure her—even though I had no money at the moment—I told her that I would pay 100,000 francs for her. And then, before we moved to Nanga–Eboko, I received 100,000 francs from someone—just the money I promised her.

Dear sisters, I regretted my lack of faith that day, for I could have asked more and the Lord could have given it to me. A day before our trip, I received 45,000 cfa from an unknown person. God was not through blessing me. Someone helped me apply for and receive a women's ministries scholarship. My faith has grown. May you too know that faith is "the evidence of things not seen." Oh, what a loving and wonderful God we have!

Mekoudjou Myriam Djia

Avoiding the Head Shot

Put on the full armor of God so that you can take your stand against the devil's schemes. . . . So that when the day of evil comes, you may be able to stand your ground, and after you have done everything, to stand.
Eph. 6:11–13, NIV.

MOST CHILDREN ARE INVOLVED in some type of sport or physical activity. While sports and games are excellent ways for children (and adults) to keep healthy and fit and to learn valuable life lessons, they can also cause serious injuries and, on rare occasions, even death.

Our son, Spencer, enjoys playing hockey, and we all know how rough that sport can be. My husband remembers a particularly anxious moment in which Spencer fell victim to a nasty "head shot." Spencer was streaking down the right wing looking for his center man, heading for the net. He made the pass and wham! He took an elbow directly to his head and went down like the walls of Jericho. Spencer was down on the ice for a few seconds but managed to get up, obviously dazed, and stagger back to the bench. Fortunately, he escaped serious injury. I shudder to think what might have happened if he hadn't been wearing his helmet and mouth guard.

Our daughter, Mikaela, has been riding horses for more than three years. While, by God's grace, she has not suffered any serious injuries, no rider should underestimate how a 1,200–pound animal might react to unexpected loud noises or quick movements. For these reasons, Mikaela must wear a helmet and also wear hard-toed boots to protect her feet from a stomping hoof.

Parents with children involved in physical activity know how it feels when their child gets hurt. Equipment is worn for a reason: protection. Hockey, skateboarding, skiing, cycling, and even tobogganing require adequate protective equipment.

God has provided us with the greatest protection of all: His Word. The Bible contains precious truths that will guide, teach, and protect us from all that life has to throw at us. It is the greatest comfort to know that, with the Lord by our side, we are taken care of, no matter how rough the game of life gets. We as Christians must also work as a team to spread His love and His promises to others so they, too, might be protected by His mighty armor.

Today and every day, put on the armor of God. Know and claim His many Bible promises and wear them like protective gear.

Janice Gibbs

Am I Ready?

Behold, I stand at the door . . . I will come in to him, and will sup with him, and he with me.
Rev. 3:20.

SIX MONTHS AGO, we got the long-awaited letter. Cousins were coming to Canada from Holland to celebrate our aunt's one-hundredth birthday. Arrangements were made by e-mail. Their itinerary was to take them through the Rockies to the West Coast. Within five days they would arrive at my house.

I removed dirty linens and replaced them with fresh sheets. I started cleaning, meal planning, cooking, shopping, and searching farm markets for ripe peaches, pears, and plums. Thursday I skipped my exercise: I had bathrooms to scrub, vacuuming to do, banking that couldn't wait, plus soup and buns to prepare for supper. I worked feverishly, for they were to arrive between 5:00 and 6:00 pm. The clock said 3:00, then it declared four. I started praying, "Lord, please don't bring them before six."

I decided what was most important, and what could be finished after they arrived. I wasn't finished cooking, but the kitchen could pass. I quickly vacuumed, then grabbed the bucket and mop. While praying for a time extension, I neared the stairs—almost finished! But alas, the clock had barely struck 5:00 when I heard car doors slamming. Here they were! The bucket and mop still stood on the landing by the door. My family had arrived, and I was not ready. I had worked hard, doing my best but . . .

All week I have been applying this preparation experience to my spiritual life. We have known for decades that Jesus is coming soon, and that we need to be ready. Have we removed the dirty thoughts from our minds and replaced them with fresh thoughts of Jesus? Have we planned nutritious times of prayer and Bible study? Do we search for the fruits of the Spirit? Have we scrubbed away the memories of secular music, movies, or books? Have we vacuumed out the dusty corners of our heart? Have we made spiritual deposits in the bank of heaven? Do we have the Bread of Life? Have we mopped up the sticky memories of disagreements with family or friends? Are we ready for Jesus to come, or is the bucket of murky thoughts and deeds still sitting on the landing? Jesus is walking toward our door. Are we ready?

Elizabeth Versteegh Odiyar

Protected Again

For he shall give his angels charge over thee, to keep thee in all thy ways.
They shall bear thee up in their hands.
Ps. 91:11, 12.

RECENTLY MY FAVORITE YOUNGER BROTHER, Gord, with whom I spent lots of time in childhood making, perhaps, a few too many memories, came to visit me after attending our fiftieth high school reunion in St. Johns, New Brunswick. It was so special to see him for the first time in 50 years.

We talked and laughed, and laughed and talked, and talked and laughed some more, making up for lost time. He told me a booklet of memories and stories from "back in the day" had been made for the reunion, and he handed me a piece of paper with one of the stories. My eyes grew bigger and bigger as I read the short paragraph, written by a school classmate from long ago. Gord remembered the story, but I didn't at all.

This is how it read: "How an Accident Was Prevented."

"One day Kenneth Sommerville was walking near where his sister was sliding. Kenneth saw his sister going down the hill onto the road just as a bus was coming. There were two poles by each other standing up. Kenneth threw a pole between the two poles. The sled hit the pole and kept going but his sister fell off and scraped her arm. The sled was run over by the bus and was smashed up. Freddie Soucy."

Wow! Who knew? It was clearer than ever—and yet another confirmation—that in my 70 years of life God is able, and that He's always there for us. Truly God has preserved my life many times. I'm aware of some of them. But I'm sure that many times death brushed up against me and I had no idea.

When we get to heaven I'm sure that we'll hear "the rest of the story." We will learn of the many times our guardian angels intervened and saved us from tragedy and even death—or when we unknowingly helped to save someone else.

I'm so thankful for our loving heavenly Father who cares for and watches over us continually, and I want to thank Him for His love, patience, protection, and guidance. I challenge you to give God a chance. He will make a difference in your life.

Christine Schneider

Like in a Fairytale

Ask and it will be given to you; seek and you will find;
knock and the door will be opened to you.
Luke 11:9, NIV.

WE WERE ON A LONG VACATION TRIP in our old VW beetle packed full with a tent, water containers, food, and everything you need for a trip from Munich, Germany, through Italy and Sicily, Tunisia, Algeria, Morocco, Spain, France, and back through Switzerland to our home town. This trip took place a long time before mobile homes.

It was past midnight. We were tired and I feared that once more we'd need to spend the night in our car. We had spent a few days camping in Algiers to rest after an adventurous crossing of the desert and the Atlas Mountains. In the morning we had set off along the coast, intending to cross over to Morocco. But we'd waited a long time at the border while our car was meticulously examined. Now, at last, we were able to continue and were on the lookout for a safe place to put up our tent and finally get to sleep.

We had gotten exact directions from the automobile club to what was supposed to be a guarded city park. But it was now the middle of the night—and almost impossible to find this park in a city devoid of streetlights. And so we considered spending the night in the car in front of a police station as a safety precaution.

But I wanted to crawl into our tent, stretch out, and just sleep peacefully. And so we studied the directions again and again. I prayed silently and earnestly that God would let us find the park. As we sat in our car, not knowing what to do, we saw something flashing at a distance. It was almost like in a fairytale, so surreal and unexpected. We focused on the other side of the street where we saw a dark figure clad in a long robe, a turban on his head.

My heart skipped a beat. "It's the park!" I cried, and we drove in the direction of this surprising apparition. When the lights of our car hit the man we saw that it was the park guardian. He opened the gates and showed us where we could put up our tent.

While I had been asking God to help us, the guardian was on his rounds and came to the gate just at the moment God made me look in his direction. Such is our God. I sent many prayers of thanksgiving to the Lord who opened the gates for us in a wonderful way.

Ingrid Naumann

God's Presence/Presents

Every good and perfect gift is from above, coming down
from the Father of the heavenly lights.
James 1:17, NIV.

DID YOU WATCH the opening ceremonies for the Beijing Olympics? I've never seen anything so amazing, filled with such incredible color and light. My senses were overwhelmed by the fluid, graceful, brilliant precision of thousands of human bodies! Such an incredible blend of technology and choreographed physical human accomplishments was mind–boggling. And because it was China, they did not pretend to be anything but what they were: followers and believers in Confucius, Buddhism, feng shui, harmony, and martial arts—or nothing at all. Their amazing opening ceremonies were filled with symbolism: the honor and glory of their feats given to their national gods and wise men and to their own human accomplishments. But after my senses were completely awed by the astounding beauty of it, I found myself profoundly sad.

Imagine if all the time, money, and amazing precision of human talents spent making this production appear so effortless and so astounding had been spent instead glorifying the God of heaven and His presence in our lives. Imagine if all that incredible technology had been used to bring the Father to the forefront instead of Buddha, or that it had been used to quote the Father's words, celebrating His presents. What if all the brilliant use of color in the opening ceremonies pointed instead to the Master Creator of color?

The Chinese repeatedly used a symbol for harmony. I can imagine the wonderful harmony all nations could enjoy if everything we had, every gift and talent we possessed, the wisdom we stored away, was presented to the rest of mankind for the sole purpose of giving honor and glory to the God of glory! What if the opening ceremonies had been presented to glorify the One who created us and manifested His love by giving His life for every single man, woman, and child on the face of this planet? God has blessed people with so much, and it is so sad that we rarely tell Him, "Thank You." Instead, we take the credit to ourselves. How sad that we take advantage of His presents and His passion for us but ignore His presence in our lives.

Whatever He has blessed you with, whatever He has created you to be, give Him the glory and honor. Use your talents and gifts for Him. The results will then be truly "Wow!"

Anita Mayes

A Miracle of Understanding Needed!

The Lord is my shepherd, I shall not be in want.
Ps. 23:1, NIV.

THE BEST TIME OF THE YEAR seems to be when we take our vacation. And this year we had decided to visit Bulgaria, the home country of our daughter-in-law. She and our son have been married for seven years and her family wanted to get to know us. After a few weeks there we became very thankful for all the comforts we had taken for granted in our simple home. The place we stayed was far from the city and the church we wanted to attend, so we prayed for a means of transportation so we could go to church. My husband and I prayed about it every day. We were thirsting for spiritual refreshment and communion, so we also prayed for the miracle of understanding. How could that happen in Bulgaria when we spoke German?

We were finally able to borrow a car. Under normal circumstances we should have been in the city within half an hour, but the car broke down continually. Our son, who was driving, had to stop every so many miles to fill up the radiator. We were sitting in the back—each with a grandchild on our laps—praying for a safe arrival.

When we finally reached the church in Trojan we could hear singing. We were speaking German as we walked to the church entrance and were greeted by the pastor's wife with a friendly "Guten Morgen!" ("Good morning" in German). Around 50 members were present, and when it was time for the Bible lesson two men joined us and translated everything for us. What a wonder! We were able to understand everything. The whole time we had brothers and sisters who helped us follow the service, and we were nourished with God's Word.

That Sabbath there was a special service; the pastoral couple was being sent to Switzerland. They had received their ministerial training 10 years before in Germany, so they spoke German. Even the conference president who was there spoke our language quite well.

God really answered our prayers for understanding. After the service they had a community meal and we were able to enjoy our contacts with the church members during this time as well. Strengthened, and with thankful hearts for this wonderful experience with God, we made our way back to our vacation home in the afternoon. Nothing is impossible for our God.

Ingrid Bomke

The Angel Drove a Taxi

The angel of the Lord encampeth round about them that fear him, and delivereth them.
Ps. 34:7.

IN THE SUMMER OF 1997, my parents had gone to Durban, South Africa, for the World Association of Veteran Athletes' World Championships. In the past they had been to many countries for athletic events such as this. However, this would be a trip they'd not forget.

The morning after their arrival they decided to share a taxi to the stadium with an acquaintance. As they climbed into the back of the cab Mom placed their duffle bag on the seat beside her. As they neared the stadium entrance, Mom took her fanny pack from the duffle bag so she could pay a portion of the taxi service fee. Their friend, who had sat in the front seat with the driver, paid the whole amount so Mom returned the pack to the duffle bag—or so she thought. Mom followed Dad out of the left side of the cab, pulling the duffle bag along with her, not knowing that the fanny pack had fallen on the other side of the duffle bag between the door and the seat.

A short time later Mom searched the bag and discovered that the pack was missing. Gripped by panic, she whispered a prayer and hurried to find Dad and tell him that the pack that held all their money, their passports, and their credit cards was gone. He asked her if she had put the bag down at anytime. When she told him that the bag had never left her shoulder, he knew what must have happened. Praying, they entered another taxi to go back to their hotel. Just as they were about to pull away, the previous taxi driver came up to the car and told them to get out because he had found their pack. When he had been unable to locate them, he had taken the pack to the hotel where he had picked them up. Now he personally took them back to the hotel to make sure they got the pack and that all the contents were still there!

God chose to use this average taxi driver to show my mother that she should never fear but only trust in Him. This experience taught her that God is ever with her in her time of need if she will but trust in Him.

Philippians 4:6 tells us to, "be careful for nothing; but in every thing by prayer and supplication with thanksgiving let your requests be made known unto God." Let us determine today that we will trust in God and turn over all our cares to Him.

Theodora V. Sanders

Raindrops and Grasshoppers

Surely the nations are like a drop in a bucket.
Isa. 40:15, NIV.

He sits enthroned above the circle of the earth, and its people are like grasshoppers.
Isa. 40:22, NIV.

HAVE YOU EVER STOPPED to observe a raindrop or dewdrop on a flower petal? Didn't it seem fragile and insignificant? And what can be said about the grasshopper that jumps here and there and suddenly ends up inside your house?

In nature, we see innumerable small, fragile species which seem insignificant. Their insignificance is increased even more if they are compared with majestic mountains that seem to touch the heavens or to the tall trees that blow to and fro as they are pushed and shoved by the wind, but nevertheless firmly remain in place.

How many times have we despised the small worm as it is attached to the stem of a plant; however, we enthusiastically relish the gigantic ocean waves that reach the beach. Likely, hundreds of times we step on tiny ants without even noticing them; meanwhile, we marvel at the immense number of shining stars sparkling in the night sky.

The defenseless slug that slowly walks along leaving its sticky trail is not often valued, but we admire the majestic pose of the roaring lion which causes us to tremble. It is intriguing to reflect on the reason that God compares us to such small things that seemingly lack in value. We, as human beings, are impressed by strength, exuberance, power. However, it seems that God thinks differently.

As I meditate on these texts I conclude that God is truly powerful and sovereign, above all things. At the same time, as Creator, He loves the small as well as the large. Whether He sees us as raindrops or grasshoppers, He cares for us kindly because He knows how weak and vulnerable we are. If, for us, a single water drop that drips out of a bucket of water has no value whatsoever, let's remember that for our loving God this single drop is very important.

I am happy because God is great and powerful. He loves me tremendously and He cares for me like He cares for all the other defenseless creatures. It is wonderful to know that I can trust in Him. Why don't you, too, place your trust in our wonderful Creator who cares for the small as well as the big?

Edileuza de Souza Meira

Jehovah-jireh

And Abraham called the name of that place Jehovahjireh: as it is said to this day.
Gen 22:14.

IN GENESIS, CHAPTER 22 (please read verses 1–18), Isaac asked Abraham about the missing lamb for the burnt offering. Abraham said, "God will provide." And Abraham named that place on Mt. Moriah Jehovah-jireh. Early in my Christian life God showed me that He was Jehovah-jireh (Jehovah will see to it) in my life, and that He was my provider!

Things changed very quickly when I got married. As a bride of only six weeks, I learned I was six weeks pregnant. My husband couldn't see how he was going to take care of a wife and child on one salary, so when our baby was about 8 months old, my husband wanted me to go back to work—after all, I did have a college degree. What he didn't know was how the Holy Spirit had been ministering to me during those months about being a stay-at-home mother. This was not an ideal I had previously considered for myself. Our plans had been to live what is perceived as the American Dream.

Now my heart had completely changed. I could think only of my baby. I wanted safety, love, and stability to surround her life. I told my husband that I was sure the Holy Spirit had revealed to me that I was to stay home. He immediately said, "Well, God didn't reveal that to me. You can work and take care of the baby at the same time like everybody else does."

I prayerfully decided to put the situation in God's hands, and I went back to work. One day when we went to pick up the baby I was shocked to see the caregiver doing things that I felt were inappropriate in the presence of our child. I grabbed up my baby and left with tears streaming down my face. My husband asked me what was wrong, and I told him what happened.

The Holy Spirit started dealing with him immediately. The Holy Spirit asked my husband three questions: Is money more important then the safety of your daughter? Who told you that you needed two incomes to survive? Don't you believe that I am a big enough God to provide for you and your family?

My husband told me that it was revealed to him that I should stop working. We have now been married 22 years and have two children. God has always showed himself as Jehovah-jireh in my life.

Chrisele Green

God's Own Land

I am sending you grain, new wine and oil, enough to satisfy you fully.
Joel 2:19, NIV.

OLIVES, MULBERRIES, almonds, figs, wild rosemary and thyme, wine, apricots, peaches, and cherry trees with boughs so laden with fruit they look like coral necklaces grow in this land. The sunflower fields are huge, the grain fields abundant. The lavender fields in their various shades of blue are so extensive you can hardly see them all. The air is filled with butterflies as blue as lavender, and the birds are as yellow as gorse. There is red, yellow, and white soil. The sun is brilliant, the sky an intense blue, the trees almost unnaturally green. The water in the wells is fresh, clear, and delicious. The pine trees exude an intensive perfume, and the sound of the crickets is associated with this land.

Is this Paradise? You could almost think so. And yet this land is in the middle of Europe. It is the Provence area in the southeastern part of France. For me, every time we go there it is like a small reflection of Paradise. It's as if God had put in this region all the good things He had left over at creation, so we could have a glimpse of what real Paradise is like. And every time I have to leave Provence I am sad and wish a time would come when I could stay there forever. My heart is filled with longing.

But then I remember that there is a place that has to be yet more beautiful. A place no man or woman has ever seen, and whose melodies no one has heard; and best of all, a place we will never have to leave. This real paradise is one that surpasses our imagination; furthermore, Jesus has promised to take us there. In the new earth He will create I will not be able to take my eyes off the wonders of nature. I will enjoy this real Paradise forever. That will finally be God's own land. He has prepared it special, just for you and me. The Bible says, "Then the angel showed me the river of the water of life, as clear as crystal, flowing from the throne of God and of the Lamb down the middle of the great street of the city. On each side of the river stood the tree of life, bearing twelve crops of fruit, yielding its fruit every month. And the leaves of the tree are for the healing of the nations" (Rev. 22:1, 2, NIV).

I am looking forward to that. What about you? The Lord says, "Yes, I am coming soon." Amen. Come, Lord Jesus! (Rev. 22:20, NIV).

Margarete Baindner

Where There Is No Way

Fear thou not; for I am with thee: be not dismayed; for I am thy God: I will strengthen thee;
yea, I will help thee; yea, I will uphold thee with the right hand of my righteousness.
Isa. 41:10.

BEING AWAY FROM THE FAMILY NEST is often difficult, and it is even more so for those, like our children, who travel to foreign countries to pursue higher education. As parents, we must encourage our children and pray that God will spare them from the dangers of this world. It is important for them to be emotionally fitted, spiritually balanced, and prepared for what is to come.

God entrusted my husband and me with wonderful children, and we tried to raise them according to His divine guidance. I want to encourage all mothers who may be worried for their children who are going away to college or will soon start living on their own. We would like to keep a watchful eye on our loved ones, but there comes a time when they must embark on life's journey. We can only prepare them to experience their faith.

When our second daughter, Deliane, left Andrews University to pursue graduate studies at a public university in Muncie, Indiana, I asked God to provide her with brothers and sisters of the faith who would sustain her spiritually. As a mother, I placed my fears in the hands of my heavenly Father and asked God to bring people into my daughter's life who could be a family to her. I was distressed by the idea of her being alone in this new environment; especially since she had been enrolled in church-run schools for most of her education. Now she was moving away from her sister, and we lived in Martinique.

God directed Deliane to a loving church. God also blessed her and put in her path a wonderful couple who welcomed her as their own. They opened their heart and their home to her, and when she had to leave Indiana to move to Atlanta, Georgia, for her internship, they did not hesitate to drive the 10 hours with her belongings and help her move into her new apartment! May God bless this local church and the Young family.

God answered a mother's plea. I encourage all mothers to rest in peace, knowing that God takes care of our children.

From their young age, I dedicated my children to the Lord and chose them for my investment plan. Be faithful and experience God's blessings in the life of your loved ones.

Flora F. Beloni

Workmen in the Trees

And take heed to yourselves, lest at any time your hearts be overcharged with . . .
cares of this life, and so that day come upon you unawares.
Luke 21:34.

IT WAS AN EXTREMELY HOT, humid summer day. My oldest son, 6 years old at the time, was at his dad's for the weekend. Divorced, with primary custody of my child, I was the usual busy single mom, so it was nice having time to myself—no cooking, cleaning, or doing anything that I didn't feel like doing. I lounged around, read a book for an hour or so while listening to music, then began to clean the apartment. After a while I realized the high heat and humidity had become unbearable. The air conditioning wasn't working properly. To get more comfortable, I took off my shorts and top and, scantily clothed, continued cleaning. I wasn't expecting anyone and I didn't plan to go anywhere, so the less I had on, the better.

While dusting, I listened to music, stopping from time to time to admire the beautiful trees adjacent to my balcony. They were overly-abundant with blooms and a lovely sight! Although the venetian blinds were mostly open, no one could see into my third-floor apartment from the ground or from the apartments directly across, so there was no danger of being spotted. I stood again and enjoyed the flowering trees before gathering up laundry to fold. The chore complete, I got a cold drink of water and sipped it while again admiring the trees.

Suddenly I saw something: two men were up in the trees just a few feet from my window, cutting off branches. I ducked down, dropped to my knees, and crawled to the bedroom, afraid they had seen me and could still see me. I put my shorts and a top back on, then returned to the living room. The men were still busily at work, no smirks or laughs to indicate they had spotted me. There was no cause for embarrassment, and I was so relieved!

After many years, in retrospect the whole situation was rather funny. But now, older and more spiritually–minded, solemn thoughts of Satan—at my door or window, busily at work in my life—plague me, for whether my life is carefree or filled with busyness, what I wear will never be the right attire for his subtle encounters. I must, therefore, be more aware, ever vigilant, and always clothed with the righteousness of Christ lest I be exposed to the world as one not fitted for heaven. *Lord, help me; Lord, help you*, is my prayer.

Iris L Kitching

Answered Prayer

Before they call I will answer; while they are still speaking I will hear.
Isa. 65:24, NIV.

IT WAS THE EVENING of October 30, and my son's pilot license would expire in the morning. In order to keep current his instrument rating as a pilot, it was necessary for him to do some flying by October 31. Two previous flying appointments had been canceled because of extremely windy weather. If he could not fly tomorrow, his instrument rating would expire, and he'd be required to retake a number of classes and rewrite the exam. This was time and money I didn't want him to have to spend.

My son had left Berrien Springs, Michigan, a year before because the weather conditions so often prevented him from flying. But moving to Boston, Massachusetts, was not the improvement he had hoped for. The weather conditions there were quite similar to those in Michigan, and good flying days were rare.

So I encouraged him to pray about the matter and reassured him that his dad and I were praying for a miracle. With faith high and prayers continually ascending to the throne of grace for calm weather, my son made another flying appointment for October 31, the last possible day to meet the requirement.

The wind blew into the night as we prayed and went to bed. The next day— calm. Praise the Lord. The God of the skies, seas, and land stayed the winds.

God shows so much love and care for us. Throughout our lives we are challenged by many and varied problems. Whether they are big or small God is ready, willing, and able to help. No concern is too small or too insignificant. So let us turn our burdens over to Him.

I have adopted the maxim for life, "Accentuate the Positive." In today's text, Isaiah is referring to the new heavens and new earth. But even here, in this sin-stained world, God hears our prayers. He can bring wonderful good out of every bad situation, however desperate or improbable it may seem at the time. We need to accentuate the positive in faith. "Do not be anxious about anything, but in everything, by prayer and petition, with thanksgiving, present your requests to God. And the peace of God, which transcends all understanding, will guard your hearts and your minds in Christ Jesus" (Phil. 4:6, 7, NIV).

Janice Fleming-Williams

Who Will Roll the Stone Away?

And they asked each other, "Who will roll the stone away from the entrance of the tomb?" But when they looked up, they saw that the stone, which was very large, had been rolled away.
Mark 16:3, 4, NIV.

SOMETHING TERRIBLE had taken place. The police had been brought in. Families were hurt; lives were exposed and dissected. The very idea that something like this could have taken place within our church community was abhorrent to us. I'd been asked to address the women of the church in order to acknowledge the whispers and half-truths that had been circulating. I was to somehow bring order to the chaotic situation that we were now a part of.

Some 50 to 60 women stayed after the morning service. I chose the text from Mark 16, because deep inside I really wanted to hand this task over to someone else. I didn't feel qualified to deal with the women and was apprehensive about how to answer their questions, how to share what little information we were permitted while still maintaining an impartial stance.

There were some tough questions, Whys?—for which I had no answer. Some felt it was wrong for us to be discussing someone else's misfortune in this way. Others understood the need for clarity and reassurance. I let them talk, because I sensed that's what they needed.

When it was time, I led them in prayer, managing only a few words before my own composure broke. Another sister continued. Taking the microphone in one hand and holding onto me with the other, she spoke in her mother tongue, and even though I was unable to follow what she was saying, I was comforted. The stone that I'd been worrying over was surely and inexorably being rolled away.

We prayed together, weeping openly, touched not just by this fresh hurt, but more by the dormant hurts from our own pasts still unresolved after all this time. At last, through our tears, God brought us cleansing as we turned to Him, pouring out our bitterness, disappointment, and anger. Who else could we turn to?

I continue to marvel at the way God brings His own peace into lives disrupted through the forces of evil. How He knit our church family back together. I thank God that He is there to deal with the things that are too big for us to handle.

Avery Davis

Best Laid Plans

Before they call I will answer; while they are still speaking I will hear.
Isa. 65:24 NIV.

*See, I am sending an angel ahead of you to guard you along
the way and to bring you to the place I have prepared.*
Ex. 23:20, NIV.

AUGUST 10, 2006, was a special day in our family. Our daughter was going to college. We awoke early as our flight was at 6:50 a.m. We had morning worship to ask God to bless our daughter as she embraced her new life in college, then left for the airport.

We arrived an hour before the flight. But little did we know that chaos filled all the airports that day as we hadn't looked at the news before leaving the house. The first thing we noticed was the long lines and armed soldiers inside the airport. I turned to my daughter and asked, "What is going on here?" Then we heard an announcement instructing us to place all liquids in our checked-in cases. We could not carry them on board with us. Puzzled by this announcement, we asked one of the security people what was going on. He explained that the day before, in London, someone had tried using liquids to bomb an airplane.

Many people didn't take the announcements seriously. They thought that by explaining why they needed them, they'd be allowed to keep their liquids in their hand luggage. Unfortunately, they ended up throwing their expensive shampoos, lotions, perfumes, and other liquids in the trash.

Because of delays we missed our Chicago connection and there were few flights to Lincoln, Nebraska. I felt impatient. I could see us spending a night in the airport, and our daughter wasn't feeling well. Just as I sent up a silent prayer an attendant came straight to me and asked where I was going then looked at the flight schedules and told us to run to the boarding gate—the last flight out was just starting to board. We were the last ones on, but God got us to Nebraska that very day.

Our best laid plans can go wrong, but God is in charge of every situation and t He will see us through—especially if we listen closely to what He is trying to tell us through His "announcements" in the Bible—we will not be disappointed.

Judith M. Mwansa

Lost and Confused

Are not two little sparrows sold for a penny? And yet not one of them will fall to the ground without your Father's leave (consent) and notice. But even the very hairs of your head are all numbered. Fear not, then; you are of more value than many sparrows.
Matt. 10:29-31, Amplified.

ONE DAY A HUMMINGBIRD flew into the firehouse garage where my husband, Mark, was working. The little bird flew up to the ceiling of the high garage looking for the way out, but the way out wasn't up there—the only door was much lower. Unfortunately, at first the crew didn't see the little bird, and it continued to fly in circles, looking and looking for a route of escape. Still no escape.

When the crew heard the little bird's twittering they opened both of the big garage doors hoping it would find its way out. Alas, the little bird stayed up near the ceiling, circling, expending all its energy looking for an escape that wasn't there. Soon, the little bird stopped more and more often to rest on the support rails. Then it happened: the little bird lay on a rafter rail in utter exhaustion, totally dehydrated. It lay there, waiting to die, unable to find the doors to freedom.

Mark burned with compassion for the hummingbird and didn't want to give up on it. He got a ladder, climbed up to the hummingbird, and gently carried it down. Then taking a little bowl of sugar water he had prepared, he gently lifted up the little head so its beak would go into the water. It took awhile, but soon the little bird started drinking. Mark carried it and the water outside, and as it finished drinking it looked at Mark as if to say, "Thank you," and then flew away. Mark said it was amazing to feel the strength and energy flow back into the small body of the little bird as he held it.

You know, that's what God does for us. We circle and exhaust ourselves in our troubles, looking for a way out when the doors are wide open with all the answers that God has provided. But we can't see it. When we give up trying to do it ourselves, God is able to restore, refresh, and carry us through each and every problem, no matter how big or how small. "Trust in the Lord with all thine heart; and lean not unto thine own understanding. In all thy ways acknowledge him, and he shall direct thy paths" (Prov. 3:5, 6).

Mona Fellers

As a Little Child

Let the little children come to Me, and do not forbid them;
for of such is the kingdom of God.
Mark 10:14, NKJV.

I LOOKED FORWARD to the day with mixed emotions. Our daughter, granddaughter, and two great-granddaughters were coming to spend the day. While we'd visited them in their home when they were younger, this was the first time the girls, ages 6 and 8, would visit us at ours. They live in a big, beautiful home in the city, while we live in a humble little house in the country. I knew from previous experience as a schoolteacher that children their age could be quite outspoken.

Since they live three hours away, I didn't expect them to arrive too early. I'd been canning tomatoes the evening before, so I needed to clean up the kitchen. Also I wanted to make a cobbler from our peaches and I was busy doing that when they arrived—earlier than I expected.

They didn't even notice the dirty kitchen. After greetings were finished, Grampa kept them busy outdoors. He showed them the beehives up on the roof and explained that the hives were up there to be out of reach of the bears that visit us sometimes. He also told them how bees make honey. A real thrill came when the girls spotted the queen bee in one of the hives.

Then they were off to visit the chicken pen and help to feed our five hens and one rooster. When Grampa demonstrated how he talks to the rooster and makes him crow, the girls thought it was great fun to do the same. After lunch, while some of us rested, Grampa took them for a ride in his golf cart and they found wild blackberries to pick and sample. Everything they did all day long was a big adventure, and we didn't have to worry about how to entertain them.

Time to go home came all too soon for them. We thought they'd surely be tired and sleep on the way home, but they were too excited about everything they'd done at Grampa and Grama's house. The next day, and for many days after, they asked their mother when they could go visit Grampa and Grama again. I'd been worried that we didn't have all the elegant things they're surrounded with at their house, but they were just as happy with the simple things.

These girls taught me an important lesson: simple things can be interesting and a lot of fun, especially true when they are out in nature as God has made them.

Betty J. Adams

How Much More Am I Worth?

Don't be afraid; you are worth more than many sparrows.
Luke 12:7, NIV.

I FELT MY WORLD crashing down around me, my orderly life spinning out of control. My husband's business was doing poorly and would likely go into receivership. Financially, we were on the brink of disaster. All our assets were tied up in our business and if we had to close its doors, my husband would have to declare bankruptcy. We would lose everything, including our home.

Every night when he came home from work the news was more bleak and discouraging than the night before. I could not begin to understand how this could be happening. Intellectually I knew that I would only be losing "stuff," but it was still, oh, so hard! The thought of losing my dream home—the one we designed and built with our own hands—was something I could hardly bear.

On a Friday morning I found myself on my knees. (I loved to pray in a special spot in my bedroom.) As I prayed, I could gaze through the sliding glass doors and marvel at the beautiful vista in front of me. We lived on a lake surrounded by low hills and every day the scene was different. I especially loved the ponderosa pine that had just been poking its head above the deck when we built the house, but now, many years later, stood tall, proud, and majestic.

This morning was different. I couldn't pray, so I just knelt there and cried my heart out. I felt so alone, so scared, so confused. I was so wrapped up in my own little world that as I gazed outside I didn't see anything. Then I became aware that we were having a major windstorm. *How apropos*, I thought. My favorite pine tree bent way over to the side. And that's when I noticed a little sparrow hanging onto the tree for dear life. At first the sparrow didn't register; God knew I needed that windstorm to catch my attention. Within moments after seeing the first sparrow, I saw another, then another, and, yes, there was the fourth. All of them riding out the storm.

Then it hit me—one sparrow for each member of my family! *Thank You, God, for providing me with a reminder that You are in control and that I can totally trust You with my life. Thank You for the peace that comes with knowing that I am as precious to You as those little birds. No,* more *precious than the sparrows.*

Jill Rhynard

The Stain on the Bed

And he passed in front of Moses, proclaiming, "The Lord, the Lord, the compassionate and gracious God, slow to anger, abounding in love and faithfulness, maintaining love to thousands, and forgiving wickedness, rebellion and sin."
Ex. 34:6, 7, NIV.

THE SUN STREAMED through the window. Its golden rays gently enveloped the couch, inviting me to take a seat. I got my book, propped up a pillow against the armrest and stretched out. In my hectic life, moments like these are precious. It was not very long before Benny, our cat, caught the idea and joined me. He sauntered over, hopped up, climbed onto my tummy, curled up, and started purring. A good book, sunshine, and time to relax: life could not be better.

After a good, long read and a short nap, I felt refreshed. I was ready to head to the kitchen and conjure up a meal. The phone rang. We would be three for dinner. Quite content and still enjoying the glow of my wonderful rest I walked into the bedroom. Should I make a pizza? Or, should I go with the new casserole recipe that I had wanted to try for some time?

Suddenly, my nose and eyes were assaulted by a huge pungent-smelling yellow stain on the freshly covered duvet. Instantly rage welled up inside me and burst forth like a volcano. "I'm going to kill that cat!" I screamed. The warm, fuzzy feeling of just a few minutes ago had been replaced with uncontrollable anger. My husband chose this unfortunate moment to arrive home. His good–natured wife had been replaced by a temper-tantrum-throwing lunatic threatening to kill "your cat." The wonderful afternoon was now a distant memory. I stripped the bed while giving a running commentary on my feelings about the feline criminal and my husband's apparent lack of understanding about the gravity of the offense. I shoved the comforter into the washing machine, releasing my frustrations on its buttons. The aforementioned dinner turned into a take-out meal. A friendly meal with friends became a tirade of cat-hate calumny.

"I would tell you more about Benny but he has fallen out of my good graces," I wrote to a friend two days later. Suddenly it hit me. God is never this way with me. Despite my pungent smelling sins and the stains on my record, Jesus always treats me with love, respect, and dignity. He is always willing to forgive me. He loves me in spite of my imperfection. *Thank You, Lord, for being patient with me—with each of us!*

Maike Stepanek

God Is With Us

Trust in the Lord with all your heart and lean not on your own understanding; in all your ways acknowledge him, and he will make your paths straight.
Prov. 3:5, 6, NIV.

WE WERE DRIVING from New Jersey to Canada when we stopped on the Pennsylvania Turnpike to get something to eat. My best friend, her husband, and newborn baby were taking my daughter and me to my hometown where we would hold a memorial service for my husband who had died unexpectedly the week before. We were all grief stricken and not thinking clearly, so it wasn't until we approached the border crossing into Ontario, Canada, that we realized my friend's purse had been left behind in the restaurant.

I had carried her purse into the restaurant and in my state of mind had forgotten it on the way out. Everything important was in her purse: money, credit cards, all of her ID, including her passport and driver's license. Since her 8-week-old son didn't have a birth certificate yet, the physician's letter verifying his parentage was also in the missing purse.

We were at least four hours from the restaurant where we'd left the purse and about an hour away from our destination, having traveled more than 12 exhausting hours with my 10-month-old daughter and the newborn infant. The thought of heading back to find the purse was unbearable.

We drove up to the immigration officer and explained what had happened. At the very least, I expected we'd be detained while they made phone calls to verify our story. But we were immediately admitted entry into Canada. We were stunned. As soon as we crossed into Canada, I began making phone calls. Using a receipt from the ATM at the restaurant, I was able to get the name of the town where we had stopped. Directory assistance gave me the phone number of the restaurant. We called. They had found the purse! When the purse reached us a few days later, everything was there: the money, credit cards, everything!

When I look back to this incident, it seems incredible. Sometimes in the midst of the worst times of your life, God gives you signs to assure you that He is still with you. If we choose to acknowledge that God has a plan for our lives, that there are no coincidences, we will be able to see His love for us. God will always find a way to let us know He is present and He cares for us—we just have to pay attention.

Melodie Homer

Kitchen Equipment

*To the weak I became weak, to win the weak. I have become all things
to all men so that by all possible means I might save some.*
1 Cor. 9:22, NIV.

MY HUSBAND AND I just visited a store for kitchen furnishings and I must confess that we were overwhelmed. What a multitude of ideas and possibilities! How many things I liked! We saw wonderful kitchen appliances and varieties of materials: glass, steel, granite, wood, and so on. There were designs with clear lines and fronts, others with many decorations and playful details. It was a good thing that we hadn't come to choose kitchen furnishings after all. It would have been difficult to make a choice.

Ever since, I have been thinking, *Why it is so easy for us to be creative as to kitchen equipment and other home furnishing matters and so difficult when we are dealing with the most important things of life?* In 1 Corinthians 9:19-22 we read how the apostle Paul wanted to be all things to all people in order to share the gospel and to reach the hearts of people. Then we wonder what that would mean for us today.

How can I be all things to all people and still be an authentic Christian? Maybe we could compare it with kitchen equipment. Every kitchen has the same basic elements: sink, stove, refrigerator, oven, cabinets. And still every kitchen is different. Every person likes different things and has different priorities. For some, the stove is most important, so they place more weight on it. For others, the design is very important and so they will be particular about that. Young people like different things in a kitchen than do older people. Everybody has different means and possibilities, and even our tastes change in the course of life and other things become more important. And yet everybody wants basically the same thing—a kitchen.

Thus it is our duty as ambassadors of God's love to meet people and their needs. When we share the gospel, we should consider that there are some important elements, and others that are only decorative. Our actions should be influenced accordingly, and we should not forget that we all like different things. One of the reasons why we are so different is so that we can reach various people with God's message. It is good there are all kinds of kitchen cabinets and all kinds of people. If we keep this principle in our hearts we will fulfill today's Bible verse.

Claudia DeJong

Garlic Gone for Good

*And great crowds gathered about him, so that he got into a boat
and sat there; and the whole crowd stood on the beach. And he told them
many things in parables, saying: "A sower went out to sow."*
Matt. 13:2, 3, RSV.

PICTURE A BEACH, waves lapping over the rocky shore while rattling the boats tethered nearby. View the low hills rising from the beach and parading low scrubby plants and scattered wildflowers. In the distance take note of the terraced farmland covered by brown rolls of earth ready for planting. Watch the people, a mass of people gathering eagerly near the beach by the small group of rough men who are standing about their fishing boats.

Several talk excitedly about the Galilean man who describes spiritual things in such a way that even the hardened and the young listen. A teenager declares that he will be the first to decipher Jesus' word puzzle for that day. Amidst all the ordinary, a melodic voice confidently rises to share a parable, teaching about seeds sown, some landing in ground ready to grow and others not.

This parable wandered through my mind as my body took on the gardener's nemesis: weeds, hundreds of them. There are weeds, and then there are good plants in the wrong place. My trowel burrowed down into the brown dirt in search of garlic bulbs. The benefits of garlic rank high in herb books, but this just wasn't the best place for garlic in my garden. Something else would make better use of that favored spot in the sun.

Thinking of the seeds parable, I decided to make a parable about garlic. Jesus used nature to illustrate, so I pictured the garlic as sins in my life. I needed to replace the garlic with something else, and then maybe those bulbs would not be able to come up through a new plant. The replacement for my garlic "sins" became a rhubarb plant, a plant with huge leaves and tart edible stems. Never again did a garlic bulb find its way into the light there. Some sins in my life need to be weeded out even though they appear to some as acceptable activities. Knowing that I needed a replacement didn't make for instant success, but the rhubarb plant did fine with only additional water and occasional fertilizer. Spiritual water and Bible study enables the Christian to replace bad habits with good.

Helen Dick Burton

Universal Language

For this is the message that ye heard from the beginning, that we should love one another.
1 John 3:11.

MY 20-YEAR-OLD twin daughters and I took a vacation to Mexico in August, 2006, with one of my brothers and his family. It was the first time we did an all inclusive vacation and it was great. I was amazed at the number of people who were there at that time of the year, considering it was not winter back home. People from Canada, the United States, England, Italy, and other countries were enjoying the hot weather and tropical environment.

One day as we lay on the beach soaking up the sun, I could not help but notice how different yet similar we were. My ears picked up the various accents. I love to hear them; it is like music to my ears. One word we all used on a daily basis was *Hola* (Hello). Since many of us could not speak Spanish we felt bilingual with that one small word.

My favorite pastime was watching families and friends splashing in the pool and swimming in the ocean, and children racing around laughing and making new friends. It dawned on me that there is one universal language that we all spoke—the language of love. It permeated the air. There was no sense of urgency but a general feeling of relaxation, fun, and frolic. Strangers were friendly and courteous with one another. Everyone seemed happy and got along. There was no road rage or drive-by shootings. Just peace and tranquility.

It was great to see parents spending quality time with their children, eating and playing together. There were 10 in our group, five adults and five children. I took the opportunity to share little snippets that showed Jesus' love for them. It was a privilege to share morning worship with those who typically did not have worship; I gave the children little love notes from Jesus with a text on it telling them daily how great God is. Like the apostle Paul, I am not ashamed of the gospel.

My Bible tells me that "God so loved the world, that he gave his only begotten Son, that whosoever believeth in him should not perish, but have everlasting life" (John 3:16). What an unconditional, unselfish sacrifice to give up a loved one who was faultless to suffer the penalty for us. He traded places with us and took what we deserve. What a mighty God we serve.

Sharon Long (Brown)

A Wonderful Country

And God shall wipe away all tears from their eyes; and there shall be no more death, neither sorrow, nor crying, neither shall there be any more pain: for the former things are passed away. Rev. 21:4.

I WANT TO TELL YOU about a wonderful country where there will be no more tears, sorrow, illness, or sadness. In this country no one will have to say goodbye, because separation will not exist.

No one can look into the future and foresee that words uttered now will come to pass at a later time. But such words from my father were expressed like this: "Dear daughter, did you know that at times people say goodbye for the last time?" And I responded with only two words, "Oh, Dad!" (Sometimes we answer quickly with whatever comes to mind.)

I was paying a visit to my elderly parents. My son and I had traveled some distance and had been with them for several days. We were preparing to return home when this conversation took place. As I sat on the bus heading homeward, and distance began to separate me from my parents, my father's words echoed clearly in my mind.

Two years later I received news that my father's health had deteriorated, and he was not well. This caught me unprepared. I did not have the funds to immediately travel to see him. When I finally got funds and began the trip, I told my dear family, "Perhaps I will be too late!" As the hours dragged by, I repeated the words of Psalm 103, "Bless the Lord, O my soul: and all that is within me, bless his holy name." It comforted me on the long 24-hour bus trip.

It was too late when I arrived. I was not able to see my dear father for he had already been lain to rest. The day he said, "Dear daughter, did you know that at times people say goodbye for the last time?" I *had* said goodbye to him for the last time. *Thank You, God, for my hope of meeting him again someday.*

Do you want to know about that country which I mentioned? It is not difficult to discover. All that you need to do is to open your heart to Jesus. He is the Way, the Truth, and the Life. If you accept Him as your Savior, after the journey of this life ends, you will go to this wonderful country and will live with Jesus forever when He comes again—no more goodbyes.

Mirian Teixeira dos Santos

He Knew the Right Time

And thine ears shall hear a word behind thee, saying, This is the way,
walk ye in it, when ye turn to the right hand, and when ye turn to the left.
Isa. 30:21.

I HAD A DEMANDING FULL-TIME JOB and was caring for my 93-year-old mother who suffered from both Parkinson's disease and dementia. Soon it became very difficult for me to manage the load on my own. Clearly I had to do something to alleviate the overwhelming strain, but what? My first instinct was to take early retirement, but I knew it was a matter to consider carefully. I would have quite a substantial loss of income if I didn't wait for full retirement. I kept going over the pros and cons of that career move. Could I afford to retire ahead of schedule? Could I afford not to, with the signs of my mother's illnesses becoming increasingly obvious? I was in a quandary. Eventually I talked to God about the situation.

At first, I decided to wait a little longer before doing anything. My mother was in an adult daycare and was doing fairly well, and at work I was fulfilling my responsibilities. Yet I could not shake the impression that God wanted me to go ahead and file the papers for early retirement right then. But considering how much I would lose by retiring early, I kept putting it off. "Everything is fine," I told myself. "Surely I can wait a bit longer."

Still I could not shake the feeling. Eventually I gave in. "OK, God, I will do it." By now I was sure that the intense urging had come from God.

At work, I announced my last day of working a 40-hour week. I agreed to work three days each week since I was now allowed only a limited number of hours. But not more than 14 days later, I had to rush my mother to the hospital. The doctors there diagnosed her with stage four colon cancer! It was too late for treatment, so they sent her home with hospice care.

Saddened, I found a silver lining in this painful experience. Since I now worked per diem, my new schedule allowed me the opportunity to spend quality time with Mother in her final days without the additional tension from my job.

Sometime after the funeral, I took a retrospective look at the events that I had just experienced. I realized then that I truly had not known what lay ahead of me, but God did. I cannot imagine what would have happened to me had I not listened to my Father in heaven.

Arline Farquharson

Out of Control

Trust in the Lord with all your heart and lean not on your own understanding; in all your ways acknowledge him, and he will make your paths straight.
Prov. 3:5, 6, NIV.

MY HUSBAND AND I had been given a large, white Alaskan Malamute. Ivy, with her thick fluffy fur and constant smile, was truly a beauty. She was also a big, loveable dog who didn't know her own strength and at times she bowled us right over.

Since Malamutes are known for flunking out of obedience school, the breeder had warned us to let her know we were boss. She'd also mentioned that Ivy wouldn't hesitate to grab a smaller animal and shake it to death. So we kept her confined.

My husband faithfully walked her up and down the long country roads. One day when he was ill, I decided to try. I grabbed the leash and headed out the door while Ivy pranced in anticipation. Soon she was hooked up and we were off. At the crossroads, we headed north. As usual, the neighbor's little dog came out, yapping furiously. I pulled hard to keep Ivy in tow, but this time little Barky got bolder and followed us. Poor Ivy was bent out of shape. I managed to keep her headed forward and Barky finally dropped behind. Eventually, Ivy and I turned around and headed back.

Ivy always pulled harder going home. And now with little Barky up ahead and a weaker hand on the leash, I was in for a challenge. I dug my huge boots into the snow and gravel and struggled with both hands to keep her down to a walk. As we neared the crossroads, she strained so hard I became desperate. Barky was back in her own yard by this time, but I knew that if I was forced into a run, Ivy would be flying after her the minute both my feet left the ground. Visions of being dragged face down through the gravel haunted me. But if I let go of the leash it would be bye-bye Barky and our rocky relations with our neighbors would become boulders.

I gasped out a prayer. My lungs ached. My body screamed. I perspired even though it was freezing. Somehow, by the grace of God, we maneuvered that corner and back up our driveway. My whole body was trembling.

It's funny how circumstances can so easily cause us to feel out of control. My desperate prayer gasped out to God was the answer. He made our path straight home and out of danger.

Dawna Beausoleil

Merry-Go-Round

*Enter by the narrow gate; for the gate is wide and the way is easy, that leads
to destruction, and those who enter by it are many. For the gate is narrow and
the way is hard, that leads to life, and those who find it are few.*
Matt. 7:13, 14, RSV.

EXCITED BUT IMPATIENT, we wait in line for our turn on the carousel, the merry-go-round. The grandchildren's hands are damp in mine. Little fingers are twitching. Our line inches along, and finally it's our turn to ride the horses up and down and around and around. We choose our stallion quickly—a white steed with a red and blue saddle. Then we buckle up for safety. The music starts and off we go, up and down and around and around. We circle once, twice, three times. Then the music slows, the pace slackens, and finally we stop. It's over. Sadly we dismount and surrender our seats to the next set of eager riders.

As I reflect on the ride we've just enjoyed, I wonder, *Where did we really go on that carousel? What progress did we make?* Of course, you know the answer. We rode around and around the same circle, returning to exactly where we began our journey.

Unfortunately, too many of us may be carousel Christians, going to church every Sabbath and returning spiritually to the same spot. We may even have enjoyed the ride, commenting on the music of the praise team and the oratory of the speaker, but was it only a carousel for us? Did we make progress on our Christian journey, or did we just go around and around, up and down, up and down, returning to the same spiritual spot where we were before?

Actually the Christian life is a journey, not a carousel. Enoch *walked* with God (Gen. 5:22). God's walk leads somewhere, and as we travel the narrow path we should be making progress on this journey. But do we? Or is it like Jeremiah wrote: "But they did not listen or pay attention. . . . They went backward and not forward" (Jer. 7:24, NIV).

It may be time to get off the carousel, to do more than simply enjoy the ride of a Sabbath celebration. It may be time for us to begin our real journey on the narrow path that leads to life eternal. It may not be fun or easy, but it won't be crowded either. In fact, there may be lonely places on that road and sometimes we may not see our way. But it will get us somewhere.

I invite you today to get off the carousel and begin your walk with Jesus.

Annette Walwyn Michael

Help Somebody Today!

But do not forget to do good and to share, for with such sacrifices God is well pleased.
Heb. 13:16, NKJV.

NOT LONG AGO I found myself humming the tune that I sang with my high school choir many, many years ago. The lyrics were written by Mrs. Frank M. Brech back in the 1930s, but are still pertinent today: "Look all around you, find someone in need, help somebody today! Tho' it be little a neighborly deed, help somebody today! Help somebody today, somebody along life's way, let sorrow be ended, the friendless befriended; oh, help somebody today."

Every day that we awaken is like a freshly-wrapped gift from God to us—an opportunity to reach out and touch a life, give a hug, a smile, share a word of encouragement, offer a prayer or a helping hand to someone in need. Sometimes all it takes is a few moments, but it could make a world of difference to someone facing difficult challenges and who just needs to know that someone cares.

At times I become so caught up in my little world that I let golden opportunities to help somebody slip by. Something happened awhile ago that still plagues my conscience. A friend visited my office and shared the devastating news that her daughter—a young mother with three children—had been diagnosed with breast cancer. I was deeply saddened. Before my friend left, I promised her that I would pray for her daughter. Sad to say, in my busyness it slipped my memory and the day went by without a prayer from my lips on their behalf.

Would my prayer have made a difference in her valley of despair? Would it have given her a measure of peace and assurance of God's presence during her therapy? I will never know. I only know that my friend was depending on me, and I let her down. Suppose it was my daughter; I would have wanted my friend to remember, but I had forgotten.

When I thought of it I pleaded with my heavenly Father to forgive my neglect. I asked Him to bless my friend and her family, to strengthen their faith and trust in Him, and to give them the assurance that He is with them always, no matter how dark the storm clouds.

My God is longsuffering and merciful. I ask Him to open my eyes to those who need my help, and that I will seize every opportunity to make a difference. For inasmuch as we help one of the smallest of His children, we've helped Him.

Shirley C. Iheanacho

Heeding the Call

There are many rooms in my Father's house . . . .
I am going there to prepare a place for each of you.
John 14:2, CEV.

WHEN CHRIST MINISTERED on earth a crisis developed at His friends' home in Bethany. Lazarus was dying, and his sisters, Mary and Martha, sent out an SOS to Jesus. But Jesus did not drop what He was doing and go to him. Lazarus died and was buried. His sisters were deeply grieved, and friends came to comfort them. Then four days later Jesus arrived. Martha upbraided Him: "Lord, if you had been here, my brother would not have died" (John 11:21, CEV). Mary said almost the same thing (v. 32). But Jesus simply asked, "Where have you put his body?" (v. 34, CEV). But Martha said, "Lord you know that Lazarus has been dead four days , and there will be a bad smell." (v. 39, CEV).

Jesus went to the tomb. The stone was removed, and He called, "Lazarus, come out!" (v. 43, CEV). Although four days late, Jesus was right on time to demonstrate the power and glory of God.

In 2005, the powerful Hurricane Katrina hit the Gulf region of the United States. This master hurricane caused death and mayhem in the area. The mayor declared a state of emergency and issued a mandatory evacuation notice. Many heeded the call. Others sought refuge in churches, hotels, and the convention center, the great Superdome. Still others refused to budge.

Katrina came, and the aftermath was grave. An SOS was sent out to FEMA, President Bush, and the National Guard. However, the president was five days late. Five days late to see the flooding, horror, deaths, grime, darkness, hunger, and frustration the people were enduring.

One day, very soon, the crises in our world will culminate in the glorious appearing of our Lord and Savior Jesus Christ. John the Baptist extended an invitation to his hearers: "Repent ye: for the kingdom of heaven is at hand" (Matt. 3:2). When the SOS was sent out in heaven, Jesus answered, "I will go to save Adam's fallen race." On the cross Jesus sealed the deal by shedding His blood for our sins.

To those who reject the call, it will be a time of fear. They will perish in their "superdome" of materialism, pride, and selfishness. For those who accept, Jesus will come quickly and "will not tarry" (Heb. 10:37). Let us heed the call today.

Bula Rose Haughton Thompson

Too Occupied to Notice

Be careful, or your hearts will be weighed down with dissipation, drunkenness and the anxieties of life, and that day will close on you unexpectedly like a trap.
Luke 21:34, NIV.

IT WAS LATE AUGUST, 1992, and my pastor husband had just received a call from our conference president that it was time to move from our home in Arkansas to Slidell, Louisiana. But we were so busy! We had just returned from vacation and school was ready to begin in three different locations for our three children. However, we very reluctantly added moving to our busy agenda. As we scurried about during the next few days we remembered hearing something about Hurricane Andrew off the east coast of Florida. But the east coast of Florida was a long way from northwest Arkansas, and besides, we were very busy with our own cares of life right then.

Finally, we put our house on the market and left early one Sunday morning to house hunt in Slidell. We were still quite oblivious to the events taking place in Florida—we were too busy with our own plans. Oh, we did hear something on the radio about the hurricane ravaging southern Florida. But that was Florida. We were headed for Louisiana.

Arriving in Slidell late that afternoon, we heard a local newscaster talking about evacuation routes out of the area we'd just come to. Slowly things began to sink into our somewhat bewildered minds. Hurricane Andrew had crossed over Florida, was out in the Gulf of Mexico and headed straight for our area!

We had been so involved, so preoccupied with our own challenges, we had completely missed the big news. We were totally unprepared for Hurricane Andrew. We rushed to a grocery store at the last minute to purchase bottled water and some food, only to discover empty shelves.

I wonder how many of us are so busy, so involved with our own hectic schedules and plans that we are missing the bigger picture and failing to see the "storm" of final events brewing in our world.

As it turned out, Hurricane Andrew took a course farther to the west of our location and all we encountered was just heavy rain and gusty wind. But we can be sure that Jesus will come to this earth as He has promised. Yes, we do have necessary cares of this life to tend to. But we have a more urgent need—to be ready for His coming.

Sharon Oster

August 30

The Shrinking Watch Frame

Like as a father pitieth his children, so the Lord pitieth them that fear him.
For he knoweth our frame; he remembereth that we are dust.
Ps. 103:13, 14.

I HAD WORN a pretty silver watch for a long time without noticing something about it—it had been shrinking. When I had first gotten this precious gift, the wristband had been too big, but I didn't mind because it wasn't so large that it slid off my wrist.

The watchband was made up of silver links fitted together. After a few months some of the links dropped out while I was in the shower. When I noticed that it clasped tighter, I ignored the lost links and just enjoyed the better fit. Then one evening while I was tidying up the kitchen the whole watch fell right off my wrist. Part of it fell on the kitchen counter. Another part fell to the floor. I noticed that the part on the counter had the watch face and two links on one side, still clasped. It had broken where the face and links attached on the other side. No trouble, I thought. I'll just have to find whatever links might be on the floor and get the watch face to snap back in place on that side.

Soon, I was on my hands and knees sweeping the kitchen floor until I found a tiny watch spring and a stopper to pass it through. While on the floor searching I felt like the woman in the parable of the lost coin. "And when she finds it, she calls her friends and neighbors together and says, 'Rejoice with me; I have found my lost coin'" (Luke 15:9, NIV). But after I found everything, I felt much worse. In vain I tried to put the watch back together. The woman in the parable had found a whole coin, but I found only pieces of a watch I could not fix.

Isn't that how our lives get spiritually broken? I thought. I had ignored each warning sign that the watch links were breaking away from the watch face—its central part—until it all fell to pieces. Likewise, if we do not keep all our spiritual links connected to God, who is the central force in our lives, we too eventually fall apart. This was like trying to get by on sermons without having personal Bible study and prayer.

We should not let this happen. God is perpetually available. Our spiritual lives should not be shrinking just because "we can manage," when He is there to keep us in top-notch condition. Let us make sure that we allow our Maker to hold us together, this and every day.

Bertlyn Gretna Reynolds

He Will Wipe Away All Tears

And I heard a loud voice from the throne saying, "Now the dwelling of God is with men, and he will live with them. They will be his people, and God himself will be with them and be their God. He will wipe away every tear from their eyes. There will be no more death or mourning or crying or pain, for the old order of things has passed away."
Rev. 21:3, 4, NIV.

IT WAS SHORTLY AFTER 8:00 one morning when I received the news from my brother that our father had collapsed and was now in a hospital. A few hours later the diagnosis was clear and we knew that Father would live only a few more hours. I got into my car, gave my husband directions for managing my shop, and drove as fast as I could to the hospital four hours away.

I can hardly explain what thoughts entered my mind, how many questions suddenly surfaced. I knew that I would be the last one to arrive at his bedside. The whole time I drove I pleaded with God to keep him alive until I could give him my personal goodbyes.

When I finally arrived I stood with my whole family at his bedside. "It is time for me to go," he said.

"Are you afraid to go?" I asked.

"No," he said in a steady voice. "I am not afraid. I know that when I awake again I will have no more pain and you will not have to cry."

I can't put into words what we felt in those minutes. But I know that his confidence and trust, his unshakeable faith in the resurrection, and his hope—this certitude of everlasting life—moved us deeply. It caused each of us to think about how sure we are, or are not, of our own salvation. On this earth, faith in a living God does not save us from illness, pain, suffering, and death. But it helps us, through hope in eternal life, to cope with pain, pass through sorrow, and manage difficult moments. "After that, we who are still alive and are left will be caught up together with them in the clouds to meet the Lord in the air. And so we will be with the Lord forever. Therefore encourage each other with these words (1 Thess. 4:17, 18, NIV).

Our pa passed on to us this confession of faith in one of his last conscious moments. He told us what is most important in life: to hold on unswervingly to the hope we profess!

Marlise Rupp

The Rosebud Hitchhiker

I have loved you, my people, with an everlasting love.
With unfailing love I have drawn you to myself.
Jer. 31:3, NLT.

I WAS HEADED TO WILLIAMS LAKE from Okanagan Falls, British Columbia, Canada, when I saw him standing alongside the road, arm outstretched, thumb raised. My first impulse was to drive by, but an impression to pick him up led me to pull over, empty the front seat contents into the back, and unlock the door. He got in, thanking me for stopping. I asked the proverbial, "Where are you going?" question. "To Kelowna." He had an appointment there. I told him I would be passing through Kelowna. And as I drove, we had an interesting conversation.

Arriving in Kelowna, I stopped where he wanted off. From his knapsack, he offered me a small, pink-red rosebud. That really surprised me. I took it and thanked him, somewhat bewildered. This was a very first! He got out, closed the door, and was gone.

My natural impulse was to shrug off the gift. It was a puny little thing—yet beautiful, delicate, velvet soft with a stub of a stem which I promptly wrapped with a wetted tissue. *Why are you here in my fingers? What is your purpose, little rosebud?*

A rainbow moment caught me up, whisking me away to where sun rays illuminate many aspects of God's promises to me from over the years. Promise after promise reminds me that I am treasured. I am precious. I am loved. I belong to a Father who never changes, who is steadfast, trustworthy. He has brought me thus far and is not letting me go now. He is my help today, tomorrow, and forever. He will bring me through everything. I'm cautioned that fear, worry, and anger separate me from His care. His promises are hugs, kisses, and yes, discipline too. They are also love notes to strengthen me.

In God's time, this rosebud will become everything He designed me to be. Everything He desires me to be. Everything He dreamed I would be and everything He knew I could be because of Him. In His care the rosebud develops in its size, its color, its scent, its texture, its purpose. Perfect in every stage of its growth, imparting its blessing by the loving hand of its Creator. "When I bring you to full bloom, June, you will be everything I created you to be. Love, Dad."

I still have the rosebud, and still remember the Rosebud Hitchhiker. *Thank You, Father.*

June Y. Powers

He Hears Our Cries

Cast all your anxiety on him because he cares for you.
1 Peter 5:7, NIV.

LIKE SO MANY FAMILIES in the mid-1800's the Hickmans and the McDowells from the Midwest decided to travel to California in search of a better life. They joined the wagon train at different towns along the way.

The Hickmans loaded their covered wagon with what they knew were necessities for the trip as well as some of their familiar belongings they just wanted to have when they arrived in the west. Other families did the same. Eleanor, their daughter, just needed to have her doll and her doll trunk along to give her comfort.

The way was hard for the travelers, hard on their oxen that pulled their wagon and hard on those who had to get out and walk for long miles. Soon parents made the hard decision to lighten the load by leaving some things beside the path. What a sad thing for Mother to see her rocking chair, then later a chest of drawers, sitting beside the way as they traveled on. But soon this wasn't enough.

Eleanor was told that her doll and the trunk must be left in the grass. What a traumatic time for the little girl. The tears flowed and she wept loudly. A teenage son of the McDowells noticed Eleanor was upset and came and asked her what was wrong. She told him that her father said she had to leave behind her favorite possessions. Alexander went back along the trail and picked up the doll and the little trunk. Then he told Eleanor he would carry them for her. How happy she must have been! We don't know if he physically carried them or stowed them in his family wagon, but when they all arrived in the Sacramento area he returned these most precious things to Eleanor.

The McDowells found that California was not what they expected and they missed their family. In a short time they were on their way back to their former home. A number of years later Alexander decided to go back west, and when he looked up the Hickman family he noticed how grown-up Eleanor was. It was not long before he asked her to marry him. Eleanor and Alexander were my husband's great-grandparents.

God, too, is just waiting to carry our burdens. He is watching, and He hears our cries.

Carol Stickle

Divine Artistry

The heavens proclaim the glory of God. The skies display his craftsmanship.
Ps. 19:1, NLT.

OUR GOD IS THE AUTHOR OF ART. When He created what is needed to maintain life on earth, He covered it all with a layer of beauty. The Great Artist showed His creative power and unlimited artistry in an exuberant variety to please every taste and preference of His children. He is also the author of light. Without light, nothing can be seen. In the shadows, we can perceive shapes and silhouettes, but not colors. But when light shines through all the beauty of the colors, forms, perspectives, dimensions, and sizes are revealed. Just so, we need the light of Jesus shining on us to be able to see and appreciate all the beauty of His creation.

The bright rainbow is an emblem of the assurance we have that God fulfills His promises, even when there are dark clouds and rain. The heavy, dark clouds warn us about the threatening presence of the evil one. The white flocks of clouds are a symbol of the presence of holy guardian angels protecting us. The gorgeous flowers reveal the smile of God, cheering us up because He accepts us. The gentle flight of the birds reminds us of the freedom we find in Jesus, and their beautiful songs bring to mind our happy praises to God. The delicate colors of birds' feathers are like a feast for our eyes, and tasty fruits invite us to eat for the glory of God.

The trees sprout from the soil and grow up, opening their branches toward the skies; their leaves are like hands lifted up, adoring the Creator. The wind and gentle breezes declare the renewal of our souls by the sweet presence of the Holy Spirit. The stillness of a lake resembles the peace of mind we can have in Jesus. The tame animals portray those who depend on us to survive. The wild animals represent our spiritual enemy, the menacing lion that wants to swallow us. The high mountains symbolize the eternal Rock on which we can find shelter and feel safe. The great seas and oceans are an expression of the huge multitude of saints saved by Jesus. The sunshine is an example of the incomparable brightness that will accompany the spectacular second coming of our Savior Jesus.

I praise God because He created infinite possibilities for us to appreciate nature and enjoy it. Today there is something in God's creation that will catch your attention, just so you can admire it and thank the Great Artist. Look for it!

Vasti S. Viana

My Best Present

I am the Lord, who heals you.
Ex. 15:26, NIV.

IN THE MIDDLE OF THE NIGHT I heard our 5-year-old son crying in the bathroom. Children often cry in the night, but this time it sounded different. I ran downstairs to find my son on his knees in front of the toilet. "Mummy, my head aches so badly," he told me. After he'd vomited several times I wanted to take him back to bed, but I noticed that he could hardly walk.

Being a nurse, meningitis came to my mind. Reduced mobility, vomiting, headache, and a rising temperature—everything fit the picture. I ran to the telephone and called our doctor. He confirmed my inkling, and soon our son was in the hospital. After a puncture of the spinal cord the doctors told us their diagnosis: our son had the worst possible kind of meningitis. Should he survive this illness he would probably be disabled. I do not remember what I thought at that moment, only that I was not overly worried. My daily communion with my Lord and Savior gave me indescribable trust and peace. My husband had similar feelings.

On the fourth day as I entered the children's ward, I looked through a window into my son's room to see many doctors standing around his bed. My heart began to pound uncontrollably, and for a moment I feared the worst. But when I entered the room I saw something incredible. Our son was sitting up in bed and talking excitedly with the doctors. A doctor I didn't know took me by my hand and said, "We don't know what has happened here, but your son is healed."

"There is no medical explanation for this," the head physician who had been in charge of the treatment told me. "I have worked all my life as a doctor but I have never before experienced anything like this." We decided to do another spinal cord puncture to be sure of our son's condition. The results were immaculate. We were able to leave the hospital with a healthy boy. When we left I told the head physician of our Christian faith. I thanked him for their rapid and professional help. But I also told him about a greater Physician who has given us life. This Creator and Physician healed our son. Unfortunately, the physician did not agree with me. Another doctor indicated that he agreed with me, but he could not say anything.

Twenty-five years later our son is a doctor himself—and I pray he will never forget what God did to save him.

Monika Machel

Do You Get It?

We haven't stopped praying for you, asking God to give you wise minds and spirits attuned to his will, and so acquire a thorough understanding of the ways in which God works.
Col. 1:9, Message.

E-MAIL, WHEN IT WORKS, is marvelous. You compose a message on your computer screen, give a simple command, and out goes your message "into space." The recipient can read it within seconds, whether you're in the same city or on different continents. Electronic communication is a marvel almost as mysterious as prayer.

But sometimes e-mail doesn't work. When I was new to the Internet (the information web that links computers throughout the world), I felt like I was casting a bottled message out to sea when I gave my e-mail address to a favorite aunt. I knew she used a computer, but just how "with-it" was she? To my delight, she responded via e-mail. Thrilled to be able to communicate quickly and at no cost, I promptly sent her an e-mail. No response. Usually when a message doesn't go through, it reverts to the sender. I assumed she got it, but why didn't she answer?

Several days later an envelope arrived the old-fashioned way. "Did you get my e-mail?" my aunt wrote.

"Yes, yes, yes!" I e-mailed back immediately, but again no reply. We resorted to the phone to discuss the problem—with no success. Even "experts" I consulted were mystified. The e-mail messages she sent continued to reach me, but mine did not reach her. We'd hit a one-way stretch on the information highway. But eventually the answer came. "Just tonight," she said, "I thought to look in another "mailbox," and there were your letters, plus letters from Japan, as well as old Christmas and New Year's messages!"

I think e-mail is similar to that not-fully-understood communication with God we call prayer. How many times do we think God is not answering our prayers when we've been looking in the wrong places for God's answers? As I pray for a friend's salvation, for example, I may feel "unheard" because she doesn't accept my invitation to hear an evangelist. But God may be reaching out to her through another, more effective means. I have often told God exactly how to answer a prayer but didn't notice God providing a different solution from the one I had in mind!

Does God have a message waiting for you in a "mailbox" you've overlooked?

Dolores Klinsky Walker

Moving Day for Grandma

Religion that God our Father accepts as pure and faultless is this: to look after orphans and widows in their distress and to keep oneself from being polluted by the world.
James 1:27, NIV.

FOR SOME TIME my mother-in-law talked about moving but put it off because when she stopped to think about it, the entire process was overwhelming. However, the time had come for her to make a change. The building she lived in was getting old and the area of the city was becoming somewhat unsafe. My husband and I made a trip to visit her and checked out several apartments close to a shopping mall. She decided on one that was newer and brighter.

Now the task of packing was at hand, and ladies from her church helped by packing boxes for her. On the morning of the move, five men from the church arrived with their trucks and vans. In less than two hours everything was loaded and moved to the new location.

Everyone left as they had other tasks at hand for the day—everyone, that is, except the pastor and his wife. The pastor helped my husband assemble the bed and move the larger furniture into place. For lunch we were invited across the hall to a lovely meal prepared by another sister in the church. Because of her age, she wasn't able to help move boxes, but she definitely knew how to prepare a delicious meal.

The pastor's wife spent the afternoon wiping out cupboards and carefully placing shelf liner in them. At the end of the day, she went home and returned with a delicious vegan quiche and salad for our supper. What a blessing she was! That evening another friend stopped in and offered to hang pictures for Mom.

As I went to bed that night I had a clearer understanding of the text in James where we are admonished to care for the widows. It wasn't as if these people didn't have other things to do for themselves that day. The head elder had his sister and husband visiting from another province but they felt it their responsibility to help. I had witnessed firsthand what a small church could do for my mother-in-law, one of their mothers and widows in Israel. In fact, many Bible texts admonish us to care for the widows and the orphans—those unable to do for themselves. And there are many biblical examples of how God took care of the widows such as Ruth and Naomi, the widow of Zarephath, and the widow of Nain. Should we not do the same?

Vera Wiebe

Conversation With My Father

Don't quit in hard times; pray all the harder.
Rom. 12:12, Message.

DO YOU BELIEVE IN PRAYER? I mean really, truly believe in prayer? Many of us are taught how to pray from early childhood, and it becomes a habit we do at least once a day, just before we go to bed and maybe at mealtimes. But what happens during the rest of the time? Do we keep in touch with God throughout the day, or is it just something we do, maybe in the morning before we leave the house and maybe, if we remember, just before we close our eyes at night?

As a child I remember praying for a special doll before my fifth birthday. It was not just an ordinary doll I wanted—oh no! I wanted one that could close her eyes and say mama! I told Jesus that and I prayed faithfully every night for a few weeks. Of course my mom was right there with me while I faithfully said my prayers.

After all my little friends had arrived for my birthday party, the doorbell rang and my mom asked me to go answer it. I didn't know it, but she and my older sisters were right behind me wanting to see what would happen. I opened the door. Just outside the door was a long white box with a ribbon on it. I picked it up. On it was written: "To Erna from Jesus!" I told everyone in the whole neighborhood that Jesus had given me that doll! It wasn't until a few years later that I understood that He had had some help from my mom and dad! I had total confidence in His mighty power, even at the age of 5. I had heard about answered prayers in my Sabbath school Bible lessons and Uncle Arthur's *Bedtime Stories*, so why shouldn't my prayer be answered too?

I know that not all prayers can be answered as easily as my long-ago request for a doll, but God is still there listening to our prayers. We can trust in His power and His love for us. He knows what's best for each and every one of us. Our text tells us to be persistent in prayer. Prayer is communicating with God. Our prayers shouldn't be ask, ask, ask, but a conversation with our heavenly Father.

I was just a child when I prayed for my special doll. My prayers of today are completely different than they were then, but my confidence in His power has strengthened since those days. Now I know from personal experience how powerful God is, not just because of Bible lessons learned as a child. May God bless us as we serve Him today.

Erna Johnson

My Do It!

I want you to trust me in your times of trouble,
so I can rescue you, and you can give me glory.
Ps. 50:15, TLB.

AT THE AGE OF ALMOST 2, my granddaughter Shae is fully enjoying exerting her independence. Any task to which assistance is offered is met with an immediate, "No, my do it!" If something is moved to within her easy reach she will immediately push it away again so that she can obtain it herself, often stretching precariously to do so.

I have the good fortune of having my granddaughters live in the same town as I do and so I can see them regularly. I especially enjoy each opportunity to spend an evening with them while their parents go out, for it's always an adventure.

Recently while I was putting Shae to bed, or rather observing while she got herself ready for bed, I was reminded of our heavenly Father's continual patience with us as well as His constant readiness, and His desire to catch us when we fall.

Shae's older sister, Jaia, has a high bunk bed in her room. Each evening, before going to her own bed Shae likes to climb the ladder to her sister's bunk. This particular evening she climbed up there and then decided she wanted to show me how she could somersault.

I cautioned her that it would be dangerous to try that up there and said that she could only do it with Gramma's help, to which I got the immediate response, "No, my do it!" With that she quickly backed up against the far wall, put her little head down, and tumbled across the bed toward me, landing with only her upper half still on the bed. As I caught her she realized what had almost happened and hugged me tightly saying, "Gramma, scary!"

As I was thinking about this later, I wondered just how often we seek to be independent, to stubbornly say, "No, my do it!" rather than accepting the guidance and support that our loving heavenly Father so freely offers. As we go somersaulting through life into one scary situation after the other, we tend to be unaware of how often He catches us, not realizing our need of Him until we start to fall.

If we would but ask Him to go with us, to guide us in our daily activities, how much safer and less frightening our lives would be.

Beverly D. Hazzard

All Things Are Possible!

For with God nothing shall be impossible.
Luke 1:37.

WHEN I ENTERED my final semester at the university, the director of student finance made it very clear that I could not register for classes because the balance I owed to the school was too great. Immediately, I became discouraged. This problem, I thought, was impossible to resolve. I thought that there was no way I could obtain this large sum of money.

But then, we Christians boast that we worship a God who specializes in accomplishing the unthinkable—even impossible—tasks. Our God has the ability to execute projects that scientists and great scholars alike would deem irrational or unrealistic. God transcends human reality and exists in a sphere where He alone determines the rules. He can do this because He created all things.

In spite of this unanimously agreed upon perception of God among Christians, in times of difficulty and discouraging circumstances, we tend to crumble under pressure. The real problem with us is that we tend to magnify our problems and lose sight of a great and powerful God who loves us so much. I eventually remembered that I should talk to this God.

I once heard someone say that when a Christian has a problem he or she usually turns to prayer for an answer, not realizing that the answer to every problem *is* prayer. I sought help from the God who—I was taught from the time I was a little child—can do things which appear impossible. Miraculously, with the help of a stepmother whom I had only met a few years before and a women's ministries scholarship, I was able to register for classes.

This experience is only one of the many which has reinforced in my mind this great truth about God: He is truly a loving Father who wants to supply our every need. The best part about it is that there are no requirements to be met. He loves us in spite of faults, failures, and shortcomings. He loves us even though we may not love ourselves or feel we are important. The Scripture says that while we were still sinning, He died for us. The love of God for humanity is a concept we may never understand, but is one which if embraced can change our lives forever.

My loving heavenly Father presented me with a reality that transcends ordinary thinking. Nothing is impossible!

Fay White

Keep Your Eyes on the Path

Thy word is a lamp unto my feet, and a light unto my path.
Ps. 119:105.

SAFETY FIRST is part of a motto at the facility where I am employed as a records administrator. One of the ways we can work safely is by keeping our eyes on the path. I had always prided myself by working safely and avoiding accidents.

However, safety and on-the-job injuries were the farthest thoughts from my mind when I attended a women's retreat in the idyllic setting of Glorieta, New Mexico, nestled in the southern edges of the Santa Fe National Forest in early September. Whenever I attend any function there, I'm reminded of what it must have been like when Jesus went with His disciples to a quiet place to pray, meditate, and rejuvenate their inmost peace of mind (see Mark 6:31 and John 18:2).

This particular retreat started out to be no different than many of the others I'd attended. They always prove to be a spiritual highlight for me, an occasion I anticipate with eagerness. Late Sabbath afternoon my roommates and I were sauntering toward to the dining hall, taking the long way around the lake. We were enthralled with the beauties around us: the tall pines, the lake, and the ducks—in general the peaceful and serene setting.

Since the sidewalk around the lake is hilly and uneven in areas, we were taking our time and for the most part keeping our eyes on the path. Then to get a better view of a mallard duck with her precious family of seven ducklings, I took my eyes off the path. In that split second I realized the cement sidewalk was rushing toward my face. I put out my hands and landed on my knees and right palm. When I regained my composure and found my feet, I thought I had only injured my pride and a good pair of pantyhose. But as the evening wore on I felt more and more discomfort and slight pain to my right forearm and elbow. By the time the evening session ended I had decided it was probably a bad sprain. Since there was some swelling to the area, my roommates helped me to immobilize it in a makeshift ice pack during the night.

I decided that as soon as we returned home I would have it x-rayed. To my dismay, I had a compression fracture. This injury resulted because I took my eyes off the path.

In our day-by-day spiritual walk, what happens when we take our eyes off Jesus? My prayer is that we will continue to remember and use today's text. God's word truly is a light unto our path.

Anna (Ivie) Swingle

The Missing Cane

There is a time to look for something and a time to stop looking for it.
Eccl. 3:6, NCV.

IT WAS A BEAUTIFUL WALKING CANE. I had prized it from the day Parker Christian of Pitcairn Island presented it to us when he was our houseguest. He had carved the cane from pecan wood, and used it until the evening before he left. I still remember the exciting stories he told around our dinner table. It was such a special treat to have him in our home, and we felt blessed.

Through the years, our moves took us from Ohio, to New York, to California. Each time, I packed Parker's cane with care to make certain it would arrive intact, but somehow, during one of the moves, the tip had broken off. I carefully saved the little piece, intending each day to glue it on. It was not just an ordinary tip. Parker's deft fingers had skillfully carved it to resemble a tiny little shoe. But days went by and it remained in my drawer.

Our next move took us to Maryland, and again I found myself holding the little "Pitcairn" shoe—a precious memory of Parker's visit. *I must glue it on right now,* I thought! And so I went in search of the cane, but it was nowhere to be found. My search continued until, after several decades, I had to accept the fact that I would never see it again. I realize the walking cane itself is not an overwhelming loss, and I smile as I discover that the little shoe is all I need to bring memories flooding back.

Occasionally, I pull my little book *The Story of Pitcairn Island*, by Norman Ferris, from my bookcase. It has survived all my moves and is an interesting account of that famous little island. However, its true value lies in our friend Parker Christian's personal autograph on the flyleaf. Then my heart warms as I remember another book that will never be discarded from my library. On every page it carries the signature of Someone who is my special friend above all others. The Author loves me more than life; I will cherish every word!

The tiny shoe is tucked safely away in my drawer. Occasionally I hold it in my hand and recall my negligence. It has become an object lesson to me that whatever our loss, great or small, our heavenly Father has a way of cheering our hearts with some precious memory. I have learned that negligence is never safe, and so I purpose daily to study His Book and stay close to Him who has promised He will never leave us nor forsake us. What a delightful and understanding God!

Lorraine Hirsch-Olson

God Still Answers Prayers

I will be with him in trouble; I will deliver him and honor him.
With long life will I satisfy him, and show him My salvation.
Ps. 91:15, 16, NKJV.

I GREW UP IN A CHRISTIAN HOME but by the time I was 18 I had decided it was not the life for me. However, after spending 26 years out in the world, I finally realized it did not give me what I was searching for. The happiness I had envisioned seemed to elude me.

One Friday night I took my two children to my mom's home because I had decided that suicide was the only way forward. Before leaving there, I kissed my kids and said goodbye to my siblings, certain that this was the last time I would be seen alive.

I arrived home and locked all the doors and windows. I didn't want to be disturbed. I soon located my bottle of painkillers and poured out every one into my hand. However, at that very moment, I remembered that my mom had taught me to pray. Immediately a pitiful cry wrenched from my very soul: "Oh, God, please send someone for me to talk to!"

It was 10:00 p.m. and I did not see how anyone could come around at that hour. However, God's ways are not our ways, and He uses any means necessary to come to the rescue of His own. In less than 10 seconds my phone rang. As desperate as I was for the sound of a human voice, I reached for the receiver and in an extremely distressed voice answered, "Hello?"

The voice on the line asked for someone by name; I replied that he had a wrong number. However, this "pest" would not go away. His next question stunned me. "When last did you go to church?" he asked. And he continued, "You sound as though you are depressed."

It turns out that this caller was a blood-washed, born again, Holy Spirit-filled Christian! His wrong number turned into an hour-and-a-half long Bible study. My mystery caller then invited me to a prayer meeting the following night. I gave him directions to my home after securing the promise of a visit from him the following day.

The following morning I got up extremely early and got ready to attend church. That same year I rededicated my life to Christ and went down into the watery grave of baptism. Fifteen years later I am still bursting with joy at how the Lord used a total stranger and one phone call to save my life.

Prisca Brouet

Singing in the Darkest Places

Though I speak with the tongues of men and of angels,
but have not love, I have become sounding brass or a clanging cymbal.
1 Cor. 13:1, NKJV.

I FELT BOXED IN and couldn't wait to get off the platform. Surrounding me was a lip-level microphone, another mic just a few inches from my guitar, and a big, black music stand. If I moved in any direction I was bound to clang into something. For an instant I wondered why I was there.

My husband, Don's, singing voice was in trouble and I wondered if the two of us would ever sing together again. The thought of the possibility that we might not made me stiffen to hold back the tears. It seemed like I cried at the littlest things these days.

Back on the platform, barely hearing myself sing, everything—including my voice—seemed strange and far away. Finally I finished the song and was very glad to relinquish the spotlight to another.

In bed later that night, I resigned myself to the fate of a 60-year-old woman aware of her limitations and relaxed and fell quickly asleep. But in the middle of the night, I awoke with an old Bible memory verse swirling in my head: "Though I speak [sing?] with the tongues . . . of angels, but have not love, I have become sounding brass . . ." *Yikes,* I thought, *that's me!* In the dark, I walked away from my thoughts and opened my laptop. Among the new e-mail I found a note from my New Jersey friend. Inside was a sweet message, blessing me and our friendship, "Help her shine in the darkest places where it is impossible to love . . . and let her know that she will always be safe." In the shadow of my disappointment, God spoke to me.

Obviously, God had not called me to shine in the spotlight capturing a youthful dream of fame but rather to stand in His light, reflecting His sweet love to the invisibles, those who passed me at school, at work, or in church, who carried their despair silently every day. I would sing again without fear or sadness, but with the refreshing of His Spirit, knowing that God dwells in my disappointments as well as in my praise. The Bible holds many other promises and reassurances, including this meaningful one that restores confidence in all of us: "Not that we are sufficient of ourselves to think of anything as being from ourselves, but our sufficiency is from God" (2 Cor. 3:5, NKJV).

Nancy Ann Neuharth Troyer

Looking for Power

*I pray that out of his glorious riches he may strengthen you with power through his
Spirit in your inner being, so that Christ may dwell in your hearts through faith. And
I pray that you, being rooted and established in love, may have power, together with
all the saints, to grasp how wide and long and high and deep is the love of Christ, and to know
this love that surpasses knowledge. . . . Now to him who is able to do immeasurably more than
all we ask or imagine, according to his power that is at work within us, to him be glory in the
church and in Christ Jesus throughout all generations, for ever and ever! Amen.
Eph 3:16-21, NIV.*

I WAS LOOKING FOR A PLACE to plug in my laptop computer during a break in the
meeting of the university board of trustees. The board room was grand, with colos-
sal brass chandeliers hanging from its high ceilings, presided over by an imposing
portrait of a pioneer educator.

"What are you doing?" asked a board member as I peeked under the heavy oak
tables and behind gold velvet curtains by the windows.

"I'm looking for power," I explained.

"Oh!" he exclaimed. Looking around at the distinguished members of the
board, he grinned and whispered, "Don't let the others hear you say that!"

How to get and maintain power is the object of the ambitious and the subject
of many a book on corporate management. Leaders accumulate power, and some
even abuse it. Power refers to many things: strength, energy, ability to get things
done, authority, rights, and national and world powers.

Beyond the corporate and political arena, there is a cosmic power struggle between good and evil. In this battle, Christ's disciples and apostles were given power
to heal, raise the dead, and expel demons. But have you seen the dead raised or
demons expelled? And why do we so often feel *powerless* in the face of evil and in-
justice? Has the power supply been cut off?

Paul reminded the Ephesians that the Spirit also expands the dominion of God
in our lives. If things don't go as fast as we might like, recall that God is at work too.
We might not be the one to raise the dead or expel demons, but we can rejoice that
God's Spirit strengthens our inner being despite the devil's daily assaults, and He
empowers us to be filled up with the very knowledge and love of God. Now that's
powerful!

Lisa M. Beardsley

I Can't Wait Until We're Together Again!

*The Lord appeared to us in the past, saying: "I have loved you with
an everlasting love; I have drawn you with loving-kindness."
Jer. 31:3, NIV.*

OUR FIRST GRANDCHILDREN were the children of our daughter Heidi and her husband, Dan. We moved through the "firsts" that new grandparents experience, squeezing out time whenever possible to go to little Ryan's home to see what new and clever things our firstborn grandson had learned. And then as time passed, Ryan was blessed with a baby sister and a younger brother—Heather and Eric. Would that be the total sum of our grandchildren? We could only wait and see.

Then after an 11-year draught in the arena of grandchildren we got the exciting news that our son, Todd, and his wife, Leesa, were going to add to our blessed anthology of grandchildren. Would it be a girl or a boy we wondered? And then Leesa went for a sonogram and came home with the news that she was going to bless the family with grandson number three—Clay.

I am so happy that we live near our grandchildren and can see them often. As I write this devotional Clay is a 7-year-old second-grader and he and I have learned to enjoy each other's company immensely. Recently, on a day when I was taking Clay home after swimming lessons, he was in a particularly loving frame of mind. And just when I thought he was about to drift off to sleep in the back seat I heard his sleepy voice call out, "Grandma, I can't wait until we're together again!" I don't think I'd ever heard sweeter words! I came home and told Clay's grandpa about these priceless utterances and he agreed that I had enjoyed a very tender moment with what appears to be the last of our grandchildren!

Ardis Stenbakken, the editor of these women's devotional books, had invited me to write a devotional but I was stumped. I wasn't sure what I should write about. But when Clay gifted me with his sweet words I knew that he had given me a reason to write. For I could almost hear my heavenly Father saying to me, "I can't wait until we're together again!" And these are my thoughts when I think of both Him and my grandson, because I look forward to spending eternity with both of them!

Rose Otis

Tests and Lies

So, if you think you are standing firm, be careful that you don't fall!
1 Cor. 10:12, NIV.

AT AGE 12, I made my decision to give my life to God, and was baptized. It was a beautiful summer day and the baptism took place outdoors on a lovely Finnish lake. My best friend, the pastor's daughter, and I waded into the water together in a rather long row of baptismal candidates. Overwhelming joy filled me to be following in the footsteps of Jesus.

My friend and I often stayed over at each other's homes and shared all our secrets as young girls do. We were both in the same grade in public high school and everyone knew we were Christians.

We had a very strict grammar and language teacher. She scared the living daylights out of all the students. Toward the end of the semester we were going to have a big Monday morning test. The teacher warned us that we must bring our own paper and pencil to the test and there was no mercy given if we failed to do so.

That Sunday I stayed overnight at my friend's house. We had so much fun talking, frying doughnuts, and staying up past midnight. Monday morning, in our scramble to get to school on time, we forgot we had to bring paper and pencils. When the teacher saw that we had none, we told her that our parents had been away and that we were not able to acquire paper and pencils for the test. She asked a few more questions and we spun a few more white lies.

Tests were later returned to us and nothing more was said, but my evening prayers seemed hypocritical, and my conscience bothered me. I suffered through the whole summer until I finally summoned up courage and wrote a card to the teacher, confessing the whole story. Now having a good conscience, I forgot the whole incident. When school started and I was back in class, the teacher cornered me and demanded to know if my parents had made me write the card. I told her that my parents didn't know anything about it. Somehow, I expected her to praise me for coming clean, but she simply looked at me and accepted my response.

This incident taught me a lifelong lesson. Honesty *is* the best policy. It is simply expected to be a way of life for God's children, nothing extraordinarily praiseworthy. And the walk of faith must be a daily commitment to vigilance or we will take our spiritual life for granted and fall.

Sinikka Dixon

What I Know

But because of his great love for us, God, who is rich in mercy, made us alive with Christ even when we were dead in transgressions—it is by grace you have been saved.
Eph. 2:4, 5, NIV.

THEY SAY YOU SHOULD WRITE about what you know. So I asked myself, "What do I know?" I know that when I leave milk sitting on the counter in the morning and return from work nine hours later, the milk will be sour. I know that if I fail to pay a bill on time, I will most certainly receive a late charge. I also know without a doubt that I must pay my taxes each year to avoid a visit from an IRS agent. I know that each year I grow older, shorter, more forgetful, and slower. I know all these things and much, much more.

On the other hand, there are millions of things that I don't know and will probably never know until Jesus comes. But one fun thing I just learned is that if you are sitting down and you rotate your right foot clockwise, then make the number six in the air with your right hand, your right foot will automatically change direction. (Go ahead. Try it. No one is looking!) See? Strange, but true. And not really that important.

Let me tell you a few more things that I know for sure. I know that Jesus Christ loves me. I know this because of what the Bible says. God is love and will be with me (2 Cor. 13:11). God loves me even while I am still a sinner (Eph. 2:4, 5). Nothing can separate me from the love of God (Rom. 8:35, 38, 39). God knew me before I was born, even as I was being "knit . . . in my mother's womb" (Ps. 139:13, NIV). God gave His only Son so that I could live forever with Him (John 3:16). God's sovereignty limits my crisis and gives meaning to my problems (Job 1:12; 2:6). God comforts me in my troubles but doesn't necessarily deliver me from them (2 Cor. 1:4). God says in His word, "For I know the thoughts that I think toward you . . . thoughts of peace and not of evil, to give you a future and a hope" (Jer. 29:11, NKJV). And, "The Lord is my helper" (Hebrews 13:6).

After reading these Bible affirmations, are you encouraged? Did you just read the words or did you absorb them? So you see, we all "know" something. Whether it is something silly or one of the more complex scientific facts of the universe, we all know something. The best thing to know is that Jesus loves you, He died for you, He forgives you, and He's coming back for you—and me!

Cathy Evenson Roberts

Two Little Dresses Hanging on the Wall

And my God will meet all your needs.
Phil. 4:19, NIV.

MY OFFICE IS CLOSE to the end of town where the charity (thrift) shops congregate. About eight of them huddle in a row, as if seeking warmth and consolation from each other, almost embarrassed to show their faces among the classier, "real" shops.

I am poorer than I am proud, and I love to browse these shops for beautiful books that are cheaper than magazines, white tableware, clothes, shoes, and other serendipitous surprises. But it must have been God who beckoned me through the door of the second charity shop one day in April.

I found a couple books I'd been wanting for ages. Then, glancing toward the back of the shop, I saw two matching flower girl dresses hanging on the wall. I could easily have walked away and not taken a second glance because I needed to get back to the office, but our daughter's wedding was approaching and our budget was very small. I was making her gown, but had no spare time to make dresses for the flower girls, and we weren't sure what to do.

Something—Someone—whispered into my heart that I should take a closer look at those dresses on the back wall. I found that the bodices were burgundy, one of the colors in Bethany's wedding, and the skirts were similar in style to her bridal gown, with layers of fine tulle over ivory silk. They looked like they'd never been worn, and were one-fifth the price of the cheapest dresses we had found. The sizes were for an 11- and a 7-year old. I knew the eldest flower girl, Asha, was almost 11, but I had never met the younger girl, Alex. I had an idea she might be about 4 or 5. I tried to call my daughter, but her cell phone was off. So I prayed and bought the dresses. The woman who took my money even offered me a refund if they weren't suitable.

That evening I showed Beth the dresses via the webcam on my laptop. The youngest flower girl was 7. We never found any other dresses that would have been more perfect for the wedding. A bride had been inspired to buy them, then inspired to change her mind and take them to the charity shop. A clerk had been inspired to hang the dresses together against the back wall, and I had been inspired to walk in and look around. Another "water into wine" miracle for our daughter's wedding.

Karen Holford

Dawn

*We have also a more sure word of prophecy; whereunto ye do well
that ye take heed, as unto a light that shineth in a dark place, until the
day dawn, and the day star arise in your hearts.*
2 Peter 1:19.

THE RISING OF THE DAWNING SUN! God cares! We are seated on our front porch, my husband, Joe, and I. We live in Sierra Leone (Sierra Leone means Lion Mountains). Our beautiful house overlooks the wide ocean to the left. To the front, a deep valley flows with streams of water, and above it a waterfall tumbles during the rainy season. Beautiful green hills with white cloud coverings greet us on the right. The gentle breeze caresses our smiling faces with clean air. Joe and I break forth in song every morning to welcome the King of kings into our hearts and home as we watch the sun rise. What a way to begin a day!

Later, driving to work, the whole town seems lit with God's light, the sun. The glistening rays remind us of the sparkle God gives to our eyes to brighten our countenances and refresh our spiritual tanks. There is hope that the day is full of life, and whatever challenges we may face at work we have a sure word of prophecy. It tells us that if we take heed, we will shine for Jesus as a light that shines in a dark place. Our God is the ever present interior designer of this earth; He provides beauty for us to enjoy, and the rising sun is a constant reminder of His presence. When we know Him, in the dawn we see the Daystar arising in our hearts.

Jesus often went to lovely places to pray. He often sent the multitudes to natural environments where they could touch flowers, watch the rivers flow, and be on mountaintops. The night of the world is almost gone, the day is coming on. It must be the breaking of the day. But before the day breaks, God has yet another reminder of His love for us. The sun is setting; beautiful white birds with long narrow beaks are returning to their homes from whence they awoke this morning. The quiet of the landscape allows us to hear the flapping of their wings as they fly above our heads. They too know their Master, and they are going to sleep until another dawn. We enjoy His beauty, but mostly, we long for the day when He will take us to our final home where we will be able to touch the birds, where all we see about us will be beauty and harmony. Till then, may the Daystar arise in our hearts each dawn.

Beryl Aseno Nyamwange

Someone Is Watching You

The eyes of the Lord are in every place, beholding the evil and the good.
Prov. 15:3.

SOON AFTER HIS RETIREMENT as director of the Public Health Laboratory in Hamilton, Ontario, Canada, my husband accepted an assignment as a lecturer to premed students at the University of Guyana in South America.

Realizing that he would be away for two weeks, I excitedly made arrangements for a mason to tile our kitchen floor, the guest bathroom, and the lower hallway. I worked out of my house all day and the mason had a regular, full-time job, so we planned that the work would be done in the evenings.

Some evenings the work continued late into the night. But the mason brought two helpers and the project progressed beautifully. The clean-up was done the evening before my husband was due to return home.

The men, who were members of my church, rejoiced with me. I was so very delighted over my intended surprise for my husband that I decided to visit the neighbor who lived opposite our house to invite her to come see what had been accomplished during my husband's absence.

As I approached her home, I saw her coming across the street to meet me. Before I could tell her why I was coming to see her, she exclaimed, "Pauline, I've noticed that men were at your home every night!" Of course, she knew my husband was away, and naturally, in her mind she was questioning why I was entertaining men each evening.

I was happy to respond, "Marie, I'm coming to invite you to see what I had done in my home during my husband's absence." When she discovered the reason that men were in my home each evening she breathed a sigh of relief. Now she realized that I would not behave in any way that would hurt my husband.

This incident made me realize that we never know who is watching us and, at the same time, judging our behavior. I thank God that I did not give my neighbor any cause to doubt my faithfulness to my spouse. The Bible verses that lifted my spirit that day were "I will instruct thee and teach thee in the way which thou shalt go: I will guide thee with mine eye" (Ps. 32:8), and the other was "All things are naked and opened unto the eyes of him with whom we have to do" (Heb. 4:13).

Pauline Belle

A Clean Smell

Purify me from my sins, and I will be clean; wash me, and I will be whiter than snow.
Ps. 51:7, NLT.

THE FIRST TIME I saw Ramesh, he was limping down a dusty road that ran through a village in South India. He was attempting to keep up with the other children who were running straight toward our car. For some reason this young boy intrigued me.

One of the most wonderful things about visiting the Indian villages is the children and this village was no exception. They quickly surrounded the car, and I had to carefully push the door open against them. Immediately, children's hands were reaching out to touch me. They would smile and echo "Hello," "Hello" as they shook hands with me. What a wonderful welcoming committee!

I looked across the children, searching for the boy whom I had seen limping along. He was nowhere to be found. I looked down the road, but he was not there. Then I felt a gentle touch on my arm and looked down into the smiling face and twinkling eyes of Ramesh. All I could do was hug him. He smelled of urine and dirt and sweat, but it mattered not. This young boy had stolen my heart.

Each day when I visited the village, Ramesh would hurry to the car and we would walk together. We became fast friends. I would purposely walk a little slower and he would limp along as fast as he could. Ramesh had suffered from polio but it did not affect his attitude or his determination.

One year later I returned to the village. I had often thought of Ramesh and shared his story with others. As the car came to a stop, I strained to see if I could see him. How delighted I was to see him hurrying toward the car. Yes, he still limped but somehow his step seemed lighter and quicker. Ramesh had the same wonderful smile and his eyes twinkled as he told me he had been baptized. Through my tears, I murmured a thankful prayer to God. Then I reached out and hugged him. But this time when I hugged him, he smelled clean.

The clean smell reminded me of how God takes us filthy, wretched sinners and cleans us up and makes our sinful hearts whiter than snow. Hopefully when God hugs me I will smell clean too.

Candy Zook

This Bus Is Going Where?

*If any of you lack wisdom, let him ask of God, that giveth to all men
liberally, and upbraideth not; and it shall be given him.*
James 1:5.

AFTER A LONG DAY of traveling, I wanted to get home. An airport shuttle would take me 90 miles closer to my destination. From that point, I would drive another 35 miles to my home. It had been a disappointing day at the airport: I had missed my flight, stood in several long lines, and ultimately, my flight was canceled.

"You'd better hurry if you want to catch that bus!" said the porter as I entered the shuttle terminal. I asked him which one would take me to South Bend. "Straight ahead," he replied.

I got on the bus straight ahead of me and told the driver I was going to South Bend. He replied that his bus stopped at Portage, and that he believed the bus behind him would take me to my destination. I rushed to the other bus. The driver was not yet on the bus, so I asked a fellow passenger where she was going. "Michigan City," she replied. That was good enough for me. The South Bend bus usually stopped in Michigan City. I sighed and took a seat. I would be home soon.

Mentally and physically tired, I was a little surprised that the driver did not come by to collect or sell tickets. Nevertheless, we were on our way and soon arrived at the last ticketing station before South Bend. "Ladies and gentlemen, this is our final transfer station. The next two stops will be Portage and then Michigan City. *This bus is going where? Portage and Michigan City? What about South Bend?* Quickly, I knew I needed to talk with the driver.

"When did you get on my bus? Do you have a ticket?"

After assuring the driver that I had not purposefully stowed away on his bus, I purchased a ticket and waited for the next bus which would get me to my destination.

At the airport I was in such a rush to get on the shuttle bus, I did not clarify which shuttle I needed. I also relied on limited information and did not ask the right source. It is comforting to know that when God gives directions, He is the reliable source; He is the source of all wisdom. I needed to slow down, ask the right questions, and clarify my information before acting. It is up to us to listen, clarify, and then make sure we're going the right way by His grace.

Faith-Ann McGarrell

God's Great Generosity

Trust in the Lord with all your heart and lean not on your own understanding.
Prov. 3:5, NIV.

OUR LADIES' BIBLE STUDY GROUP, Faith Lift, was studying the book *The Organic God* by Margaret Feinberg. We had just finished the chapter on God's outrageous generosity. We learned of God's joy when we, too, give, and the author recounted the abundant generosity God bestows on us all the time.

The following week there was a preholiday bazaar at the retirement facility where I live. My friend, Diane, would be selling handcrafted cards and "Stampin Up" supplies. Charla, a friend of hers who was sharing table space, was selling beautifully crafted miniature fold-out picture albums. She had made these specifically to sell to help raise funds for her grandson's mission trip, and I was told that she had prayed that God would help her sell them. She was asking $15.00 each, but no one was buying.

As I stood there admiring the exquisite detail, I wondered how I could use one. Finally I decided to buy just one to help her. She was ecstatic! She announced that I was the answer to her prayers. Seeing how much the sale meant to her, I decided to buy one more.

I had not brought any money with me, so as Diane walked with me to my apartment to get the money, she explained how discouraged Charla had been, and how she had kept wondering why God hadn't answered her prayers. Diane had told her not to give up, and within five minutes I had come by and made the purchases. I listened and thought how often I help young people on their mission trips. Why not help this one? So I added $50.00 to the check, sent it back with Diane and said, "Tell Charla not to cry."

I'm sure there were tears of joy and thankfulness. A few days later I received a lovely thank you card and the news that the grandson was able to go on his mission trip. God had answered her prayers!

A simple act of sharing God's resources became a feeling of God's outrageous generosity. This kind of giving works in a circle of love. God gives and gives and gives again. And who gets the greatest blessing? Everyone in the circle, including God—who has told us it is more blessed to give than to receive.

Mary Paulson-Lauda

Doors

Listen! I am standing and knocking at your door. If you hear my voice and
open the door, I will come in and we will eat together.
Rev 3:20, CEV.

HAVE YOU EVER NOTICED how something can move from the sidelines of your attention to take a prime spot when you happen to need it. That's how it was when we needed to replace our front door.

It is not to say that doors were not always all around us before. We reached for the doorknobs to go in and out of homes, offices, restaurants, and countless other places, but now, suddenly, everywhere we went we noticed the doors. Prior to this if they were open, we'd just walk right through with scarcely a thought to the design, color, dimensions, material, or anything else for that matter. It was simply something to go through. Now as we were in the market for a new door, it all took on new meaning. The hardware to open the door, the way the doors hung, whether they swung in or out, each was something to notice.

There were major considerations too: double doors versus single-hung doors, vintage doors (I still say that they're just *old doors* that were kept as scraps from construction sites—sorry), French doors, glass doors, solid wood doors, fiberglass doors, prefabricated versus custom-built doors. So many types! Some looked like they led to a castle; others, you'd expect to find Little Red Riding Hood behind— you get the picture. To complicate things even further, since the doors we needed would be the front doors, a permit and inspection to meet hurricane code would be required. Who knew?

A door: it provides protection and a sense of safety to those within from the world outside. A door separates and divides. It's meant to control access. So how does one get in? Using force is possible—breaking in. Using a key to unlock it and let yourself in is another option. Then, of course, it can be opened and you are invited in and welcomed. I like Jesus' willingness to stand at the door of our hearts and knock. He waits for us to allow Him entry into our hearts—never forcing, but steadily knocking. May we answer and welcome Him today.

Dear Lord, today I open my heart's door to You as I welcome You into my heart—
Your home in which to dwell.

Maxine Williams Allen

Out of Captivity

You will seek Me and find Me, when you search for Me with all your heart. I will be found by you, says the Lord, and I will bring you back from your captivity.
Jer. 29:13, 14, NKJV.

THERE IS A CHORUS that states, "When I think about the Lord,/ How He saved me, how He raised me,/ How He filled me, with the Holy Ghost./ How He healed me, to the uttermost./ . . . It makes me wanna shout!" If you're a Christian, you recognize that these words exemplify a converted relationship with God. However, conversion is not an instantaneous experience. Saul didn't suddenly become Paul at the Damascus experience. The disciples had to be in the presence of Jesus before they could comprehend and receive the Holy Ghost. It behooves us to be cognizant that the Holy Spirit has been wooing us with subtlety—perhaps all of our life.

I cannot say when the first inclination for the Lord entered my life, but I recall my first Communion when I was 6. I was dressed all in white: I wore a white dress and veil, white shoes and leggings, and carried a white rosary and Bible. I remember feeling as though I was being married to Jesus. Did I really know who Jesus was? Unfortunately, no! The love of Jesus was never taught; I heard only condemnation. I believed that I must be a good girl and not sin—all on my own.

I didn't understand how sin could send one spiraling to depths of despair. But I do remember when I became a captive to a particular sin. When I was 21, I ate of the forbidden fruit that removed my status as a "good girl." I believed I was marred for life, a sinner destined for eternal condemnation. Too ashamed, I turned away from Jesus and kept looking for love in all the wrong places. The Holy Spirit had to woo me to a point where I was ready to accept the truth of God's love. I needed to be taught about His compassion, His forgiveness, His mercy, His grace. I needed a conversion!

If you were to ask me when I took my stand for Jesus and was baptized, I can recall where, when, and how. But, if you asked me when I became a converted Christian, I cannot vocalize the moment it occurred. I only can testify that somewhere along my life's journey, I searched for Him and found Him through the power of the Holy Spirit, and in so doing I found peace. I found forgiveness. I found healing. I found true love. Yes! Out of captivity and into the glorious light of Jesus Christ. And the good news is—so can you! Let's shout together!

Evelyn Gertrude Greenwade Boltwood

Rattlesnake Story

Cursed are you above all the livestock and all the wild animals!
You will crawl on your belly and you will eat dust all the days of your life.
Gen. 3:14, NIV.

FOR A WHILE when my sister, Jane, and I were in high school, we lived with our grandparents in an old-fashioned farmhouse. I can still taste the oatmeal Pap fixed for us every morning. But it was Granny who had a delicious, hot meal on the table when we got off the school bus. One day I came home, went through the front door, dropped my books on the horsehair sofa, walked through the kitchen, out the back door, and "up the road a piece" to the outhouse. Considering the creepy crawlers that could be hiding there, I was in and out quickly.

And then I saw it—something stretched about halfway across the road. You might be surprised at how many things can run through your mind in a split second. Since it was lying close to Pap's collection of scrap metal, I thought it might be an iron tool of some kind. Or a tree limb fallen onto the road. Or maybe Granny's clothesline pole? And then I knew—it had eyes and it was looking at me—a snake! It never moved a muscle so I convinced myself that it must be dead. I felt weak-kneed and a little nauseated . . . even if it were dead!

I went in the kitchen door and saw that they'd started supper without me. Knowing it wasn't polite to interrupt, I hesitantly asked, "Pap, did you kill a snake today?"

Jane said, "Don't talk about things like that when I'm trying to eat." But I knew if she had seen it she would have said something too. Pap went to the closet at the foot of the stairs, got his gun, and made sure it was in order. I said, "I'll show you." But he shook his head "Tell me." Needless to say, the snake had moved, but my grandfather, never once doubting my word, stood in the middle of that scrap pile, watching until he sensed a movement, then blasted the snake. It was a rattlesnake—more than eight feet long, with 18 rattles on its tail.

Pap has passed away, but I've always had a special feeling knowing that he risked his life for us, *for me*. I am reminded of Someone else who not only risked His life for others but freely gave it. However, death could not hold Him. He was resurrected and went back to His home. But He has promised to come again, in clouds of glory, so we can go home with Him. I want to be ready when Jesus comes, don't you?

Carol Wiggins Gigante

The Calm Before the Storm

Always giving thanks to God the Father for everything, in the name of our Lord Jesus Christ.
Eph. 5:20, NIV.

I SO LOOKED FORWARD to attending the meeting in South America. The invitation to make a presentation had been extended almost two years before the scientific event, and I was excited at the prospect of seeing colleagues and friends after more than 30 years. Diligent preparation was made: adequate research on the topic coupled with our own work on the national scene. My former student and protégé, as is our custom, helped with the development of an excellent PowerPoint selection of pertinent material. Some reading was done on the history and present–day situation (economic, political, cultural) of the country to be visited, and a list made of the people I hoped to see at that international conclave.

The day for travel dawned a bit cloudy with bursts of rain, but cleared up nicely by take-off, with an uneventful—in my opinion, the best kind—flight to the host country. Upon arrival, I, along with other delegates, was met by congress collaborators (scientists, professionals, medical students), given a tour of the city with a lunch stop, then taken to our hotel which had fine accommodations. After all, it was the congress venue. Things were going well.

The following four days were packed with congress activities, highlighted by an impressive opening ceremony, numerous sessions and presentations, lunches with professors, and visits to sites of interest such as the botanical gardens, and a municipal parade. We delegates were recipients of every kind of attention and showered with various souvenirs of the event. It was truly an outstanding and totally satisfying experience, both scientifically and culturally. I returned home in good health and very pleased with all that had transpired.

So far so good. Then without warning, illness raised its unwelcome head, forcing me to be hospitalized on two separate occasions in less than a month. As I writhed in pain and was totally miserable, I reflected that if I had to fall sick it was so much better to be at home to have the support of family, to be close to my personal physician, and not abroad. The previous calm helped me to weather the storm, for which I was grateful, and I feel constrained to say with the apostle Paul, in all things give thanks.

Marion V. Clarke Martin

Crop—Dusting

And it shall come to pass, that before they call,
I will answer; and while they are yet speaking, I will hear.
Isa. 65:24.

SEVERAL YEARS AGO we did something a little different in our fall farming operation. Instead of spending the usual several days preparing the ground, planting, and hoping rain would be delayed, we had our winter wheat seed scattered by a crop duster. When my husband called in the order he was told that no exact date could be given, but the job would be done in one to two weeks.

About a week later our daughter and her friend stopped by to see us. Our niece and her two small children were also visiting. We were all in the yard enjoying the beautiful fall weather when we heard a dull droning off in the distance. As it got louder and louder, my husband remarked that it was probably our wheat coming. Sure enough. As the plane circled around to line up with the field, my niece lifted Zachary, not quite 2 years old, from his stroller and pointed up in the air. He watched, as we all did, as the plane dipped dangerously close to the ground and began spraying the seed on the field. The duster was coming straight for us and getting louder and louder. With a look of terror, Zach buried his face in his mama's neck and squealed, "A hug, a hug." As the plane shot up over the house and past, Zach again watched it circle, but as it came toward us, once again he repeated, "A hug, a hug." We all smiled and thought how cute it was, but I would like to draw a comparison.

Satan is also doing a planting job. He's doing it the best he can. You can hear his droning noises and watch his moves throughout the world. You can see him working all around and his circles get smaller and closer to home. You watch as he circles your friends, your neighbors, your loved ones, all the while dropping seeds of pain, doubt, and despair, and the noise gets louder and louder. Then one day you look up and he's headed straight for you. With terror in your eyes you realize there's no place to run and no place to hide. Isn't it great that at a time like that you can simply turn your face toward heaven and say to your Father, "A hug, a hug"?

Not only is He waiting to give us a hug this very day, but He was ready long before we even thought to ask.

Diana Inman

A Portrait of the Master Artist

But we all . . . are being transformed into the same image from
glory to glory, just as by the Spirit of the Lord.
2 Cor. 3:18, NKJV.

I HAVE VISITED MANY GALLERIES and museums, and I am always fascinated by the enormous diversity of colors, styles, and topics chosen by the painters to express themselves. Each painting subtly reveals something about its creator. Once I read about an artist who stated, "I paint my portrait each day." Actually, a work of art is a statement made by the artist using paint, pencil, clay, stone, or words. One could say it is the life of that creative individual being visually expressed in a chosen medium.

While I thought about the words of that artist, I considered God and how He exhibits His art in such a magnificent way through nature. However, His preferred work is painting His portrait in human lives. He is the Master Painter and we are His chosen means of expression. God uses an unfathomable variety in His creative art. None of His "portraits" are the same. Each one has its own personality, style, and talent that reflect the Artist in an exclusive manner.

In the same manner that the artist works to obtain the precise mixture of colors, the right quality of light and shadow, and the perfect expression on the face of a portrait, the heavenly Artist also tirelessly works. God paints from the inside out. Through the Holy Spirit, our thoughts, our motives, our desires are purified. The internal life commands the external actions.

God did not merely begin to paint His portrait in us when we were born—or even after our rebirth in Jesus. His brush strokes continue to transform us from what we were previously to what He wants us to be today. In today's text the apostle Paul gives us an idea when he states that as we contemplate our Lord we are transformed into His image through the Spirit.

Years, and even centuries, may go by before the works of a painter are truly valued. However, artists do not give up. They continue to produce art. God, in the same manner, is tireless as He applies His creative power in us. He does not give up because you and I are still not everything that He wants us to be. He patiently creates His art within us, knowing that if we grant Him creative freedom to work in our lives, the masterpieces that He has planned will emerge and make us portraits of the Master Himself.

Rosemeyre Gianne Pereira

From Death to Life

"For I know the plans I have for you," declares the Lord,
"plans to prosper you and not to harm you, plans to give you hope and a future."
Jer. 29:11, NIV.

"OH, NO! I'VE KILLED MY BOUGAINVILLEA!"

I've had plants die before, but this one was special. My mom had given me a cutting from her thriving plant and I was pained to see it doing poorly. For years it had been lush with green, healthy leaves, but now it was losing leaves at an alarming rate. When I shook the stems, almost all the leaves ended up on the floor. Within days all that remained were spindly stems sticking this way and that way while one leaf hung on tenaciously. It looked so sad!

It reminded me of my life. My life had been full—a life rich in family and friends; all had seemed well with the world. I was content, happy, and at peace. How quickly everything changed. We had recently lost our home in a bankruptcy, and then, as if that weren't enough, my husband left me for another woman. Like my bougainvillea, I felt spindly, ugly, exposed, and of little value, but I was tenaciously trying to hang on.

For some reason I continued to water my plant. Even though it seemed all but dead, I just couldn't bear to throw it out. It was still precious to me. Little did I know what was going to happen next. I told my mom what had happened, and she suggested that I be patient and wait for the surprise.

Much to my delight I discovered buds on the plant. I awoke one morning to discover a beautiful jewel-red flower on a bare stem! It was paper-thin and so translucent one could almost read through the petals. Within a week the plant was awash in flowers and the leaves started to grow back denser and fuller than before. Once again God had visually shown His love to me. How I had wanted to die during this painful time. (In fact, I had thought I was dying.) But God had different plans for my life—plans that made my previous life pale in comparison. No, He did not discard me when I was looking ugly and felt as if I had no worth or value to anyone. He sustained and nurtured me with His love and tender care.

"The reason I wrote you was to see if you would stand the test and be obedient in everything" (2 Cor. 2:9, NIV). Today I have bloomed and blossomed into the woman He always wanted me to be. Praise God!

Jill Rhynard

Jesus, I Heard

In my Father's house are many mansions: if it were not so,
I would have told you. I go to prepare a place for you.
John 14:2.

ONE OF MY FAVORITE television channels is HGTV—the home and garden channel. I like watching the transformations of houses and rooms that go from old to new. I marvel at the creativity of the designers and often come away with new ideas for my own house. I imagine what my kitchen could be like if I made the changes. It's good to have brand new things—eventually I figure I'll use them. You see, I live in a country where real estate is, well, expensive to say the least. Although I am content with my two bedroom apartment I would like to get a place with a few more rooms for my growing family. More room. More space. That would be my dream home.

Oh, I have had a dream home—for the past 30 years. Constructed in 1978, it had six rooms and came on the market for a mere $100 plus. My parents lovingly bought it for me as a Christmas present when I was about 6. My oldest cousin helped me put it together. Yes, it was the ultimate dream house at that time—*the Barbie Dream House.*

Around that same time my parents introduced me to Someone who had a bigger house. They bought me a record by Bill and Gloria Gaither, "Jesus, I Heard You Had a Big House." "Jesus, I heard you had a big house,/ Where I'd have a room of my own/ Jesus, I heard you had a big yard,/ Big enough to let a kid roam,/ I heard you had clothes in your closet/ Just the right size that I wear,/ And Jesus, I heard if I give you my heart,/ Then you would let me go there."

Well, I am glad to say that although I still have my Barbie Dream House (which has been passed on to my daughter), I am looking forward to getting another dream house. Unlike my last dream house, this one will be real. I won't have to worry about getting a loan from the bank or paying the mortgage. I won't have to worry about space or storage. It will be far better than anything I have even seen on HGTV. Beyond all that, I'll have a bigger yard than now, where I'll have the garden of my dreams. I can't even imagine what it will be like, but I know it will be perfect—just for me. The furnishings and the décor will be just what I have always wanted. Make sure you're there. I want you to see it.

Dana M. (Bassett) Bean

God's Grace Is Sufficient for Me

Let us then approach the throne of grace with confidence,
so that we may receive mercy and find grace to help us in our time of need.
Heb. 4:16, NIV.

WE ARE SAVED by the grace of God which He freely gives us. But we humans, who are part of this sinful world, do not always extend grace.

I am thinking back to my high school days when I appeared for my ninth-grade final exams. I had done exceptionally well in all the subjects except one: mathematics. I was not comfortable with the subject as it was the year they introduced modern math. Some of my classmates also had the same fear, and we wondered whether we would get through our class, or if we would fail.

Our worst fear came true when six of us were called into the principal's office. He was feeling sad and sorry to talk to us, for we each had scored higher than 60 percent as aggregate marks in all our subjects except math. He further informed us that when the promotion committee met, our teacher refused to give us the two grace marks required for us to pass, and so we would have to repeat the ninth grade in the following school session. Or we could attend some other school.

This incident had a great impact on our minds. We could not understand the reason our math teacher had refused to give us the grace marks, as the other teachers had given grace marks to the other students and promoted them. This question continued to trouble me even into my college days.

God never does that to us. His grace is for all. Everyone. Even though we don't deserve it, He renders it to us freely. We have not done anything for Him, but He still confers grace sufficient for us.

If I had not failed the math class, I don't believe I would have ever understood the meaning of grace. But now I do. Grace is God's gift to us as sinners. It is an undeserved, unmerited, and unexpected favor given to me, though I am unworthy. I am very thankful to God for sending His son to die for me, a sinner, as well as for the whole world. We need to believe Him in faith and accept His gift of grace. I think of the song that says, "Amazing grace! how sweet the sound, that saved a wretch like me!" *Thank You, Lord, for Your grace. It is sufficient.*

Rebecca Singh

Buttered Bread

Cast your bread upon the waters, for after many days you will find it again.
Eccl. 11:1, NIV.

AND YOU MAY FIND IT BUTTERED.

I am writing from the Sahmyook University campus in South Korea. I am visiting here for three weeks; my husband has come to teach in the seminary for four months. Officially retired from teaching, he was asked to return for one semester—exactly 50 years after we first came to this campus as missionaries, a young couple with a 16-month-old son.

We had not sought a mission call. My husband spoke a few romance languages but not Korean. Was God really behind the call? The church officer who sent the call wisely suggested we take two months to think and pray about it. As we did so, God sent indicators pointing toward Korea—not the least of which was a Sabbath school Bible lesson on Jonah!

But God knew Korea was just right for us. It was a great place to raise our toddler and the three children born to us there. We gained many solid friends, and my husband developed skills as a college professor. Not only did God use him to train many pastors here, but he has since been able to serve Korean students in the Philippines and then in the United States.

These students have gone on to leadership positions in Korea, America, and around the world—as foreign missionaries, teachers, medical professionals, and in other ways. We are in our 70s now, and it is gratifying to look back at the ripple effect of our work. We know clearly that it is not from our bumbling attempts at mission, but from God's grace to us and through us.

Upon our return, former students have treated us like royalty, with gifts, meals, and trips that we know are costly. Koreans are a gracious and generous people. Our children also have fond memories of their early childhood here. One daughter and her family returned here the same day I did (because of her husband's work). During her few days here we enjoyed a reunion and some wonderful hospitality from Korean friends.

Our old house on this campus is gone—torn down, replaced by a large apartment building to house foreign teachers, as the campus has grown tremendously. But our warm memories remain. God has blessed us, our family, the church and its many phases of work here, and our former students. He has indeed returned our bread with butter—and even jam on it.

Madeline Steele Johnston

Inside the Wood

Be diligent to present yourself approved to God, a worker
who does not need to be ashamed, rightly dividing the word of truth.
2 Tim. 2:15, NKJV.

IT WAS OCTOBER and we were spending the weekend at a singles' retreat in Pennsylvania. On Sabbath morning during worship we were all told to pair up with someone we didn't know, find out as much as possible about them, then introduce them to the rest of the group. At the conclusion of this exercise we were to go on a nature walk with our new friend. But we had an assignment: to collect items to bring back and share with the rest of the group.

Many pairs of new friends went out on the walk, and one pair brought back a piece of wood that housed honey bees inside. The beehive remained intact and the bees undisturbed. Those showing the wood explained the relationship of the wood and the bees to nature. We were very impressed that this group was able to share so much and that their "find" included bees that were apparently asleep for the winter inside the wood. They received first prize for their presentation.

After the presentations, we went about the rest of the day's activities. All the items we'd brought in to share remained in our main meeting place. And as the building warmed up, to our surprise—and consternation—the bees warmed up, woke up, and flew out of the wood and into the main meeting room. We scrambled for protection as the wood was taken out and, sadly, the bees destroyed for our safety.

The lesson I learned from the sleeping bees was that, brought into a building, they were out of their natural habitat. They got warm, awoke, became confused, and apparently didn't know where they were. Let us not become confused in these last days of earth's history. Things are winding down, prophecies are being fulfilled, and many have gone to sleep to await Jesus' return. Let's remember Paul's words in 2 Timothy 3:1: "But know this, that in the last days perilous times will come" (NKJV). He also said, "I do not count myself to have apprehended; but one thing I do, forgetting those things which are behind and reaching forward to those things which are ahead, I press toward the goal for the prize of the upward call of God in Christ Jesus" (Phil. 3:13, 14, NKJV).

That provides a direction for the future!

Bessie Haynes

Lost My Connection

But they that wait upon the Lord shall renew their strength;
they shall mount up with wings as eagles; they shall run, and not
be weary; and they shall walk, and not faint.
Isa. 40:31.

RECENTLY I CHATTED with a dear friend, Helen, my sister in ministry, by way of her cell phone to my land phone. We were having a wonderful visit, sharing our latest endeavors and of course talking about our children and grandchildren. We'd been talking and laughing very happily for about 10 minutes when I asked her a question. There was no response. I checked my phone and saw that we were no longer connected. In our attempts to reconnect, we kept missing each other. We each waited a few moments, then one of us tried again. We reconnected and resumed our conversation where we'd left off.

Whenever you start your day without getting some transmitted power through prayer to God, you stand to loose your connection and your way. However, the Lord is our ever-present help whenever we call Him. I ask that He will teach me how to be patient and to wait for Him.

For cell phones, we know that transmission towers along the way help carry our voices to the other phone. But if you are out of bounds—not near enough to a tower—a disconnect can occur. If your signals are crossed and go to another tower you may have a better connection. Helen and I lost connections again later, but were happy that we had spent that time together.

Sometimes in our travels along this Christian journey, we may loose connection with our Supreme Provider. Continuing to travel on your own without any supreme transmission support—which is yours for the asking—can be hazardous. When you have reached just so far the Lord, in His own way, allows you to reconnect with Him simply through prayer. When you think you have lost connection, stop and pray for a recharge and thus get back in touch.

It is a joy to talk to the Lord, to tell Him all about my concerns, even though He already knows. He cares about me and gives me food for thought—even an object lesson from cell phones. I can talk to Him anytime, any place, as He always works out things out that are best for me. Continual communication with Jesus increases my strength and faith—it will yours too.

Betty G. Perry

Stranded

There is the sea, vast and spacious. . . . There the ships go to and fro.
Ps. 104:25, 26, NIV.

WE WERE ENJOYING another delightful family vacation, staying at a waterfront apartment on Queensland's beautiful Sunshine Coast. From the living room we could look out over the calm waters of Pumicestone Passage to a low-lying sand island and beyond to the open sea. The waterway was busy all day with small fishing boats and pleasure crafts scurrying back and forth. A fleet of pelicans went about their daily routine—always with an eye out for any fishermen who might be willing to share their catch—and over in the main shipping lane large cargo boats and container ships passed by at regular intervals. A couple of times a day a small local cruise boat filled with sightseers would also meander past and call in at the nearby jetty.

I noticed that the cruise boat seemed to take a very indirect route when crossing from the far side of the Passage to the jetty. I thought the captain was simply trying to prolong what would otherwise be a rather short trip—until the day the cruise boat reached a spot opposite our apartment and came to a sudden unscheduled, shuddering stop. The Coast Guard volunteers quickly launched their inflatable craft and buzzed over to bring back the stranded passengers. But for the rest of the afternoon the cruise boat stayed right where it was. Every so often the captain, no doubt embarrassed, would get out to survey his vessel, walking gloomily around it in knee-deep water. Yes, the boat was sitting firmly on a sandbar. Attempts by the Coast Guard to tow it free were without success. There was no choice but to wait for the returning tide.

We learned later that the sparkling waters of Pumicestone Passage hid many sandbars, a trap both for sailors unfamiliar with the area and for those who might have become over-confident or inattentive. This small episode was also a reminder of how much we each need God's guidance as we navigate the waters of life. It's reassuring to know that He has promised, "When you pass through the waters, I will be with you; and when you pass through the rivers, they will not sweep over you" (Isa. 43:2, NIV).

Thank You, Lord, for keeping us on course and for patiently coming to the rescue whenever we foolishly take our eyes off You and run aground.

Jennifer M. Baldwin

Arrested Development of the Mind

And be renewed in the spirit of your mind.
Eph. 4:23.

THERE WAS A TIME when the only peace I could find was when I was sitting and hearing the Word of God, and when I was in fellowship with other Christian brothers and sisters. The atmosphere of God was—and is now—my refuge. Back then my mind was under continual attack. I was in a constant battle to keep control of my mind, and I literally walked around praying without ceasing. I was in my 30s before I was able to come to a conclusion about what was causing this battle in my life.

The story began when I was 12 years old and something extremely traumatic happened to me. Most of us face experiences such as abuse, neglect, abandonment, fear, sadness, hurt, or disappointments in our lives—yet we must go on. And so this pain manifests itself in anger, hate, depression, and rebellion. In my case the emotional pain was so severe that a portion of my mind literally shut down—and my ability to learn certain things went with it.

It was simply a miracle that God, from the moment I accepted Christ, began teaching and healing my mind. As a baby Christian I went to counseling with one of the leaders at my church. When I told him the struggles I was having, He advised me to first start with little things that I could overcome; then from there I could gain strength for the greater battles.

So I opened up completely to God and He began to work things out in my life, taking my struggles one by one and defeating them. Yet this came through great struggles to overcome a weak and damaged mind. I felt literal pain in my mind as I desperately fought to change.

It was years later that I recognized my need of *total* deliverance. So I went back to the same leader and told him I was ready. I wanted to be free to serve God. He told me to fast, pray, and seek God for one week. After one week he asked if God had revealed anything to me. And at that moment the Holy Spirit revealed to me the source of my struggles. I had totally suppressed the incident. The leader anointed me with oil, laid hands on me, and prayed in the name of Jesus, and my mind was healed.

To this very day I conscientiously take care to protect my mind. God has taken my greatest weakness, a weak and damaged mind, and transformed it for His service.

Chrisele Green

Jesus Built a Bridge

God is our refuge and strength, a very present help in trouble.
Ps. 46:1.

I'M OFTEN IN AWE at the grandeur and strength of great and magnificent bridges. But then, there are others: those that look too spindly and fragile to support their immense weight. It is then that I think of the knowledge behind the architecture. It isn't the builders who are keeping the structure up: it is the plans they created and put together that make it all possible.

No records exist of the people who first conceived the idea of spanning a stream, a river, a gorge, or a chasm with logs, rocks, or vines, but today we find bridges all over the world.

Bridges are many things to many people. To the traveler, a bridge is a means to cross a chasm or river from one side to another. To an engineer a bridge is a problem in stresses and strains. An artist sees a bridge as an expression of the urge to create. There is also more than one way to use a bridge, for bridges link communities and nations, they shorten distances, and they generate commerce.

There are three basic types of bridges: the arch bridge, the truss bridge, and the suspension bridge. Aqueducts are bridges for water. A drawbridge divides and raises to let large boats pass under and fits back together so cars and people can pass over. A bridge for pedestrians is called a footbridge. There are covered bridges, cantilever bridges, deck bridges, and moveable bridges. Bridges are made from many types of material: aluminum, timber, masonry, iron, steel alloy, reinforced concrete—and even vines and other natural materials.

What does this have to do with God, you ask? Bridges make me think of what Jesus did for me. With three rugged nails and two pieces of wood, Jesus built a bridge that you and I can cross to reach heaven.

Have we been guilty of trampling across that Bridge to do the things that we want to do, regardless of the plan that Jesus has for us? My Jesus is not a covered bridge that hides His grace and forgiveness. He is not a moveable bridge that picks up at any whim and moves to another location if He does not like the way I approach Him. He is not made of cold, hard material. He is light, strength, goodness, and all that is perfect. It is the plans built at Calvary that make it possible for me to be held together and held up when things seem to go wrong. It is then that I give it all to my Father to carry across the bridge He built for me.

Vidella McClellan

Welcome Home

*He will call upon me, and I will answer him; I will be
with him in trouble, I will deliver him and honor him.*
Ps. 91:15, NIV.

MY HUSBAND RETIRED from the US Navy in October after 25 years of service. We decided it was time to move and enjoy life away from the busyness and stress of city life. Moving often has simply been a part of being a Navy family, but as the children got older, moving became a bit more complicated as it was harder for them to leave their school and friends behind. We had lived in apartments and military housing, and we had enjoyed our own homes in California and Maryland. As we faced the uncertain future, we looked forward to the Blue Ridge Mountains in South Carolina.

Together with our dog, Hercules, we began an eight-hour drive from Maryland to Greenville, South Carolina. All of us were excited and could hardly wait to get there. Our daughter, who had never seen the house we were moving into, started asking questions about it. We assured her that she was going to love it so much she might decide not to go back to college in Maryland.

As we neared our destination, we noticed dark clouds hovering over South Carolina. We prayed that God would hold back the summer storm until we arrived safely. It would be difficult to travel in the rain especially with the car fully packed and blocking the rear view. My husband had to focus on the road using his side-view mirrors to help him change lanes. Driving in the rain would be treacherous at this time of the night. We arrived and had barely settled in when the rain started pounding on the housetop. Thank God for His protection and traveling mercies!

I am looking forward to heaven, and am very excited about seeing the home that God is preparing for me. The travel may be long and tedious, with frustrations and failure along the way. However, I can count on God's promise that He will see me through as long as I keep my eyes focused on Him. The road can be bumpy and full of potholes, but my God has promised to give me a smooth ride if I put my trust in Him. Aren't we blessed to serve an all-powerful God who holds the future in His hands? He has promised to take care of our needs as we journey to our final destination. I can't wait to hear His loving voice say, "Welcome home, my child, enter into the joy I have prepared for you!"

Rhona Grace Magpayo

God's GPS

The Lord is good and does what is right; he shows the proper path
to those who go astray. He leads the humble in doing right.
Ps. 25:8, 9, NLT.

FOR THE CANADIAN Thanksgiving weekend my husband and I planned a drive down from Toronto, Canada, to visit my mother in Nashville, Tennessee. We planned to cross the border at Lake Huron instead of going through Windsor as we normally do, as crossing the border there would be a little faster. Since we were not too familiar with this route, and the trip would be more than 700-plus miles (1,120 kilometers) long, we decided to use our new GPS (Global Positioning System) to help us navigate the journey.

All went well at first. It was a beautiful fall morning and the sky and air were clear. The leaves of the trees along the way were rich with changing colors: bright oranges, yellows, and browns. This made it a restful, yet spectacular, drive. Crossing the border was no problem, and we were fine until we reached Detroit where we met a lot of road construction and detours. We knew that the GPS does not know where the detours are, but if we followed the detour signs or made a wrong turn, the GPS would recalculate and give us an alternate route to follow.

Unfortunately, our trust in the GPS was weak. We trusted our own judgment instead, and the result was chaos. We became hopelessly lost and found ourselves constantly going around in circles. In desperation, and realizing that time was going by very quickly, we decided to trust the GPS and see what would happen. The result? You guessed it. We found ourselves on the right path again.

Reflecting on this trip made me reflect on God's Book, the Bible. The Bible is God's GPS to us. In it He has given us the direction for our journey through this life, including the pitfalls to stay away from. But so many times we stop trusting His instructions and follow our own path. The results can be wasted time, bitter disappointment, sorrow, and unhappiness.

Too often it is only when we have nowhere else to go that we remember God's GPS, where we find instruction for our happiness in this life's journey, even if the path is rough.

Heavenly Father, help us to really trust Your Word. Thanks for always being there to help us get back on track when we try to follow our own way.

Marion Newman Chin

Daisies, a Butterfly, a Kiss

Oh, taste and see that the Lord is good; blessed is the man who trusts in Him!
Ps. 34:8, NKJV.

I SAT WRITING BIRTHDAY GREETINGS to my two sons. Pausing a moment, contemplating words to encourage, I glanced out the open door. Just then a white butterfly, its wings etched with black, lit upon the daisies that grew wild outside my door.

I was drawn to it, so I went outside and stood to watch it. Just then a spirited breeze blew in and caught the butterfly, lifting it higher and higher as if it were inviting the butterfly to partner in a dance. And dance they did, with such grace and beauty. A pure joy to behold. The dance ended all too soon when the breeze took its leave.

The butterfly paused a moment, then flew straight toward me, landing on my upper lip. It lifted and circled me once before lighting once again on the daisies. I was so shocked I just stood there. The moment of impact seemed to freeze my whole body. I was standing in a moment of time, conscious of only two things: the Lord's presence and having just been kissed by a butterfly!

Wonder of wonders! You see, the night before I had spent hours with the Lord, reasoning together regarding the many things, past and present, that weighed heavily on my heart. I had seen myself as a broken pot, its fragments scattered over a battlefield, quite beyond repair. In every area of my life, I felt, I was nothing but a big screw-up. I knew my relationship with God was terribly lopsided: all of Him, precious little of me. Trust, love, and surrender were long-standing mega issues.

Precious Lord, today I am blessed with Your presence through nature—which in my wildest imagination I could never have envisioned happening to me. A butterfly! How exquisite! Its metamorphic stages akin to spiritual growth. In Your exhaustless, creative way You let me know You listened and heard me last night. I am impressed that I need to let my heart soar like the eagle, and let my spirit dance with the wind like the butterfly. To let go. Jump. You will catch me.

Thank You, my Father, for the daisies, the breeze, the butterfly kiss—all orchestrated by You that I may taste and see that You truly are very present, very involved, very real. Thank You for loving me the way that You do. With love, Your daughter, June.

June Y. Powers

His Name

I will set him on high, because he hath known my name.
Ps. 91:14.

WHAT'S IN A NAME? A name is our main source of identification. It denotes our historical background or family line. When a baby is born, society expects that the parents or guardian will name the child. Often a baby boy is named after his father, sometimes to the fourth generation. Parents may use the names of loved family members for their baby's name. The name may be misspelled during the registration process, but everyone must have a name. They say a good family name can take you far.

In some cultures, a baby's name is based on the day it was born, while in other cultures the name's meaning is of paramount importance. Some parents choose from the names of athletes or movie stars that they admire, or the name of someone especially important in their society such as the prime minister or president. Others want to be original so name their child Affinity or Tuesday or who knows what else. Without a doubt, names are important.

In the spiritual realm, a name is no less important. The book of Genesis tells us that "In the beginning God created" the sun, moon, stars, trees, flowers, birds, all the animals, and then He made man and woman. He is our heavenly Father and we are His children. By virtue of this—believe it or not—He has given us His name.

The many forms of His name give us clear evidence of the kind of God He is: *Elohim*: Lord God or creator; *El Elyon*: God most high; *Adonai*: my Lord; *Jehovah–Jireh*: provider; *Jehovah–Rapha*: healer; *Jehovah–shalom*: my peace; *Jehovah–tsidkenu*: our righteousness; *Jehovah Sabaoth*: Lord of Hosts; *Jehovah Raah*: Lord my Shepherd, and the list goes on. When we accept Him as our personal Lord and Savior we take His character, His likeness, His Name. As such, He expects us to live up to His good name. In 2 Chronicles. 7:14, God says, "If my people, which are called by my name, shall humble themselves, and pray, and seek my face, and turn from their wicked ways; then will I . . . forgive their sin, and will heal their land." It is only as we live up to His good name that we give Him the authority to act on our behalf, on behalf of our family, and our country.

Remember that "The name of the Lord is a strong tower; the righteous run to it and are safe" (Prov. 18:10, NKJV).

Thamer Cassandra Smikle

While Still Speaking . . .

Before they call I will answer; while they are still speaking I will hear.
Isa. 65:24, NIV.

A PLETHORA OF STUDIES allude to the benefits of prayer and meditation, and a myriad of anecdotal reports from all corners of the globe (if a globe has corners) spotlight answered prayers. But when you personally experience a surprising or clearly supernatural answer to prayer, there is a totally different impact on your mind and heart.

Six a.m., and still dark. I had prayed off and on during the entire 45-minute commute to work. My request was different from any I had made before: "Please put someone in my path who can point me in the right direction." Walking into the hospital it was patently obvious—even to me who tries to put the best spin possible on almost everything in life—that the arthritis in my left hip was progressing. Even with the aid of my elegant walking stick (OK, an essential cane), a frisson of pain accompanied every step. But who should I see? Selecting a surgeon can be nearly as important as picking a life-partner. During the surgery you are quite literally in the surgeon's hands!

The hospital conference room. Seven a.m. I took my place at the table for the surgery steering committee. Not three minutes later the operating room supervisor slipped into a chair next to mine. (There were a half dozen open spaces, and in several years of committee meetings this was the first time she had sat beside me.) I shifted my position to relieve the pressure on my hip. The woman leaned toward me and whispered, "Looks like you need to have that hip replaced."

I smiled and nodded. "I am afraid so."

"I expect you're going to ask Dr. _____ to be your surgeon. I worked with him when he started the hip-replacement program, and he's the best there is."

I blinked in surprise, both at her comments and at the fact that her beeper was already sounding. Getting to her feet, she whispered in parting, "Say hello to him for me. You'll be in good hands." Then she was gone.

I sat there, stunned. *Please put someone in my path who can point me in the right direction,* I had prayed. Oh my! While I was yet speaking . . .

Arlene Taylor

Life's Little Dilemmas?

Behold, I go forward, but he is not there; and backward, but I cannot perceive him: On the left hand, where he doth work, but I cannot behold him: he hideth himself on the right hand, that I cannot see him: But he knoweth the way that I take: when he hath tried me, I shall come forth as gold.
Job 23:8-10.

I HAVE A LITTLE DILEMMA. You know those occasions when God gives you something wonderful? You have absolutely no doubt that it came from Him because it is something you never had before. That happened to me. I have always wanted to paint. Going up or down the highway, I'd see these picturesque little scenes and wished I could paint them. I got the opportunity when God just literally dropped the talent in my hands. Now I don't know what He wants me to do with it. That's the dilemma.

I have all these dreams and aspirations. I start taking classes. I want to get my art degree, but it seems every time I try something, the door closes. So I ask, *Lord, what do you want me to do with this ability?* I've been invited to exhibit at galleries a few times and I joined some online art forums. No pieces were sold, so I ask again, *Is it that I want too much? Do I expect too much of myself? I don't want to be a millionaire, but I would at least like to be able to sell enough pieces so that I could finance this habit. Art supplies are expensive and money is tight.* No response. *What's the lesson I should be learning?* I ask myself. *What direction am I supposed to go in?* I become dissatisfied with my work and frustrated with the silence (or seeming silence) because it means I'm not getting the lesson.

At the time of this writing I am supposed to be getting ready for a few exhibitions. But I can't seem to get it together. Nothing I do is good enough for me. I've given up the brush and called it quits a few times, because of my constant frustration. But when you love something, it always calls you back.

So what's the message? What's the lesson? For me right now it's to lean on Jesus—all the time. Let go, and let God lead me through the process; learn to trust that He knows best even when I'm not hearing Him. It's not about me—it's about Him. In His season He will come through. After all, He wants the best for me. Our dilemma is to enjoy the now and know how to follow.

Greta Michelle Joachim-Fox-Dyett

Delight Yourself in the Lord

Delight yourself in the Lord and he will give you the desires of your heart.
Ps. 37:4, NIV.

AT THE BEGINNING of our ministry my husband and I faced many challenges. With little experience, my husband ministered to six churches and I was the principal at one church's school. We had just married and were adapting to a new personal and professional life.

Since my childhood I had been instructed that in everything I did, I should seek the presence of God for success. Now that I was a housewife, a school leader, and a minister's wife, I frequently thought, "Little prayer, little power; much prayer, much power." However, I considered a routine prayer and a quick Bible study to be enough.

But as I listened to my husband's sermons, I noticed he always used the same expression in his appeals. "To be successful, there is only one secret: Bible study and prayer!" This was not new to me, so finally after one of his sermons I told him I was tired of hearing that the secret to success in life was Bible study and prayer. With a surprised look he said, "Rosinha, try this in your life. Take time for God. Read the Bible more, pray more, get up earlier, and then come and talk to me about this again." Getting up early was not for me! Reading a few chapters in the Bible and praying could be done for a few minutes before going to sleep. Besides, my husband and I did family worship together.

But as my challenges increased I decided I would get up early and spend more time with God. Gradually, changes began to take place. I began to understand that success comes as we indeed walk with God, just like Enoch (see Gen. 5:24). And as I read the Bible I recognized that in spite of having faults, Noah, Abraham, David, and other biblical greats reached success because they walked with God. David himself wrote that he wanted to "walk before the Lord" (Ps. 116:9, NIV). Of David, God said, "I have found David . . . a man after my own heart; he will do everything I want him to do" (Acts 13:22, NIV).

In my own life I saw that it is possible to be victorious when we walk in the presence of God. Friend, there is no other way to overcome the struggles in this life. The secret is dedicating time to Bible study and prayer. You will see the difference in your own life too.

Rosinha Gomes Dias de Oliveira

Mr. Snake

For the battle is not yours, but God's.
2 Chron. 20:15.

"COME ON, RYAN. Let's go get some jars from downstairs," I called to my 4-year-old son as I headed to the basement. We were living in a country home that boasted a half basement and much of our food came from our garden. We did a lot of canning during the summer months, and the half basement was a perfect place to store our bounty.

This particular day I needed several things so asked for Ryan's help. We clasped hands as we went down the stairs. In the basement, I pulled the light string and waited the several seconds it took for our eyes to adjust to the dim light, then looked up and down the heavily-laden shelves for the jars I planned to use for supper.

Suddenly my eyes opened wide and I gasped. At the same moment, Ryan squealed, darted behind me, wrapped his little arms around both my legs, almost knocking me down, and cried, "Get him, Mama! Get him!"

Intertwined around the tops of some of the jars and looking at us was a very large black snake. We stared at him and he stared at us.

"I think we will let Daddy take care of him, sweetheart," I responded quietly as I slowly unwound Ryan's arms from my knees, never taking my eyes off the snake.

We backed up the stairs and shut the door. Throughout the rest of the afternoon I watched the door to make sure the snake didn't decide to come up into the house.

We never saw Mr. Snake again, but I was reminded of this incident recently when reading 2 Chronicles 20:15. Though we're told, "The battle is not yours, but God's" (NIV), we try to fight the devil ourselves and end up much worse off than when we started.

Satan has had many years of practice in getting our eyes off Jesus and luring us away from our heavenly Father. We have no power against him—but Jesus does. Jesus gained the victory on Calvary and He offers it to us freely.

Again and again the Bible says, "The Lord wrought a great victory." He will do the same in our lives today if we just ask. So when Satan comes at us, we need to do as Ryan did: hide in Jesus and say, "Get him, Jesus! Get him!"

Gail Bremmer

Heavenly Makeover

I am making everything new!
Rev 21:5, NIV.

I LIKE GETTING NEW THINGS, don't you? When we were children our mother, who was an excellent seamstress, made all our clothes. They were pretty, well-made dresses which fitted perfectly but I used to long for just one new store–bought dress, and I'd look longingly at the mannequins in shop windows and at pictures in mail order catalogues.

When I got married and we bought our first house, it was nearly new. Later we bought a brand–new house. There was something extra special about choosing new furnishings for our new home. Stepping into the house for the first time, I loved the scent of newness everywhere. I loved knowing that no one else had cooked in its kitchen before or eaten at that breakfast bar.

Speaking of new, I enjoy several interesting house makeover programs on TV. In one, someone buys a dilapidated building and sets about renovating it for resale. They get advice from an expert who comments on their progress, and the success or failings of their project. I particularly enjoy the before-and-after photographs shown at the end, seeing the transformation from old and worn to new, modern, and bright. Finally the house is valued, and comparisons made with the original purchase price and cost of renovation. The success of the project is determined by the amount of profit made on a quick resale.

In another TV show, viewers follow someone who is building a home on a grand scale. Money is no object in achieving the home of their dreams. The end product is always so large and lavish that in our wildest dreams I, and most other viewers, could never aspire to live in it. For me, the entertainment value of these programs is in enjoying the creativity of people who can take an idea and turn it into reality. I also like to comment on what I like or dislike about what they've done and whether I would enjoy living in the house or not.

Jesus, the Creator of the universe tells us He is making everything new—and that re-creation begins with you and me. He is making me a new person, created in God's likeness (Eph. 4:24). He is also preparing for me a new home in heaven that will be perfect in every way (John 14:2, 3). Furthermore, I will be able to design and build whatever I can wish for in the earth made new (Isa. 65:21). What a privilege that will be to live with Him forever in a world where nothing will ever become old or decrepit again!

Antonia Castellino

God's Smiles

Observe how the lilies of the field grow; . . . that not even
Solomon in all his glory clothed himself like one of these.
Matt. 6:28, 29, NASB.

THE FAST-MELTING SNOW all about us was filling ditches, creeks, and sloughs with water. We knew spring would soon be upon us. Our spirits brightened as we shed layers of clothing, especially the long underwear and brown-gartered stockings. But one needed much covering to get through the cold, blizzards, and snow that came with living in North Dakota.

Now we watched for the first sighting of the purple crocus that would cover hill and prairie. When they were in full bloom, we spent our recesses picking these dainty, pretty blossoms, filling every container in the schoolroom that would hold water. Our room looked like a flower garden. In my mind, nothing could be prettier. Remembering the bouquets and corsages of orchids, gardenias, or roses I have received, I don't think they carried the same message as did the crocuses. They told me that North Dakota was "a fine place" to live though others thought there was "only a picket fence between us and the North Pole." Ridiculous!

Next in the season came the dandelions—just in time for Mother's Day. I also remember a bright yellow bouquet I made for my mother. She accepted it in admiration and love.

And by June, and for the remainder of the summer, a cacophony of brilliant colors and a variety of flowers romped through the garden. Mother always saved a special space for her flowers. It was much too big, we children thought, as we spent hours under the hot sun weeding and hoeing. But we were proud to carry large bouquets to church to set on the piano each week.

Today I have access to flower shops and they to me. Last Mother's Day I had a bouquet of 50 flowers from my daughter in London and pink and white blossoms from my son in California. I am delighted with the beauty of the flowers and cherish them, but somehow the memory of specialness of the spring crocus still remains. It was God smiling on me.

I have heard it said that flowers are a reflection of God's smiles for us. How beautifully He has made the whole array for His children to enjoy and be blessed by. Our smiles are like God's flowers—important to make the world a better place. We must not forget them as we go about our daily lives—regardless of the season.

Dessa Weisz Hardin

Dark Glasses

*If any of you lacks wisdom, let him ask of God, who gives to
all liberally and without reproach, and it will be given to him.
James 1:5, NKJV.*

TO MAINTAIN MY GOOD HEALTH I try to walk at least five evenings a week. But one summer evening was a little different. My walking partner had gone out of state so I walked alone. Taking a more public route, I followed the sidewalk for an uneventful two miles, and since the sun was still high and the glare intense, I wore my prescription dark glasses.

The next day as we got into the car to run some errands, my daughter handed me the glasses case that I'd left in her room the night before. But when I opened the case, it was empty. Thinking that I'd laid the glasses down somewhere, I went back into the house to search for them. No glasses. Using an older pair, we continued our mission, praying that we'd find them. That evening I decided to walk the same route I'd used the day before so I could look for my glasses. But I quickly noticed something that devastated me. The grass beside the sidewalk had just been mowed. "They'd have been mangled by the mower," I mused, more to comfort myself than anything else. Still distressed, I turned to my God. "Please, Father, help me find the glasses. And if anyone else finds them, please see to it that they need that very prescription."

I used my old sunglasses again the next day when I went out in the car. Driving back into the garage, I noticed a glint in the sunlight in the passenger seat. Surprised, I looked again. There on the seat were my dark glasses, tightly wedged into the farthest corner.

God answered my prayer on two levels. First, He showed me where the glasses were, and then He made sure that I, the person who needed that prescription, found them. Reflecting on that God-blessed incident, I saw a striking similarity between myself and the woman searching for a coin in the gospel parable (Luke 15:8-10). We both were diligent searchers, but the objects of our search were inanimate and thus totally unaware that they were lost. It took special light to find them. She used a small clay lamp, but in my case, it was more than that: it was a spiritual light, His light—a light that never goes out when God searches for us.

Shower us with Your light, heavenly Father, so that we radiate Your love. Thank You that I can actively search for You when I lose my way.

Carol J. Greene

Used by God

Let the words of my mouth . . . be acceptable in your sight.
Ps. 19:14, NKJV.

SO OFTEN WE YEARN to be used by God—even in a little way. It thrilled me when I recently experienced this event in my own life.

For some time I meant to take a special cookie to a neighbor. She had lost her dog in the fall and really missed her pet. This cookie was designed and shaped to look like "Mortimore Mouse." It was so cute with ears made of half a peanut, and a thin licorice tail. I knew she would get a smile out of it. Finally, one day I felt I should delay no longer so I carefully wrapped the cookie in gold paper and put it in a small Ziploc bag.

Before I went on an errand, I stopped by her house. When she opened the door I said, "Hi, Mary Lou. Here's a little gift from Mortimore."

She immediately said, "How did you know?"

"What do you mean?" I inquired.

"It's my birthday!"

I was stunned. "I didn't know, but God knew!" And God had used me, sending me on exactly the right day. That time I didn't really have to say any words.

Another day as we were walking, a neighbor drove by. She stopped her car and rolled down her window. "As you are walking, would you please keep an eye out for our lost cat? She's 12 years old and is black and white with a sort of 'mask' face." We replied that we certainly would, and we would pray that she would be found soon. The neighbor said that she was grateful.

The next day as we were backing out to leave for church, there to my right, on the sidewalk, sat a most beautiful black and white kitty. I called out, "Honey, there's the kitty! Please try to catch it." My husband got out of the car and slowly walked to the cat, talking softly to her, and she let him pick her up! We were so thrilled to see an answer to our prayer. My husband carried her to the end of the cul-de-sac and a woman came out who said, "I know where that cat belongs." We were certain kitty's owner was very happy. Not many words, just actions.

We felt pleased to have been used by God to help one of His children. God can use each of us to His glory! We just need to be open to His leading.

Frieda Tanner

Pajama Runs and Other Detours

The race is not to the swift or the battle to the strong, nor does food come to the wise or wealth to the brilliant or favor to the learned; but time and chance happen to them all.
Eccl. 9:11, NIV.

GRAY CLOUDS DOMINATED the sky as the wind whipped the trees into a frenzied dance. I sat over the heating duct in my purple Garfield pajamas, laptop resting on my knees as I prepared the seminar for the evening. Wind-propelled leaves and branches forced the cat inside while I happily watched nature's circus unfold. Then the postman arrived. I'd been content to stay inside, but the fear of losing our mail to the elements forced me from my warm resting place.

Pulling on my sneakers I decided to risk a pajama run to the letterbox. It was only about 50 feet (15 meters) and I'd be back before my computer could do an auto-save. As I retrieved the letters, I heard a mighty *thump*. My super running speed proved pointless as my fears were confirmed: the front door was locked, and I was outside in my purple Garfield pajamas. I had securely locked all the windows to keep the wind out, so there was only one course of action left.

The real estate agent was almost a mile away down the road in a small local shopping center. I jogged self-consciously down the street smiling and greeting people as they gave me unusual looks. By the time I made it to the real estate agent most of my neighbors had seen my pajama run and local shoppers were giggling at my attire. Our real estate agent smiled as I swept into her office. "New wardrobe I see," she smiled.

"Well, I believe the world would be a happier place if we could all wear our pajamas all day, but sadly, this is a forced appearance. The wind blew my door shut."

Life has many unexpected twists and turns. We envision our future and make plans to arrive there well dressed, with hair styled, and breath minty fresh. However, more often than not we end up taking detours, our clothes get creased, and we arrive in our future a little worse for wear. Ecclesiastes states that despite the plans we make, time and chance happen to us all. So while we are on this journey of life, we may as well smile and enjoy the ride. The real estate agent laughed understandingly as she went to get my keys. Getting home and out of the wind and the starring neighborhood was a relief, though I still smile when I think of it. When time and chance throw you a detour, remember to smile.

Susan Magaitis

Lady Lost

Two sparrows cost only a penny, but not even one of them can die without your Father's knowing it. God even knows how many hairs are on your head. So don't be afraid. You are worth much more than many sparrows.
Matt. 10:29-31, NCV.

THE FIRST HINTS OF FALL COLORS and sunshine shimmered through the trees as we made our way to the car. Lunch conversation had been the usual banter, but now my thoughts were focused on what to do first when I got back to the office.

Opening the car door, I sensed eyes on me. I heard no sound, just had a feeling that someone was there. I turned and there she walked, shoulders crouched, her approach at the same time tentative yet intentional. My ears began to hear the words, "Husband left . . . , job lost . . ." Oh my, I've heard these words before.

My first impulse was to ignore, to move along as I have often done. I looked at her again, her face anguished, her voice so small against the big, empty parking lot. She was so alone.

She was still talking as I walked toward her. She acted embarrassed, eager to see me come, yet trying to slink back from my approach. Before I could put my token gift into her hands, the words spilled out, "I'm so hungry . . . I'm so hungry," and she began to weep, tears spilling onto half-washed cheeks.

Her body shook with emotion. I asked her name and told her I would pray for her. She thanked me again and again, then said again, "I'm so hungry." I hugged her, then watched her walk to the fast food restaurant across the parking lot. She was gone.

I wish I could share with her that Jesus said, "Two sparrows cost only a penny, but not even one of them can die without your Father's knowing it. God even knows how many hairs are on your head. So don't be afraid. You are worth much more than many sparrows" (Matt. 10:29-31, NCV). What a promise!

Jesus gave these promises for one such as she; they are also commands for us: "Then the King will answer, 'I tell you the truth, anything you refused to do for even the least of my people here, you refused to do for me'" (Matt. 25:45, NCV). May God always open my eyes and ears and arms for those hungry, hurting, lost ones He entrusts to my path.

Debra Clements Brill

Rumors

Take heed that ye be not deceived.
Luke 21:8.

THE RUMORS BEGAN when our beloved senior pastor and his family decided to relocate after more than eight years at our church, leaving a vacancy to be filled.

The church and a boarding high school are on the same campus and all worship together on Sabbath, along with many people from the adjoining retirement community. With such a wide range of ages, from Beginners to those of us with gray hair, some compromise in worship style is necessary. The first rumor was that there was a plan to change our fairly conservative church into something much more informal and modern. When asked if that were true, the conference president, our church's state leader, assured the inquirer that it was not. One rumor put to rest!

My husband, Ted, teaches an adult Bible class, and in introducing a lesson on women in the Bible, he asked how we would feel if a woman pastor should be brought in to fill the vacancy. The following Thursday night a friend called to ask where Ted got the information that we were getting a woman pastor! The interesting thing is that the friend goes to a different church in the area, and he got his information from a neighbor who goes to still another one!

It reminded us of the old game of Gossip, in which the first person in a line of people whispers a sentence to the next in line, and that one to the following one, and so on to the end. Each one tells what he heard, and then they compare with the original sentence to see how it changed from person to person.

The rumors have been alarming to some people and amusing to others. But the day is coming when there will be much more serious rumors, stories, and reports inspired by Satan himself. The Bible tells us clearly that when Jesus comes again "He is coming with clouds, and every eye will see Him" (Rev. 1:7, NKJV). So "if they shall say unto you, Behold, he is in the desert, go not forth: behold, he is in the secret chambers; believe it not" (Matt. 24:26). When that time comes, let's be among those who can say with certainty that we know how Jesus will come again; we will not be swayed by rumors or exciting stories. We can say when He comes, "Lo, this is our God; we have waited for him, and he will save us: . . . we will be glad and rejoice in his salvation" (Isa. 25:9).

Mary Jane Graves

Count It All Joy!

My brethren, count it all joy when ye fall into divers temptations; knowing this, that the trying of your faith worketh patience. But let patience have her perfect work, that ye may be perfect and entire, wanting nothing.
James 1:2-4.

HAVE YOU EVER BEEN FRUSTRATED with situations in your life and wondered why God "allowed" them to happen when He has the power to prevent them from happening? I found a quote that really stopped me in my tracks, but it was what I needed at the time: "Each one has his own battles to fight, his own Christian experience to gain, independent in some respects from any other soul; and God has lessons each to gain for himself that no other can gain for him. . . . Our heavenly Father measures and weighs every trial before He permits it to come upon the believer. He considers the circumstances and the strength of the one who is to stand under the proving and test of God, and He never permits the temptations to be greater than the capacity of resistance" (*Our High Calling*, p. 323). Imagine that—God measures and weighs every trial. So if He gives me a trial, He must know that I can get through it.

I discovered this quote when I was questioning the death of a dear friend and colleague, a wonderful Christian gentleman who died in the prime of his life, leaving a young wife and two beautiful baby girls. About a year later we lost another young colleague to cancer, leaving his wife with three young sons. *Why, Lord, do You permit Your children to go through these trials?* Now I realize that God allows suffering—that Satan causes, not God—that we may see the result of sin and turn to God. James said it well in our text for today—count it all joy!

Learning to worship God through my trials has enabled me to "count it all joy," to accept that I may not understand what I'm going through now, but I know that my heavenly Father has everything under control. It's amazing how the Lord used these incidents to prepare me to deal with the rapidly-growing cancer and death of my own mother. In the midst of this, our family was still able to "count it all joy"; she was not in pain, nor did the chemo make her sick. She died knowing that the next voice she would hear would be that of her heavenly Father welcoming her home.

Lord, help me to see our suffering as God sees it—as a refining fire that purifies us and makes us more like Christ.

Lynn Smith

Old Clothes Contentment?

*Keep your lives free from the love of money and be content with what
you have, because God has said, "Never will I leave you; never will I forsake you."
Heb. 13:5, NIV.*

I WAS TAKING OUT my well-worn, well-kept clothes that had grown two sizes too big since I lost a few pounds. The five-day ministerial retreat for pastors and their wives was approaching, and I had no money to purchase new dresses, so adjusting my old clothes was necessary.

Confident that my special seamstress was able to do the job, I called her to make an appointment. To my surprise she couldn't do it. However, she was kind enough to adjust two of the outfits. I tried a second person, then a third—no help. I could not believe it. Three of the best seamstresses I knew were not able to do the job? Disappointment flooded my mind.

I yelled at myself, *I can't believe that my contentment with my old clothes could have led me into such a predicament!*

Calmly, yet reluctantly, I decided to get the phone numbers of a few more seamstresses.

Then like a silent whisper I heard, "Dyhann, haven't I always provided and cared for you?" I recognized that voice. It always sneaks into my thoughts when I am in desperate need.

One month before my wedding I was in a car accident. Semiconscious, I asked God to send someone to take me to the hospital immediately. Without skipping a beat, God sent a Good Samaritan who took me from the disfigured vehicle and drove me to the emergency unit. To this day, I cannot find this person.

Then, in 2008, I was rushed to the hospital accident and emergency unit. The type of attention I needed was not forthcoming, so I whispered another prayer, "Lord, I need Dr. Henry." Once again, without skipping a beat, God sent Dr. Henry to my rescue. My life was saved.

My gratitude to God reminded me of today's text. I felt assured that I would soon find a reliable seamstress. One month later a cousin came from Canada to visit, and yes, she brought her sewing machine! You could say I stepped out in style each day of the retreat.

I thank God for keeping His promise. He met my contentment with a far greater surprise—new clothes for old. I am deeply touched by the miracles He unfolds. Truly, these blessings are new every morning.

Dyhann Buddoo-Fletcher

Have Faith

Daughter, you took a risk of faith, and now you're healed and whole.
Live well, live blessed! Be healed of your plague.
Mark 5:34, Message.

HAVE YOU EVER EXPERIENCED an event so dramatic that the only thing left is faith? Have you faced a situation where the only thing you have to hold onto is belief in a miracle?

I was prepared to endure the eight-hour flight from Amsterdam to Tel Aviv. During a flight, I usually look over my presentations (all organized in one binder) to make sure that everything is ready. On this trip, after looking through my binder, I placed it in the seat-back pocket in front of me. Then, as I usually do, I spent some time in prayer, enjoying the quietness to talk to God, feeling that I was closer to Him. That is how I feel when I am on a plane.

When we landed, I had to hurry. I had just two hours to get ready and go to the central church to preach that evening.

Reaching the hotel, I dashed to my room and hastily dropped my luggage and computer case. I had barely enough time to have a quick shower, pick up my Bible and materials, and get to the church. As I gathered my materials, I suddenly realized that my binder with all my presentations was not in my computer case. Frantically, I searched my personal belongings—twice—looking in every possible pocket. Nothing! I begin to cry, asking God for help. Then, looking toward the window, I prayed a radical prayer: "Lord, please bring my binder back."

For a moment I hoped the flight attendants might have found it, but I knew in my heart that was nearly impossible. So without sermon notes or binder, I left the hotel, becoming calm as I reached the church. That evening I preached with all my heart, knowing that God had a plan in mind, not only to teach me a lesson but also to grow my faith. Peace came to my heart. I felt intense, utter calm. The assurance that God would teach me what to say in all my seminars gave me courage to keep going.

Back at the hotel I was organizing my things when I decided to look in the computer pocket *again*. To my utter amazement the binder was there. How? I do not know. The only thing I know is that God showed His love and care for me even when what I asked seemed impossible to my little faith. He's the Hope-giver and the answer you need in times of trouble. Have faith.

Raquel Queiroz da Costa Arrais

Joy in the Lord

For unto you is born this day in the city of David a Saviour, which is Christ the Lord.
Luke 2:11.

FOUR DOLLARS AND EIGHTY-FOUR CENTS—not all that much money for a Christmas CD, so why couldn't I just forget it and stop the search?

Earlier, while October still hosted autumn leaves, I had cozied myself by the fireplace with the scent of spiced candles and my new CD. I had all the elements of a Christmas moment. Several nights later my husband and I attended a Selah concert. Redeeming our coupon from a church school auction we sported a Miata from a local rental. Sometimes they tuck in CDs but this time we brought our own music, my new Christmas CD. The evening was great.

The following day dawned with a long to-do list. With the Christmas season launched, Christmas tunes would inspire the chores, but where was my new CD? I checked behind the speakers. Not there. Surely it was still in the Miata. I called the rental company—no CD. The search became more about the mystery than the find. The CD could be replaced.

My daughter called the next day suggesting we take a walk and then go to Wal-Mart to replace my CD. You guessed it—not a single copy left. I had an agenda, and a host of things to do, but for some reason I felt lost and immobile.

Dear Lord, the CD hunt is silly. I don't need it. But somehow it isn't about the CD anymore. It's about finding You. My days have been full, pushing aside my thoughts. My son is on the road, my husband's job is hanging, my health feels fragile, and my friends seem distant. Lord, could it be Your will to give me this small sign that affects no one but me. Oh, how I need to feel Your presence, Lord. Amen.

A few more moments of searching and then, for some unknown reason, I opened the door. There in the middle of the porch floor was the lost CD. In that one small disc I saw my God as awesome. I was freshly aware that He loves my children more than I do. He cares about my husband's job, my family, and every part of my life. In the month of October no less, I give you my Christmas thoughts: "The joy of the Lord is your strength" (Neh. 8:10). "For unto you is born this day in the city of David a Saviour, which is Christ the Lord" (Luke 2:11). He is *my* Lord! He is *your* Lord.

Judy Good Silver

Beauty in Disguise

But I fear, lest by any means, as the serpent beguiled Eve through his subtilty,
so your minds should be corrupted from the simplicity that is in Christ.
2 Cor. 11:3.

EVEN THOUGH I HAD lEFT THE CITY on numerous occasions to visit family and friends, I had failed to realize the extreme differences between city and rural living. Since moving to the country I've come in contact with animals that aren't generally seen in a city: raccoons, rabbits, squirrels, foxes, opossums, skunks, moles, and deer. I've witnessed a number of beautifully-colored birds of different species. The air is much cleaner and there is less noise.

Recently, I was talking to Bob on the phone about taking a package to my son Andre since Bob and his wife Tina were going to visit him. "Can you please hold a minute?" I asked.

"Yes," Bob replied. I turned on the light and raced down the stairs to the basement to retrieve another item to send to Andre. As I was about to step onto the basement floor, I broke my pace and stood on the bottom step looking at what I thought was a beautiful black necklace with bright red ornaments lying on the newly installed carpet. *I don't own a necklace*, I realized, and no one had visited me lately wearing one. Taking a second look, it dawned on me that it wasn't a necklace at all—it was a baby snake about a foot long. I told Bob I would call him back as there was a snake in the basement.

Bob suggested that I put it in a jar. I quickly found an empty jar and grabbed a twig from the fireplace. The snake wiggled and squirmed and did all it could to keep from being confined to the empty jar. Finally, after about five minutes of trying to capture the critter, I placed the jar over it. That exposed its beautiful orange-colored belly.

I thought of Eve and how she was deceived by Satan. What a beautiful deadly creature. This is the way sin presents itself. Sin is deadly and often comes beautifully decorated, unexpected and in disguise. Sometimes one may not be as fortunate as I. I had turned the light on over the stairs before going into the basement, but sometimes we step into sin because we haven't allowed Christ to illuminate our pathway. Once we step into sin, we can be forgiven if we repent and ask for forgiveness. As the snake was contained in a quart jar, Christ contained sin and sealed it on the cross with the shedding of His blood. Thank God for Jesus!

Cora A. Walker

Answered Prayer

Train up a child in the way he should go: and when he is old, he will not depart from it.
Prov. 22:6.

I WAS ONLY 6 YEARS OLD when I knelt by the chair in my class at church and asked Jesus to come into my heart. It was a serious matter to me—and still is.

When we arrived home from church that afternoon, I wasted no time in inviting my friends next door to come over and play. Out in the backyard I preached my first sermon to my girlfriends, telling them to pray because God loved them and could see right through the roof! I don't know what impression that had on them at the time but I thought it was important.

That winter was particularly severe. As always, I was the first in the family to get sick. After three days of a high fever and sore throat, Mom had Dad take me to the children's hospital clinic. It was extremely busy that day, and we waited in an examination cubicle for what seemed like hours. At last Dad went out to the desk to find out how much longer we would have to wait. While he was gone, I jumped down from the table and peeked through the curtain into the next cubicle. I had heard a cry coming from there and I wanted to see what was going on. There on the table sat a teenager; a doctor was sticking a long needle into his nose. It scared me so much I turned from the curtain and got back on the table, shaking. "Please, God, I prayed, don't let him do that to me. Please send the doctor away or let me go home."

My dad returned and said he couldn't find anyone at the desk. Just as he sat down a nurse entered the cubicle and said, "The doctor has been called away on an emergency, and you will have to leave until tomorrow, or you could go to the emergency room." I assured my dad that I was feeling better and we went home. From that day to this, I am convinced that the Lord answered my prayer. Through the years when I would become discouraged I would think of how God had answered my prayer as a child and my doubts and misgivings would flee.

God has answered many of my prayers since then—not always the way I wanted, but as time passed, I found it to be what was for the best.

Thank You, Lord, for answering this child's prayer so many years ago. I know You are always aware of every aspect of our lives and are willing to help in time of need. Amen.

Margaret E. Fisher

A Song of Grace

But unto every one of us is given grace according to the measure of the gift of Christ.
Eph. 4:7.

SEVERAL YEARS AGO I worked as a hospice referral coordinator. I did not work directly with the patients; I only knew them through what the other hospice team members shared with me. I was delighted when our volunteer coordinator stopped one morning and asked me if I would go sing for one of our inpatient residents. "She loves church hymns," she explained. "In fact, she has her own hymnbook at her bedside!"

Mrs. Morris was a delightful lady. She looked well, not like someone dying of a terminal illness. She was very alert, sitting contentedly in a lounge chair with a crocheted afghan tucked neatly about her lap.

At first we chatted for a while, just as a matter of introduction. I quickly discovered that she was very knowledgeable about music. She especially loved church music history and sacred classics. She also loved choirs and had sung in many over the years. I suggested a few songs we might sing together just to get started, but she overruled me, selecting songs she wanted from her hymnal. The book was a well-worn treasure to her and many of the pages were marked to what were obviously her favorites. "Today," she pronounced, "we will sing songs of grace!"

And so we did. We sang for nearly an hour, "Amazing Grace," "Grace Greater Than All My Sins," and on and on. I sang soprano and she harmonized with me. We sang until it was time for supper. I helped her with her meal and afterward read a favorite passage of Scripture from Psalm 91 and had prayer. It was such a blessed hour.

"Will you come back again?" she asked as I prepared to leave.

Of course I would. So when I returned two weeks later I brought two of my choir members to sing with me. But Mrs. Morris wasn't in her chair. Her condition had declined and she lay quietly in her bed, a flower fading. It saddened me to see her that way, and I stood there for a while saying nothing. She looked at me and weakly smiled. I knew she couldn't sing with us. We quietly sang three hymns and left the room as she slept. She died a week later.

Sometimes it is good for us to step into someone else's world, even if just for a moment. We will always find God there, and perhaps a song of grace.

Marcia R. Pope

The Flood That Never Came

*Bring ye all the tithes into the storehouse. . . . and I will rebuke
the devourer for your sakes . . . saith the Lord.
Mal. 3:10, 11.*

WHEN I WAS APPROXIMATELY 10 years old, our home needed a new roof. My mother made the arrangements with the contractor to begin work the following Sunday morning. Sunday was also the day she traveled to town to purchase merchandise for our business. The roofing crew arrived very early and began work before she left.

Rain had fallen almost every day for a week—from light, few-minute showers to sudden heavy rains that caused minor flooding. In spite of that, the men quickly removed the old roof. And sure enough, we looked up and saw storm clouds gathering in the sky. Some of the neighbors came out and started to forecast doom, predicting that our house would be flooded since the roofers did not have tarpaulins large enough to cover the entire roof. I looked at my mother with fear in my eyes because I knew she would soon be leaving us alone to the taunts of the neighbors.

My mother was faithful about paying her tithe, so with her arms akimbo she said, "Well, I'm a tither so God will have a chance to keep His word. He is doing His work, so let me get to mine." With that, she was off. I can remember wanting to go somewhere to hide but being the eldest, I tried to act as if I echoed her sentiments.

We lived on the west bank of a very wide river. The crew was now working feverishly in order to escape the inevitable. Within half an hour the rain started on the east bank of the river. All heads now turned toward the river. The large drops of rain hitting the water sounded like an army marching toward our house. The neighbors hurriedly retreated to their houses. They'd view the disaster from their dry homes.

After about five minutes, everyone realized that there was no tell-tale sound of the rain hitting the galvanized zinc roofs. Something unusual was happening. You'll never guess! The rain had advanced to the middle of the river—and stopped. It was as if God had said, "Thus far and no farther." What a relief for me and a testimony to the goodness of God who kept His promise to rebuke the devourer. The neighbors could not wait to tell my mother about it when she returned home, even sending their offerings to the church. God honors those who honor Him.

Vashti Hinds-Vanier

Metamorphosis

*Do not conform any longer to the pattern of this world, but be transformed
by the renewing of your mind. Then you will be able to test and approve
what God's will is—his good, pleasing and perfect will.*
Rom. 12:2, NIV.

IT WAS SUMMER and the lush vegetation along the Atlantic coast of Brazil produced mangos and cashew fruit as well as other lush native delicacies. The little house where we were staying was simple but comfortable. The sun was very hot, but a constant breeze came from the ocean and increased in the afternoon, cooling the house at night.

One day I saw a larva attached to the inside of the kitchen window. What a pleasant discovery; now I could follow its step-by-step metamorphosis. For the next several days I took care of the regular and necessary household tasks, but I didn't forget to take a peek at the larva once in a while. The days seemed to pass slowly because of my curiosity and my desire to observe the change that would take place with "my larva." One day I noticed a color change; it was now a chrysalis. What a difference! My visits were more frequent as I did not want to miss the final stages of the metamorphosis. After the necessary number of days for the process to be completed, the chrysalis shook in sudden movements, and then an insect emerged—a beautiful butterfly. Smiling happily, I felt victorious. The limp insect seemed tired and rested near the window. After what appeared to be a nap, the butterfly opened its wings in brief movements and flew for the first time, going through the window and lifting high in the backyard.

After witnessing this scene, I mediated on God's power that can transform us into another person. This same transformation took place with Saul, the first king of Israel: "The Spirit of the Lord will come upon you . . . ; and you will be changed into a different person" (1 Sam. 10:6, NIV).

That butterfly never again returned to the chrysalis or larva stage; unfortunately, however, Saul returned to being the "old man." What a sad and tragic ending for this king.

May we keep our eyes fixed on our Lord and may our prayer each day be, "Do not cast me from your presence or take your Holy Spirit from me" (Ps. 51:11, NIV). "Can the Ethiopian change his skin or the leopard its spots? Neither can you do good who are accustomed to doing evil" (Jer. 13:23, NIV).

Noemia das N. Carvalho

Come Home

All we like sheep have gone astray.
Isa. 53:6.

I'VE ALWAYS LIKED COLLIES and wanted to own one sometime in my lifetime. The Lord has blessed me with Max. One day I saw an ad in the paper saying, "Collie free to a good home." I answered the ad, and when I got to the address Max jumped up on me. I knew then that he was mine—the one for me.

I brought Max home, walked him around the yard, let him run on the dog run, and got him a doghouse. Soon he became used to his new surroundings as well as our routines. Then he decided he wanted to explore outside of his immediate surroundings. So he worked and worked until he broke loose. The first time he just ran around the house several times and then came up on the porch and lay down until morning. Then he broke loose several more times, and each time he went just a little farther. Each time we put him back and tried to make him more secure. The last time Max broke loose, he was gone for three days. I was just sick. I told my husband, "Someone has him," so we went to the neighborhood store and put up a lost dog sign. The next day we got a phone call from a woman who said she had the collie. I took her number and told her I would call back when my husband came home. When we called her back, she said, "He's gone. I had to leave so I untied him and he went running with some neighborhood dogs." She apologized and said that if she saw him again, she would call us.

We decided to look around again ourselves, but no Max. Finally, as we were heading for home our granddaughter said, "Look, there he is!"

"Where?" my husband and I both gasped. Sure enough, there was Max. We called for him and he came running. The lady of the house where he was came out to meet Max's owners. She said he was a well–mannered dog, and she had purchased some dog food for him and was going to put an announcement about him on the radio.

Like Max, we sometimes get the idea that we want to explore beyond our surroundings. We break loose and get caught up in the things of this world and then become lost. We stray from our Maker. Thank God we have a Father who wants us back home. In the parable of the lost sheep, it says, "Rejoice with me; for I have found my sheep which was lost" (Luke 15:6).

Elaine J. Johnson

Little Sister

And God shall wipe away all tears from their eyes; and there shall be no more death, neither sorrow, nor crying, neither shall there be any more pain: for the former things are passed away.
Rev. 21:4.

I AM SITTING in the same church where only five months before I attended the wedding of my youngest sister, Barbara. It was fun to see her get married and to see the rest of my family. It had been a long time since I had been back to my home state of California. But now I am back again, and it is not for the happy reasons that I was here before.

I still vividly remember the day Barbara told me that her husband had died. I still cannot believe it. But yes, I must believe it. I am at his funeral with his family and friends. I look around and see familiar faces for most of the people at the funeral attended the wedding. Sitting next to me is Barbara. She is sad beyond words. Her future will undoubtedly have more heartache as she faces financial and other challenges. It makes me think of my husband. How many times have I snapped at him or used not-so-positive words with him. I have my husband, and all my sister has are memories of the short time that she and her husband had together.

We often take for granted the blessings that God gives us. Whether it is goods or people, we tend to be less than the best stewards of what He has put in our care.

Today is very sad for me and my family, but I find a few lessons in it for me. First, I am thankful my immediate family came to the wedding. We almost didn't come due to financial reasons. But then, we would have missed a major part of my sister's life, and I would not have been as connected to the situation if I had missed the joy of the wedding. God is amazing. He thinks of the little things that can become major in the future. Second, I have been trying to see my husband in a different light. Don't get me wrong. He's a good man, but even a good man has things that bother a wife—such as leaving cupboard doors open, clothes strewn everywhere, forgetting to pick up the children, and the list goes on. Under the current circumstances this all seems so small. So today I recommit my life to God . . . and to my husband, and look forward to more adventures with both of them. I have witnessed the alternative, and it is heart-wrenching.

Thank You for accepting me despite my flaws. And please comfort my sister.

Mary M. J. Wagoner-Angelin

Footprints in the Snow

And anyone who does not carry his cross and follow me cannot be my disciple.
Luke 14:27, NIV.

IT WAS A BEAUTIFUL WINTER DAY. Together with some friends we decided to hike in the snow. After first following a road, we then set off across a field. The snow had formed a crust during the cold winter nights, so we stamped along to break through the crust. We followed each other: the man, his wife, and then I trod in their footprints. I wanted to keep up with their pace but it was difficult to walk in their footprints so I decided to leave their path and make my own way. I thought it would be easier, but it didn't take me long to realize that it was easier to follow in their steps rather than to tread my own way in the deep snow.

What about following Jesus? Are we on the right path, following in His footprints, or have we gone our own way? It is not always easy to follow Jesus. When we decide to follow the Lord with all our heart, we have to fight difficulties and temptations. Jesus knew this and said, "Anyone who does not carry his cross and follow me cannot be my disciple" (Luke 14:27, NIV), and "Anyone who does not take his cross and follow me is not worthy of me" (Matt. 10:38, NIV). Those are hard words. What do they mean to us?

It's a pivotal decision. Whoever makes it will not regret it even though people and circumstances can make following Him difficult. But we must think of Jesus who is our example and who has walked the road before us. He suffered for us, taking our failure and sins upon Himself so that we could follow safely in His footprints. The path Jesus took was not easy—it even cost Him His life. He did this because He loves you and me.

In the poem "Footprints in the Sand," Mary Stevenson writes, "The times when you have seen only one set of footprints in the sand, is when I carried you." We are not alone. We have someone with us who cares for us intensely. No matter what your life looks like, Jesus knows your troubles and is walking with you. He carries you when you can go no farther on your own. When you don't know how to continue, when your cross seems too heavy, He will help you carry it. It is easier to place your feet in the footprints in the snow than to make your own path. It is easier to walk in Jesus' footprints than without Him. Decide to follow Jesus today. Don't give up!

Katharina Heise

The God Who Answers Before We Call

And it shall come to pass, that before they call, I will answer;
and while they are yet speaking, I will hear.
Isa. 65:24.

WE HAD RECENTLY MOVED into a new town, and understood from new friends that the area was almost crime free. However, things changed rather quickly. One day I came home from work to find our house totally ransacked. A thief had taken a number of valuables, including a cassette tape recorder with all our religious tapes. Our food for the week was gone too.

I was distraught. I was pregnant so I did not want to become unduly upset. My husband had gone back to school, so financially it was already difficult. I was the sole breadwinner. I began to pour out my soul to the Lord. As I continued to talk to the Lord, I began to thank Him and praise Him because He allowed us to be absent at the time of the robbery and that saved us from harm.

Just then the telephone rang. It was my husband, calling from the college and the sound of his voice brought peace to me. He told me that the police had caught the burglar, and told my husband to come to the police station. There he'd been asked to identify a number of items—which all belonged to us. Before he'd even reached home to find out that we'd been robbed, everything taken had been retrieved. Surely our God is good.

A woman had come into the police station with the items. She told the police that her wayward son had recently returned from the city. While he was sleeping, she heard religious music playing in his room, which was quite unlike him. Quietly slipping into his room, she saw the bags of stolen goods and our names written on the tapes. So she simply picked up everything and took it all to the police station. Before we had even called upon God, He had worked out the situation for us.

That son did not give up, however. One year later he again broke into our home. This time our neighbors came with their guns. I cried again to my God and asked Him to save the young man; to simply let us have our things back. God came through a second time. The stolen goods were found and returned to us; the young man was never caught. I believe that my prayers and those of his mother saved him from certain death. Indeed, God is on time. Before we called, He answered, sending help while we were yet speaking.

Shirnet Wellington

No Mistake!

And my God will meet all your needs according to his glorious riches in Christ Jesus.
Phil. 4:19, NIV.

MY HUSBAND WAS A PASTOR in Midland, Texas. Our son had just gone away to a Christian boarding school, and our older daughter was in the church's parochial school. I was a stay-at-home mom with our younger daughter who was just a baby. Every month was a financial struggle. We had even taken over our son's paper route to help meet expenses. One month when it was nearly time for the school bill to arrive, my husband informed me that we owed the school about $200 and we didn't have the money to pay it.

As soon as he received his monthly paycheck, my husband always paid a faithful tithe. He was also very generous with the church budget and other offerings. To keep back any money from tithe or other offerings to pay a school bill—or any other bill—would have never entered his mind, and this month was no different. He would simply trust God to supply the needed money.

The bill arrived. My husband opened it and studied it for a very long time. Finally, he handed the bill to me and said, "I think the school has made a mistake on Brian's account. The statement shows we have a $200 credit. But I know we owe the school $200."

Later that day he wrote a letter to the school, telling them he was certain they had made a mistake; we were certain we owed $200.

We no longer have the reply the school sent to us, but I remember it well: "We are happy to inform you that we have not made a mistake. A very generous friend of yours, who wishes to remain anonymous, has sent the school money for Brian's account. The statement is correct and you owe us nothing. Have a great day!" And indeed we did!

Jesus has promised that He will supply just what we need when we need it. The widow in Elijah's time was not given a year's supply of flour and oil all at once. She was given only what she needed for one day at a time. Jesus has told us not to worry about tomorrow: "Therefore do not worry about tomorrow, for tomorrow will worry about itself. Each day has enough trouble of its own" (Matt. 6:34, NIV). He wants us to trust Him only for today.

Sharon Oster

A Song on the Radio

Be careful for nothing; but in every thing by prayer and supplication with thanksgiving let your requests be made known unto God. And the peace of God, which passeth all understanding, shall keep your hearts and minds through Christ Jesus. Phil. 4:6, 7.

I WAS ON MY WAY TO WORK and crying so hard I could barely see the road. It was a glorious Florida winter morning, my favorite time of day, my time alone with God. But today was different. I had thought that God was leading my family and that He had opened a door for me, but now I was not so sure. Seven months before, my husband, Steven, and I had made the painful decision to move from New York to Florida. Our youngest daughter, Cassandra, suffered from severe asthma and life-threatening food allergies. Her only respite came during her summer vacation in Florida with my family. So wanting her to have a better quality of life, we decided that I would move with the children to my parent's home in Florida to determine if living there year-round would be advantageous for Cassandra. Steven would stay in New York until we knew the outcome and then, if favorable, he would apply for a transfer. It was difficult leaving my childhood friends and church family, but leaving Steven was the hardest.

The transition was smooth for Lillian and Cassandra as they were accustomed to being with my parents. But as everything else was changing, I decided I should change careers. I prayed about it and stepped out in faith. I was excited to learn that I had enough credits to qualify for a Florida's educators' certificate. But just before the courses started I was informed that there'd been a mistake and I did not qualify. I was devastated. I questioned why God would bring me to this point and then forsake me.

About two months later, I was accepted into the program. I was never so overwhelmed in my life. I worked full time, cared for two girls, spent long distance quality time with Steven, and completed my assignments for school! Thus the tears. I was at my breaking point and God knew it. I cried so hard it hurt. Slowly, I became aware of a song on the radio. The lyrics said to hold on, that help is coming—God will save the day.

I felt as if God had gently touched me. He knew I was in need of His touch and comfort. I knew the road ahead would not be easy, but I knew that my God was looking after me. I knew God would sustain me—regardless.

Tamara Marquez de Smith

A Lesson in the Checkout Line

It is good for me that I have been afflicted, that I may learn Your statutes.
Ps. 119:71, NKJV.

I WAS IN THE GROCERY STORE for the third time that Friday, very upset with myself for forgetting a most important ingredient for my favorite recipe that I was preparing for Sabbath. I had invited several people to dinner and wanted everything just right. The long line moved slowly, and I felt just miserable because I was caught in the rush before sunset. To make it worse as we all waited, a woman ahead of me kept telling jokes that were not even funny. It appeared she was the only one laughing at her jokes as others were preoccupied with their own thoughts. I wished she would just keep quiet, and I was glad I wasn't near her.

As she reached the cashier, I saw that he was kind and concerned, asking her quite sympathetically how she was doing. I strained to hear her reply, curious to know why she was behaving as she was. What she said took me by surprise and I'm sure I will remember her answer until the day I die. She said, "I try to keep laughing because if I don't, I will start crying." The cashier encouraged her to do the best she could and keep doing well. As she left the store, I found myself hurting for her. As the next person stepped to the checkout, the cashier shared with him that just two weeks before, this woman's 15-year-old son was found behind their apartment building shot to death. I felt sick, guilty, and on the verge of crying myself.

It seemed that a sudden gloom had descended on the entire store, for nothing nor anyone seemed the same. After paying for my groceries, I walked outside in a daze. Even the outside looked different because of the way I felt inside. The scene kept replaying over and over in my mind and I was miserable. I prayed for that woman that night and continue to hold her up to God in prayer every time I remember that Friday at the grocery store.

That Sabbath as I ate lunch with my guests, I repeated the story of the woman in the checkout line who was trying to cheer herself up. I tried to think how often we get annoyed at things that people do or say, having no knowledge of the reason for their actions. I pray that not only I, but all of us, will understand that people are driven to some behavior because of a need in their life. I thank God for the lessons that teach me to accept everyone I come in contact with, whether I know the reason for their behavior or not. We are all God's children and He loves us.

Irisdeane Henley-Charles

The Power of Prayer

Be joyful always; pray continually; give thanks in all circumstances,
for this is God's will for you in Christ Jesus.
1 Thess. 5:16-18, NIV.

If you believe, you will receive whatever you ask for in prayer.
Matt. 21:22, NIV.

WHENEVER I READ 1 Thessalonians 5:16-18, I feel ashamed of myself, remembering how many times I have grumbled at God rather than thanked Him. One day I really wanted to change my attitude, and as a way to do that I started writing prayer notes. At the beginning, I wrote both things I was thankful for and prayer requests in my notes. A few weeks later, Matthew 21:22 caught my attention, and helped me to realize that believing should be the first step. It says, "If you believe." I don't believe because I received what I asked for, but since I believe, I receive it.

Since then I have changed the way I write my prayer requests. For example, if I had an exam the next day, previously I would write, "Lord, please give me Your wisdom for tomorrow's exam." But now I write, "Lord, thank You so much for giving me Your wisdom for tomorrow's exam." Surprisingly, most of my prayers have been answered.

One of my eager prayer requests was for my father to attend church. He was baptized before my husband and I went to the Philippines to study and we went to church together. But after we left, he stopped going. Whenever I urged him to attend church, he got angry. In fact, my dad was a heavy drinker and smoker. He smoked a pack of cigarettes a day for more than 30 years, and all of us suffered from the smoke. One day I heard amazing news. He was trying to quit. What made him change? It was God. Once a week I checked whether he smoked or not, and found that he did not have even a desire to smoke. Six months passed. My dad permanently quit smoking.

Moreover, I had good news from my mom. My dad never liked for church members to visit him at home. If he learned they were coming, he left and came back after they were gone. But yesterday Mom told me that church members visited and Dad worshipped with them.

I cannot fully express my heart filled with thankfulness to God in words. Everybody said it was impossible for my dad to quit smoking and to be converted. However, I have learned God has never given up on my dad. There is nothing impossible for God. There is no prayer that God ignores. How amazing God's love is!

Romi Chae

No More Tears

And God shall wipe away all tears from their eyes; and there shall be no more death, neither sorrow, nor crying, neither shall there be any more pain: for the former things are passed away. Rev. 21:4.

MY HUSBAND AND I were at the hospital. The dialysis center had recommended that he come in since they hadn't been able to get enough fluid out of his body following congestive heart failure. As we sat in the hospital waiting room I watched others who were waiting too.

Sitting by herself was a woman, maybe in her twenties, in a wheelchair. She had a huge black eye, and as I watched she began to cry. Though the waiting room was filled with people, no one seemed to notice her. I felt so badly for her and when I saw that she had no tissues to wipe her tears I went over to her, put my arm around her, and handed her a tissue.

"Is there anything I can do for you?" She shook her head. "Is there something I can get for you?"

"A drink of water would be good," she offered.

So I located a vending area, purchased a bottle of water, and took it to her. She thanked me and I went back to my seat. But I kept an eye on her as she kept crying.

Soon an older woman came and sat with her. I felt better that she actually wasn't alone now. Then a younger man came. It seems quite natural that we sometimes think the worst in some situations and I wondered if he might be the one who had given her the black eye. I hoped not.

My husband's name was called and we left the waiting room. I didn't see the woman again and chances are I will never see her again. But I have thought about her many times.

Tears are a way to express our sorrows when there is a death, when our bodies are in pain, or when our hearts hurt. They express our joy and happiness for the many things that make our hearts glad. I will never know the circumstances, but I do know the woman's tears got to me, and I felt a need to help her.

Someday soon there will be no more tears. God will wipe them away. There will be no more pain or sorrow, only joy and happiness. Where there is joy and happiness, there Jesus will be. I'm looking forward to that day and I am sure you are too.

Donna Sherrill

The Lost Doll's Dress

*If we confess our sins, he is faithful and just and will forgive
us our sins and purify us from all unrighteousness.*
1 John 1:9, NIV.

NOT LONG AGO when I was asked to tell the children's story at church I told about something that happened when I was a little girl. As you know, things were very different then. People didn't have the wealth of things like they do now. There was no TV or video games. I had only a couple dresses to wear to school and a church dress. I had one pair of school shoes and a pair of church shoes. We weren't poor—that's how everyone lived.

One day a little girl who attended kindergarten with me came over to play and brought her doll. I had my doll, too. This girl had two dresses for her doll. Two dresses! One doll with two different dresses. Wow! We had so much fun changing the dolls' clothes. As my friend played with my play oven and dishes I changed my doll back into her own dress from one of my friend's doll's dresses. I kept thinking how much fun it would be if my doll had two dresses. In a flash I poked my friend's doll's dress way down in the side of the couch—way down.

Before long my friend's mother returned and my friend picked up her doll to go home. But where was the other doll dress? No one knew. We all looked for it. Her mom. My mom. My friend. Even me, but no one could find it. Soon they had to leave without the dress. Later I retrieved the dress and took it to my room, but I hardly ever played with it because I was afraid Mom would see it on my doll, and would know what I had done. Now, I was 5 or 6 years old, but I knew what I had done was wrong.

The next time I remembered that dress was when I wanted to be baptized. I didn't know where the girl—or the little dress—was! How could I make it right? I decided to give all the money I had—$1.16—in the offering to pay for the dress. The next time that doll dress came to mind was when I was in church and the minister talked about making amends. Sometimes Satan likes to tap us on the shoulder and say, "Remember the doll dress?"—or whatever it is that we may have done. But Jesus says, "Ask, and you will be forgiven." We don't have to keep paying.

I will tell you the three "Go's" I gave the children: If you do (or have done) something wrong, go to the person you wronged and say you're sorry. Go to Jesus and ask Him to forgive you. And tell Satan to *go away* for Jesus has already forgiven you.

Judy Gray Seeger Cherry

He Dropped It!

So do not worry, saying, "What shall we eat?" or "What shall we drink?" or "What shall we wear?" For the pagans run after all these things, and your heavenly Father knows that you need them. But seek first his kingdom and his righteousness, and all these things will be given to you as well. Therefore do not worry about tomorrow, for tomorrow will worry about itself. Each day has enough trouble of its own.
Matt. 6:31-34, NIV.

I LAUGH AT MYSELF at times when strange things happen to me because of my forgetfulness, when things happen that I least expect. There was a period in my life when I was at my lowest ebb with finances. Perhaps you have been there too, trying to do little things here and there to make ends meet.

One day while preparing a lesson plan for my son's home–schooling, I realized I had a lot of little things to do so I decided to look on my bookshelf for a notebook. I was going to write down some projects and get organized. Sure enough, I found a new notebook but when I pulled it out, something fell to the floor. I looked down and saw—a stash of folded dollar bills! I was amazed, hardly believing my eyes. "God, is this for me?" I shouted in glee. "Where did this money come from? Did You drop it?" I bent down quickly, picked it up, and then proceeded to count: 10, 20, 30, 40 . . . I was astonished to tears when I reached the last bill and found $310 in my hand. *Where did all of this money come from?* I wondered as I sat down in a daze. Then it came to me.

I remembered that while working on a project I decided to put some money aside simply because I did not want it to be spent on my everyday expenses. But I totally forgot that I had placed the money there. Silly me. How I could have forgotten that—only God knows. But all I can say is that He dropped it right when it was needed. And I am so blessed. *Thank You, God, for Your mercies every day. They are new every morning.*

When hope is gone and frustration has taken over, when the spirit is low and we stop asking because our faith has also departed, be confident and trust Him. He will drop it in front of you—showers of blessings. That's all He has. Just as the song writer said, "Just when I need Him, Jesus is near; . . . Just when I need Him most."

Shelly-Ann Patricia Zabala

Jesus Shines Through

You are my lamp, O Lord; the Lord turns my darkness into light.
2 Sam. 22:29, NIV.

AS WE WALKED DOWN the village road that Friday evening, we did not need a flashlight to find our way. All we had to do was listen. The beautiful music was our guide. Voices of young people who had gathered to worship Jesus Christ and begin the Sabbath together filled the night air. Their voices were the lamp that led us through the darkness.

There is always something special about Friday evening services in the villages of India. Music can continue for hours, and warmth and love radiate in the churches and meeting places. This Friday was no exception.

My message that evening was on the love of Jesus Christ. As I began to share with the congregation, the electricity went off. This was nothing unusual, and candles were quickly brought out and strategically placed throughout the church. This is a process well known to the villagers. That night the candlelight added something special to the atmosphere.

Young people were packed into the mud and bamboo hut. Many stood against the back wall, and those standing outside listened through the windows and at the doors. In the dim light I could see them smiling and nodding. My heart soared when I realized how hungry they were to hear the Word of God and to worship Him. I continually prayed that the Holy Spirit would speak through me so they would hear just what the Lord wanted them to hear. When my translator and I finished, the music once again started, and I knew something wonderful had happened that night. How I praised God for allowing me to be a part of it all.

I had been invited to this northeast Indian state to witness the baptisms that were going to take place that Sabbath. It was my privilege to speak on both Friday evening and Sabbath morning. How wonderful and exciting to mingle with these young people and watch them follow the example of Jesus by being baptized. Their beautiful music is now being used to spread the gospel of Jesus Christ and bring others out of the darkness and into the light. "For you were once darkness, but now you are light in the Lord. Live as children of light" (Eph. 5:8, NIV).

Here in this primitive village I learned that even in the darkness, the light of Jesus Christ shines through. He is in charge even in the darkest hours and places of our lives.

Candy Zook

Trust in the Lord

I waited patiently for the Lord; he turned to me and heard my cry.
Ps. 40:1, NIV.

THERE WAS NO WAY out in the face of some trials. I began to ask God, "Why?" Facing such anguish, I wanted to know why the apostle Paul was inspired to write Romans 8:28, "All things work together for good to them that love God." How could such anguish come to those who love God? I do not understand, Lord!

I began pleading for Divine help, praying more than ever. The presence of the spirit of forgiveness was necessary in my life, and these prayer requests became part of my daily life. I struggled against hurt and resentment and asked for the fruit of the Spirit mentioned in Galatians 5:22, 23. How I needed to be transformed! I wanted my prayers to be heard! I thought I was bothering God by praying so much. Then I thought, *If He says that we should pray without ceasing, He is not going to be bothered by my praying for help every moment.*

Unsupportable conflicts surrounded me, but there was hope of one day having happiness. Happiness—such a difficult word. However, I know today that it exists. Happiness in this world alone is not what is important—Jesus makes a difference. We must believe and trust in the promise that He has made, "I am with you always" (Matt. 28:20, NKJV).

The "whys" that I had used to question God turned and began to question me. Today, I can affirm that only God is perfect, only God does not deceive us. We err and suffer because of others' faults. Even so, God hears our cries and answers our requests. At times we think that our prayers do not go through the ceiling, but this is just our impression. In my limitation, I thought that God took a long time to hear me. Today, in the face of the certainty that He heard me, I have to thank Him. *Lord, thank You for Your love, for being present always in my tribulations. Praise be to the name of God because He hears us, regardless of the timing.*

We should be patient as we wait on the Lord, patient for the right moment to receive. For God there is no delay. We should not require Him to answer us as soon as we ask. We should believe that He will help us. As the psalmist wrote: "I waited patiently for the Lord; he turned to me and heard my cry." *Thank You, Lord, for saving us, although we do not deserve it.*

Marivan de Oliveira Almeida

Africa River Crossing

Behold, I send an Angel before you to keep you in the way
and to bring you into the place which I have prepared.
Ex. 23:20, NKJV.

WE HAD DRIVEN all that Friday to the Masai Mara game park in Kenya. Most of the road was rough and tiring. We'd been back in Africa for only three weeks and this was our first "safari" after living for 14 years in Sydney, Australia. Along the way to the Mara we had willingly given rides to a few hitchhikers, and by the end of the day we were praising God for the passenger with the bag of potatoes. For a tall Masai man, returning home with food for his family and with his trusty long red-leather covered knife—something a Masai man always carries with him for protection— was with us when the storm broke.

The rain rushed down in torrents and soon we found ourselves facing a raging river—which had been the road! We stopped on an "island" in the midst of all this water. My husband had intended to drive into it and continue on in our four-wheel-drive vehicle but I was terrified to do so. The Masai man, James, said, "Let's turn around and go back up to the top of the plain and find another way." I anxiously agreed and he led us up and across a "lake" of water. There was almost zero visibility and no road marks. He said, "Turn left, turn right, this way, that way," and we carefully and slowly guided the car wherever he directed, even though there was absolutely no evidence of any road. Eventually we came to his house where we dropped him off with his potatoes. We thanked him. I believed—and told him—that God sent him to us.

The rain had eased a little but we still had farther to go. In front of us, creeping down the road toward the swollen river, was a small white station wagon. We said to each other, "If that car can make it, we certainly can in our four-wheel-drive vehicle!" So we slowly inched our vehicle over the rocks and torrent just like the car before us did. We reached the bridge across the Mara River, thankful that it was not under water, for the river teemed with crocodiles and hippos. We crossed over and up the side of the hill and, after passing a few grazing zebras and giraffes, we found our tented campsite as the African night descended. What a relief! I know God put James there to guide us and the white car in front to lead us. Praise Him.

It was so reassuring to have the assurance that God hears our prayers and cares for us as we began our mission service. What a blessing to trust Him.

Joy Butler

Grace Cleaners

*Blessed are they that do his commandments, that they may have right to
the tree of life, and may enter in through the gates into the city.*
Rev. 22:14.

*A blessing on those whose robes are washed, so that they may have a right
to the tree of life, and may go in by the doors into the town."*
Rev. 22:14. Basic English.

GRACE CLEANERS NESTLES next to the Giant Food grocery in Chillum, Maryland, across Eastern Avenue from Washington, D.C. A sidewalk sign outside its door declares: "Grace—Our purpose is to make you look good. All work done on premises. Dry cleaning, Laundry, Alteration."

People didn't always need to get clothing dry cleaned or altered; in fact, people didn't always need clothing. In a sense, our original foreparents, Adam and Eve, needed only innocence to wear. Then sin replaced their innocence with feelings of shame. After that they knew they were naked. God killed an animal—one of the animals named by Adam—and from its coat made garments for Adam and Eve. There its body lay, an innocent animal which they knew sacrificed its life to make them look good again.

For millennia, people sacrificed animals for sin offerings, for clothing, for food, for protection, for sport. Each animal sacrificed dulled the shock of killing a bit more. God had to write the Ten Commandments because people had forgotten the basics of being good. Soon sin offerings became routine; animals became mere chattel.

Then Jesus came.

Jesus lived with people. Jesus lived a life innocent of sin. His innocence shocked, irked, and enraged people. Who wants to live around someone who makes you feel dirty and cheap when you are longing to look good? Soon Jesus was crucified; He died as a sacrifice to make people look good again. Three days later, Jesus came back to life, visited His friends, and went to be with God.

Anyone who wants to look good, to feel good, to be good, can ask Jesus directly through prayer. I love Grace Cleaners! It is a reminder that grace is a big favor. God's grace tailors the spotlessly clean, wrinkle-free innocence of Jesus to fit you perfectly, to make you look good.

Carol June Hooker

His Truth Endures to All Generations

Enter into his gates with thanksgiving, and into his courts with praise: be thankful unto him, and bless his name. For the Lord is good; his mercy is everlasting; and his truth endureth to all generations.
Ps. 100:4, 5.

IT WAS FRIDAY EVENING. Four-year-old Jo Ann watched her mother, Ethel, as she sat in the kitchen, her purse on her lap. Ethel searched in every compartment of the purse then, for the second time, poured its contents out on the table. Perhaps a dime had fallen behind the purse lining and she had overlooked it. But there was nothing there. Finally she told Jo Ann that they might not be able to go to church the next morning for she had no money for streetcar fare.

Jo Ann sat on the floor at Ethel's feet. She felt badly to think they wouldn't get to go. After all, they were ready. Their hair had been shampooed and set, and they already knew what they were going to wear. Looking up at her mother's face, she saw that she was just as disappointed. Jo Ann was surprised that a grown-up could feel as badly as she did. But she knew that for both of them, the high point of the week was Sabbath school and church—and now it looked like they'd have to stay home. To walk to church was out of the question. St. Louis was a big city and the church was miles away. They even had to transfer between streetcars. Ethel was confident that if they could just get there someone would be kind enough to bring them home. All she needed was a dime for streetcar fare.

All that week, as Jo Ann played in the kitchen, she'd noticed a small raised place just under the edge of the linoleum next to the door. She had meant to look under there to find out just what was making that bump but for some reason she hadn't—until that moment. As she looked at the concern on her mother's face, something caught her eye. There was that little bump. She crawled over to the raised place and pulled back the linoleum. There, to her delight, lay a dime! She ran to Ethel and held it up. Ethel's face broke into a smile. "We *are* going to church tomorrow!" she announced. One dime was all they needed.

No one knew how a dime got under the linoleum but it was waiting. Incidences like these produce faith in small children, letting them know that God is interested in the smallest detail of the lives of those who desire to please Him. And it shall come to pass, that before they call, I will answer. (Isa. 65:24).

Jo Ann Wetteland

Meet Jesus

In God I trust; I will not be afraid. What can man do to me? I am under vows to you,
O God; I will present my thank offerings to you. For you have delivered me
from death and my feet from stumbling, that I may walk before God in the light of life.
Ps. 56:11-13, NIV.

I WAS BORN IN JAPAN and grew up in a Christian family. My parents instilled in me respect for God. I am very thankful for them.

When I was 15, my father went to the United States to study for his doctorate. For various reasons, I enrolled in a church-sponsored boarding high school far from the family, living in the dormitory. Everything I saw was new to me. People around me were kind and friendly, but I had a hard time because of the language barrier. I was often bewildered, lonely, and scared. When I felt alone I talked with Jesus through prayer. He understood my words and thoughts, and became my best friend.

One morning a rash broke out all over my legs. The school nurse took me to see a doctor and he diagnosed poison ivy. He suggested I take a soapy bath, and gave me some pills. But a week later, the rash had spread over my whole body, except on my face. It was extremely itchy. I couldn't sleep at night, and during the day I was miserable. I prayed to God to help me.

Several months passed but there was no improvement; it became worse. I visited another doctor and tried other medications as well. At the same time I started reading about Job, who suffered from painful boils, in the book of Job. When I look back I see that God was preparing me to humble myself before Him. He was taking all my human pride and strength from me.

One day I returned from class and went into my room where I could be alone. I closed the door and wept silently. I was afraid someone might overhear me crying. Then suddenly I saw Jesus sitting on a stone in the olive garden. It was the middle of the day, but around me it became dark as evening. A dim light shone from His body and I saw myself on His lap. I heard His soft voice saying, "Fear not. Be at peace." At that moment, all my sorrows and bitterness disappeared, and perfect peace came into my mind. I was satisfied with His presence and wanted no more.

There is a God who knows me and loves me, and He loves you too. He gradually restored my health; I am thankful that He sustains my life even today.

Eriko Suzuki

He Loves Me!

For God so loved the world, that he gave his only begotten Son, that
whosoever believeth in him should not perish, but have everlasting life.
John 3:16.

JOHN 3:16 is probably the most memorized and well-known scripture verse in the Bible. We Christians have repeated these words so often, but how often do we stop and meditate on what the verse means? God loved us so much that He left heaven to come down to this sin-cursed earth to die for me! That is an amazing love!

God has given me many experiences that provide a glimpse of what His love is like—the grasp of a baby's hand while nursing, a smile and a wave from a happy child, a Mother's Day card from a young-adult daughter thanking her mom for making her home one filled with love. But my most amazing examples have come from my husband. He has done many things through the years to show me how much he cares for me, but two times stand out in my memory. One was on our twenty-fifth anniversary. We had wanted to do something extra special, but a sudden call for my pastor-husband to move to another city necessitated a number of changes. I was disappointed—the timing could not have been worse. But on our anniversary my husband "kidnapped" me and whisked me away to a place I had always wanted to go. He had taken care of everything—packed my suitcase, arranged for our daughter to stay with a friend, got my boss to give me a few days off, and arranged for all the amenities at the hotel.

Then the very next year he pulled off another surprise, this time for my fiftieth birthday. Money was tight, and we discovered that he had to be away. He suggested that I meet him in Miami and we could spend a few days there. You'd think I would have been suspicious this time, but I was just looking forward to having some time with him. And my loving husband did it again. He arranged for a week in New York City. I attended concerts and saw places I'd always wanted to see. What a week!

When I reflect on these occasions and realize that my husband did a lot of planning and budgeting to pull off the surprises, I think of all that God has done to make eternal life available to me. I remember the promises in Scripture that He will come back one day to "whisk" us away to His heavenly home where we'll spend forever with Him. Oh, I can't wait for this surprise party!

Lynn Smith

There Will Be No More Tears

He will wipe every tear from their eyes. There will be no more death or mourning or crying or pain, for the old order of things has passed away.
Rev. 21:4, NIV.

MY HUSBAND AND I were in the Greek Islands on the trip of our dreams. The weather was great, and the sea a blue we had never imagined. There were wonderful outings and days filled with happiness. Everything was perfect. However, a storm was brewing.

One day, to get news from home, I called my daughter Neila. "Is everything fine, dear?" "Here everything is wonderful." But I heard sadness in her voice.

"What's the matter? You're sad."

"Mom. I just found out I have a tumor on my pancreas."

Tumor? Pancreas? How? My world seemed to crumble in an instant.

As she realized my anguish, she said, "Don't get scared, Mom, it could be benign."

We returned home immediately. A succession of dark days began, followed by even sadder days of surgery, chemotherapy, a few days of rest, and then a new series of chemo. We wanted to keep up our hope, but we felt that the disease was spreading.

"O God," I prayed, "I am not ready to loose my daughter. Please save my daughter!" The difficult part was to say, "May Your will be done."

There were the long days in the hospital: pain killers, morphine, then increased doses of morphine to help her endure the pain. "Mother, if God loves me, why am I suffering like this?"

How could I answer? How could I make her—and me—understand that although we did not see the sun, we knew that it was there? Although we could not understand, we had to trust and know that God was with us during those times of extreme pain; that He suffered with us, and He wiped away our tears. My prayer changed: "Father, do not let her loose her belief in You. Help her to hold on to her faith!" Finally she asked, "Mother, pray for God to forgive my sins." She had given her life totally to Jesus! Then like a boat that sailed farther and farther from the shore, her life slipped away.

But that is not the end. One day death will be swallowed up in victory. Then we shall proclaim, "Where, O death, is your victory? Where, O death, is your sting?" (1 Cor. 15:55, NIV).

Eunice Michiles Malty

Pay Attention to the Signs

He replied, "You know the saying, 'Red sky at night means fair weather tomorrow; red sky in the morning means foul weather all day.' You know how to interpret the weather signs in the sky, but you don't know how to interpret the signs of the times!"
Matt. 16:2, 3, NLT.

I WASN'T FEELING WELL THAT DAY—I had contracted the flu while on a trip—but nevertheless I was heading home to St. Lucia from Trinidad. When the plane made a landing in Barbados en route to St. Lucia, I exited the plane ahead of my traveling companion, Carmen, a work colleague and friend. We normally waited on each other, but I was hurrying a bit, anxious to rest my aching body. In my haste, I just followed the crowd of persons ahead of me. Shortly, I found myself standing in a customs line. I looked around for Carmen. She was no where to be found. Was I in the wrong place?

I approached a customs officer, handed her my documents, and inquired if I were in the right place. She confirmed my worst fears. She pointed me back through the doors I had entered. A very large sign read "Arrivals," but I was in transit. How could I have missed that sign!

I entered another set of doors, praying as I walked. This time I was sure I would see Carmen, but she was nowhere to be found. I began to get really concerned. How could I be so lost in such a short time? I looked through the transparent glass windows and recognized the area where I needed to be, but somehow I could not find my way there. The airport was under construction and the regular exits and entrances were blocked. I looked at my ticket and realized it was time to board. I prayed, *God, please don't let me miss my flight home!*

Just then a flight attendant came through a door and I asked her how to get to the correct gate. She signaled to the exit. I quickly rushed through it and down the walkway to the gate. Halfway there, I saw Carmen approach the large automatic glass doors. I was so relieved!

If I had only paid attention to a number of important signs rather than follow the crowd, I would not have gotten lost. What should have been an easy, short walk to the next plane turned into an unnecessary panicking plight. I almost missed my flight home. As the coming of Jesus approaches, let us not follow the crowd but pay special attention to the ominous signs around us so that we don't miss the only flight to our eternal home.

Cavelle S. Regis

Attitude of Gratitude

Give thanks to the Lord, for he is good. His love endures forever.
Ps.136:1, NIV.

THANKSGIVING IS AN ATTITUDE of gratitude. In 1 Thessalonians 5:18 it says, "Give thanks in all circumstances, for this is God's will for you in Christ Jesus." Unlike the Western thanksgiving culture where tables are laden with turkey, mashed potatoes, stuffing, and pumpkin pie, my grandparents bundled a tenth of their harvest and gave it to the church. This demonstrated their spirit of gratitude. Witnessing their faithfulness every year while growing up grounded my understanding of what it means to be thankful to the Creator of the universe, the Provider of life to every plant that grows and every living creature that breathes.

One time I gave a Thanksgiving morning speech centered on the essence of gratitude compared to the birth of a butterfly. A butterfly does not start out as a happy, flying, beautiful creature. It starts as a caterpillar that crawls. At the right time it spins a cocoon around itself, and then, while in the cocoon it is transformed into a beautiful, colorful, flying butterfly, seemingly saying, "Thank you, thank you."

The growth of us humans follows the same pattern. Babies, created in the image of God, are dependent upon nurture and love. As they grow, God is busy shaping and molding them into His character through the experiences—including the crucibles—of life.

Visiting the Murano glass factory in Venice, Italy, I saw an authentic picture of how God shapes me. Watching the glass placed under fire and shaped in the way the blowers want it to be reminded me that every tear that flows indicates God's way of molding me into His character. Those beautiful chandeliers and lamps were authentic creations tried in fire. Having been tried in the fire makes me come out like pure gold. In fact, 1 Peter 1:7 tells us that our genuine faith is even more precious than gold.

Knowing that God is busy transforming and molding me to fit me for heaven gives me that spirit of gratitude as a breath of life. Job in his turmoil said, "Blessed be the name of the Lord" (Job 1:21, NKJV). In response to his friends, he said, "Though he slay me, yet will I hope in him" (Job 13:15, NIV). Being thankful means walking the road of gratitude, for thanksgiving is born out of the adversity and difficulties of life.

Edna B. Bacate-Domingo

God Is in the Canning Business

And my God shall supply all your need according to His riches in glory by Christ Jesus.
Phil. 4:19, NKJV.

WHEN I WAS IN MY EARLY TEENS, our family experienced some of the hardships of the Great Depression. To augment our rather scanty food supply, we sometimes made trips to parts of the state where fruit was less expensive—or even free—to those who picked it for themselves.

The trip I remember best was to the blueberry bogs. Before daylight that morning, we were all up and ready to go—Mother, Father, my brother, my little sister, and I. Buckets and a couple of washtubs had been loaded into the car in hopes that all of them would be filled with blueberries by the end of the day. Just as the sun came up, we reached the marshy areas where the wild blueberries grew. With a homemade rake that my father had invented, he soon filled a washtub with berries—plus quite a few twigs and leaves to be removed later. The rest of us each took a bucket and picked as fast as we could.

The next day at home all hands were busy canning blueberries. We used what was then a new way of canning: the new-fangled Kerr lids. The directions told how to seal the jars. Then, the directions instructed us to carefully remove the rings when the jars were cooled and to reuse those rings to seal the next jars. We canned 200 quarts, carefully carried them down into the cellar, and arranged all in neat rows on the shelves. How we thanked God for those berries!

That winter was a severe one in Wisconsin. Temperatures dropped down as low as -46°F. The first morning of that cold spell, we went down into the cellar to check our precious food supply. When we looked at the shelves of blueberries, our hearts fell. Every jar had frozen solid and the Kerr lids stood an inch or more above the top of the jar. Not a jar broke.

The severe cold spell lasted three weeks. Then an amazing thing happened. As the jars thawed, the lids settled back into place on top of each jar. Mother carried one upstairs to open for breakfast and discovered that it had resealed itself. No, it did not reseal itself! God had mercifully saved our 200 quarts of blueberries—every jar—by resealing the lids as they settled back into place. Every time we ate blueberries that winter, we said an extra "Thank You" to God for resealing them.

Naomi Zalabak

Thanksgiving Tapestries

I so want to be there to deliver God's gift in person and watch you grow stronger right before my eyes! But don't think I'm not expecting to get something out of this, too! You have as much to give me as I do to you.
Rom. 1:11, 12, Message.

EACH YEAR WHEN SUMMER winds down and autumn moves in I take inventory while preparing our holiday mailing list. It's my time to make a census, not of things but of friends. It's not that I've ignored my friends—they are ever in my prayers—but because the celebration of Thanksgiving comes along with autumn and I'm especially thankful for my friends. Isn't it great the way friendship threads itself into our lives, making us living tapestries? Together we become a part of the Tapestry Maker's design.

There's nothing that pleases me more than to have a friend drop in for a visit or as a traveling guest. When my husband and I lived in Kansas City, Kansas, we enjoyed visits with a lot of traveling friends. But when we lived in northern Michigan we discovered that few travelers came through there. Though a beautiful area, it was quite out-of-the-way.

But wherever we've lived, even if visits weren't possible, letters and telephone calls have kept our friendships close. These missives have been a comforting presence. I consider every letter that I have received or every one I have written a form of honor, an "I love you."

When one moves around a lot, as we have done through the years, one must work at keeping the tapestries in good repair. I have many friends whom I haven't seen for perhaps 40 years but our communication still holds tight. We still call each other on the telephone and laugh the same way we did when we were young. Laughter never goes out of style or shape! But sometimes those connections carry grief and we cry together. Can anyone understand our tears better than a friend? Even Jesus wept at the death of his friend Lazarus, regardless that He knew He would soon raise Lazarus from his sleep. He cried with compassion for the sorrowing family.

I've never had a real tapestry hanging on my home's wall. But I do have many beautiful tapestries hanging in my heart—my friends. Sometimes life gets bogged-down-busy and you don't have letter writing time. However, that doesn't mean you aren't thinking of your friends. I count each one as a special gift from the Tapestry Maker, so I don't dare let any frayed edges happen to these valuable works of His art.

Betty Kossick

Thanksgiving Day, Canada Geese, Lost Mates

For your Maker is your husband, the Lord of hosts is His name; and your Redeemer is the Holy One of Israel; He is called the God of the whole earth. Isa. 54:5, NKJV.

IT WAS THANKSGIVING DAY. I heard them long before I saw them. Huge flocks of Canada geese flying south, looking for a place to stop for the winter. I saw one mournful goose turn back—perhaps to look for a lost mate? It finally turned again and joined the last of the flocks, still with its mournful cry.

I sympathized if it missed its mate. I lost my own more than a year ago. I still miss him; I will always miss him—until the Lord returns. You get used to a comfortable relationship after almost 57 years of marriage. I have read that Canada geese mate for life. Most of my family never married again after losing a husband, and I don't believe I will break that tradition.

We are told in the Bible that the Lord is our husband, and I will be content with that. One could not ask for a better replacement husband if it becomes necessary. God promises to always be there when we need Him, He never fails us, and He has promised to come back and take us home with Him.

I find it hard to make decisions without the one who always helped me make them. I miss my husband's expertise, but I am learning to depend upon the Lord, and He finds ways to impress me with the way that I should go.

I live in a great retirement area and there are many widows in my church while just a few widowers. Statistics tell us that the husband is often the first to pass away. It has been that way in my church and in most of the churches around me. I value my church family more than most, since, unlike many others, I am left with no close relatives. My husband and I lost a baby boy at birth, and a 28-year-old daughter. My parents passed away years ago, and both of my brothers are gone. I have two nieces, one nephew, and an 88-year-old great-aunt who lives in Canada, as well as quite a few cousins.

Those who attend stress seminars soon learn that the number-one stressor of life is losing a spouse. I am looking forward, as are many others, to that day when our Lord will return to give us back all of our loved ones who have passed away. May the day soon come when He will return.

Loraine F. Sweetland

Strange Noises

He who dwells in the shelter of the Most High will rest in the shadow of the Almighty.
Ps. 91:1, NIV.

IT WAS PAST MIDNIGHT when I woke up and my husband told me he had heard a strange noise at one of our bedroom doors. He said it sounded like someone trying to open the door. I didn't take it too seriously as our house is big and it's common to hear different sounds in the night. So we switched out the light and settled back to go to sleep. Then after some minutes, when all was silent, I clearly heard the sound of someone touching the door key lock. I jumped to my feet, switched on the light, and looked in the direction of the door. Although we had the impression that someone was on the other side of the door, all became very silent. We waited a long time, then again switched out the light, but this time remained seated to wait. After some seconds the noise began again. It sounded like someone was using a screwdriver to loosen the screws of the door. We switched on the light again.

I was shaking and shivering with fear so hard that neither my husband nor I remembered that the screws of the door were on the inside so no one could loosen them from the outside. It also was strange that our dog was sleeping peacefully outside under the window. We wanted to call the reception desk of the condo where we live, but were a bit apprehensive. Maybe there was nobody behind the door and the next day all the neighborhood would laugh at us.

While we waited for what could happen I suddenly looked to the floor and saw a mouse run from the door to hide under our bed. It came from I know not where, and as it felt trapped it made scraping sounds at the door like someone trying to open it. This was too much for me. I jumped up and ran into the closet, shutting the door behind me. My sweet husband was left alone to catch the mouse.

This experience taught me a lesson. Although we pray and ask God for protection, we actually don't trust Him as we should. When we let Him lead us, we don't feel so scared. Sometimes we even end up having fun and laughing about the problem later, as was our case, even though it was scary at that moment. We all need to grow in Christian maturity. We need to fully trust in our heavenly Father so that in frightening times we can feel peace.

Ani Köhler Bravo

God's Deliverance

Oh, magnify the Lord with me, and let us exalt His name together. I
sought the Lord, and He heard me, And delivered me from all my fears.
Ps. 34:3, 4, NKJV.

THE FIRST OF THE MONTH can be nerve racking, especially if you don't have all the funds needed to make your rent or mortgage payment. I prayed earnestly all week, counting down to the first of the month, and crying out to God for help. I reminded Him several times that I had no one else to call on but Him. There was much talk in the news about a stimulus check which the U.S. government was going to issue to all taxpayers and I pleaded with the Lord, "Please don't let it be dispensed in A-B-C order—the letter V would be very far away."

I am usually paid twice per month. Ideally I need to save a portion from each check to cover my rent, but the preceding month saw drastic increases in gas prices. After buying gas and groceries, paying for parking, and returning my tithes and offerings, I was unable to save the required amount. May 1 arrived. I had not received a stimulus check, and my rent was now short $200.

By faith I went to the business office and submitted the rent check, knowing full well that if it got to the bank before I did, my account would show insufficient funds. I kept hoping there'd be money in the mail, but when I went to my mailbox I found the mail carrier still sorting the mail. As I walked back to my apartment my faith started shaking, and doubts started creeping in. I prayed, "Lord, it's in Your hands. I'm doing the best I can. I'm trusting You to catch me as I just took a leap of faith." By the time I got to my apartment, a sense of calm enveloped my spirit and I stopped worrying about it.

A few hours later I remembered that I had not checked my mailbox and the banks would close in another hour. I grabbed my keys and hurried back down the stairs. Reaching into the mailbox, I found lots of junk mail and just as anguish was about to engulf me I noticed an envelope from my insurance company. Quickly opening it, I found that they had finally honored my claim to replace items which were water damaged four months before.

"You need to persevere so that when you have done the will of God, you will receive what he has promised" (Heb. 10:36, NIV). God can do anything but fail.

Desrene L. Vernon

Engraved

I will not forget you! See, I have engraved you on the palms of my hands.
Isa. 49:15, 16, NIV.

"WHAT A PRETTY SERVER," Debra said as she placed slices of pumpkin pie on dessert plates. "What does the engraving say?" "Oh, those are my parents' names. They used it for their wedding and their fiftieth anniversary. On the back are the names of their grandchildren—my son and two nieces and their spouses. Each couple used it at their wedding reception."

Talk swirled around the Thanksgiving table, but my thoughts were on the cake server.

Dorothie and Delbert, May 29, 1939. In my mind I saw my mother's grin and my dad's proud smile as they greeted their friends at their golden anniversary. But my memories didn't stop there. I recalled an ancient home movie of their wedding reception, held on my grandparents' front lawn: Mom holding up her train as she navigated the steps; Dad looking proudly at his bride. And greeting the guests were my beloved grandparents, much younger than I had ever known them. They were quietly celebrating their twenty-fifth anniversary on the same day.

Lauren and Robert, May 6, 2006. I heard notes of a choir soaring to the golden dome of the church and envisioned Laurie and Rob, serious yet joyful, as they said their vows. Stephanie and Garrick, September 3, 2006. I heard again my son's exclamation when he realized his dad was actually wearing a tie for this occasion. I saw Garrick and Steph, their faces lit with laughter, sharing a cupcake emblazoned with the words "I Do."

Liane and Jason, July 28, 2007. I saw my niece and her husband walking hand in hand along the sea cliffs under a shower of rose petals.

If words engraved on a cake server can engender such strong, immediate memories, what would happen if I wrote the names of my loved ones on the palm of my hand? Every time I chop an onion, I'd think of my son. Each time I reach for the computer mouse, I'd pray for my nieces. When I weeded the garden, I'd remember my mom. When I shook hands, I'd recall my dad. My daughter-in-law would be with me as I graded papers, and my nephews-in-law would be on my mind when I paddled a canoe or wrote notes in the margins of my textbooks.

Every time I use my hands I would think of each one. How much more must God remember and care for us. He holds our hopes in His heart and hands.

Denise Dick Herr

A Healthy Baby

For thou hast possessed my reins: thou hast covered me in my mother's womb.
I will praise thee; for I am fearfully and wonderfully made: marvellous are
thy works; and that my soul knoweth right well.
Ps. 139:13, 14.

SINCE I TURNED 14, I've suffered from a chronic intestinal disease and have simply learned to live with it. I have even gotten used to swallowing my daily pills. With time everything becomes routine.

In the beginning, there were times when I felt great, but there were also times when I felt very uneasy. Finally I'd have to change my treatment and then I'd get used to the new schedule. So I learned to take my medicine according to my physical condition.

When I got pregnant my condition changed rapidly. Since the medicine was harmful to the unborn baby I wasn't allowed to take it anymore. I lost weight rapidly. I had intensive bloody diarrhea and I vomited as well. I could survive only by lying in bed. Finally I was sent to the hospital as my life and the life of my unborn baby were in great danger. I was too sick to even eat so we were both nourished intravenously. A few days later I had a catheter put in to help my body more quickly take advantage of the medicine and without any harm for the baby. This is how we managed another two weeks. Regular examinations were made for the child's sake.

Thank God, the baby was doing fine! Even my physical condition improved, although the baby was still at risk. I then received a different medical treatment which wasn't supposed to harm the baby's health. And finally, after five weeks in the hospital, I went home with my newborn son. My husband and I were so happy! We're very thankful to God that He protected us from great danger. Our son is completely healthy!

Regardless of our own birth experience—whether thinking about when we were born or when we gave birth or when we were reborn into Jesus Christ, we can claim the promises of Isaiah 44:2, 21, 24 (NIV): "This is what the Lord says—he who made you, who formed you in the womb, and who will help you." "O Israel, I will not forget you." "This is what the Lord says—your Redeemer, who formed you in the womb: I am the Lord."

Sandra Widulle

What Is Your Worth

For ye are bought with a price: therefore glorify God
in your body, and in your spirit, which are God's.
1 Cor. 6:20.

DURING A SERMON, a pastor pulled a crisp, new bill from his wallet and said, "This is a brand–new $100 bill which I picked up at the bank for this demonstration." He folded the bill in half and asked his congregation, "Now that I have folded this in half, is it worth half as much?" Of course they said, "No!"

He kept folding the bill into squares until it was the size of a quarter or less. After each fold he asked, "What is the bill worth at this size? The answer always came back, "It is still worth $100." He stressed that no matter how small he folded the bill, its value remained the same.

He opened up the bill to full size and crushed it into a wad in his hand. "What is it worth now?" he asked. Then he threw the crushed bill on the floor and stomped on it. Again he asked the congregation, "What is it worth now?" Back echoed their prompt answer, "The same!"

"You may be like this $100 bill," the pastor continued. "Perhaps you have been belittled. You may feel worth less than a quarter. On the other hand, you may have been crushed by some devastating gossip, sickness, or bereavement. You may have been stomped on by abuse from a family member or a so-called friend. Remember, like this $100 bill, none of these dealings or occurrences in your life change your value in the eyes of Jesus. His love for you never changes. His love never varies. He is always the same. He bought you by excruciating pain on the cross. You are priceless to Him."

Even though you have been belittled, crushed, or stomped upon, Jesus bought you with an extreme price. You belong to Him no matter what experiences come your way. Remember the belittled, crushed, and stomped-upon $100 bill illustration. No matter what abuse it endured, it was still of the same value.

This reminds me of Matthew 10:29-31, "Are not two sparrows sold for a farthing? and one of them shall not fall on the ground without your Father. But the very hairs of your head are all numbered. Fear ye not therefore, ye are of more value than many sparrows."

Nathalie Ladner-Bischoff

Have You Checked Your Oil Lately?

Watch therefore, for ye know neither the day nor the hour wherein the Son of man cometh.
Matt. 25:13.

IT WAS ON A COLD December evening that I drove from the Atlanta Airport north on Interstate 75. It had just turned dark when I realized that there was something wrong with the car. It made a rattling noise whenever I pushed the accelerator. Then I saw the "Check Gauge" warning appear on the panel. Since I was already late for my appointment, I chose to ignore the warning, not wanting to admit that I might have bigger problems ahead. Sure enough, as I drove on the noise became louder and louder. All of a sudden, the oil gauge plummeted to zero and my engine broke down.

Now I had no choice other than to park on the shoulder. It didn't take me too long to realize that I could be in serious trouble, and immediately some disconcerting thoughts flooded my mind. Here I was, a woman, all by myself on this freeway in a foreign country. It was dark and I didn't even have a cell phone on me. I knew I had to do something so I started waving to the cars flying by at 70-plus miles (113 kilometers) per hour. Not too long after, a friendly couple, followed by a truck driver, stopped in response to my frantic gestures to check if I was OK and to inspect my car. It was determined that my car would have to stay, but by God's providence the truck driver was heading to Nashville, Tennessee, and my destination was on his way! So he gave me a ride and dropped me off exactly where I needed to go.

I later found out that I had been driving a car that had not had any oil, thus ruining the engine. The oil gauge was broken and erroneously indicated that there was plenty of oil!

This incident reminded me of the parable of the 10 virgins told by Jesus. Like the five foolish virgins, I failed to ensure I had enough oil; I believed I had enough. In the same way, Satan likes to deceive us into thinking that we are doing just fine and don't need to grow in our daily walk with Jesus. The five wise virgins knew the source of their supply and ensured they had enough oil. Through daily prayer and Bible study we also can be filled with the oil of the Holy Spirit. Praise the Lord— through Him we can overcome sin. I don't want to play the foolish virgin again. What about you?

Daniela Weichhold

The Red Amaryllis

Oh, worship the Lord in the beauty of holiness!
1 Chron. 16:29, NKJV.

AT CHRISTMASTIME I love to decorate my living room with bright red amaryllis. They are tall, elegant plants with huge seven-inch flowers. After they finish blooming, I plant the bulbs outdoors and for many years am rewarded with more brilliant red beauty each spring.

Last year in early December I purchased an amaryllis plant with shoots that were about six inches tall. I knew that by Christmas, or New Year's at the latest, I would have several large red blossoms. I set the pot in bright, indirect sunlight and sure enough, I was rewarded with four huge blossoms before Christmas and two more in January. I was too busy at Christmastime to do more than occasionally water the plant and admire the blossoms from across the room. However, in January I had a bit more time to enjoy the gorgeous flowers. One day I stopped to examine them closely in the sunlight and discovered something I'd never noticed before. The petals appeared dusted with fine particles of red glitter, similar to a woman's dress or jacket that is woven with metallic threads that make the garment sparkle.

I was so amazed by my discovery that I stood in disbelief, gazing at the plant for a long time. I even took photos, trying to capture the glittery phenomenon to show others.

For many years I had grown red amaryllis at Christmas, but I had never taken the time to examine them closely in direct sunlight. Only then did I get the full impact of their beauty. As strikingly beautiful as the flower is, the amaryllis has hidden treasure that can be enjoyed only by close observation in direct light.

It occurred to me that God reveals much about Himself in His creation. In some ways He is very much like the amaryllis. The more we get to know Him, the more intricacies of His divine character we discover. Only by taking time to develop an intimate relationship with Him can we begin to appreciate what an amazing God we serve.

God rewards us as we take time to marvel at the glory and radiance of His character each day, just as I gazed at the amaryllis in the sunlight. He will not fail to delight us as we turn our gaze upon Him. Then we will worship God as we are instructed in 1 Chronicles 16:29—in the *beauty* of *His* holiness.

Carla Baker

Be Thankful for Accidents?

And we know that all things work together for good to them that love God, to them who are the called according to his purpose.
Rom. 8:28.

I REMEMBER THAT WINTER DAY that my husband and I went exercising on the jogging trail of our age-55-plus community. It was already 38°F, which meant it was above the freezing point. Besides that, we thought that all the snow had melted. Then, after covering three-fourths of the jogging trail, we reached a little area on the pavement covered with black ice. I slid right across the ice and my whole body landed on top of my left arm. Oww-ch! I realized I had a Colles fracture or wrist fracture. The result: surgery to set the break and external screws to hold the bones in place. What an irony! Wanting to be healthy, we were exercising out in the open air. The result? A fracture!

I had a choice to make—I could complain or be thankful for the accident and count my blessings. With His help, I chose to be thankful.

First, I am thankful that the fracture was a plain left wrist fracture as I am a right-handed person. Second, I am thankful I had the opportunity to learn to be more patient because I had to do everything at a slower pace. Third, I also developed more empathy for people with limited movement. Fourth, I am thankful that although my husband had to leave for an itinerary because no one could replace him at the last minute, the Lord touched the hearts of many family members and friends to support me. They called me, sent e-mails, cards, flowers, plants, soothing CDs, various fruit, and food. Some accompanied me to church, to orthopedic checkups, and physiotherapy. Some were even willing to clean my condo. So much food was delivered that I finally had to say, "Please stop. Don't bring any more food!" However, they didn't listen to my plea, and I had to throw away some of the food that turned bad, asking God for forgiveness. Fifth, I am thankful to be alive and to experience the outstanding support—for the dead know nothing.

Last, I realize that the suffering I went through when the external screws were taken out of my left hand without anesthesia is nothing compared to what my loving Jesus went through at the cross to save me. This motivates me to love Him all the more and serve Him as best as I can despite the limitations I have.

Kathleen H. Liwidjaja-Kuntaraf

Waiting

For the Lord himself shall descend from heaven.
1 Thess. 4:16.

I PEDALED HARD on my bicycle for 1½ miles to get there. A crowd had arrived ahead of me, but I still found a good spot—standing firmly on the sloping bank of Hope Road. It was just the right place, high above the roadway, for a full view of Princess Elizabeth and Prince Philip when they came by. In my 16 years, I had never so eagerly awaited an event.

As I stood there, my hands resting on my bicycle's handlebar, my eyes dancing from face to face, I soaked up the mood. Everyone was waiting, waiting for a glimpse of the princess and her prince who had come all the way from England to visit our island. Soon we would see them.

Police officers in their starched white tunics and black pants with a bright red seam down each side were on hand to keep order, but their services were not needed. Nobody pushed. Everyone stood or sat on the bank in an orderly fashion. The Union Jack fluttered in the breeze in the hands of small children as well as grown-ups eager to show their love for the royal couple. Four o'clock came. We waited. A slow-moving line of police cars drove up the road. At the sight of the police officers, the buzz along the roadway rose an octave higher. Five o'clock. We still waited.

Then it began, way down the road—faint squeals and the toot of horns. A murmur passed along our bank of watching people. Slowly it came closer and closer. Then we saw what looked like the enchanted coach in a fairytale. The crowd burst into cheers.

Right there before our eyes was the black Rolls Royce bearing the smiling princess and her prince. As the coach glided by, the princess waved a white-gloved hand. The jeweled tiara on her head shimmered in the soft light inside the automobile. In the dusk, with the gentle light inside, the limousine was transformed into the fabled glass coach. The coach did not stop, but slowly glided past the cheering, waving throng. It happened just for a brief moment. Then, like a breath, it was gone.

We're waiting, standing on the banks of time, waiting for the Prince to appear. We are eager. Our eyes are fixed upon the skies from where He will come, riding on a cloud of angels, trumpets heralding His glorious appearing. He's coming. He's near. We are excited. Our hearts wait with joyful anticipation. Our King will come!

Judith Nembhard

The Holy Spirit Will Take It From There!

And my message and my preaching were very plain. Rather than using clever
and persuasive speeches, I relied only on the power of the Holy Spirit.
1 Cor. 2:4, NLT.

EXHAUSTED WOMEN filed into the homeless day shelter. Shoulders sagged under backpacks. Others held onto grimy hands of wide-eyed children. I was one of 20 volunteers helping with a one-day "God-in-Shoes" hands-on, spa-and-shoe-store inner city outreach. I'd been asked to share a 45-minute devotional.

"I'm not the right person for that," I'd countered several weeks earlier. "I've been neither homeless nor abused. You need to ask someone with whom they can identify."

The outreach leader responded, "Simply tell them how God has made a difference in *your* life. Then pray, and the Holy Spirit will take it from there."

Now I stood before 40-plus destitute women and tried not to be distracted by the armed guards who were directing the streams of homeless coming through the front doors toward the shelter's main desk. At first, most of the women watched from behind a veneer of suspicion. A couple couldn't keep their eyes open. Many were coughing and sneezing. All appeared disheveled. Ten minutes into my devotional, I saw a tear slip down a woman's cheek. Averting her eyes, she swiped at it. Then to my astonishment, more women began to weep. For a moment I could barely speak through my own choked voice. A sad-eyed woman on the front row commented, "She's telling my story—*our* stories. She understands what we're going through."

But I didn't—not fully. Yet Someone was whole-heartedly empathizing with their desperate plight. And somehow the women suddenly felt His compassion.

Ending my testimony, I felt impressed to lead the women in the "sinner's prayer." I cried when a former computer analyst who'd lost her job confided she'd just accepted Christ for the first time in that little service. The volunteer coordinator found a Bible for her.

During the next few hours we volunteers held babies, passed out lunches, gave massages and manicures, played with children, listened, prayed, and cried some. As we left, I silently agonized, *Oh, God, we've only scratched the surface. How can we ever hope to make a difference in anyone's life?* As if in response came the wise, comforting words of our team leader from several weeks earlier: "Just pray, and the Holy Spirit will take it from there."

Carolyn Sutton

Listen Up

And He said to them, "Come aside by yourselves to a deserted place and rest a while."
Mark 6:31, NKJV.

IF YOU FEEL OVERWHELMED TODAY, you are not alone. There were times when even Jesus felt that way. The Gospels tell us that at times He invited His disciples to get away from the crowds for a short time to rest. In my hectic schedule, I realize how much I need to get away, to have quiet for a while. It is during these times that God speaks to my soul, illuminates my heart, and exposes my sins. I really need His words of love and mercy when He corrects me. I need His words of hope and healing as I face my fears. I need His voice to say, "Raquel, this is the way. 'I am the way and the truth and the life'" (John 14:6, NIV).

We need to learn to trust the quiet wisdom that comes from God. We must learn to trust the whisper of the Holy Spirit. We need to learn to retreat into the presence of God. The more time we spend in His presence, the more we will realize our need to let Him have full control of all aspects of our lives.

As we study the life of Jesus through the Gospels we learn that He had a deep relationship with the Father. This was the secret of Jesus' life: those times with God. In communion with Him, Jesus had the time to focus His mission and the time to be restored. We too must live in the Father's presence. But what does that mean? It means taking time to spend with Him. Everything flows from that relationship. Not from what we do, but from what we are in Him.

Some mornings, I find myself overwhelmed by so many responsibilities that the "come aside" time with God gets pushed to later in the day. But God is so good to me. He always has a kind way to interrupt me and call me to rest for a while.

When Jesus first spoke the words in today's text, He was speaking to the disciples soon after they learned of the death of their friend John the Baptist. But within the context of our own lives, it's as if Jesus is issuing a personal invitation to you and to me. *Come away. And let Me give you rest.*

Rest. Is it not wonderful to have a God who invites us to rest with Him and in Him? Are you ready to accept His invitation?

Raquel Queiroz da Costa Arrais

Endless Joy

However, as it is written: "No eye has seen, no ear has heard, no mind has conceived what God has prepared for those who love him."
1 Cor. 2:9, NIV.

OUR REFRIGERATOR DIED on Monday. No gasps or sighs to indicate that its condition was terminal. It just stood there dignified-like and slowly leaked its vital juices all over the floor. A kindly undertaker, disguised in a gray Tompkins Appliance shirt, solemnly bore it away for burial or whatever happens to dead machines. The premature ending was unexpected. On the heels of Thanksgiving and with Christmas bearing down, it was, well, in a word, funereal.

I faced it squarely. Life is a tenuous business. Not that I sank into woe-is-me-for-I-am-undone. I can stand up to compressor failures or buying a new mattress; then, after a few sleepless nights on its unforgiving surface, I dig for the manufacturer's tag to be certain it says Beautyrest®, not Gibraltar. But I've lived long enough to know harder things than a Gibraltar mattress in life. Tragedies come. Life mows us down like late-summer wheat. We despair. How can we negotiate this vale of tears with our courage and faith intact?

Paul knew a bit about tough times. He shivered from exposure, slept on rocks, in chains, in dungeons, the raw stripes and cuts on his back oozing pus. Yet, as he quoted the words from Isaiah, his eyes gleamed with hope.

The hard things in life pale when we know that God is so like parents who want Christmas to be beyond their children's expectations. He longs to lift our spirits and fulfill our dreams.

Our planet is barely hanging on to the orbit into which God flung His masterwork. It needs love and compassion. How can we tell our fellow travelers that there is One who is all compassion, all the time, and that He will never leave us? We can take the mercy and love that God pours into us and share it with others. Our smiles and prayers will brighten somebody else's life.

Disappointments and sorrows abound, and the complete picture that awaits us has never entered our heads. In our limited capacity even our imaginations fail us. Take courage. Look up. Commit yourself and your loved ones to the loving Parent who is planning a celebration that exceeds a thousand Christmases!

Marilyn Joyce Applegate

A Week of Turmoil— and Then a Miracle!

Why do you look for the living among the dead? He is not here; he has risen!
Luke 24:5, 6, NIV.

FOR YEARS I HAD BEEN SEARCHING for direction from the Lord. I can remember a bright sunny day when I was about 7 years old. My grandmother sat on the front porch reading her Bible and I was curious to know what she was doing. So in time I found a Bible and tried to follow her example, but being a child I couldn't understand it, so that was short-lived.

Years passed. School was difficult for me but I improved as I went along. After high school my life seemed at a standstill; everyone was moving forward but me. As they begin to mature into adulthood most people have dreams of what they want to become. I had no particular ambitions at the time, but in the back of my mind I envisioned myself as a wife and mother taking care of the children while my husband provided for us. And when I was 16 I met the man I would marry at a party at his cousin's. That was 44 years ago.

During these years, I have always searched for the Lord's guidance. Through this search, I came upon several radio and television broadcasts and took their Bible studies. For a while nothing changed in my life, but eventually through these studies the Lord took hold of me.

The week of turmoil began when the Holy Spirit fell upon me mightily and I began telling my husband what joy I was experiencing through the grace of God. I told him so much about the Word of God that he thought I had lost my mind. He went to everyone he knew, trying to get some help for me, but to his dismay no one could assist him.

It had been the week before Easter. My husband did not attend church with me and our son, but he would drop us off and pick us up again. That week when he picked us up from church he told me that he'd gone to the cemetery, intending to go in, but the gate was locked. As he told me about this he looked over at the church bulletin I'd brought home. On it was a picture of a tombstone and the caption: "Why Seek Ye the Living Among the Dead? He is Not Here. He is Risen." With those words the Holy Spirit was able to touch his heart and life. Today my husband and I are in the church serving the Lord. God has led through the years and my search has ended.

"But seek first his kingdom and his righteousness, and all these things will be given to you as well" (Matt. 6:33, NIV).

Lenora Franklin

An Awesome God

*Who is like the Lord our God, who is seated on high, who looks
far down upon the heavens and the earth?
Ps. 113: 5, 6, RSV.*

I HAVE BEEN SITTING in a hotel room in Athens for the past three hours, just gazing out at the beautiful, calm Aegean Sea. We have just returned from a cruise around the Greek islands.

The sea has always fascinated me. The day that I boarded the ship thoughts ran through my mind of ships lost at sea, storms and earthquakes at sea, stories of persons disappearing at sea, and even human errors in navigation. I whispered a prayer to the One who created the seas and calmed the storms and asked for His protection. I was then able to go aboard in faith that everything would be fine. Our voyage was uneventful except for one night when the sea became somewhat choppy—my faith was tested. Maybe I was taking Him for granted, so I whispered a prayer and He brought us through.

I was equally fascinated by our shore excursions. We visited rocky, barren Patmos, and our guide informed us that water had to be brought there by boat as there was so little rainfall. I was amazed that John survived his exile in a cave on what was an apparently uninhabitable island. However, God was in control. We visited the grotto where John is supposed to have lived, and were amazed at John's endurance, God's sustaining power, and the Revelation that John left us.

Mars Hill, where Paul first preached, was described by our guide as the birthplace of Christianity in Athens. This reminder of Paul's missionary journey also remains intact.

In contrast, however, in Rhodes, where once stood the Colossus, one of the Seven Wonders of the Ancient World, only two columns remain. This 110-foot (35-meter) statue was destroyed by an earthquake in 226 B.C.

As I gaze at the sea, I ponder how awesome and totally in control of this world my God is. He creates, sustains, and destroys. He controls the winds and the waves, and suspends the smallest of islands sitting in the largest oceans. These islands, that seem so small and even insignificant, are important to Him. He preserves places like John's grotto and Mars Hill, lest we forget. However, it is interesting that the Colossus, that played no role in our salvation, no longer stands. What a wise and awe-inspiring God we serve.

Cecelia Grant

Let Go!

Jesus saith unto him, Rise, take up thy bed, and walk. And immediately the man was made whole, and took up his bed, and walked: and on the same day was the sabbath.
John 5:8, 9.

MY ORGANIZATION HELD a four-day staff retreat in the Drankensberg Mountains in KwaZulu-Natal Province in South Africa. The place was beautiful, surrounded by mountains and rivers. We enjoyed hiking, swimming, and all sorts of games.

One morning the organizers took us to an adventure park where we would do team building games and exercises. Upon arrival, we were oriented and divided into groups of 10. The games were very exciting and challenging at the same time. The ultimate game was the king swing, although it was optional. I opted to swing because I love swinging. As I approached the king swing the assistants fastened all sorts of gadgets on me for safety. Then on a ladder I climbed 55 feet (17 meters) up a tree. When I reached the point where I was to jump off, an assistant gave me instructions. He assured me I was safe and that his duty was to protect me. But when I looked down I was gripped by fear. The assistant told me to hold on to the ropes in front of me as I let go of the supporting ropes. But I couldn't let go. I was losing my balance and didn't trust the assistant or the encouragement of my team members. I almost gave up.

But the assistant was patient. I struggled for about 15 minutes before I could let go—with a struggle. In a fast free-fall, as I neared the ground I swung up at an even greater speed. I was shaken. But when I realized I was safe, I gained strength and courage. I got hold of the ropes, put my feet forward, and enjoyed my swing.

As I reflect on this incident, I realize there are times when I have failed to trust God and have also failed to let go. In most cases I have relied on my own wisdom and power. This particular incident was a great lesson for me. When everybody else was laughing at me for failing to jump immediately, I was rejoicing because God had given me a lesson I would never forget. God was telling me to deal with my inner self and see if there were areas that were not pleasing to Him. For He says in Hebrews 11:6, "But without faith it is impossible to please him: for he that cometh to God must believe that he is, and that he is a rewarder of them that diligently seek him." I am convinced that I need to trust Him even in small things—in play and everything.

Caroline Chola

Sold for 8,000 Rupees

This is the Lord's doing; it is marvelous in our eyes.
Ps. 118:23.

IN THE MID-1980S my husband, Gordon, and I were members of the staff and faculty at Spicer College in India. A few months before my son's first birthday we bought an old 3-to-4-foot baby grand piano for Rs.2,000. My family loves music and acquiring a piano was very, very special. What prompted us to sell the piano five years later, I can't remember, but we sold it for Rs.8,000.

Recently I made a trip to Khurda, Orissa, to write about our church's school and its beginnings. The principal of that school, a former student of Gordon's, has often expressed his gratitude to us for helping him while he was studying for his master's degree. Prabhudas was one of the few students who regularly visited our home as he was Gordon's reader for the undergraduate level. He made it a point to visit us even during his graduate work at the neighboring university.

One day he told Gordon that he had applied for work in Sweden selling books for the summer, and asked for his recommendation. Sometime later Gordon inquired about his plans for Sweden. Prabhudas said that he'd been accepted but he didn't have the money for the fare—so he wouldn't be able to go. "How much do you need?" Gordon asked.

"Sir, I need a large amount. I need 8,000 rupees."

My husband thought for a moment then said in wonder, "We just sold a piano for 8,000 rupees. You can borrow the money and pay it back when you are able."

Prabhudas did go to Sweden, repaying the loan as soon as he had enough money to send. Gordon and I often thought about the piano, especially since both of our children play the piano and would have loved to have a baby grand. But after my trip to Khurda, I realized how crucial that Rs.8, 000 was to Prabhudas. I'm glad we sold the piano when we did.

I feel so honored that God used us to fill the gap, and I am very glad that we responded. It took many years to fully understand the why, but it was well worth it. Prabhudas is now an ordained minister and a very successful and dependable worker and leader in his area. It was truly the Lord's doing that we had the money to loan him, and marvelous in our eyes!

Rosenita Christo

Guided by an Angel

For he shall give his angels charge over thee.
Ps. 91:11.

OUR CHURCH YOUTH GROUP in Manhattan had been invited to fellowship with a like society in New Jersey. We would have a joint meeting Sabbath afternoon and a social after sundown. We young people met at our church and took the trip to Jersey together.

I was a recent member of the church and was quite naïve. I thought everyone was serious about keeping the Ten Commandments, so I was surprised when I overheard the conversation of some young men seated beside me on the train. Instinctively, I blurted out my shock. "But we are commandment-keepers! How can you have such ideas?" I asked.

They looked at me and laughed. "These are modern times," one said, and continued to express their immoral ideas. Being a new convert, and filled with fervor, I foolishly tried to straighten them out. The conversation resumed when we headed home. When we got off the Jersey train these boys took the lead and I walked along in front, hoping still to correct their outlook. Because I was in front I did not see that they were leading me away from the group. Then suddenly I realized that they were getting ready to leave the station. We were still downtown and needed to get another train uptown. Sensing my danger, I hastily turned around.

Prior to this, knowing that we would return late from Jersey, I had made arrangements to spend the night with two young ladies in the group. When I turned around, expecting to join them, I discovered to my chagrin that there was no one in sight. These two girls, seeing me so engrossed with these boys, had misjudged the topic of our conversation. Without questioning me, they got on the train and went on their way without me.

Now I was lost! I was just a teenager, recently arrived from the Caribbean, and did not yet know my way around. I walked around in the station until I saw some train tracks and stood on that platform, hoping I was standing in the right place.

Suddenly a man stood beside me and asked, "Do you want to go to 116th Street and Lenox Avenue?" I said that I did. "Well, you are standing in the wrong place." Then he told me how to get to the right train. *How does he know where I am going?* Suddenly I remembered that I hadn't thanked him and turned my head toward him. He had vanished.

H. Elizabeth Sweeny-Cabey

Trust in Jesus

Trust in him at all times, O people; pour out your hearts to him, for God is our refuge.
Ps. 62:8, NIV.

CRISES, CRISES EVERYWHERE! Calamities here and there. Wars, cyclones, floods, and other dreadful stories. People are homeless. They lose loved ones. Some suffer from hunger and poor health. There is much pain: physical, emotional, financial, mental, and even spiritual—because they have no hope, no one in whom to put their trust. What a disaster! Hopelessness! Why are most men and women so fearful? It is for lack of trust and hope. But for the faithful Christian, we have Jesus—our only hope. We don't have to be afraid; we can trust in Him.

When I received a call to be the director of women's ministries and pastors' wives coordinator for all of Southeast Asia, I realized I was the most fearful of women. I was afraid—afraid to talk up front, afraid to leave my garden, afraid to travel alone in places unknown to me, afraid of new cultures, afraid of failure, afraid I might get sick and die in a foreign land without my family. And it almost happened—or so it seemed.

I was conducting a women's ministries leadership training in Malaysia. After administering a quiz to the participants, my head ached. I had never had such an experience before. The pain was unbearable. Two loving women's ministries leaders took me to the hospital. While on the way, I threw up three times. Of course, I was afraid. I was getting weak, and I thought that was my last moment and as I'd feared, I would die in a foreign land.

Normally my blood pressure is 110/70, but when it was checked in the hospital it was 170/90. Too high! What's more, I was terrified. I prayed, *Lord, please save me, forgive me, and help me to trust in You from now on. I know You called me for a purpose. Just allow me to go home. Thank You, in Jesus' name. Amen.* The doctor gave me two shots and told me to rest. I felt so close to God, and He reminded me to trust in Him no matter what. When the storm raged one night on the sea, and the disciples saw Jesus walking on the water, they were very afraid. Jesus said, "It is I; don't be afraid" (see John 6:16-20, NIV).

The following day I flew back home to Manila, Philippines, as normal as could be. Praise God. He is our refuge. Let us trust in Him.

Helen Bocala-Gulfan

Open My Eyes That I Might See

And all things you ask in prayer, believing, you will receive.
Matt. 21:22, NASB.

NOW WHERE IN THE WORLD did I put those tickets? I grumbled to myself, diligently searching around my apartment for the two unused BritRail passes I had left after a recent trip to England. I had carelessly misplaced them though I'd planned to return them to my travel agent one evening after work. I remembered seeing them in the "stuff" bag that I carry to work every day. I was certain that's where I'd left them until a thorough search proved that theory incorrect.

I retraced my steps in thought, then searched for the passes everywhere I could think of—at work and home. Again I searched everywhere I might possibly have left them, to no avail. I could not imagine what had happened to them. All I could do was pray.

At my desk at work I have two stacked organizer trays to the left of my computer. I use them for current and follow-up projects. One morning, after exhausting all the search possibilities on and around my desk, I decided to check in the top organizer tray. I looked through all the papers at least three times, removing them from the tray and sorting through them one by one. No tickets.

After lunch, I sat back at my desk feeling a little discouraged that I still hadn't found the tickets. With them was also the credit card bill I thought my travel agent might possibly need to see. But refusing to be defeated and give up on God so quickly, I prayed again for the Lord's help. When I opened my eyes I was looking directly at the top tray. Lo and behold, I saw the tickets and the credit card bill—in plain sight. Why didn't I see them earlier? Of course I smiled and thanked God for His never-failing love and guidance.

I think we can be that way with people. In the stress and rush of life, we can be blind to the spiritual and emotional needs of others. We miss a golden opportunity to share the Lord and receive a special blessing He has for them and for us. When He answers our prayers in such an amazing way it gives us an opportunity to share about prayer and faith with those who may be struggling also. I encourage you to invite God to make you alert to His divine appointments. Be a fulfillment to the promise given in 1 Peter 3:15: "Be ready always to give an answer to every man that asketh you a reason of the hope that is in you."

Joan Green

Oh, Yes, He Cares!

But perfect love casts out fear, because fear involves torment.
1 John 4:18, NKJV.

MY DEAR CANADIAN HUSBAND had put a great deal of thought and planning into his trip to Canada. Weeks were spent pouring over maps, and numerous phone calls were made to accommodate the work schedule of the various family members he planned to visit.

I was not yet retired and did not have the three weeks vacation available. My job was to care for the cat and dog and keep the home fires burning. I planned several fun things to occupy myself during his absence. However, I realized that I would miss him at home very much.

We have had a loving, trusting relationship in our 25 years of marriage. I had no reason to doubt his faithfulness. I understand his need to visit his relatives, even though I cannot always travel with him. He planned to spend time with his brother and sisters to catch up on all the family news and enjoy all the good Canadian food they prepare especially for him.

Two weeks after his departure I was awakened at 3:30 a.m. by a dream. In the dream my husband said he had found someone else and asked for a divorce. I pled with him to reconsider; he became angry and left, taking with him our German Shepherd, Buddy. I awakened with tears streaming down my face. *This is ridiculous,* I thought, but I was unable to fall back to sleep and just laid in bed until the alarm rang. As I prepared for work I could not shake the feelings of fear and sadness.

Later that morning the hospital chaplain stopped by the nurses' desk on his morning rounds. He asked how I was and pressed a small card into my hand. "Open and read it. There's a special message in it for you today," he said. On the outside there was a picture of a kitten; inside the message read as follows: "May the Lord keep watch between you and me when we are away from each other" (Gen. 31:49, NIV). The thought below read: "God is interested in my relationships and holds them together by His love." I turned to thank him but he had stepped on the elevator. Comfort and love filled my heart at his kind gesture.

When my husband returned home on the scheduled date I told him of my dream. He was kind and understanding. We both agreed that Satan attempted to plant doubt in our relationship.

Rose Neff Sikora

My Dear Friend

Ask, and it shall be given you.
Matt. 7:7.

TRUST IN THE LORD with all your might and He will bring it to pass. That was my belief. It is so good to do good, and good will attend to you—another belief.

She came into my life out of nowhere. I cannot recall the occasion when we first met, but I am very glad that we did. She came to my rescue many times. My friend was very close to me in every way. Then suddenly she was gone. She did not know when she'd return. Nevertheless, it was our custom to pray with and for each other, so she continued in my prayers.

Time passed, and I often wondered what had become of her. One day my doorbell rang, and there she was on my doorstep. We embraced for a few minutes and then sat down side by side. I was overcome with joy, and I could hardly believe she was there. Suddenly tears rolled down her cheeks. "What's the matter?" I asked.

She smiled through her tears. They were, she explained, tears of joy. She then told me her remarkable story. "A couple of years ago I came very close to death, but here I am alive and well. I was diagnosed with cancer. My son and daughter came and took me back to New York where they live so that I could be near them when I had my surgery. I was very afraid." She continued, explaining that before the surgery she had gone for a walk alone and found herself in an old abandoned building. There she fell on her knees and face and prayed. "Suddenly it seemed as if two hands lifted me up," she told me. "I looked around, but no one else was there. Again I knelt and, with a loud cry I thanked God for lifting a heavy weight from my shoulders.

"I hurried home, sure that my family was concerned about me. Of course, they were alarmed at my absence. I told them I was ready to go for the surgery; that we should hurry since it was getting late. In the car I hummed my favorite tune; they looked at me curiously but said nothing."

Before the surgery the doctor checked her one last time. After a thorough exam, he said he could find no cancer. My friend told me, "I know without a shadow of a doubt that the hands that raised me up in that abandoned dump also healed me with His loving touch." Since that day she has been healthy and happy. Jesus promised that if you ask, you shall receive. I believe that!

Daisy Simpson

On Being Rude

It [love] is not rude.
1 Cor. 13:5, NIV.

RUDE. MY FAMILY WORD FINDER describes "rude" as discourteous, inconsiderate, disrespectful, impolite, insulting, unmannerly, unladylike, ill-bred, abrupt, surly, and uncouth. Other synonyms encompass words like crude, without refinement, vulgar, and uncivilized. All behaviors unbecoming to a Christian.

Rude behavior irritates others and makes us disagreeable to be around. This might include foul language, poor table manners, always being late. It could mean cutting in front of others while in line, taking for granted a gift or favor, or blasting a car horn. To those who do it, the behaviors seem insignificant, but if you're on the receiving end—they're not!

The bottom line is that love minds its manners, and embracing this concept could add a breath of fresh air to your day. I am in final negotiations with a group who has invited me to conduct a family seminar. The tag line at the bottom of the coordinator's e-mails reads: "Manners are a sensitive awareness of the feelings of others. If you have that awareness, you have good manners, no matter what fork you use" (Emily Post). I am truly looking forward to working with a woman who uses such a quote as her mantra.

Incorporating good manners into your home life may well revolutionize your marriage as well as your relationship with your children. We often blow up or use language at home that we'd never use on a stranger. Why do we show our better side to those we don't know, and our worst side at home? Two big reasons people are rude are ignorance and selfishness—they are unaware that that their words or actions are rude and/or quite aware, but don't care or want to make the effort to change. A Christian will surely attempt to live above such behaviors. The real test of Christian character, as I see it, is how you respond when someone is rude to you.

Are you a rude or courteous person? Here are some questions you might ask yourself: How does my family feel about the way I treat them? How does my behavior affect their self-worth? Would my husband and kids say my behavior is a blessing or an embarrassment to them?

Just for today let's determine to practice the Golden Rule. Treat others the same way you want to be treated (see Luke 6:31).

Nancy L. Van Pelt

Don't Let Your Senses Deceive You

But without faith it is impossible to please Him, for he who comes to God must believe that He is, and that He is a rewarder of those who diligently seek Him.
Heb 11:6, NKJV.

WE ALL HAVE TIMES when there seems to be very little light. It's then that we must grasp tightly to God's Word. It's often difficult to walk by faith, not sight, but we must if we are to please God and have victory. We come into this world ruled by our senses: what we see, hear, taste, touch, smell, and feel emotionally. But once we come to Christ the way we deal with the natural world and events must change. Our senses may be e very things that keep us from entering into the promises of God.

Genesis 15 tells of the promise the Lord made to His servant Abraham. God promised him a son. You see, 75-year-old Abraham and his 65-year-old wife, Sarah, had no children. Every man wanted a son, but more than that, people believed that if a couple was childless the wife had been cursed by God. They were the power couple of their generation and yet they could not have a child. Against all physical odds, Abraham believed the promise that the Creator of the universe made to him. He knew that the Lord whom he served was not limited in His ability to take that which was dead and give it new life. The lack of a child was not the issue for Abraham—it was a matter of faith. Though the promise took 25 years to fulfill, God kept His word and Abraham's faith developed in ways he couldn't have imagined. Abraham's faith was counted to him for righteousness.

Are there areas in your life that seem to be dead? You have been calling on the Lord to give life to those situations, yet it seems nothing has changed. Just remember that there is no failure in God. He longs to bring into your life what you need most: the faith to reach places in Him that you never dreamed of. The inheritance that Isaac received was more than material—it was spiritual. That spiritual gift had eternal consequences. The next time your feelings cloud your ability to see clearly, remember that things are never as they appear. Ask the Lord to open your spiritual eyes so that you can see from His perspective. Give your faith the freedom to grow in spite of how you feel and it will be counted to you for righteousness (see Rom. 4:3).

Lord Jesus, I come to You. Yet my five senses are in the way of my ability to see from Your perspective. Help me to turn my eyes up to You and trust You by faith.

Eilean L. Greene

He Is Able

Oh that men would praise the Lord for his goodness,
and for his wonderful works to the children of men!
Ps. 107:8.

THESE DAYS, I AM STILL PRAYING—for my children, my grandchildren, my fellow church members, our missionaries, and God's work going on around the world. But I am also spending more prayer time in praise—for my prodigal son who has come home!

Will was a sweet, loving boy but it seemed like it was always a little difficult for him to do exactly as he was told—especially by the male figure in his life. So he was subject to many disciplinary measures—some unique, such as spending hours in a barrel!

When he was ready to go to high school he attended the church-run boarding school where his older sister had studied earlier. But he was always having to dig out stumps—the preferred method of discipline at this school. And it was always for the same offense—talking to the girls.

One day I asked one of the professors why my son—who is not tall, dark, nor handsome—had so much trouble with the girls. His reply: "He makes every girl feel like she is queen for the day."

After his exit from that school, Will attended public school and eventually became an x-ray technician—and, by the way, all his patients love him. But he was on my prayer list, day and night, that he might come back to God and to the church he attended with us when he was growing up.

So imagine my delight the day he called me to tell me that he was attending church again—and not only that—he was teaching a Sabbath school Bible class! Since my birthday was coming up very soon, I asked my daughter and son-in-law to take me to Will's church for Sabbath school. They agreed, and what a wonderful birthday present it was!

My joy knows no bounds! And now you will understand why I praise the Lord every day for His wonderful works to His children. What in your life makes you praise God? "I will extol thee, my God, O king; and I will bless thy name for ever and ever. Every day will I bless thee; and I will praise thy name for ever and ever" (Ps. 145:1, 2).

Rubye Sue

Wedding on a Shoestring

*Now to him who is able to do immeasurably more than all we ask
or imagine, according to his power that is at work within us.
Eph. 3:20, NIV.*

OUR DAUGHTER, SANDY, and her boyfriend, David, announced they planned to be married at Christmastime. A wedding? Then? Both were music students in college. Because of illness my husband hadn't worked in some time, and I barely had part-time work. In addition to the usual financial concerns, we had two daughters in a church-run boarding high school. I started planning for the wedding with serious prayer. This is how God worked it out.

Our sister-in-law, Mary Lou, offered to cater the reception at the church at no cost to us. It would be a gift. Lyle, a photographer, offered to take the pictures as his gift. The date of the wedding was December 20—a time when red poinsettias would decorate the front of the sanctuary and lanterns tied with greens and red bows would hang from the ceiling. The father of the groom would perform the ceremony, and family and close friends would provide the music.

We found a wedding dress, a discontinued one, at an unbelievably low price. Its sleeves and neckline were trimmed with fur-like white marabou feathers. It was beautifully Christmassy. I was able to buy an additional length of marabou and made a gorgeous muff by lining an oatmeal box with white satin and winding the marabou around the outside. For the wedding we attached one red poinsettia to the front—and that was the bridal bouquet. We borrowed my sister's veil and put marabou across the headpiece. Stunning!

For the bridesmaids, we found, on sale, plain long, berry-red dresses. The flower girl had a red and white dress and carried one poinsettia.

But what to do for the bridesmaids' bouquets? The Lord gave me an idea. I cut branches off our spruce tree, wired them together, and made candleholders in them. We wired red berries to the branches and whipped soap snow to frost them. We tied them with red bows and put a white candle in each. The candles were lit for the bridesmaids' walk down the aisle.

The only flowers we bought were for the groom, groomsmen, and all the wedding helpers. I wore a dress I already had, and a friend made a beautiful wedding cake. We found invitations and napkins for half price. The wedding cost was so very small. Only the Lord could have put on such a wedding!

Darlene Ytredal Burgeson

A Christmas Prayer

Jesus Christ the same yesterday, and to day, and for ever.
Heb. 13:8.

IT WAS GETTING LATE and Robert, my husband, was not yet home. He was often late, but this time it was different: he had promised he would be home early to take the children Christmas shopping. He knew how important this was to the children, and he seldom broke a promise to them.

As I sat down at the table I was reminded of another Christmas Eve some 30 years earlier when I was 12 years old. My sisters and brothers were decorating the Christmas tree. Most of the gifts that would go under the tree had already been wrapped and my mother was in the kitchen cooking and baking. Everyone seemed happy except my mother—she seemed worried.

Mother was concerned about my dad as he was not yet home and it was getting late. Father worked in the city, and as his commute was about 60 minutes each way, we were used to him being late. But this time was different. Because it was Christmas Eve, he was going to stop at the produce market to get fruits, nuts, and spices for my mom to use in finishing her baking. It wasn't because he was bringing goodies that we were concerned—he wasn't—but just to have him home safely. We children always said good night to him before we went to bed. My mother tried not to show that she was worried, but she couldn't hide it very well. And Mom had every right to be concerned—my father worked in the worst part of the city so she was worried about his safety. Finally she sent us all to bed though we protested, wanting to wait up for our dad.

Just as I climbed into bed, I could hear my mother in the kitchen praying that God would bring my father home safely because we needed him. So I got out of bed and knelt, and started to pray. Before I could get back into bed I heard the front door open and my mom greeting my dad. My brothers and sisters must have heard it too because we all ran downstairs at the same time and gave our dad a big hug.

So as I put my own children to bed this Christmas night, I whisper the same prayer I had prayed 30 years before, believing that God will hear my prayers to bring my husband and father of my children home safely once again.

Avis Floyd Jackson

The Angel

The angel of the Lord encampeth round about them that fear him, and delivereth them.
Ps. 34:7.

A FEW DAYS BEFORE CHRISTMAS, my husband, Cecil, our two daughters, and I left Washington, D.C. to drive to Toronto, Canada. The Lord answered our prayer for a safe trip and we arrived without problems. Then, after visiting my sister for a few days, we said goodbye to go to New York to visit another sister.

We were on the New York Thruway when our car suddenly skidded on a damp, oily surface. The car spun halfway around and whooshed across the highway into the left lane and then down a slight incline. The right front fender stuck under a railing. This railing stopped the car from toppling farther. As we'd slid across the highway, what I saw took my breath away. Standing in the middle of the thruway, with extra long arms extended wide, an approximately eight-foot-tall man faced oncoming traffic. Behind him, as far back as I could see, was a long line of cars stopped on the right side of the thruway. My daughters' two pillows were on the roadway not far from the man's feet—smashed.

I thought my girls were dead. They'd been asleep in the middle of the backseat, their heads on those pillows. But now they were sitting up, bewildered, fearful, and silent. Our firstborn did not speak for days. The driver's door had jammed on impact and Cecil struggled with it until he was finally able to get out to check the front of the car. As he got back into the car I saw that the same huge man was bending over, holding the right front side of our car. I never saw his face, but I heard a voice say, "OK, start!" At that moment my husband turned on the ignition and I felt the car lift and jerk backward. The car was free—and the man was gone.

I said to my husband, "Cecil, did you see that big man?"

"What man?" he replied. He had not seen anyone. The awesomeness of what had happened struck me. My mind raced. There was no doubt that God had sent His angel to deliver us. Was he Gabriel? Or an ordinary angel? There could have been a pile up of cars on us if all those cars had not been divinely stopped. No one was hurt, praise God! The right back door had swung open, but the dresses hanging there were still hanging, undisturbed. God kept our girls safe, but permitted two small pillows to slip out and onto the road.

Thank God for His angels. What an amazing God!

Joyce O'Garro

Christmas Interlude

So here's what I want you to do, God helping you: Take your everyday, ordinary life—your sleeping, eating, going-to-work, and walking-around life—and place it before God as an offering. Embracing what God does for you is the best thing you can do for him. Don't become so well-adjusted to your culture that you fit into it without even thinking. Instead, fix your attention on God. You'll be changed from the inside out. Readily recognize what he wants from you, and quickly respond to it. Unlike the culture around you, always dragging you down to its level of immaturity, God brings the best out of you, develops well-formed maturity in you.
Rom. 12:1, 2, Message.

THE HOLIDAY SEASON sometimes snuffs out our spiritual and devotional life. Life becomes hectic. Emotions run high. There are places to go, shopping to be done. Money to buy the needed gifts is scarce. Frustration sets in. Short tempers are apparent. Sometimes the fuse blows.

Our households become alive with Christmas decorations strewn all over the place. Chaos takes a new shape. "Yikes," we yell, "not enough time for anything." It is our excuse for not spending time with Him.

Jesus woke me up—again—this morning. Before going to sleep last night, my prayer (one I pray almost every evening) was, *Lord, You know what is ahead of me tomorrow. Give me the time You want me to have with You.* I sigh, hoping that it won't be too early. But He woke me up—again—at 4:15.

Today's passage filled my heart and soul this cold, crisp morning. *What an unearthly hour,* I mumbled to Him. Then I laughed at myself because that's what I usually say to Jesus when He wakes me up "in the middle of the night." Somehow He provides extra rest spiritually—which boosts me physically. Do I miss my sleep? Oh, sometimes yes. Most of the time—no!

Jesus more than makes up for the physical sleep when He gives me the banquet (holiday-style) for my spiritual soul, as He did this morning.

What I wish to share with you is that while you are still sleeping God is working on you. Isn't He an extraordinary God? He lovingly crowns the day "extra" ordinary—because I've given Him my day. Place your life before God today.

Mary L. Maxson

The Best Christmas Gift

"Is Ephraim My dear son? Is he a delightful child? Indeed, as often as I have spoken against him, I certainly still remember him; therefore My heart yearns for him; I will surely have mercy on him," declares the Lord. Jer. 31:20, NASB.

LAST YEAR OUR FAMILY got together for Christmas and I got the best unexpected gift ever. It all started five years ago when I was enjoying the company of my father and one of my sisters. Dad was telling us that the only thing he wanted after Grandpa passed away was Grandpa's Bible. Immediately I said that what I wanted was my father's Bible, and one of my sisters could have Grandpa's Bible when the time came. Eliana, my baby sister, didn't waste any time and said, "Me, too." Childhood moments came to mind when we children said things like "I asked first," and "It's not fair," but soon we changed the subject and the whole thing was forgotten, or so we thought. Dad, on the other hand, had an inspired idea. He decided to copy all the marks, studies, and notations from his Bible to four other identical Bibles. And for the next four years, using red, green, and blue pencils to mark verses (and the computer to print on Bible-thin paper the extra references and studies) he spent uncountable hours preparing his gift.

Christmas Eve came, and after all the presents were opened Daddy called us together. He started telling us about that conversation five years before. He reminded us that when we were growing up he taught us not to fight with each other, and he didn't want us to fight over his Bible. Also we would each have "his" Bible while he was still alive. After asking each of us to choose one Bible, he told us that the only difference between them was that he wrote each owner's name close to one of his favorite verses—so we didn't know if we'd chosen our own Bible or not. At that moment time stopped. Page by page the four of us searched for our names. Nothing could distract us—not even the fireworks. Nancy, the firstborn, found a name first. Then Neyde found a name. I had picked my own Bible. After the exchange of Bibles, Daddy told us to read the verse with our names and see how beautiful and reassuring what God said was: "Is Eunice My dear daughter? Is she a delightful child? Indeed, as often as I have spoken against her, I certainly still remember her; therefore My heart yearns for her; I will surely have mercy on her."

I invite you to personalize Bible verses and share a most wonderful gift this Christmas.

Eunice Passos Molina Berger

Ties to Jesus

So humble yourselves under the mighty power of God, and at the right time he will lift you up in honor. Give all your worries and cares to God, for he cares about you.
1 Peter 5:6, 7, NLT.

WHEN JESUS HONORS His people they know it, and He made my Christmas, 2007, extra-special. First off, the Lord, my cherished Friend, gave me a wonderful job at the Salvation Army Thrift Store. The store was in the process of moving to a new location, so throughout November and December we had clearance sales. The citizens in our community are very generous and donate nice things. A large percentage of my wages returned back into Thrift Store profits, and this money was recycled back into the community to help people in need. It delights me to see how Jesus blesses what I call, "our play money." Previous to Christmas Day, I made an announcement to my church friends during prayer and praise time that if anyone ever receives a gift from me which is not to their liking, then please just recycle it back through Goodwill where my son, Sonny, who is developmentally disabled, works.

On the morning of November 23 I went to work hoping that we'd have a Bag Day Sale—all the clothing items you can fit into a bag for just $10.00—because I felt impressed that Jesus wanted Sonny/me to buy neckties as Christmas gifts for some of our male friends. Yes, it *was* bag day! To my total surprise I found that my coworker and precious friend, Heather, had filled the tie racks the day before with brand new ties. I purchased 58! They were all the same design; the original price tags were $29.00, totaling $1,682.00. But I paid $5.00 for half a bag full. Wow! Sonny gave these ties to men whom I believe often pray for Sonny, our family, and other persons with developmental disabilities. The brand name on the ties was Structure; its design was a multi-printed picture of an ancient gateway. This picture makes me think of a gateway leading to the courts of justice and how Jesus is our personal representative before God's throne in heaven.

There are other types of ties as well. Every devotional I write and publicly share is done in the spirit of friendship and is a gift from my heart to everyone that heaven connects me with, creating invisible "ties to Jesus." As we reach out to others, we establish ties. It is my prayer that this will tie them to Jesus as well.

Deborah Sanders

My Guardian Angel and My "New" Honda!

Then no harm will befall you, no disaster will come near your tent. For he will command his angels concerning you to guard you in all your ways.
Ps. 91:10, 11, NIV.

I DROVE MY WHITE NISSAN QUEST VAN to Atlanta so that my daughter and I could visit my cousin for the Christmas holidays. The van had never given me any major trouble, but it did have a lot of mileage on it. I asked my cousin if she knew of any mechanic who could do a basic oil change, and she told me of a man who owned his own shop. He did the job on Christmas Eve.

The day after Christmas we took the 6½-hour journey home. As I neared my hometown I remembered the mechanic telling me that when I returned to North Carolina, I should consider getting my timing belt changed. Since I was still on vacation, I knew I had time to see how much a timing belt would cost to replace. But when I tried to park at the service department of an auto repair shop, I noticed something strange: I couldn't put the van in reverse!

Bewildered, I hurried inside to describe my dilemma to a mechanic. He checked the van and told me, "Someone must have poured oil instead of transmission fluid into the transmission. The fluid is extremely black." I was stunned. I had been driving for 6½-hours with no transmission fluid! I thanked God and our guardian angels for the protection He had poured out on my daughter and me. But the blessings didn't stop there. Now I needed a new transmission. But I figured with all the miles on the old van and the cost of replacing the transmission, I might as well put the little money I had toward a different van. I started the search.

Mr. Wilson, the father of one of my daycare children, told me he knew an honest car salesman who would give me a good deal. When I went there, Mr. Jackson already had a vehicle picked out for me: a Honda with low mileage. He told me that Mr. Wilson had said that his son was in a great daycare and that the teacher needed a reliable vehicle to transport the children safely. He added that his friend had advised him to give me a good deal since I was limited by a teacher's salary.

I smiled in agreement, and he took my old van. I drove off with a "new" silver Honda Odyssey without putting any money down!

How did that happen? Only God could have done it. To God be the glory!

Cheryl Henry-Aguilar

The Lost Bag

And we know that all things work together for good to them that love God.
Rom. 8:28.

THE BIGGEST SALES of the year are the day after Christmas and our family looks forward to shopping for bargains during these sales year after year. It's fun to shop together and lots of fun to get some good buys. We went on our special shopping spree December 27. My son was especially excited because he had a $100 gift card for Hecht's department store. My daughter and I also had gift cards—an exciting shopping trip for all of us.

We went directly to the Hecht's store at the mall and all got some good deals there—especially my son. He bought six good dress shirts and a tie for less than $100.

From Hecht's we stopped at Burlington's to return and exchange some things. After shopping there my children went on home and I stayed longer at the mall.

A few days later my son asked, "Have you seen my shopping bag from Hecht's?"

"It may be in the basement," I told him. He must have thought I knew what I was talking about for he didn't bother to check immediately. After a week, he again asked about the bag. When we all said that we hadn't seen it he became a bit perturbed, searching high and low. At last he realized it was truly lost. He went from worried to being sad that he'd lost everything and, no doubt, mad at himself for not doing a thorough search earlier.

We tried to figure out where he may have left the bag. He remembered carrying it out of Hecht's, and the only other stop he'd made was Burlington's. He had to work the next day so he asked his sister to please go to Burlington's and check for him. Since a week had gone by, our hopes of finding the bag were very slim. Anyone could have easily walked out with it. I said the only thing that he could do now was to earnestly pray to find it—and he did pray.

My daughter did go to Burlington's and asked the manager if they'd found a Hecht's shopping bag. At first the answer was no, but after checking in a back room they found the bag intact. My son was so thrilled that God had answered his prayer!

Even in small matters, our great God is so kind and helpful to us. I love today's text: "And we know that all things work together for good to them that love God" (Rom. 8:28).

Stella Thomas

Stars Through the Window

Do not worry about tomorrow; for tomorrow will care for itself.
Matt. 6:34, NASB.

THE VIEW WAS MAGNIFICENT: my husband and I were surrounded by snowy mountain peaks silvered by moonlight. The weather was ideal—not a cloud in the sky and temperatures perfect for our long-anticipated cross-country skiing jaunt. The accommodations were luxurious—accustomed as we were to pitching a tent, the comfortable mattresses, flannel sheets, and thick down comforter were several steps above our usual standards. We didn't mind that they were spread out in the back of our vehicle.

Wanting to enjoy the silent world, we parked at the trailhead and walked. Our boots creaked over the dry snow and clouds of condensation bloomed in front of us as we talked. Half an hour later, we returned to the car, our cheeks glowing.

I didn't expect to sleep solidly through the night, so when I awoke shortly after midnight, I wasn't surprised. I simply turned over sleepily, pulled the covers up to warm my nose, and looked out the window to enjoy the brilliant stars. They weren't nearly as clear as they'd been a few hours before. Obviously it was clouding up. I drowsed for an hour, opening my eyes from time to time to look at the stars, and noting that the cloud cover seemed to be thickening. And then I slept.

Near 4:00, I awoke again. This time I could see no stars. It wasn't snowing, but, I thought, we might want to change our plans. After all, we didn't want to be caught in a whiteout. And then I pulled the covers over my head to warm my ears and fell asleep.

Several hours later, I awoke to sunlight flooding through the car windows. Rubbing my eyes, I wondered what had happened to the clouds. I tried to peer through the windows, but it was impossible—they were coated in a thick layer of sparkling frost created from our condensed breath. The "clouds" that had threatened to darken my day and spoil our plans had been an illusion.

Laughing, I pulled on my boots, cap, mitts, and jacket and opened the door to see clear skies, our skis propped in the snow bank, and my husband saying, "It's a glorious day. As soon as we can, let's hit the trail!"

Denise Dick Herr

Under His Wings

But those who hope in the Lord will renew their strength. They will soar on wings like eagles;
they will run and not grow weary, they will walk and not be faint.
Isa. 40:31, NIV.

MY HUSBAND, PARENTS, children, grandchildren, great-grandchildren, and I had spent a glorious Christmas vacation in California. Upon our return home to North Carolina, we checked our finances to make sure we had taken care of every little thing. On viewing our checking account, I noted we were in the red and wondered how this could be as we had carefully planned.

I searched the checking account and discovered we had authorized our mortgage payment to be deducted twice on the same day and for the exact same amount—that was the problem. It was now Saturday night and the banks would be closed for the holidays until Tuesday. My plan of action was to first ask for divine guidance, then send an e-mail to the bank confessing my error, and asking for a stop-payment remedy.

On Sunday morning a representative from the bank called in response to my e-mail. He explained that ordinarily they respond to e-mails the next business day. But our mail got his attention. "I was impressed to bring a little holiday cheer by calling and listening to your explanation before I sent a written acknowledgement," he told me. This was news too good to wait. We praised the Lord for this. God is on time, merciful, and loves us unconditionally. Sometimes we allow ourselves to do things without thinking through our options, but God knows our intentions, whether they are good or bad, and He shelters us like the mighty eagle hovers over her young.

I called the mortgage company that Tuesday. They thought that we had paid in advance on next month's payment and had therefore saved the check in their files. After my explanation they mailed back my check. The extra funds were restored to our checking account.

God in His tender mercy desires to make us whole again. In our heavenly homes we will not have concerns about overpayments nor underpayments. Our new lives will be sweeter than ever imagined; these little earthly trials will not affect us at all. I want to see Jesus and my new home, don't you?

Dear Jesus, thank You for Your blessings. All of these trials are getting me ready to see You in my heavenly home where everything will be taken care of. Hallelujah!

Betty G. Perry

Heaven at Last

Then I, John, saw the holy city, New Jerusalem, coming down out of heaven from God, prepared as a bride adorned for her husband.
Rev. 21:2, NKJV.

MY DAUGHTER AND I had spent several happy hours visiting with our friends from out of state. They were spending the Christmas holidays with their relatives who live in the southern California mountains.

When it was time for us to leave, we were asked if we knew how to find our way down the mountain as it was now night. We laughed and assured them we had been there once before, and we would be just fine.

However, an hour later we knew we did *not* know where we were. Nothing looked familiar, and we were worried. We decided to turn around and try to find where we had gone wrong. Almost another hour passed before we came to a small village where we could stop to ask for help. A pick-up truck entered the parking lot ahead of us. Since my daughter was doing the driving, she said a quick prayer, then got out and went to the truck to ask for directions. The driver was very kind and carefully told her what to do and what to look for. He even walked her back to our automobile.

Within a short time we could see bright city lights below us and we recognized where we were, and we knew how to get home. We thanked God for His mercy in sending a human, or a heavenly angel, to give us the exact directions. I remembered an old hymn about viewing heaven just over the mountains, and I longed for the day when all of us will look up and see the glorious lights of the beautiful New Jerusalem.

Then I thought about the Lord's care for His children. Sometimes life presents us with uncertainties and problems. Everything around us seems dark and we are lost in the mountains of our difficulties. We wonder what to do. But God is ever ready to help us. The answer may not come as quickly as He directed us that Christmas season, but in His time—and when it is best for us—He will show us the way. We may have to wait for heaven to learn about some of the times He has directed us, or why He has not answered as we think He should at other times. But someday we will understand. "Even so, come, Lord Jesus" (Rev. 22:20).

Mildred C. Williams

The Little Light Along the Way

*The people walking in darkness have seen a great light; on those
living in the land of the shadow of death a light has dawned.
Isa. 9:2, NIV.*

IT WAS THE AFTERNOON of the last day of the year. We women were attending a singles retreat in the mountains. We had visited a home for the elderly that was in the vicinity, singing songs for the residents, and now were on our way back to the retreat center. It was dusk, and about halfway up the steep mountainside we hit dense fog. Visibility was less than 65 feet (20 meters), and we were scared. I could only navigate by looking for the reflecting posts at the roadside. I drove slowly, my car lights reflecting one small light after the other. The road was very dangerous and without those light posts we would certainly have come much too close to the precipice. During this dangerous drive we realized how frightening and dismal our lives would be without God's light, direction, and leading.

Even though these light posts only reflected a little light we were able to continue on our journey because they showed us the way. A little light is often a big help in darkness.

The psalmist says, "The Lord is my light and my salvation—whom shall I fear?" (Ps. 27:1, NIV)

Of course we are often afraid of what the future may bring. We deal with the question, "How will things go?" Unemployment, sickness, existential worries will not come to a halt just because we are believers. It can become dark in our souls. We may not see a way out. And yet we realize that in the year gone by the Lord has held our hand, led us, and helped us when we needed Him most. He has consoled us and encouraged us through His Word.

When we look back at our lives we can only be amazed at how great and wonderful God is and how He has always intended things to work out for our good.

My wish is that in the coming New Year we will be on the lookout for God's light, hold on to His outstretched hand, and walk joyfully with Him. He knows the best way for me and for you. He will lead us all to our goal.

Jesus says "I am the light of the world" (John 8:12). The psalmist says, "Your word is a lamp to my feet and a light for my path" (Ps. 119:105, NIV). We have here two great sources of light for our lives. What else do we need? Let us look for this light and we will be safe.

Katharina Heise

Betty J. Adams is a retired teacher, a mother of three, plus two stepchildren, grandmother of seven, and great-grandmother of five, plus three step-great-grandchildren. She has written for *Guide* magazine and her church newsletter, and is active in community services. She enjoys writing, her grandchildren, scrapbooking, and traveling—especially on mission trips. **Feb. 14, Aug. 16.**

Maxine Williams Allen currently resides in central Florida with her husband and two fast-growing sons, Brandon and Jonathan. She's a licensed real estate professional who enjoys reading, writing, and traveling, and she has a special interest in family life ministries. Considering each day a true gift, she endeavors to discover and live God's plan for her life. **May 8, Sept. 24.**

Marivan de Oliveira Almeida writes from Brazil. She is married with three children and five grandchildren. She enjoys poetry and walking. **Nov. 14.**

Claudette Joy Andrews is married to Pastor Maurice Andrews and is the mother of three adult sons. She is a nationally certified counselor, licensed psychotherapist, and commissioned pastor. She serves as director of women's and children's ministries in the Caribbean Union. Her hobbies include reading, gardening, cooking, entertaining guests, and people watching. **June 13.**

Marilyn Joyce Applegate who writes from Walla Walla, Washington, enjoys writing, serving as a deaconess in the Walla Walla University church, and mission trips with her husband. **Feb. 27, Dec. 7.**

Raquel Queiroz da Costa Arrais is a minister's wife who has developed her ministries as an educator for 20 years. Currently she works as associate director of the General Conference women's ministries department. She has two sons and one daughter-in-law, Paula. Her greatest pleasures are to be with people, sing, play the piano, and travel. **Oct. 26, Dec. 6.**

Lady Dana Austin writes from Georgia, where she is a women's ministries leader. A product of both public and Christian education, she attended Southern Adventist University. She is a clinical project manager, and her passions are writing, travel, tea ceremonies, and women's ministries. She is also a certified tea consultant, an author, and entrepreneur. **June 25.**

Edna B. Bacate-Domingo is a member of Loma Linda Filipino church in California, where she has served as an elder. She is also on the church's nurture council and the women's/family ministries council. Edna is a nursing professor at American University of Health Sciences, School of Nursing. She retired from California State University, College of Nursing. She is the mother of three daughters. **Nov. 22.**

Margarete Baindner was born in Tübingen, Germany, where she still lives. She loves her husband, her three adult sons, and music. She takes loving care of the church building and is active in women's ministries. **Aug. 9.**

Carla Baker is women's ministries director for the North American Division of Seventh-day Adventists. Her special areas of interest in women's ministries include reclaiming inactive members, ministries to teens, and abuse prevention and education. Carla enjoys traveling, reading, cooking, and walking. **Dec. 2.**

Jennifer M. Baldwin writes from Australia, where she works in risk management at Sydney Adventist Hospital. She enjoys church involvement, travel, crossword puzzles, and writing, and has contributed to a number of church publications. **Oct. 6.**

Tammy Barnes-Taylor lives in Pell City, Alabama, where she attends the Pell City Adventist Church. She is active in women's ministries in her church and conference. Married 23 years, she has three sons and one daughter. Tammy enjoys photography, writing, and scrapbooking. She owns Little Cherubs Christian Center where she has been teaching for 13 years. **Jan. 2, May 27.**

Dana M. (Bassett) Bean, a primary teacher, lives in Bermuda with her husband, daughter, and son. Dana loves being a writing instrument through which God can spread His love. She enjoys reading, travel, swimming, and photography. **Oct. 1.**

Lisa M. Beardsley is associate director of education for the General Conference of Seventh-day Adventists. She works with the Adventist Accrediting Association and is editor-in-chief for *Dialogue* journal which is published in English, French, Spanish, and Portuguese for Adventist university students around the world. **Mar. 22, Sept. 14.**

Dawna Beausoleil and her husband, John, have recently moved out of the wilderness to a charming little town in Northern Ontario. She's a former teacher who enjoys singing, reading, scrapbooking, and her two spoiled kitties. **Aug. 25.**

Joan Beck has written for *Adventist Review* and the church's children's magazines for 35 years and worked in Pathfinders and children's Sabbath schools for 40 years. She also served in the church's community outreach programs. She enjoys family, writing, and gardening—and has time for all, now that she is retired from the Alabama state law enforcement community. **Mar. 29.**

Ginger Bell resides in Brighton, Colorado, with her pastor husband. They have two married children and four grandchildren who live in the area. Ginger is the administrative assistant and women's ministries leader at her church and the women's ministries director for the Rocky Mountain Conference. She enjoys gardening, reading, traveling, and being with family. **May 23.**

Pauline Belle writes from Canada. Now a senior citizen, she served the community as a public health nurse, then a social worker, and finally a hospital chaplain. She retired in March, 1995. Her hobbies are Scrabble, crossword puzzles, and word searches. She takes time to minister to the elderly both in a retirement home and a nursing home. **Sept. 20.**

Flora F. Beloni is a confirmed nurse working for the government. She lives in Martinique, French West Indies, and is in charge of women's ministries in her local church. Her husband, Pierre A. Beloni, is first elder of the church. Their two daughters are studying and living in the United States and their son is studying in Jamaica. **Aug. 10.**

Eunice Passos Molina Berger was born in Brazil, but has lived in Canada with her husband, Marcus, for more than 19 years. She is a dentist, and also helps with Sabbath school and women's ministries at her church. She enjoys music, sports, nature, and friends. **June 12, Dec. 24.**

Ingrid Berker is married and has an adult son. She is a chiropodist. Her hobbies include reading, singing, and the love of nature. **Feb. 24.**

Undine Binder-Farr is married and has a daughter. She works as publicity manager for the German city where she lives and writes many news articles for daily and weekly newspapers. Her main interest in church is in the children's department. **Mar. 16.**

Alice K. Binns writes from Madison, Alabama, and is a woman on the move for God. She is an inspirational speaker for prayer meetings, women's conferences, Woman's Day, women's club meetings, church services, Sabbath school, and community service meetings. **Apr. 30.**

Dinorah Blackman writes from beautiful Panama where she lives with her husband and daughter, Imani. **Jan. 26, June 16.**

Juli Blood has been happily married since 1994, and is the mother of two young boys. She loves to read, write, and bake. Her greatest joy is to serve the Lord through writing, storytelling, and sharing His truth with all who will listen. She dreams of heaven where she will have all eternity to fellowship with the Lord and all His children. She wants to hear their testimonies first hand. **Feb. 28.**

Helen Bocala-Gulfan is the shepherdess coordinator and women's ministries director of the Southern Asia-Pacific Division of Seventh-day Adventists. She and her husband have three grown children and one grandson. She delights in organizing programs, gardening, sports, traveling, making and writing to friends, encouraging women, and sharing God's love and plan of salvation. **Dec. 13.**

Julie Bocock-Bliss is pursuing her master's degree in Library and Information Sciences (MLISC) at the University of Hawaii at Manoa. She is an active member of the Manoa Japanese Seventh-day Adventist Church, being especially involved with the primary division of 7- to 10-year-olds. She is "mommy" to three cats, and loves reading and traveling. **July 20.**

Fulori Bola is originally from the Fiji Islands but is now a lecturer at the Pacific Adventist University, Papua New Guinea. A single mother, she enjoys working with women and is the women's ministries coordinator of the Koiari Park English church. She is the mother of Sala, Terri, and Josh, and grandmother of Yvonne and Rafa. **Apr. 21.**

Evelyn Gertrude Greenwade Boltwood is a mother of two young adults and grandmother of one grandson. She is the Pathfinder and Adventurer area coordinator for Western New York. Her passions are youth ministries, camping, reading, writing, and traveling. She is a member of the Akoma women's community gospel choir which raises money for scholarships for young women. **July 19, Sept. 25.**

Ingrid Bomke is married and has three sons and two grandchildren. She was leader in a nursery school for many years. Since 1997, she has had a ministry counseling teens and young people. She presents seminars on Christian education. Her second audio book will be presented shortly. **Aug. 5.**

Althea Y. Boxx, a Jamaican, is a registered nurse. She has published her first book, a devotional entitled *Fuel for the Journey*, an inspirational nugget for life's uphill climb. Althea believes that nothing is as contagious as enthusiasm. Her hobbies include reading, writing, traveling, and photography. **June 29.**

Elizabeth Boyd graduated from Loma Linda University in physical therapy. She founded the company, Traveling Medical Professionals, Inc., placing traveling therapists in positions throughout the United States. She mentors teens of the Northern New England Conference of Seventh-day Adventists and loves to bring them together at her old farm house for prayer, Bible study, and service. **June 23.**

Laura L. Bradford seeks to encourage others by writing of the countless ways God has touched her life. Some of her stories appear in *A Cup of Comfort for Families Touched by Alzheimer's* and *Life Savors for Women*. She resides in Walla Walla, Washington. **Mar. 19.**

Ani Köhler Bravo is a retired secretary who worked at the Brazil Publishing House and wrote the 2007 daily devotional book for juniors. She lives with her husband and son in Engenheiro Coelho, Brazil, and serves her church by leading women's ministries. She enjoys reading and says that a day—or a year—doesn't have hours enough to read all the books she wants. **Nov. 26.**

Gail Bremmer lives in western North Carolina with her husband and mother. She is the mother of two boys, the stepmother of two girls, and has reared a niece. She is a graphic designer and bookkeeper. Gail enjoys time with family, is active in women's ministries, and loves preaching on ShareHim mission trips. **Oct. 16.**

Debra Clements Brill is vice president of the North American Division of Seventh-day Adventists. "Mimi" loves reading to Reese, Ivan, and Avery and introducing them to God's creatures, especially the birds she and husband, George, enjoy watching anytime, anywhere. **Oct. 22.**

Prisca Brouet, a single mother of two adult children, is presently rearing two other children. Born in the Caribbean island of St. Lucia, she is a qualified general education teacher. She taught for 32 years, teaching grade six for 21 years. She now teaches special needs children, as she is also qualified in this field. Prisca is very active in church, and loves witnessing. **Sept. 12.**

Dyhann Buddoo-Fletcher hails from the parish of St. Catherine, Jamaica. She is outgoing and loves taking road trips across the island as well as hiking, biking, gardening, reading, writing, and making great meals for her family. She shares in a team ministry with her husband, Pastor Gary. They have two children, Victoria and Carrington. Dyhann is a secretary. **Oct. 25.**

Darlene Ytredal Burgeson is a retired sales manager, and caregiver for both herself and her husband. Although they are not well, they spend much time with their great-grandchildren. They thank God they have time to take them to many interesting places, even some lengthy car trips. Their family is their hobby and Darlene also loves to write. **Dec. 20.**

Helen Dick Burton, after home, church music, and Sabbath school activities are finished, enjoys dreaming up artistic and writing projects—which she may never complete. She taught elementary school for several years, and now works in a finance department paying bills for developmentally challenged individuals. **Aug. 21.**

Joy Butler, originally from New Zealand, is administrative secretary at the East Central Africa Division of Seventh-day Adventists, located in Nairobi, Kenya. She is a wife and the mother of three grown children, and has lived in various countries where she served as a teacher, chaplain, departmental director, fundraiser, speaker, and writer. She has a passion to help the hurting women of the world. **Nov. 15.**

Elizabeth Ida Cain works as an administrative officer with a new motor vehicle company. She attends the St. John's Seventh-day Adventist Church where she is a member of the women's ministries association, and also serves as a Sabbath school teacher. She enjoys writing and is a designer of floral art. **June 30.**

Noemia das N. Carvalho is a retired school teacher who worked in the state education system in Brazil. She is the mother of two adult children and joyfully helps in her church when requested. She enjoys gardening and crocheting. **Nov. 1.**

Antonia Castellino is married and lives in the English midlands. She has two grown children and two grandchildren—her pride and joy. She works part-time as an elementary teacher and enjoys walking, nature, listening to music, visual arts, and Bible study. Antonia is active in her local church. **Oct. 17.**

Joelcira F. Cavedon was introduced to Christ through the community work of the Hong Kong Adventist Hospital. She lived in Southeast Asia for 18 years, working in more than 15 countries, training executives. She was baptized when she returned to her roots in Porto Alegre, Brazil. An active member of her church, she has two children. **Mar. 21.**

Romi Chae writes from the Philippines where she is studying in a Ph.D. program in education and her husband (Kim Jong Hwan) is taking the MDIV course in the Adventist International Institute of Advanced Studies. They are Korean, and do not yet have a child. Romi loves singing, as it encourages her to keep moving forward. She and her husband praise God who guides their steps. **Nov. 9.**

Judy Gray Seeger Cherry graduated from Union College where Ardis Stenbakken was her roommate. She and her husband, Earl, live on a farmstead in Nebraska. Between Judy and Earl, they have six children and six grandchildren. Judy is an accountant and the church/school treasurer as well as church organist. She enjoys visiting grandchildren, doing puzzles, and watching car races. **Nov. 11.**

Marion Newman Chin lives in Canada and is one of the organists at her church. Her husband has his own financial business and she works with him. She has three grown children and five grandchildren. Marion enjoys reading the women's devotional and calls the women writers her friends because she identifies with them so well. **Oct. 10.**

Lyndelle Brower Chiomenti is the editor of *CQ: A Devotional Bible Study for Young Adults* published by the Seventh-day Adventist Church. **July 13.**

Caroline Chola lives in Pretoria, South Africa. She is the women's and children's ministries director for the South Africa-Indian Ocean Division of Seventh-day Adventists. She and her husband, Habson, have five sons and one granddaughter. She enjoys gardening. Her passion is to see women discover their potential and use it to the glory of God. **Dec. 10.**

Birol Charlotte Christo is a retired teacher. During her active service she also worked as an office secretary and statistician in the Southern Asia Division of Seventh-day Adventists. She lives with her husband in Hosur, India. The mother of five adult children, Birol enjoys gardening, sewing, and creating craft items to finance her projects for homeless children. **Feb. 7.**

Rosenita Christo is married to Gordon and they have two children: Gerald, married to Naphirisa; and Cheryl, married to Andre. She has been a teacher and department head at Spicer College in India. She is the editor of the Southern Asia *Tidings* and coordinator of Adventist Volunteer Service for the Southern Asia Division of Seventh-day Adventists. Rosenita likes to sing and currently directs the church choir. **Dec. 11.**

Rosemarie Clardy's roots are in Queens, New York, but she now lives in the mountains of North Carolina and loves it. She has three boys, two cats, and one dog. She loves to garden, take walks, and write little stories to share with others. **July 29.**

Debbie Clarke-Grant, a registered dietitian, coordinates the dietetics program at Northern Caribbean University, Jamaica. She and her husband, Leroy, have two children, David and Leigh-Ann. Debbie loves the Lord and serves in various capacities in her local church. She believes that each day is a gift from God. **July 21.**

Naomi N. Coleman and her husband operate the Intermountain Adventist Bookmobile. She is the proud mother of three, stepmother of six, and grandmother of 13. She has served nationally in singles ministries, as a leader in family life ministries, and she created the Blended Family Ministries. She has also served as secretary-treasurer for Enterprise Academy alumni association. **July 17.**

Patricia Cove celebrated her fiftieth wedding anniversary in 2008. She is a mother of five, grandmother of 17, and great-grandmother of one. She is head elder of her church, a freelance writer, does substitute teaching, and spends much time in her gardens. Her hobbies are sailing with husband George, outdoor pursuits, and reading. **May 22.**

Celia Mejia Cruz is a pastor's wife, mother of five adult children, and grandmother of seven. She moved to the Tennessee Highlands in 2009. She is a church elder, a Shaklee distributor, and local women's ministries leader. She is also a public speaker and seminar presenter. **May 18, July 27.**

Carol J. Daniel is director of career development services at the University of the Southern Caribbean in Trinidad and part-time lecturer for the School of Behavioral Sciences. Carol holds an MA in educational psychology and has a background in business education and management. She spends free time reading motivational literature, traveling, and listening to music. **Jan. 18.**

Avery Davis, over the years, has been actively involved with both children's and women's ministries in her local church. The mother of Theresa, Sarah, and Grace, she is currently working on a collection of family stories. **Jan. 21, Aug. 13.**

Claudia DeJong is married and works as a manager for a large software company. She is also the leader of the women's ministries department in southern Bavaria. **June 20, Aug. 20.**

Sinikka Dixon has just retired on Prince Edward Island with her husband. She is a sociologist with a Ph.D. from the University of California, Riverside. She is multicultural and multilingual, with publications in her professional field of social inequalities, aging, and community studies. She loves to read, travel, and participate in water and snow sports. **Sep. 16.**

Mekoudjou Myriam Djia writes from Cameroon where she is a student at Adventist University Cosendai, majoring in accounting. She wrote this devotional after receiving a scholarship from the General Conference Women's Ministries funded by these devotional books. She wants to encourage others to have more faith in God to supply their needs. **July 30.**

Leonie Donald thanks God every day for the beauty of Queen Charlotte Sound, New Zealand, where she lives. She enjoys long walks, devours books, and admits to spending more time in her garden than doing housework. Leonie and her husband of 43 years attend the Blenheim Adventist Church. **July 24.**

Susan Drieberg lives in Grand Terrace, California, with her husband, Denver, and her youngest daughter. She has four daughters and three grandchildren, and is a school nurse. Her hobbies include oil painting, gardening, and music. **Mar. 23.**

Louise Driver, now retired, lives in Idaho where three sons and four grandchildren also live. She works a few days a week at the Family Christian Bookstore enjoying the opportunities to help others in their walk with the Lord through Bibles, books, and music. Her hobbies are singing, music, reading, gardening, and traveling to historical places. **Mar. 8.**

Trudy Duncan, a medical technologist, has found a new love: American Sign Language. Her hobbies include traveling, singing, nature activities, and now ASL. She has two children, and resides in northern Virginia with her family. **Feb. 18.**

Margaret Duran is a writer of Christian material and has published four books: one of them is an autobiography and two are inspirational. Although she grew up in a very strict Christian home God allowed her to wander in the desert for many years to bring her to a total submission to His will. She is 75 years old, but has been an Adventist for just a few short months—and loves it. **Apr. 13.**

Joy Dustow is a retired teacher who enjoys taking part in the spiritual and social activities of the retirement village in Australia, where she and her husband now live. **Mar. 12.**

Pauline A. Dwyer-Kerr has served the Seventh-day Adventist church as an elder, head of Sabbath school, in communication and family life, on social committees, as receptionist, and as a church clerk. She has sung in the church choir and led their singing group. Pauline has a doctorate and is a professor. She loves travel and the outdoors. A native of Jamaica, Pauline now resides in Florida. **July 25.**

Regina Fackler is a nurse and chiropodist. She is a deaconess in her church and loves to take care of elderly persons. Her other hobbies are cooking, hiking, and creating personalized cards. **Apr. 4.**

Fartema M. Fagin, a family service worker, is married with two adult sons. In her leisure time she enjoys reading and writing. She is actively involved in her church where she participates in the women's ministries programs and sings in the choir. Fartema lives in Tennessee. **May 12.**

Susana Faria, writing from Brazil, enjoys volunteering her time in children's ministries at her church. She has been married to Marco Faria for 23 years and they have two sons, Marco, 22, and Jorge, 20. Susana has worked in a hospital for 21 years, and enjoys reading, embroidery, and walking. **Mar. 30.**

Arline Farquharson writes from Florida, where she is music coordinator at the Palm Bay Adventist Church. She has three adult children and four grandchildren. Arline is a medical coder, and in her spare time enjoys singing, painting, and brisk early morning walks. This is her first submission. **Aug. 24.**

Gloria Stella Felder lives in Atlanta, Georgia. She and her retired pastor-husband share a family of four adult children and five grandchildren. Gloria works in the treasury department of the South Atlantic Conference of Seventh-day Adventists. She enjoys music, writing, speaking, and spending time with family, especially the grandchildren. She has written magazine articles and is working on a second book. **Jan. 22, May 10.**

Mona Fellers is married and has a grown daughter. She is a paramedic and has been an EMS since 1984. She teaches EMS part-time, and is now training to be a deputy coroner. She is the women's and children's ministries leader at her church. And her favorite thing to say is that God has blessed her in that she lives at 10,300 feet and every year gets to feed about 100 hummingbirds. **Aug. 15.**

Margaret E. Fisher and her husband, Floyd, live in Dayton, Tennessee. They have five children and 16 grandchildren. She loves to write, especially poetry. Margaret has had several poems published, as well as articles, one for *Guidepost* and several for *Southern Tidings*. She enjoys playing the piano in church and is still nursing part-time. Her hobbies are knitting and crafts. **Oct. 29.**

Edith Fitch is a retired teacher living in Lacombe, Alberta, Canada, and volunteers in the archives at Canadian University College. She enjoys life and thanks God for every new day. Her hobbies include writing, traveling, needlework, Sudoku, and cryptograms. **Mar. 5, May 24.**

Janice Fleming-Williams, an elementary school teacher and a certified family life educator, has been teaching for more than 30 years. Her hobbies include reading and keeping in touch with friends. Janice and her husband live on St. Thomas, United States Virgin Islands, and are the parents of two adult sons. Her motto is "Accentuate the positive." **Aug. 12.**

Lana Fletcher lives in Chehalis, Washington, with her husband. They have one married daughter; their younger daughter was killed in a car accident in 1993. Lana is the church clerk. She loves gardening, does the bookkeeping for her husband's business, makes Creative Memories albums, helps with a Loss-of-a-Child support group, and journals her prayers. **Mar. 20, May 5.**

Lenora Franklin lives in Detroit, Michigan. She has one son, Lamar, who is married to Lisa, and two grandchildren, Janee and Tashanique. Lenora and her husband have been married for 44 years. Lenora has written an acrostic for her name (which means light of the sun and shows her passions) Light, Ever, New, Onward, Rising, Always: to let His Name Be Praised! **Dec. 8.**

Janice Gibbs writes from Canada and is a first-time contributor. She is a freelance medical editor who lives in Seaforth, Ontario, with her husband, two children, and a cat. She enjoys reading, playing tennis, and spending time with her family. **July 31.**

Carol Wiggins Gigante, a former day-care provider, is a teacher at heart. She is an avid reader, photographer, and flower and bird lover. Carol resides in Beltsville, Maryland, with her husband, Joe, their dog Buddy, and new kitten Suzannah. They have two grown sons, Jeff and James. "Even so come, Lord Jesus!" **Sept. 26.**

Evelyn Glass and her husband, Darrell, live in Minnesota on the farm where Darrell was born. They have three grown children, Rod, Peggy, and Judy, a daughter-in-law, Dawn; a son-in-law, Darin; and two grandchildren. Evelyn writes a column for the local paper and is active as a speaker and volunteer. She recently authored a series of Bible studies, *Women in the Bible and Me.* **Jan. 23, June 19.**

Hannelore Gomez, who is from Panama, teaches Spanish in a high school in Virginia. Her hobbies are reading and traveling. Knowing the gospel since she was born has been her greatest blessing. **Feb. 15.**

Cecelia Grant is a medical doctor who retired from government service but works part-time at Andrews Memorial Hospital in Kingston, Jamaica. Her hobbies are traveling, gardening, and listening to good music. She has a passion for young people, to whom she often gives advice. **Apr. 20, Dec. 9.**

Charlotte S. Grant writes from Florida and is currently a school social worker and family therapist. She attends Mount Calvary Adventist Church in Tampa. **Apr. 10.**

Mary Jane Graves and her husband Ted are retired and living in North Carolina. She is the church librarian and is involved in women's ministries. Other activities include delivering Meals-on-Wheels once a week, gardening, reading, and occasionally writing. **Oct. 23.**

Chrisele Green accepted the Lord as her Savior in 1985. She has a bachelor's degree from Eastern Michigan University, and is married and has two children. In her church she sometimes preaches, teaches a Sabbath school Bible class, is a women's ministries leader, sings in the choir, and serves on the hospitality committee. Her passion in life is to bring God's healing to women. **Aug. 8, Oct. 7.**

Ellie Green is a retired registered nurse and serves as the Sharon Church head elder and as a lay pastor's assistant in the Carolina Conference of Seventh-day Adventists. Evangelism is her passion and she has conducted 16 evangelism series. Her husband is retired from NASA. They have two children and three grandchildren. **Feb. 22.**

Joan Green is a secretary in Idaho and the director of Green Light Women's Ministries and their annual women's conference. She has been published in several publications, is a retreat speaker, an inventor, and creator of the board game Cross Pix Challenge. Her passions include her grandchildren and children, encouraging women in the Lord, traveling, writing, and speaking. **June 26, Dec. 14.**

Carol J. Greene praises God for every year with which He extends her life. A grandmother of four and an active member of the prayer chains at the Palm Bay church in Florida, she delights in her rose garden and the cooling breezes of April. **Oct. 19.**

Eilean L. Greene, who is retired from active ministries, is an ordained elder in the African Methodist Episcopal Church. She enjoys writing and intercessory prayer. **Dec. 18.**

Glenda-mae Greene is a frequent contributor to the women's devotional book project. A former university educator, she revels in interacting with young adults and mentoring those women who want to share their testimonies on the printed page. **Jan. 17, Apr. 23.**

Gloria Gregory is a minister's wife and the mother of two young adult women. She works as director of admissions at Northern Caribbean University in Jamaica. She believes that each person is precious in God's sight and is born to fulfill a special mission. She is convinced that her mission is to help others unearth their full potentials and use them to honor God. **Jan. 25.**

Edith Haberzeth-Grau is a health and relaxation educator. She is married to a Lutheran pastor and has three adult children. She lives in southern Germany. **May 16.**

Diantha Hall-Smith is a daughter of God. She is wife to a Christian husband, who serves in the U.S. Air Force, and is the mother of two children. Born in New York, she has had the honor and privilege of visiting and living in interesting places domestically and globally. She enjoys writing, traveling, and spending time with her family. **Jan. 29, June 17.**

Dessa Weisz Hardin lives in Maine with her husband, where she greatly enjoys the ocean. She is also interested in traveling, writing, art, and music, and is teaching herself to play the piano. An added dimension to her life is grandparenting. She enjoys the women's devotional book and hearing from friends who have been blessed through it. **May 2, Oct. 18.**

Marian M. Hart, a retired elementary teacher and nursing home administrator, works with her husband in property management. A member of the Battle Creek Seventh-day Adventist Tabernacle for 35 years, she has served in many different capacities. Six grandchildren make her a proud grandmother. Marian enjoys knitting, reading, growing flowers, and winters in Florida. **May 17, July 23.**

Bessie Haynes is a semi-retired teacher living in South Korea, working as an English teacher. She has three grown children—all of them live in different countries. Bessie's hobbies are reading, writing, traveling, and meeting people. **Feb. 26, Oct. 4.**

Beverly D. Hazzard was born in England but grew up in Jamaica, Ohio, and British Columbia. She now lives in Kelowna, British Columbia, Canada. She worked as a registered nurse for many years but recently retired from healthcare administration. She has two grown children and three grandchildren—whom she enjoys very much. She loves travel, church activities, missions, poetry, and gospel songs. **May 13, Sept. 8.**

Katharina Heise lives in Schramberg in Germany's Black Forest. She teaches Sabbath school for children. She is also actively engaged in an organization for singles and single parents. Her hobbies include being creative, singing, reading, talking, laughing, and writing devotionals. **Nov. 4, Dec. 31.**

Irisdeane Henley-Charles is a nurse consultant working in Washington, D.C. She is married to Oscar, and they have three children. Through the years she has worked in many areas of the church, and enjoys serving the Lord. Some of her hobbies include arts and crafts projects, sewing, playing the guitar, and reading. **Nov. 8.**

Cheryl Henry-Aguilar writes from Wilmington, North Carolina, where she owns and operates a five-star daycare center and an after-school program. She and her preteen daughter, Antannia, spend a lot of time in Pathfinder activities. Cheryl enjoys photography and travel in her spare time. **Dec. 26.**

Denise Dick Herr teaches English at Canadian University College in Alberta, Canada. She loves to travel with her family and rejoices in the power of words. **Nov. 28, Dec. 28.**

Vashti Hinds-Vanier was born in Guyana, South America, and is presently retired in New York after a nursing career that spanned 40 years. This story was edited from Vashti's published work, "School Daze and Beyond." Her hobbies include travel, cake decorating, gardening, and crocheting. **Oct. 31.**

Patricia Hines writes from Florida where she is a member, a deaconess, and the music director of the South Orlando Adventist Church. A teacher, she enjoys working with children. Her Christian walk has been a struggle with many challenges, but she has had many wonderful experiences as a friend of God. She hopes that the devotional she wrote will touch some heart. **Mar. 24.**

Lorraine Hirsch-Olson (was Hudgins-Hirsch) recently married and lives in a delightful retirement community in Loma Linda, California. She has worked at Faith for Today, the Voice of Prophecy, and the General Conference of Seventh-day Adventists. Her articles and poems have appeared in various publications. She is the grateful mother of five adult children. **Sept. 11**

Roxy Hoehn writes from Topeka, Kansas, about her first grandchild. Now retired after 15 years in the women's ministries department of the Kansas-Nebraska Conference of Seventh-day Adventists, she has more time to spend with her 11 grandchildren. **Jan. 16.**

Karen Holford is married to Bernie and works with him as the associate director of children's and family ministries in southern England near London. They have three adult children. She likes to write, create multisensory worship experiences, make quilts, and dream up unusual things to feed her family. Karen has written more than a dozen books. **May 31, Sept. 18.**

Melodie Homer resides in southern New Jersey with her two children. A registered nurse, she currently works as a clinical nursing instructor in pediatrics. She also runs a non-profit organization in her husband's memory. In her spare time, she is an avid reader and enjoys spending time with family and friends. **Aug. 19.**

Carol June Hooker is a registered nurse who teaches community health nursing and serves in the diaconate of the Sligo (Maryland) Seventh-day Adventist church. She adores her husband and two adult children, and she enjoys studying wildlife of the eastern United States. **Nov. 16.**

Jacqueline Hope HoShing-Clarke has been an educator since 1979, as principal, assistant principal, and teacher. She is now director for the pre-college department at Northern Caribbean University, Jamaica, and is reading for a Ph.D. She is married to Pastor Bylton Clarke and they have two adult children, Deidre and Deneil. Jackie enjoys writing and gardening. **Mar. 28.**

Shirley C. Iheanacho and her husband, Morris, are enjoying retirement and find joy traveling to new and interesting places. However, she still finds time to write, serve as elder in her local church, sing in the choir, play hand bells, and encourage fellow travelers. Shirley and Morris always look forward to spending time with their three daughters, and especially their grandsons. **Aug. 27.**

Diana Inman was born and raised in a family of nine siblings. She is the mother of two adult children, grandmother of five, and lives with her husband on a farm in mid-Michigan. She enjoys antiques, growing herbs and flowers, reading, and sometimes writing. She is working toward certification as a master herbalist, and coauthored *Eden's Bounty*, a vegetarian cookbook. **Sept. 28.**

Avis Floyd Jackson, mother of five, lives in Pleasantville, New Jersey. She runs a party planner business out of her home. Avis has been the women's ministries director in her local church for the past five years. She says she is an Adventist by calling. **Dec. 21.**

Joan D. L. Jaensch is married and lives with her husband in Murray Bridge, South Australia. They have two married sons, two granddaughters, and two grandsons. Gardening and potted plants are her hobbies. **May 29.**

Wilma C. Jardine, a retired supply technician, lives in Fort Washington, Maryland. She has six children, seven grandchildren, and four great-grandchildren. A member of the women's ministries council at her church, she is also a soloist and choir member. Wilma enjoys reading, playing the piano, and spending time with family. She is originally from Panama. **Apr. 19.**

Greta Michelle Joachim-Fox-Dyett is married to a God-fearing man and is the mother of one daughter. She is an artist, an art teacher at Southern Academy, and an active member of the South Caribbean Conference women's ministries council. Presently, she is working on becoming a serious artist. **Oct. 14.**

Elaine J. Johnson has been married for 41 years to her best friend, Peter. They have four adult children and 12 grandchildren. Active in her local country church, she enjoys writing and communication in all its forms. Elaine recently retired after working for 30 years in preschool. **July 1, Nov. 2.**

Erna Johnson was born and raised in Iceland. She is married to Eddy, a minister, and they have worked for the Seventh-day Adventist Church all over the world. They have two children and eight grandchildren. Since 1997, Erna has served as women's ministries director in different places, and is now director for the South Pacific Division. She has a passion to help women reach their potential. **Sept. 7.**

Madeline Steele Johnston is a retired missionary to Korea and the Philippines. She is a grandmother of six, mother of four and their spouses, and wife of one seminary professor. She and her husband serve jointly as associate head elders of Pioneer Memorial Church at Andrews University. Her hobbies include photography, bird watching. and travel. She has written several books and numerous articles. **May 14, Oct. 3.**

Emily Felts Jones began Bring Forth Ministries in 1996. Through music, writing, and speaking she loves to share God's infinite power to work in and through each one of us, whatever our age. **Mar. 17.**

Gloria Josiah is originally from Trinidad, and has served with her pastor-husband for more than 40 years on seven Caribbean Islands. Now retired from a career in education, she lives in the Virgin Islands. She enjoys writing, and has published several articles and a book, *Ministries Adventures in the Caribbean*. She has three children and seven grandchildren. **Apr. 29.**

Aila Rehumäki Kauhanen lives in Finland where she teaches German, Swedish, and French. Her husband is a nature researcher in Lapland. **May 20.**

Bridgid Kilgour is a registered nurse specializing in aged care. She writes from Sydney, Australia. Her passion for writing was born when she started writing scripts for puppet plays while she, her husband, and two sons were leaders in children's ministries. **July 11.**

Iris L. Kitching is a mother, and grandmother, and with husband, Will, enjoys their blended families—five sons, one daughter, four daughters-in-law, and 10 grandchildren. She works in the presidential section of the General Conference of Seventh-day Adventists, and is communications leader and editor/designer of *Church Matters*, the monthly newsletter, at her local church. **Apr. 12, Aug. 11.**

Melissa Irene Koeffler lives in New Jersey where she is a student working toward a degree in the medical field. She has three passions: writing, her heavenly Father, and compassion for those in need. **July 28.**

Hepzibah Kore writes from Hosur, India, where she is the women's ministries director and shepherdess coordinator of the Southern Asia Division of Seventh-day Adventists. Her husband, Gnanaraj Kore, a minister, is a director in the same division. Her passion is to open the eyes of the women of her country to read the Word and see the world through adult literacy programs. **April 25.**

Betty Kossick moved to Ocala, Florida, in 2008. She writes locally as a freelance correspondent feature writer for Ocala *Star-Banner* and the Ocala *Business Journal*, as well as the *Senior Times* in Gainesville. She also writes for *Adventist Review* and *Renewed and Ready*. During her 38 years as a writer she's had the opportunity to give honor to the Giver of talents. **Nov. 24.**

Patricia Mulraney Kovalski lives in Collegedale, Tennessee, but spends many months each year with her family in Michigan. She enjoys walking, swimming, crafts, reading, and traveling. **July 22.**

Juanita Kretschmar, a mother and grandmother, has been in ministries in Brazil, the northwestern USA, Greater New York, and now in the Florida Keys. By the mercy of God she writes, counsels, preaches, and prays. God is now her only husband and He provides human support continually. Juanita lives with gratitude in her heart and a sure expectancy of His return. **Jan. 13.**

Mabel Kwei, originally from Ghana, West Africa, now lives in New Jersey. She is a retired university and college lecturer, a pastor's wife, and mother of three. She loves to read, write, paint, and garden. **Jan. 28, Mar. 26.**

Nathalie Ladner-Bischoff, a retired nurse, enjoys homemaking, gardening, volunteering at Gospel Outreach and the local hospital gift shop, reading, writing, knitting, and crocheting. She's had several magazine stories published, as well as three books: *An Angel's Touch, Touched by a Miracle,* and *Through It All—Then God*. **Nov. 30.**

Maria Lamprecht-Schmid lives in southern Germany. She is married and has four adult children and five grandchildren. For her seventieth birthday her children presented her with a flight to Paraguay to visit her daughter. **June 6.**

Iani Dias Lauer-Leite writes from Brazil where she is a college professor. She is currently on a leave of absence to finish her doctorate in psychology on economic behavior of children and teens in Brazil. She likes to read about different topics, especially prayer, and is involved in the prayer ministries of her church. **Mar. 10, Apr. 6.**

Loida Gulaja Lehmann spent 10 years selling religious books in the Philippines, then went to Germany and married. She and her husband are active members in the International church in Darmstadt. For years she worked in the Adventist military center in Frankfurt/Main. Her hobbies include traveling, collecting souvenirs, nature walks, and photography. **Apr. 11.**

Ruth Lennox and her husband celebrated their fiftieth anniversary in 2008. They have three married children and four granddaughters. Ruth is totally retired from medicine and is now also retired from leadership of the British Columbia, Canada, conference women's ministries. Her hobbies are watching her granddaughters grow and helping with the local Parkinson's group. **Feb. 23.**

Nair Costa Lessa is a retired educational counselor. She dedicates herself to her family and social causes and helps with a children's home which gives a home to 14 girls. She participates in the Brazilian Adventist Laymen's Association and in various church activities. She enjoys reading, writing, traveling, and spending time with her children and grandchildren. **May 28.**

Kathleen H. Liwidjaja-Kuntaraf, MD, MPH, has been the associate health director at the world headquarters of the Seventh-day Adventist Church since 1995. Prior to this, she worked in the Far East in Adventist hospitals and as assistant ADRA director and health director. She and her husband, Jonathan, have authored five books. They have two adult children, Andrew and Andrea. **Dec. 3.**

Bessie Siemens Lobsien is a retired missionary librarian who worked for 21 years in foreign missions as well as in the United States. Throughout her adult life her writings have been published in church papers. She now enjoys her fast-growing great-grandchildren, sews for outreach concerns, and volunteers in church work. Her hobbies include relaxing! **Mar. 7, May 26.**

Sharon Long (Brown) was born in Trinidad, West Indies, but now lives in Canada with her husband, Miguel Brown. She has been a social worker for 29 years and is assistant director with Alberta Children and Youth Services. She has four adult children and two granddaughters. Sharon is active in her church. She enjoys writing, singing, entertaining, cooking, and baking. **Mar. 6, Aug. 22.**

Monika Machel is married and has three adult children. Her husband is a church administrator. Monika takes care of her elderly parents. **Sept. 4**

Ezinwanyi Madukoma is from Nigeria where she and her husband live. She works in the library at Babcock University. She is a first-time contributor and a scholarship recipient from the General Conference women's ministries. It is her hope that this devotional will bring encouragement to others. **June 2.**

Susan Magaitis is wife to Steven and mother to Tuvok—a RSPCA rescue cat—and domestic goddess. Susan spends her spare time working as a local church pastor and women's ministries director in the North New South Wales Conference of Seventh-day Adventists in Australia. Susan loves traveling and believes everyone needs to visit the Acropolis and eat authentic Greek food. **Oct. 21.**

Rhona Grace Magpayo, a Virginia-licensed optician, resides in Laurel, Maryland, with husband, Celestino, Jr., a retired master chief in the U.S. Navy. Both their daughter, Celesti, and son, David, are attending college. Rhona and her husband attend Sligo Seventh-day Adventist Church where they are greeters. They are active members of the Filipino-American Christian Association. **Oct. 9.**

Eunice Michiles Malty was a congresswoman for 16 years, being the first female senator in Brazil. She actively participates in women's ministries in the Central church in Brasilia and, with her second husband, Gerson, participates in the senior citizen ministries. She enjoys traveling, reading, social work, and making flower arrangements. **Nov. 20.**

Tamara Marquez de Smith writes from sunny Florida where she lives with her husband, Steven, and their daughters, Lillian, age 11, and Cassandra, age 6. As the family just relocated, they currently do not have a home church, but they allow the Lord to use them wherever He sees fit. **Nov. 7.**

Marion V. Clarke Martin, M.D., retired from professional and academic pursuits in August, 2007. She is active in her church where, among other duties, she serves as an elder, pianist, and organist. She is an avid reader, enjoys music and interior decorating, and considers herself greatly blessed with two adult sons, one granddaughter, and a grandson. **Feb. 11, Sept. 27.**

Julienne Lumière Ngo Massock, the fourth-born of five children, writes from University of Consendai, Cameroon, where she is studying nursing. She is one of the General Conference women's ministries scholarship recipients, and is committed to contributing and providing full support to this important program. **Mar. 2.**

Delores Pohle Master and her husband have been married for 52 years. They have three children, seven grandchildren, and one great-grandchild. She worked as a registered nurse for 21 years. She is now retired but is the secretary-treasurer of their small business. Delores enjoys sewing, writing poems, playing the piano for church, puzzles, and flower gardening. **June 24.**

Mary L. Maxson is the associate pastor of a church in Paradise, California. Her responsibilities include six ministries and discipling 12 young adult women. For creativity, she makes sure her landscaping isn't demolished by the deer which often pass through their property. She loves flower gardening and creating computer cards to send to church members. **June 11, Dec. 23.**

Anita Mayes lives in Lovell, Wyoming, at the foot of the Big Horn Mountains with her husband and their two dogs. They have twin adult daughters and a 3-year-old granddaughter. Anita enjoys gardening, writing sermons and Bible lessons, photography, and family history and stories. **Aug. 4.**

Retha McCarty enjoys crocheting, designing counted cross-stitch bookmarks with inspirational quotes, sewing, and bird watching. She has made 24 quilt tops for Bags of Love. Since retirement, writing is her new hobby. She has had a few articles plus two poems published. Church involvement includes more than 31 years as church treasurer. **Feb. 17.**

Vidella McClellan is a married senior and a caregiver for the elderly in British Columbia, Canada. She is a mother of three with seven grandchildren, one great-grandchild, and seven step- grandchildren. Her current hobbies are gardening, crosswords, Scrabble, and writing. She also loves cats, reading, and instrumental music. She often speaks in nearby churches. **June 21, Oct. 8.**

Faith-Ann McGarrell is a former high school English teacher. She enjoys drama, creative writing, playing the piano, reading a good book, listening to good music, and spending time with her family and friends. Currently, she is an assistant professor of curriculum and instruction at Andrews University. **June 15, Sept. 22.**

Raschelle Mclean-Jones is an elementary teacher in Haines City, Florida. She and husband John, have two sons, Aaron and Josiah. She loves to cook, sing in the choir, and write. **June 8.**

Edileuza de Souza Meira is a teacher and mother of three young children. She enjoys reading, listening to and telling stories, walking, and cooking. **May 15, Aug. 7.**

Gay Mentes is a sister to three brothers and mother to two adult children. She and artist husband, Alex, live in Kelowna, British Columbia, Canada, where they do their art. Gay is a published author and is learning watercolor and calligraphy. She continues to add to her heart rock collection which now nears 200 pieces. She enjoys working with flowers. **Feb. 25, June 9.**

Annette Walwyn Michael is a former English teacher who, along with her pastor-husband, Reginald, has recently retired. She loves to write, work in her garden, and read good books. She is the mother of three and the grandmother of four. **July 14, Aug. 26.**

Sharon Michael, M.D., a family physician in Pennsylvania, enjoys scrapbooking, reading, writing, and traveling. She also enjoys teaching lifestyle change to her patients and spending time with her parents, nieces, and nephews. **May 6.**

Quilvie G. Mills is a retired community college professor. She lives with her husband, Herman, in Port St. Lucie, Florida. She serves her church as Bible class teacher, board member, minister of music, and member of the floral committee. She enjoys traveling, reading, music, gardening, word games, and teaching piano. **Feb. 19.**

Cheryol Mitchell, Ed.D., is an assistant high school principal to eleventh-grade students in the second largest school district in St. Louis, Missouri. She has been an educator in both parochial and public school systems for 22 years. She is an avid reader and enjoys spending time with friends and family. **July 4.**

Susen Mattison Molé grew up as a missionary child in India and enjoyed moving around. She has two girls, both in college, and enjoys hiking, writing, reading, painting, playing her cello, and eating food from different cultures. She still travels around with her Navy doctor-husband as she has for the past 28 years. **Mar. 27.**

Marcia Mollenkopf is a retired teacher who lives in Klamath Falls, Oregon. She enjoys church involvement and has served in both adult and children's divisions. Her hobbies include reading, writing, music, and bird watching. **July 2.**

Esperanza Aquino Mopera is the mother of four adults and grandmother of five. She enjoys gardening and being a traveling nurse. **June 27.**

Frances Osborne Morford married her high school sweetheart 60 years ago and spent 30 of those years in South Africa, Uganda, Ethiopia, Lebanon, Egypt, and South Sudan. She taught English and Bible alongside her math-instructor husband. They have now retired to beautiful Colorado. They have two children, three grandchildren, and one great-grandson. **July 18.**

Bonnie Moyers lives with her husband and three cats in Staunton, Virginia. She has two adult children and two granddaughters. She is a musician in her local church and plays for a Methodist church and a Presbyterian church on Sundays. She writes freelance, and has been published in many magazines and books. **Jan. 9, Apr. 28.**

Lillian Musgrave and her family continue to enjoy the beauty and uniqueness of northern California, close to family and friends. She belongs to Sierra Christian Writers, and enjoys writing stories, poems, songs, and music, as well as being involved in church responsibilities and family activities. **Feb. 21.**

Judith M. Mwansa comes from Zambia and currently lives in Maryland with her pastor husband, Pardon, and their children. She enjoys traveling to new places, spending time with her family, baking, reading, and helping those she meets to know the King of peace. She also maintains the intake and data base for this devotional book series. **Aug. 14.**

Ingrid Naumann lives in Grafing, Germany. She has one son, a daughter-in-law, and a grandson. She is the women's ministries director for the South German Union of Seventh-day Adventists, which does not leave much time for her hobbies—sports, reading, and traveling. **Feb. 1, Aug. 3.**

Anne Elaine Nelson is a retired teacher who works with testing for schools. She has written the book, *Puzzled Parents*. Her four children have blessed her with 14 grandchildren and three great-grandchildren. Anne lives in Michigan where she stays active in her church. Her favorite activities are sewing, music, photography, and creating memories for her grandchildren. **Jan. 7, Apr. 26.**

Judith Nembhard was born in Jamaica and received her early education there, later studying in the United States. A former college and university instructor and administrator, she is now retired and lives in Chattanooga, Tennessee. **Dec. 4.**

Ann Northwood is a wife, mother, and grandmother of 10. She was a stay-at-home mom, teacher, and social worker. She loves to quilt, paint, and teach. **Mar. 18.**

Beryl Aseno Nyamwange and her husband, Joe, enjoy working with the youth in their local church. Beryl is the ADRA country director for Sierra Leone and Gambia. She is a good swimmer and enjoys the outdoors, especially beach walks with her husband. Writing is her passion, and she is an avid reader. She has written a collection of poems. **Sept. 19.**

Elizabeth Versteegh Odiyar of Kelowna, British Columbia, has managed the family chimney sweep business since 1985. She has three adult children. Beth enjoys mission trips and road trips. She loves being creative, sewing, decorating, and cooking vegan. She has filled many positions in her local church and is still a Pathfinder at heart. **Aug. 1.**

Joyce O'Garro, a retired laboratory technologist of 20 years, took care of cancer patients. She is a qualified teacher who has taught from kindergarten to college, and a pianist who, at 78 years of age, still teaches piano. She has two grown daughters, one son-in-law, and three grandchildren. Her mother was still living, at age 103, at the time of this writing. **Dec. 22.**

Rosinha Gomes Dias de Oliveira has a degree in biology and enjoys her work as women's ministries director in the Central Rio Grande do Sul Conference of Seventh-day Adventists. She and her minister-husband have two sons. Her hobbies include reading, writing, traveling with her family, and swimming. **Oct. 15.**

Jemima Dollosa Orillosa lives in Maryland with her husband, Danny. They have two daughters and two sons-in-law. Her passion is organizing mission trips. She loves children. Her greatest happiness comes from experiencing the joy of people accepting Christ as their personal Savior, and seeing the joy of service and the changed lives of team members. **Jan. 10, June 7.**

Sharon Oster lives near St. Louis, Missouri, with her pastor-husband Jerry. They have three grown children and six grandchildren. Diagnosed with multiple sclerosis several years ago, Sharon has taken medical retirement from the Special School District. She enjoys reading, cross stitch and embroidery, and spending time with her family. **Aug. 29, Nov. 6.**

Rose Otis started this devotional book series and the scholarship program when she was the director of the General Conference women's ministries, a position she held from 1990 to 1997. Now a full-time grandmother, she and her husband, Bud, live in Middletown, Maryland, near their children and grandchildren. Rose enjoys gardening, travel, visiting friends and family, the ocean, and some golf. **Sept. 15.**

Brenda D. (Hardy) Ottley was born in Guyana, South America. She is married to Ernest, a Trinidadian, and lives in St. Lucia where she works as a secondary school teacher and e-tutor in the University of the West Indies open campus. She and her husband are involved in radio ministries at Rizzen 102 FM. **Mar. 1.**

Hannele Ottschofski is of Finnish origin and lives in southern Germany. She has four adult daughters and a recently retired pastor-husband. She loves reading and writing, and is actively involved in her local church and women's ministries. **Feb. 20, July 16.**

Ofelia A. Pangan lives in central California with her husband of 48 years. They have three adult children and nine grandchildren. She likes reading, gardening, traveling, and playing word games. But even more than these, she loves visiting with her children and their families. She goes to Central Valley Fil-Am Adventist Church and enjoys teaching her Sabbath school Bible class. **Jan. 27.**

Revel Papaioannou works with her retired-but-working pastor-husband of 52 years in the biblical town of Berea, Greece. They have four sons and 13 grandchildren. She has held almost every local church position and at present is Sabbath school superintendent, teaches the adult Bible lesson, cleans the church, and cares for the tiny garden. Free time is filled with visiting, Bible studies, and hiking. **Jan. 19, Apr. 17.**

Mary Paulson-Lauda lives in Gladstone, Oregon, and is retired after 47 years in healthcare work. She has served on various church and community committees, and was involved with children's ministries in Pathfinders and summer camps. She tutors first-grade reading, handcrafts greeting cards, and enjoys visiting her family. She was named in *Notable Adventist Women* and *Energized.* **Sept. 23**

Betty A. Pearson is a great-grandmother now living in College Place, Washington, spending her days with her husband of three years, Dorsett Feyen. She gardens, writes, and attends the Christian Writers' Club. She has three children in western Washington, and courtesy of her "new" husband, has three "new" children in the area, and one on the California coast. **Mar. 13.**

Virginia Eggert Pearson grew up in Michigan and now lives in North Carolina. She is a retired registered nurse and was the communications secretary of three churches and beginner and kindergarten Sabbath school leader until illness forced her to give up all her church jobs. She still does some Bible studies with prisoners, encouraging them to keep hanging on to God and His Word. **Mar. 9.**

Lois Rittenhouse Pecce and her husband are "retired" in Centerville, Ohio. She is active with the Dayton Christian Scribes writers' group which she co-founded with friend Betty Kossick 31 years ago. Her favorite role is grandma, but she also enjoys gardening, conducting nursing home chapel services, and teaching beginner Sabbath school. **Feb. 10.**

Naomi J. Penn, the proud parent of two adult children, currently attends the Shiloh Adventist Church in St. Thomas, Virgin Islands. An accountant by profession, she served in women's ministries for several years at her former church. She enjoys reading, baking, and gardening. **July 8.**

Rosemeyre Gianne Pereira was a psychologist who enjoyed art, books, and festivities at her church, the Arab Adventist Community in Brazil. Rosemeyre died in October, 2007, at 40 years of age. **Sept. 29.**

Betty G. Perry lives in Fayetteville, North Carolina, with her active-retired pastor-husband. There are three adult children and six grandchildren in their family. An anesthetist for 35 years, she is now semi-retired. Hobbies include playing the piano and organ, doing arts and crafts, trying new recipes, quilting, and yearly contributions to the women's devotional. **Oct. 5, Dec. 29.**

Angèle Peterson lives in Ohio where she works as an administrative assistant and serves her church in several capacities. She enjoys spending time with her family, especially her niece and nephew, and looks forward to Christ's soon return. **June 22.**

Birdie Poddar and her husband live at Maranatha Colony in South India with families of other retirees. They have two adult children and four grandchildren. Her hobbies are gardening, writing, composing poems, and stitching. She has a card ministry for encouraging those in need of prayers and encouragement. **Apr. 18.**

Marcia R. Pope is a registered nurse living in Westminster, Colorado. She has three sons and one daughter-in-law, and attends Chapel Haven Adventist Church in Northglenn. She is very active in her church, teaching a Sabbath school Bible class, and directing the choir and praise singers. She enjoys music, teaching, writing, crocheting, and drawing. **Oct. 30.**

Kimone Powell is a medical student at Loma Linda University in California. She enjoys community outreach and music. Kimone likes to travel but does not like to fly. She loves meeting new people, learning new languages and about different cultures. **Mar. 15.**

June Y. Powers is a "country gal," a wife, Mom to six grown children, and Grama to 14. She enjoys nature walks, hikes, canoeing, and time-out with girlfriends. She lives in OK Falls, British Columbia, Canada. **Sept. 1, Oct. 11.**

Judith Purkiss is a secondary school teacher living and working in London, England. She loves reading and working with words. Judith serves in Sabbath school and women's ministries in her local church. **Feb. 2, June 1.**

Gustavia Raymond-Smith lives with her husband in Maryland. She is a former teacher, a staff development specialist, and a freelance writer. She enjoys traveling, knitting, and floral arranging. **June 18.**

Louise Rea, author of *Quick Trips to the Wallowas,* has moved to a tiny town only 10 miles from Wallowa Lake and countless mountain trails in the Wallowa Mountains in northeast Oregon. Here, more of her retirement time from teaching and office work can be spent in God's beautiful outdoors. She is always looking for hiking companions. **Apr. 5.**

Cavelle S. Regis is a native of St. Croix, US Virgin Islands. She is married to Pastor Marcellinus Regis and they have two children: a son, Malachi Joel and a daughter, Eboni Jayden. Cavelle is the children's ministries director and shepherdess coordinator of the St. Lucia Mission. She enjoys reading, crafts, sewing, singing, and meeting people. **Nov. 21.**

Barbara Horst Reinholtz is a happily retired senior citizen who is enjoying the luxury of spending quality time with her husband. They have three married children, two grandchildren, six grand dogs, and a grand horse. She's enjoying choosing her own daily projects: family, and cooking and baking for ailing or lonely members in her church. She also serves as a deaconess. **May 4.**

Bertlyn Gretna Reynolds is a Ph.D. student in Michigan. She is originally from Guyana, South America. She enjoys reading, writing, photography, sewing, and music—especially the type of music that fills her imagination with heavenly things. **Aug. 30.**

Darlenejoan McKibbin Rhine was born in Nebraska, raised in California, and schooled in Tennessee. She holds a B.A. in journalism and worked in the plant at the Los Angeles *Times* for 21 years before retiring in 1995. She now lives on an island in Puget Sound, Washington, spending much of her time writing and attending the North Cascade Adventist Church. **Jan. 11.**

Jill Rhynard has her Masters in Public Health and works for a health authority in British Colombia, Canada. She writes a health column for 32 newspapers and does health promotion newsletters. She is active in her local church as an elder, a member of the worship committee, and head of the healthy relationship team. Both of her sons are married and live in the United States. **Aug. 17, Sept. 30.**

Sweetie Ritchil writes from Bangladesh where she is the treasurer for the Union Mission and has served the church in different financial areas. She has been involved with children's Sabbath school, and is women's ministries and Dorcas director. She loves Bible reading, composing religious songs, poems, writing articles, and especially finding ways to help the helpless. **Mar. 11.**

Cathy Evenson Roberts has recently returned to the great plains of Nebraska. She has traveled to a wide variety of places and experienced many cultural settings. Each one has contributed to her experience with God. "Without valley experiences the mountaintop encounter is not as rewarding." Cathy enjoys writing, gardening, visiting with friends, and making new ones! **Sept. 17.**

Avis Mae Rodney is a justice of the peace for the province of Ontario, Canada, where she resides with her husband, Leon. Avis is the mother of two young adults and continues to be awed by the blessings of her beautiful grandchildren. She enjoys early morning walks, gardening, reading, and spending time with family and friends. **Jan. 6.**

Agnes Chepkorir Rotich writes from Kenya where she is a church assistant at the University of Eastern Africa Baraton and a student as well. Her hobbies are singing and reading Bible texts. She is a first-time contributor and the recipient of a women's ministries scholarship. **Mar. 31.**

Marlise Rupp, who lives in Germany, is married with three adult children. She has one granddaughter who lives much too far away in the United States. For many years she was active in women's ministries and is now one of the elders of her local church. She has a shop offering floral arrangements. She loves nature—especially the mountains, and she enjoys sports. **Aug. 31.**

Deborah Sanders lives in Alberta, Canada. In 2007 Deborah and her husband Ron wrote a book, *Our Journey Through Time With Sonny.* Sonny has significant developmental disabilities. The book is a collection of sacred memories shared in hopes of spiritually encouraging others in the family of God until Jesus comes for His people. **Apr. 14, Dec. 25.**

Theodora V. Sanders lives in Huntsville, Alabama, where she moved to attend Oakwood College, and where she met her husband, James. When James was diagnosed with a progressive muscle disease she quit her job to care for him and to home school their five young adopted children. She enjoys reading, writing, playing Scrabble, and spending time with her six grandchildren. **Apr. 3, Aug. 6.**

Andrea de Almeida Santos is a dental surgeon and substitute professor at the Federal University of Bahia. She also works in an Adventist community center teaching, preaching, and sharing Christ with underprivileged children and teens. She enjoys nature, animals, caring for her home, and studying. **Apr. 1, July 3.**

Mirian Teixeira dos Santos enjoys music, poetry, painting cloth, and crocheting. At 72 years of age, she continues giving Bible studies, making missionary visits, and offering personal and spiritual support to those she comes in contact with. **Aug. 23.**

Valquiria Teixeira dos Santos was born in a Christian home and, following the example of her mother, has held various positions in local church leadership. She enjoys music, poetry, the ocean, and good books. She also likes to talk with friends, write letters, and compose poetry. She resides in São Paulo, Brazil. **May 1.**

Christine Schneider is a busy mother of three and a grandmother of 10. She lives in the country near Kelowna, British Columbia, Canada, with her husband Arnie. She loves to do puzzles, and is a master at laughing contagiously. She sings and loves helping people. Her hobbies are crocheting, sewing, biking, and nature. **Aug. 2.**

Angelika Schöpf is a widow with two adult children and one grandchild. She likes to laugh and enjoys walking with her dog. She lives in Germany. **July 5.**

Donna Lee Sharp enjoys using her music in her home church, other churches, and at three care homes, as well as the Christian Women's Club. Her hobbies include gardening, flower arranging, bird watching, and travel—mainly to visit family members scattered across North America. **May 7.**

Donna Sherrill manages a small country store in Jefferson, Texas, which takes most of her time. At home she takes care of an invalid husband. Donna loves to read. **Nov. 10.**

Rose Neff Sikora and her husband, Norman, call the beautiful mountains of North Carolina their home. She retired in 2009 from a 45-year career as a registered nurse. She enjoys walking, writing, and helping others. Rose has one adult daughter, Julie, and three grandchildren—Tyler, Olivia, and Grant. **Dec. 15.**

Luciana Barbosa Freitas da Silva is a member of the Casa Amarela Seventh-day Adventist Church in Recife, Pernambuco, Brazil. She is secretary to the personal ministries department in the Pernambuco Conference of Seventh-day Adventists in northeast Brazil. She is married to Elias, and enjoys crocheting, embroidering, swimming, and traveling. **Mar. 3.**

Judy Good Silver (Jonah and Mary's "Meme") is so grateful the Lord is still blessing the years within her "dash"(1953-20—). She and Phil share 33 years of marriage and friendship. Her joys include family, friends, home, writing, gardening, the replenishing gift of Sabbath, rocking chairs, porches, and a little piece of heaven nestled in the Shenandoah Valley. **Feb. 3, Oct. 27.**

Daisy Simpson, a member in a local Seventh-day Adventist church in Queens, New York, for more than 40 years, has been active as a choir member, deaconess, Sabbath school secretary, treasurer, and teacher. She has worked as a counselor and instructor in prison ministries for more than 30 years. She enjoys gardening and giving Bible studies. **Dec. 16.**

Rebecca Singh is teacher-in-charge of the Adventist school which opened in the newly constructed school building at Varanasi, Uttar Pradesh, India. Most of the population of this city is Hindu as it is a pilgrim center for Hindus. She has been working in this organization for more than 28 years. Her husband is the treasurer of the Adventist Church headquarters there. **Oct. 2.**

Cinda Lea Sitler shares the joys and sorrows of ministries with her pastor-husband, David. They have one son, Nehemiah. She enjoys digi-scrapping, cooking, and serving in the home and school at her son's school and on the Illinois Conference of Seventh-day Adventists' women's ministries committee. **June 3.**

Heather-Dawn Small is director for women's ministries at the General Conference of Seventh-day Adventists. She has been children's and women's ministries director for the Caribbean Union Conference located in Trinidad and Tobago. She is the wife of Pastor Joseph Small and the mother of Dalonne and Jerard. She loves air travel, reading, and scrapbooking. **Feb. 6, Apr. 24.**

Yvonne Curry Smallwood is a mother, wife, and grandmother. She is a scientist who has worked for more than 20 years in science administration. When she is not entertaining her granddaughter, Jordan, she enjoys crocheting, knitting, and writing. Her stories and articles have appeared in several publications. **July 6.**

Thamer Cassandra Smikle writes from Jamaica where she is an auditor at the Jamaica customs department. She has completed a master's degree in business administration (specializing in financing) at the Northern Caribbean University and is an active member of Portmore church. Her hobbies include reading, singing, relaxing, and laughing. **Oct. 12.**

Lynn Smith was born on the beautiful island of New Providence, Bahamas. She has been a teacher and principal and has been married to a pastor/conference administrator for the past 27 years. They have three young adult daughters. Lynn loves to read, cook, travel, shop, sing, play the piano, conduct choirs, and spend time with her extended families. **Oct. 24, Nov. 19.**

Martha Spaulding is now widowed and lives in a retirement center after working for many years in Christian education. She enjoys reading, writing, scrapbooking, and volunteering. **Mar. 14.**

Candace Sprauve is a retired educator who serves her church as personal ministries leader and as an elder. She and her husband, Roy, have four adult children (three sons and a daughter) and four grandchildren. **July 7.**

Heike Steinebach is a trained nurse who lives with her husband, Mathias, and their three children in Ratekau in northern Germany. They are active in a church planting project in Bad Schwartau. Her book, *Doch die Hoffnung bleibt* (Hope Remains) was published in 1997 by the Saatkorn Verlag. **June 14.**

Ardis Dick Stenbakken considers editing these devotional books to be her primary ministry to women. Now retired, she lives in Colorado, enjoying the view of the Rocky Mountains from her home. She is very proud of her husband, Richard (the Dick in her name is her maiden name—not his name!), their children, four grandchildren, and most of all what Jesus has done in her life. **Jan. 3, Apr. 22.**

Maike Stepanek is German, born and raised in South Africa. She and her husband, Brian, have lived in Korea since 2001. She enjoys nature, meeting people, experiencing new cultures and foods, artistic expression in its various forms, and adventure. She loves to laugh and sing, and she draws great satisfaction from encouraging people. **Apr. 7, Aug. 18.**

Rita Kay Stevens works as a medical technologist in Albuquerque, New Mexico, and is a church administrator's wife in New Mexico and west Texas. They have two adult sons, a daughter-in-law, a grandson, and a granddaughter. Rita enjoys traveling, spending time with family, exercising, and meeting and entertaining people. She is active in women's ministries and enjoys planning retreats. **June 28.**

Carol Stickle has enjoyed an interesting life, including being a registered nurse, having an antique store, and other side careers. She loves doing flower arrangements for her church. Making a tasty Sabbath dinner and inviting people over to enjoy fellowship is something both she and her husband love to do. She is a happy mother of three adult children and five grandchildren. **June 4, Sept. 2.**

Rubye Sue lives on the campus of Laurelbrook Academy with her husband. She is the retired secretary to retired president Robert D. Zollinger. When he needs something typed he calls her, and she enjoys still being active and using the one talent the Lord gave her. **Dec. 19.**

Carolyn Sutton lives with her husband, Jim, on a small farm in Tennessee. They are field representatives for Adventist World Radio as well as being involved in their local church, prison ministries, and community events. Carolyn enjoys grandparenting, writing, speaking, music, and herb gardening. **Dec. 5.**

Eriko Suzuki is a graduate student at Sahmyook University in Korea, completing her master's degree in public health. Her great interest in music led her to devote 2007 to a singing ministry with the Golden Angels of the Northern Asia-Pacific Division supporting evangelism in Hong Kong, Japan, Taiwan, Mongolia, Macao, and Korea. She serves her church as a pianist. **Nov. 18.**

H. Elizabeth Sweeney-Cabey is a retired widow. She has worked as a schoolteacher, sample maker for party frocks, and a mental health worker. She has home schooled many of her grandchildren. Her hobbies include reading, writing, sewing, carpentry, and especially in-depth Bible study. She is involved in community service and has published a book, *'Twas Worth It All.* **Dec. 12.**

Loraine F. Sweetland is retired in Tennessee. She recently began an Adventist Food Buying Club for her church and community. She enjoys writing; computer surfing; reading; her church; and the deer, woodchucks, and birds in her backyard. She lost her husband of almost 57 years and now lives alone with her three little dogs for companions. **Jan. 8, Nov. 25.**

Anna (Ivie) Swingle and Stan will be married 43 years in 2011. They have two adult children and one grandchild. She is a records administrator for a United States government facility and is the church clerk, church organist and pianist, in the choir, and involved in women's ministries. Her hobbies include camping, counted cross-stitching, knitting, crocheting, scrapbooking, and music. **Sept. 10**

Frieda Tanner, a retired nurse, moved to Eugene, Oregon, 21 years ago to be near her daughter and family. She spends most of her time making Sabbath school items for children all over the world—90 countries so far. She will be 93 on August 31, 2011. **Oct. 20.**

Arlene Taylor is risk manager and director of infection control for three Adventist Health hospitals in northern California. A brain-function specialist, she does research through her nonprofit corporation Realizations, Inc. and presents a variety of seminars internationally. Web site: www.arlenetaylor.org. **Jan. 4, Oct. 13.**

Audre B. Taylor, a published writer, is a retired administrative assistant for Adventist Development and Relief Agency International. One of her hobbies is choral conducting, and she won an Angel Award for one of her choral and orchestral performances in a national media competition. She is also a practicing psychotherapist in the Washington, D.C. area. **Jan. 20, March 25.**

Rose Thomas is a wife and grateful mother of two children. She is a passionate teacher and works at Forest Lake Education Center in Longwood, Florida. **Feb. 9, Apr. 2.**

Stella Thomas works in the Office of Adventist Mission/Presidential of the General Conference of Seventh-day Adventists. Her motto in life is to share God's love with the world. **Dec. 27.**

Bula Rose Haughton Thompson is a dental assistant who works at the Bellefield, Cross Keys, and Pratville Health Centers in Manchester, Jamaica. She also works at the Mandeville Comprehensive Clinic. In addition, she is a *couturière par excellence* whose other hobbies are singing, reading, and meeting people. **July 9, Aug. 28.**

Gloria Lindsey Trotman is a commissioned minister and women's and children's ministries director of the Inter-American Division of Seventh-day Adventists. She and her husband, Pastor Jansen Trotman, have four children and six grandchildren. Gloria enjoys writing, music, and laughter. Her motto is "Making a difference." **Feb. 16.**

Nancy Ann Neuharth Troyer grew up in California, graduated from Lynwood Academy and Andrews University, and married a "cute guy" who became a military chaplain. They have traveled to faraway places, sung in crowded chapels and empty cathedrals, and now live in Sun Lakes-Banning, California. Nancy is often called "the notetaker." **Jan. 15, Sept. 13.**

Nancy L. Van Pelt, is a certified family life educator, best-selling author, and internationally-known speaker. She has written more than 20 books, and has traversed the globe teaching families how to really love each other. Her hobbies are getting organized, entertaining, having fun, and quilting. Nancy and her husband live in California and are the parents of three adult children. **Feb. 8, Dec. 17.**

Desrene L. Vernon is a communications practitioner. She has taught communication courses at Andrews University, Indiana University South Bend, and Columbia Union College. She enjoys traveling, public speaking, reading the Bible, and playing Scrabble. **June 5, Nov. 27.**

Vasti S. Viana is the widow of Pastor José M. Viana; mother of two adult children, Ricardo and Joyce; and grandmother of Raissa Lynn. Recently she wrote and published a book about effective prayer. She likes music, writing, reading, and jogging. **July10, Sept. 3.**

Tammy Vice and her family attend the Hendersonville Adventist Church. She is a singer and songwriter. She promotes autism awareness and understanding through her music and testimony. She became an advocate after her younger daughter was diagnosed at age 3. Tammy works at the Autism Society of Middle Tennessee. For more information, please visit: www.tammyvice.com **Apr. 8.**

Carolyn Voss, Ph.D, is a widow and a retired nurse educator. Her hobbies are sewing, quilting, crafts, walking, golf, and studying God's Word. **Jan. 30.**

Nancy Jean Vyhmeister grew up as a missionary kid in Uruguay, married a Chilean, raised her two children in Argentina, and taught in the United States and the Philippines. In retirement, she corrects theses written by African students, superintends her local Sabbath school, and pretends that she keeps house. Of course, all of this with the support of her husband, Werner. **May 30, July 26.**

Mary M. J. Wagoner-Angelin lives in Ooltewah, Tennessee, with her husband and their two daughters. Mary is a stay-at-home mom and a part-time social worker at a psychiatric hospital. She volunteers for Make-A-Wish Foundation, is council coordinator for MOPS (Mothers of Preschoolers), and a church youth leader. Her hobbies include humor therapy and working out. **May 3, Nov. 3.**

Cora A. Walker is a retired nurse, editor, and freelance writer who lives in Fort Washington, Maryland. She is an active member of the church she attends in Charles County, Maryland. She enjoys reading, writing, swimming, classical music, singing, and traveling. She has one son, Andre V. Walker. **Jan. 5, Oct. 28.**

Dolores Klinsky Walker, having launched her three children into adulthood, found great satisfaction in mentoring released prisoners and tutoring English-as-second-language students. A prolonged convalescence temporarily switched her from "doing" to "being." She and her husband have been married for 49 years. She is a United Methodist member in Washington State. **May 25, Sept. 5.**

Anna May Radke Waters is a retired administrative secretary from Columbia Adventist Academy, and served for many years as an ordained elder and greeter at church. She has too many hobbies to list, but at the top are her eight grandchildren, two great-granddaughters, and her husband with whom she likes to travel and make memories. She and her husband are now "snowbirds." **Jan. 31, Mar. 4.**

Dorothy Eaton Watts is a freelance writer, editor, and speaker. She was a missionary in India for more than 28 years, founded an orphanage, taught elementary school, and has written more than 26 books. She enjoys birding and has more than 1,600 in her world total. She continues to write from her home in Maryland. **Jan.1, Apr. 16.**

Daniela Weichhold is originally from Germany, but works as an administrative assistant at the European Commission Headquarters in Brussels, Belgium. She enjoys the cultural diversity both at her workplace and in her adopted hometown. In her free time, she likes cooking, the outdoors, playing the piano and singing, and doing medical missionary work. **June 10, Dec. 1.**

Lyn Welk-Sandy, from Adelaide, South Australia, is a mother of four, and has 12 grandchildren. She works as a grief counselor, and assists young offenders attending court. Lyn spent many years as a pipe organist and loves church music, choir work, and helping Sudanese refugee families. She enjoys photography and caravanning the outback of Australia with her husband, Keith. **Feb. 12, Apr. 15.**

Shirnet Wellington, an administrative assistant in Miami, Florida, is Jamaican by birth and a teacher by profession. She served as an education officer before immigrating to the United States with her pastor-husband, Leon. They have two sons. Her hobbies include writing, reading, gardening, and encouraging fellow ministers' wives in their role as shepherdesses. **Jan. 12, Nov. 5.**

Jo Ann Wetteland taught registered nursing students both in Illinois and in Indiana, and later was vice president for nursing at Platte Valley Medical Center. She and her husband, Weston, have been married for 53 years. They live in Colorado and have three grown children and two grandchildren. She finds painting, writing, and quilting to be enjoyable pastimes. **Nov. 17.**

Penny Estes Wheeler initiated a rivalry with her son as to who logs in the most airports. She's ahead—but not by much. The founding editor of *Women of Spirit*, Penny is a book editor for the Review and Herald Publishing Association. She enjoys reading, scrapping, and travel, and has fallen in love with beautiful Kenya. She and her husband have four adult children and two grandchildren. **May 9, July 15.**

Fay White, age 26, graduated from the University of the Southern Caribbean in 2007 with a bachelor's degree in English, and is now pursuing a master's degree in English at Andrews University in Michigan. An identical twin, her twin sister is Pastor Kay White, a Seventh-day Adventist minister. Fay enjoys reading about ancient civilizations. **Jan. 24, Sept. 9.**

Sandra Widulle is married and has two children. She loves to express her thoughts in writing. She is involved in children's ministries in her local church and uses her creativity to decorate the church showcase. **Apr. 27, Nov. 29.**

Vera Wiebe, a pastor's wife for more than 30 years, enjoys entertaining and traveling with her husband. Music has played a big part in her life, and she continues to organize music for her church as well as for camp meeting. Four grandchildren bring her a great deal of joy. **May 21, Sept. 6.**

Anna Williams is the women's ministries coordinator of a local church. She loves reading, crafts, faith-booking, and being around people. Anna lives out in the country with her husband, Michael. Her passion is making visitors and members feel comfortable in the house of God so that they feel loved and will return. **Jan. 14.**

Mildred C. Williams is a widow and retired physical therapist living in southern California. She enjoys studying and teaching the Bible, writing, gardening, public speaking, sewing, and spending time with her adult children and granddaughter. She likes writing for the devotional books as it gives her a chance to share God's love with others. **Dec. 30.**

Josefine Wimmer is a widow living in Germany although she is originally from Sicily. She has three adult sons and three grandchildren. She is active in ministering to singles and is creatively engaged in women's ministries. **July 12.**

Anne-May Wollan was born in Norway but lives and works in England at the Trans-European Division of Seventh-day Adventists where she is women's and children's ministries director and shepherdess coordinator. She is a music and art teacher by profession, and was a missionary with her family in Liberia and Bangladesh. She has two married children and five granddaughters. **Feb. 5.**

Charlene M. Wright is an active prison ministries federation officer in her local church conference, conducting Bible studies and participating in worship services in both mens' and womens' prisons in the state of Maryland. A widow, Charlene enjoys studying the Bible and spreading the good news of Jesus Christ. **May 19.**

Aileen L. Young enjoys art, music, and her three grandchildren: Spencer, Ashley, and Liliane. She is a retired teacher, a church and community helper, and has traveled extensively. Her current occupations are e-mailing, reading, writing, singing, and playing the organ. She plays Rook, Chinese checkers, Scrabble, and Make a Million. **Feb. 13, May 11.**

Shelly-Ann Patricia Zabala writes from Puerto Rico where she is a registered nurse who is currently a stay-at-home mom with her sons, Elias and Patric. A minister's wife, she enjoys children's and women's ministries. Her hobbies include singing, gardening, and entertaining. With her husband, Florencio, she serves in the East Puerto Rican Conference of Seventh-day Adventists. **Nov. 12.**

Naomi Zalabak graduated from Emmanuel Missionary College in 1951 with a degree in elementary education, and in 1959, from St. Helena School of Nursing as a registered nurse. She taught for 11 years in the United States and for 19 years in the Far Eastern Division of Seventh-day Adventists. She is now retired but keeps busy in Avon Park, Florida. **Apr. 9, Nov. 23.**

Ursula Ziegler lives near Tübingen, Germany, where she is involved in women's ministries in her church. **Feb. 4.**

Candy Zook, originally from Nebraska, now serves the Southern Asia Division of Seventh-day Adventists as director of Adventist Child India. She has traveled extensively in India, working in the villages and schools. She has three children and five grandchildren who live in America. She is an elder in the North Platte, Nebraska church. **Sept. 21, Nov. 13.**

Prayer Requests

_____

_____

_____

_____

_____

_____

_____

_____

_____

"Be devoted to one another in brotherly love.
Honor one another above yourselves."
—Romans 12:10, NIV

Prayer Requests

_____

_____

_____

_____

_____

_____

_____

_____

_____

_____

*"Whatever you ask for in prayer, believe that you
have received it, and it will be yours."*
—Mark 11:24, NIV